Lecture Notes of the Institute for Computer Sciences, Social Informatics and Telecommunications Engineering 244

More information about this series at http://www.springer.com/series/8197

Fisseha Mekuria · Ethiopia Enideg Nigussie
Waltenegus Dargie · Mutafugwa Edward
Tesfa Tegegne (Eds.)

Information and Communication Technology for Development for Africa

First International Conference, ICT4DA 2017
Bahir Dar, Ethiopia, September 25–27, 2017
Proceedings

 Springer

Editors
Fisseha Mekuria
Council for Scientific and Industrial
  Research
Pretoria
South Africa

Ethiopia Enideg Nigussie
Information Technology
University of Turku
Turku
Finland

Waltenegus Dargie
Dresden University of Technology
Dresden
Germany

Mutafugwa Edward
Aalto University
Helsinki
Finland

Tesfa Tegegne
Bahir Dar Institute of Technology
Bahir Dar
Ethiopia

ISSN 1867-8211   ISSN 1867-822X (electronic)
Lecture Notes of the Institute for Computer Sciences, Social Informatics
and Telecommunications Engineering
ISBN 978-3-319-95152-2   ISBN 978-3-319-95153-9 (eBook)
https://doi.org/10.1007/978-3-319-95153-9

Library of Congress Control Number: 2018947454

Printed on acid-free paper

This Springer imprint is published by the registered company Springer International Publishing AG
part of Springer Nature
The registered company address is: Gewerbestrasse 11, 6330 Cham, Switzerland

Preface

We are delighted to introduce the proceedings of the first edition of the 2017 European Alliance for Innovation (EAI) International Conference on ICT for Development for Africa (ICT4DA). This conference brought together researchers, developers, and practitioners from around the world who are leveraging and developing ICT and systems for socioeconomic development for Africa. The theme of ICT4DA 2017 was "The Application of ICT for Socioeconomic Development for Africa." The conference consisted of keynote speeches on current important topics in ICT and relevant research areas in ICT, technical papers on relevant topical areas accepted after a technical review process, and workshops addressing specific issues in ICT for development in Africa.

The technical program of ICT4DA 2017 consisted of 26 full papers in oral presentation sessions during the main conference tracks. The conference tracks were: Track 1 –Natural Language Processing; Track 2 –Intelligent Systems; Track 3 – e-Service and Web Technologies; and Track 4 –Mobile Computing and Wireless Communications. Aside from the high-quality technical paper presentations, the technical program also featured four keynote speeches, one invited talk, and two technical workshops. The five keynote speakers were Prof. Mammo Muchie from Tshwane University of Technology, South Africa; Dr. Timnit Gebru from Microsoft Research, New York, USA, "The Importance of AI Research in Africa"; Prof. Michael Gasser Indiana University, Bloomington, Indiana, USA, "ICTs, the Linguistic Digital Divide, and the Democratization of Knowledge"; and Prof. Fisseha Mekuria from CSIR, South Africa "5G and Industry 4.0 for Emerging Economies." The invited talk was presented by Ms. Alexandra Fraser from mLab, South Africa on "Mlab Innovations and Creations of Mobile Applications." The two workshops organized were Affordable Broadband DSA and 5G and Innovations in ICT for Building the African Knowledge Economy. The DSA and 5G workshops aimed to address the question: "Will 5G support the efforts of emerging market countries for digital inclusion and participation in the Industry 4.0?". The DSA and 5G workshops tried to address also how rural areas access broadband connectivity from unlicensed spectrum. The ICT innovation workshop aimed to address how an ICT-supported innovation system can be organized to plan, manage, and implement the transformation of the African economy and service sector.

Coordination with the steering chairs, Imrich Chlamtac, Tesfa Tegegne, and Yoseph Maloche, was essential for the success of the conference. We sincerely appreciate their constant support and guidance. It was also a great pleasure to work with such an excellent Organizing Committee team and we thank them for their hard work in organizing and supporting the conference. In particular, the Technical Program Committee, led by our TPC chair, Prof. Fisseha Mekuria (CSIR, South Africa), and co-chairs, Dr. Ethiopia Nigussie (University of Turku), Dr. Waltenegus Dargie (Technical University of Dresden), and Dr. Mutafugwa Edward (Aalto University), who completed the peer-review process of technical papers and created a high-quality technical program relevant to the conference theme. We are also grateful to the ICT4DA conference managers, Alzbeta Mackova and Dominika Belisová, for their support, and all the authors who submitted their papers contributing to the success of the ICT4DA 2017 conference and workshops.

We strongly believe that the ICT4DA 2017 conference provided a good forum for all staff and graduating researchers, developers, public and private industry players, and practitioners to discuss all the science and ICT technology trends and research aspects that are relevant to ICT for socioeconomic development. We also expect that future ICT4DA conferences will be as successful, stimulating, and make relevant contributions to the local and global knowledge in ICT4D as presented in this volume.

June 2018

Fisseha Mekuria
Ethiopia Nigussie
Waltenegus Dargie
Mutafugwa Edward
Tesfa Tegegne

Organization

Steering Committee

Imrich Chlamtac (Chair)   Create-Net, Italy/EAI, Italy
Tesfa Tegegne (Member)   Bahir Dar University, Ethiopia
Yoseph Maloche (Member)   University of Trento, Italy

Organizing Committee

General Chair

Tesfa Tegegne   Bahir Dar University, Ethiopia

General Co-chairs

Mesfin Belachew   Ministry of Communication and Information
                                 Technology
Mesfin Kifle   Addis Ababa University, Ethiopia
Yoseph Maloche   University of Trento, Italy

Technical Program Committee Chair

Fisseha Mekuria   CSIR Council for Scientific and Industrial Research,
                                 South Africa

Technical Program Committee Co-chairs

Waltenegus Dargie   Dresden University of Technology, Germany
Mutafugwa Edward   Aalto University, Finland
Dereje Hailemariam   Addis Ababa Institute of Technology, Ethiopia
Ethiopia Nigussie   Turku University, Finland

Web Chairs

Getnet Mamo   Bahir Dar University, Ethiopia
Belisty Yalew

Publicity and Social Media Chair/Co-chairs

Fikreselam Garad   Bahir Dar University, Ethiopia
Haile Melkamu   Bahir Dar University, Ethiopia

Workshops Chair

Dereje Teferi   Addis Ababa University, Ethiopia

Publication Chair

Ephrem Teshale Bekele   Addis Ababa Institute of Technology, Ethiopia

Panels Chair

Tibebe Beshah   Addis Ababa University, Ethiopia

Tutorials Chair

Abiot Sinamo   Mekelle University, Ethiopia

Demos Chair

Elefelious Getachew   Bahir Dar University, Addis Ababa University,
                            Ethiopia

Posters and PhD Track Chairs

Silesh Demissie   KTH Royal Institute of Technology, Sweden
Ahmdin Mohammed   Wollo University, Ethiopia

Local Chair

Mesfin Belachew   Ministry of Communication and Information
                            Technology

Conference Manager

Alžbeta Macková   EAI (European Alliance for Innovation)

Technical Program Committee

Gergely Alpár   Open University and Radboud University Nijmegen,
                            The Netherlands
Mikko Apiola
Yaregal Assabie   Addis Ababa University, Ethiopia
Rehema Baguma   Makerere University, Uganda
Ephrem Teshale Bekele   Addis Ababa University, AAiT, Ethiopia
Waltenegus Dargie   Dresden University of Technology, Germany
Vincenzo De Florio   VITO, Vlaamse Instelling voor Technologisch
                            Onderzoek, Belgium
Silesh Demissie   KTH Royal Institute of Technology, Sweden
Nelly Condori Fernandez   VU University Amsterdam, The Netherlands
Fikreselam Garad   Bahir Dar University, Ethiopia
Samson H. Gegibo   University of Bergen, Norway
Elefelious Getachew   Bahir Dar University, Ethiopia
Fekade Getahun   Addis Ababa University, Ethiopia
Liang Guang   Huawei Technologies, China

Tom Heskes	Radboud University, Nijmegen, The Netherlands
Laura Hollink	Centrum Wiskunde & Informatica, Amsterdam, The Netherlands
Kyanda Swaib Kaawaase	Makerere University, Uganda
Mesfin Kebede	CSIR Council for Scientific & Industrial Research, South Africa
Mesfin Kifle	Addis Ababa University, Ethiopia
Khalid Latif	Aalto University, Finland
Surafel Lemma	Addis Ababa University, AAiT, Ethiopia
Fisseha Mekuria	CSIR Council for Scientific and Industrial Research, South Africa
Drake Patrick Mirembe	Uganda Technology and Management University, Uganda
Geoffrey Muchiri	Muranga University College, Kenya
Edward Mutafungwa	Aalto University, Finland
Ethiopia Nigussie	University of Turku, Finland
Walter Omona	Makerere University, Uganda
Gaberilla Pasi	Università degli Studi di Milano, Italy
Erik Poll	Radboud University Nijmegen, The Netherlands
Peteri Sainio	University of Turku, Finland
Abiot Sinamo	Mekelle University, Ethiopia
Ville Taajamaa	University of Turku, Finland and Stanford University, USA
Woubishet Z. Taffese	Aalto University, Finland
Dereje Teferi	Addis Ababa University, Ethiopia
Nanda Kumar Thanigaivelan	University of Turku, Finland
Theo van der Weide	Radboud University, Nijmegen, The Netherlands
Dereje Yohannes	Adama Science and Technology University, Ethiopia

Contents

ICT4DA Workshops

ICT4DA Demos & Exhibits

ICT4DA Main Track

Is Addis Ababa Wi-Fi Ready?

Asrat Mulatu Beyene[1][(⊠)], Jordi Casademont Serra[2],
and Yalemzewd Negash Shiferaw[3]

[1] Department of Electrical and Computer Engineering,
College of Electrical and Mechanical Engineering,
Addis Ababa Science and Technology University, Addis Ababa, Ethiopia
asrat.mulatu@aastu.edu.et
[2] Universitat Politècnica de Catalunya, Barcelona, Spain
jordi.casademont@entel.upc.edu
[3] Department of Electrical and Computer Engineering, Addis Ababa University,
Addis Ababa, Ethiopia
yalemzewdn@yahoo.com

Abstract. As we are heading towards future ubiquitous networks, heterogeneity is one key aspect we need to deal with. Interworking between Cellular
and WLAN holds a major part in these future networks. Among other potential
benefits it gives the opportunity to offload traffic from the former to the latter. To
successfully accomplish that, we need to thoroughly study the availability,
capacity and performance of both networks. To quantify the possibility of
mobile traffic offloading, this work in progress presents the availability, capacity
and performance investigation of Wi-Fi Access Points in the city of Addis
Ababa. Analysis of the scanned data, collected by travelling through the highly
populated business areas of the city, reveals the potential of existing Wi-Fi
coverage and capability for many application domains.

Keywords: Wireless networks · Performance evaluation · Urban areas
Heterogeneous networks

1 Introduction

Currently and for the foreseeable future, there is an increasing pattern of mobile
connectivity penetration [1], mobile devices usage and ownership [2], and computing
capability of mobile devices like smart phones, laptops and tablets [3]. All these facts
have an impact on the demand for a greater bandwidth and better ubiquitous connectivity from the existing mobile infrastructures, primarily, from cellular telecommunication networks. The increased usage and acceptance of existing and new
bandwidth hungry services exacerbates the already-saturated cellular networks.

Operators, academia and the industry are working on many solutions to alleviate
this global problem [1]. Among these is the idea of offloading cellular traffic to
Wireless Local Area Networks (WLANs). It is attractive, mainly, because WLANs
provide a cheaper, immediate and a better short-range solution for the problem [4, 5].
Nowadays, Wi-Fi Access Points (APs) are being deployed in urban areas, primarily, to
extend the wired network Internet access or to avail intranet services. As the price of

© ICST Institute for Computer Sciences, Social Informatics and Telecommunications Engineering 2018
F. Mekuria et al. (Eds.): ICT4DA 2017, LNICST 244, pp. 3–13, 2018.
https://doi.org/10.1007/978-3-319-95153-9_1

Wi-Fi devices is getting cheaper, the technical expertise to install them becomes trivial and, more importantly, since WLAN is based on the unlicensed ISM (Industrial, Scientific and Medical) band their availability is expected to sky-rocket in urban and semi-urban areas [1–3].

Therefore, exploiting these Wi-Fi hotspots for the purpose of redirecting the traffic primarily intended for the cellular infrastructure is one of the main research areas in the trade. In this work we made Wi-Fi AP scanning of Addis Ababa metropolis, the capital city of Ethiopia, using mobile devices by making many drives and walks around the main streets of the city. This is primarily done to see the potential of Addis Ababa city to use mobile offloading applications exploiting the already deployed Wi-Fi APs. We analyzed the data collected in terms of availability, capability and performance to see the possibility and potential of offloading some of the traffic intended for the cellular infrastructure. This paper is organized as follows. Section 2 briefly summarizes related works. Section 3 shades some light on how the real-time Wi-Fi traffic data is collected. The availability and capacity analysis of the collected data is presented in Sects. 4 and 5, respectively. Finally, Sect. 6 enumerates the contributions while Sect. 7 made conclusions and points future directions.

2   Related Works

Many studies are being made on IEEE 802.11 technologies as they are one of the corner stones in ubiquitous future networks having various potential application domains. Many of these studies involve in the investigation of the availability and performance of public Wi-Fi APs deployed in urban and semi-urban environments.

In [6] public Wi-Fi hotspots coverage of Paris, France, was mapped by making several bus routes for the purpose of mobile data offloading. They found that, on average, there are 3.9 APs/km^2 of public Wi-Fi hotspots on areas that have at least one AP. Moreover, they obtained 27.7% of the APs being open, there is at least one AP with in every 52 m, and -80.1 dBm as the average RSSI during reception. They concluded that up to 30% of mobile traffic can be offloaded using the exiting Wi-Fi APs. Another study for similar purpose was made in [7] at Seoul, South Korea. They found 20.6% of spatial coverage and 80% of temporal coverage concluding that the already deployed Wi-Fi APs can offload up to 65% of the mobile data traffic and can save 55% of battery power. This is achieved mainly due to the reduced transmission time via the use of Wi-Fi APs. Yet another similar undertaking was made by Balasubramianian et al. in [8] where they found out on average, Wi-Fi and 3G are available around 87% and 11% of the time across three US cities. They also studied the comparative usage of Wi-Fi and 3G across certain geographic areas of the cities which gave an insight of places where Wi-Fi is under- and over- utilized with respect to 3G.

A huge history of Wi-Fi data collected over a very long period of time through war-driving covering the entire USA was analyzed to see the availability of Wi-Fi APs in [9]. They found as high as 1800 APs/km^2 in some cities like downtown Manhattan. They also found that around 50% of the APs are unsecured. Berezin et al. in [10] tried to study the extent of citywide mobile Internet access exploiting the exiting Wi-Fi APs in the city of Lausanne, Switzerland. They found that about 40% of the APs have

−70 dBm or better signal strength during reception, around 63% of the APs use channels 1, 6 and 11 and less than 20% of the APs are open for association. They highlighted that the existing Wi-Fi coverage can be used for many applications guaranteeing the minimum QoS requirements. Another interesting study was made in [11] on public Wi-Fi networks deployed by Google Inc. in Mountain View, California, USA. Most locations in the city can reach at most 4 APs at any given time. Even at late night, 80% of the APs are identified being used by at least one client. They also investigated that usage depends and varies with user traffic type, mobility pattern, and usage behavior. In our study, the availability and capacity analysis of Wi-Fi APs is made on data collected by travelling around the city of Addis Ababa. We focused only on the major public areas and streets to see the extent of coverage and the possible usage of the exiting hotspots for various applications, especially for mobile traffic offloading.

3   Methodology

In this work, commercial-grade 51 mobile devices that are based on both Android and iOS systems on top of which freely available network scanning and monitoring apps are used to collect Wi-Fi AP data for three consecutive months. It's focused mainly on highly populated business areas, like market places and city centers, where more people are engaged in their daily work, streets and places like bus and taxi stations where considerable all-day traffic is present. The scanning of the city for Wi-Fi APs was made through war-driving by walking and driving through the city covering approximately 157 km of distance and quarter of the area of the whole city, which is covering 527 km^2.

Totally, more than 15000 individual Wi-Fi APs where scanned in this process. For each Wi-Fi AP the scanned data contains, among others, the time stamp, MAC address, RSSI in dBm, location information, AP security configuration, frequency configurations, TCP and UDP uplink and downlink throughput for a given traffic load, and RTT values. Mobiperf, GMON and OpenSignal third-party apps are used to collect real-time traffic data. More specifically, default configuration of the apps is used except varying packet sizes and server addresses, whenever possible. The scanned data has three different file formats, .csv, .kml and .txt which are analyzed using spreadsheet applications, MATLAB and GoogleEarth.

4   Wi-Fi AP Availability

To see how much the city of Addis Ababa is populated with Wi-Fi APs, coverage heat maps for specific locations are generated from the .kml data set. In addition, AP densities, distance and time between APs as the mobile user travels along the streets of the city, are calculated from the .csv data.

4.1 AP Density and Coverage Heat Maps

The density of Wi-Fi APs in the main streets of the city is analyzed based on the number of APs within a given area. This is calculated by counting the number of APs within 1 km × 1 km area making the scanning mobile device at the center as it moves along the streets of the city. Figure 1 and Table 1 summarize the result. Figure 1 shows, as a sample, some areas of the city that are highly populated during working hours, specifically, between 8:00 AM to 6:30 PM. Each dot represents the geographic position where an AP signal is received with the maximum power (RSSI) along the route of travelling. Each AP can be seen from some meters before this location is reached and to some meters afterwards. This coverage area, among others, depends on the distance from the real position of the AP to the point where its signal was detected by the scanning devices.

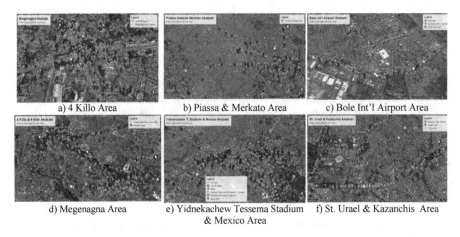

a) 4 Killo Area   b) Piassa & Merkato Area   c) Bole Int'l Airport Area

d) Megenagna Area   e) Yidnekachew Tessema Stadium   f) St. Urael & Kazanchis Area
                              & Mexico Area

Fig. 1. Heat maps of APs on the major streets/areas of Addis Ababa. On the graphics, APs are colored based on their security configurations, in *Red*, *Yellow* and *Green* pins signifying *Secure* (either WPA or WPA2), *Less Secure* (WEP), and *Open* (no security), respectively. (Color figure online)

An attempt has been made to find out the number of APs available on a given area. The measurement is done by simply counting each and every Wi-Fi AP enclosed within a given perimeter. The result is populated in Table 2. It shows that *4 Killo Area* (Fig. 1a) is highly populated with 223.84 APs per km^2 whereas; *Merkato Area* (Fig. 1b) has less number of APs per km^2 which is 48. Having these extremes, the number of APs per km^2 is found to be around 133, on average, in the main streets of the city.

The average linear density of APs on the major streets of the city has been found to be around 50 APs per km. That means someone moving along the major streets of the city can get around one AP within every 20 m, on average. In addition, the path from *Bole Int'l Airport* to *Mesqel Square* has, relatively, the highest APs/km which is 104.89 whereas; the path from *Piassa* to *Autobustera via Merkato* is less populated with only 44.67 APs/km. To have a glimpse of the above results and discussions, Fig. 1 depicts the heat maps of the available Wi-Fi APs on the major areas (avenues and streets) of Addis Ababa.

Table 1. Area density of APs found on the main streets of the city

№	Area/Akababi	Density (AP/km^2)
1	6 killo	139.80
2	4 killo	223.84
3	Piassa	94.36
4	Mexico and Yidnekachew Tessema Stadium	195.12
5	Bole Int'l Airport	123.99
6	Megenagna	187.27
7	St. Urael Church	80.65
8	Merkato	48.98
9	Kazanchis	116.28

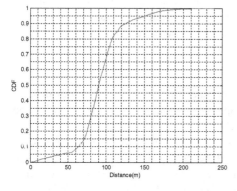

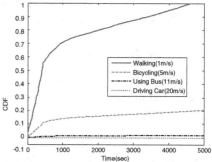

Fig. 2. Shows the cumulative percentage of distances between locations where the RSSI of scanned APs is maximum.

Fig. 3. Cumulative distribution of the time between Wi-Fi access points for various user speeds.

4.2 Distances Between APs

Greatest Circle Distance (GCD) is the shortest distance between two points over spherical surfaces like that of our planet. Based on the location data collected the Haversine Formula [6] is used to generate the distance between the street locations with maximum RSSI of consecutive Wi-Fi APs as shown in Fig. 2. In the same figure, around 10% and 80% of the APs are found within, approximately, 55 and 100 m of the mobile user, respectively. Moreover, it is observed that the deployment of Wi-Fi APs has no regular pattern or topology in the city.

4.3 Time Between APs

Extending the previous analysis, it's tried to generate the minimum amount of time required for a mobile user to get another Wi-Fi AP as it moves in city at various speeds. Figure 3 shows how soon a mobile user, who is either walking or using a bicycle or a bus or driving a car, gets a Wi-Fi AP to get associated with. The graph clearly shows the slowest mobile user, who is walking around, on average, at one meter per second gets the next access point within 20 s, on average. This doesn't tell about the real performance of the AP but confirms the availability of another AP to get connected with. As expected the faster the mobile user moves the lesser the time getting another AP. This effect of mobile user speed on the performance of the Wi-Fi AP should be investigated further to understand its effect on the QoS requirements of various services.

5   Wi-Fi AP Capacity

Based on the collected .csv and .txt data, further analysis was made to determine the capacity of the-already-deployed Wi-Fi APs in the city. To this end, the security configuration, the channel/frequency used, signal strength, the number of APs within a given distance from the mobile user, TCP and UDP throughput analysis, and round trip delay analysis are made and the results are presented hereafter.

5.1   Security Configurations

The security configuration of Wi-Fi APs determines their availability. In our dataset, more than half of the APs are identified as open for anyone to associate as long as the user is within the coverage area.

As presented in Fig. 4 around 40% of the APs are configured with WPA (Wi-Fi Protected Access) and WPA2 (Wi-Fi Protected Access 2) with varied combinations of the available encryption, authentication and other security algorithms. From this, half of them are configured with the strictest security configuration in the trade – 802.11i or WPA2. And, only 1 in around 10 APs are found to be configured with WEP (Wired Equivalent Privacy), the old and weakest security protocol in the realm of WLANs.

5.2   Channel/Frequency Usage

Figure 5 shows the channels together with the center frequencies assigned to the scanned Wi-Fi APs. All the APs are found to be 802.11 b or g types using the 2.4 GHz frequency band. In this standard, each channel is 22 MHz wide and channels 1, 6 and 11 are non-overlapping with 25 MHz separation between the respective center frequencies. Basically, this is what makes them the ideal choice by networking professionals during deployment of WLANs.

That is exactly what can be observed in Fig. 5. Channel 1, 6 and 11 are used approximately in the 27%, 37% and 16% respectively, totaling around 80% of the APs. That leaves only around 20% for the rest of the channels. The use of these three channels not only minimizes the inter-channel interference within a WLAN but also the interference between neighboring WLANs. However, a better way of assigning channels for wireless nodes deserves a critical analysis of channel assignments and the resulting interferences [12].

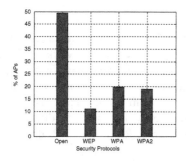

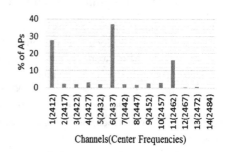

Fig. 4. Distribution of AP security configurations

Fig. 5. Channels and frequencies used by the APs

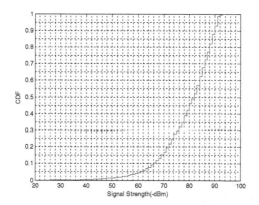

Fig. 6. Received signal strength of the Wi-Fi APs.

5.3 Signal Strength

When talking about signal strength one need to differentiate between the transmitter signal transmission power and the received signal strength. As a standard, the transmission signal power of Wi-Fi equipment, specifically, for 802.11b/g ranges from 1 mW (0 dBm) to 100 mW (20 dBm) [13]. The standard also specifies that the sensitivity will be at least −94, −89 and −71 dBm for data rates of 1, 6 and 54 Mbps, respectively [13]. The last values are only for 802.11 g.

In this work, as depicted in Fig. 6, the RSSI (Received Signal Strength Indicator) ranges from −26 dBm (2.5 mW) to −94 dBm (0.398 nW). Moreover, around 40% of the APs have RSSI value greater than −78 dBm. This value is above the minimum required to achieve full data rate for 802.11b which is 11 Mbps. The same RSSI value can be used to achieve 12 Mbps data rate for 802.11 g based networks. From the overall APs, only 754 APs have RSSI values lower than −90 dBm, which suggests that all APs can perform above the minimum data rate.

5.4   Number of APs Within a Given Distance

Here an attempt has been made to estimate how many APs are deployed in the vicinity of certain locations. The locations presented in Table 2 and two typical working distances, 40 m and 100 m, were chosen. Using a free space outdoor propagation model, for the sake of simplicity, and considering a transmission power of 100 mW at 40 m the received power is −56 dBm, and at 100 m it is −73 dBm. On this basis, Table 2 presents how many APs are received with RSSI equal or higher than −56 dBm and −70 dBm at the chosen locations. It also presents the average RSSI of the APs that are at 40 m and 100 m or closer.

Although, the aforementioned propagation model were used, further analysis should be done to obtain more precise results taking into account the fact that the variability of the signal strengths with distance depends on many factors specific to the environment where the APs are deployed and many parameters of the mobile user.

Table 2. Number of Wi-Fi APs within 40 and 100 m of the mobile device with their corresponding average signal strength values.

Main city area	40 m	Avg. RSSI (−dBm)	100 m	Avg. RSSI (−dBm)
4Killo (AAU Campus)	16	−58	48	−78
6Killo (AAU Main Campus)	14	−56	42	−78
Piassa (Cinema Ethiopia)	16	−62	52	−77
National Theatre (In front of)	19	−68	48	−76
Y.T. Stadium (Taxi Tera)	21	−70	51	−72
Kazanchis (Taxi Tera)	20	−69	43	−73
Megenagna (Kaldis Cafe)	22	−70	45	−75
Bole Int'l Airport (Bole Mini)	21	−70	52	−74
Merkato (city bus station)	9	−70	21	−80
22 Mazoria (Golagul Bldg)	16	−58	57	−72
Le Gare (Legehar)	14	−56	47	−71
Saris Abo (@ EBG)	16	−60	49	−75
Averages	*17*	*−63.9*	*46.3*	*−75.1*

As it is presented in the same table, within 40 m of the mobile device, the received power from Wi-Fi APs is much below the minimum RSSI required to achieve the maximum data rate. Moreover, even at 100 m radius of the mobile device the signal strengths of deployed APs can be used for many services and application domains.

5.5   TCP and UDP Throughput Analysis

Here, TCP and UDP throughput analysis is presented where the data is generated at selected spots of the city by initiating the data traffic from the mobile device to the servers located in Gaza and Libya which are automatically selected by the traffic data gathering app. data traffic of various bytes were generated for those APs that are openly available. The TCP and UDP throughput performances are measured for each traffic load, from smaller to larger values, repeating averagely 100 times for each location. This is done separately for both uploading and downloading scenarios. Figure 7 presents the plot of the average TCP and UDP upload and download values for each traffic load. The average TCP and UDP throughput performances obtained are, approximately, 5.7 Mbps and 6.4 Mbps for download and 7.9 Mbps and 8.8 Mbps for upload, respectively. In both cases the results show that the downstream flow of data shows more variability and, on average, lower performance when compared to the upstream flows. That could be due the uploading is mainly depends on the APs device performances while the downloading is depends on the mobile devices performances.

5.6 Round Trip Delay and Loss Analysis

Using the MobiPerf app the RTT delay were measured for three most common servers on the Internet; YouTube, Facebook and Google. Ping is initiated with 100 packets load for each of the three servers repeating 10 times almost every second. This is done for 12 selected areas of the city. As shown in Fig. 8, the overall maximum and minimum round trip delay times are found to be 257.2 and 105.3 ms, respectively. The average is 224.0, 197.6 and 161.5 ms for YouTube, Facebook and Google, respectively. It's also found that there is no packet loss in all the ping attempts. These results show that the Wi-Fi APs are reliable enough even for services like voice communication which is very sensitive for delay. It is good to remind the reader that mouth-to-ear delay of conversational voice ranges from 20 to 200 ms and for VoIP is between 20 to 150 ms.

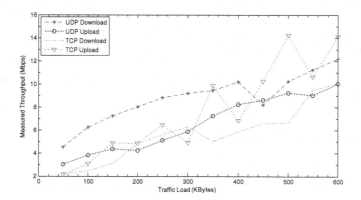

Fig. 7. TCP and UDP performances

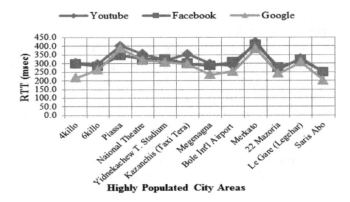

Fig. 8. Ping results of the main areas of the city.

6   Contributions

Based on the data gathered, the analysis made and the discussions presented lots of valuable and unique contributions can be harvested from this geographically pioneering, and yet preliminary, work.

First, users can delay the use of costly services using the slower cellular infrastructure for delay tolerant and non-urgent tasks like email and text messages. *Second,* AP owners may come to know the resource they owe and its economic and social potential prompting for utilizing it effectively and efficiently. *Third,* retailers and importers can pursue procuring new and improved Wi-Fi APs, like 5 GHz based ones, as long as they market based on its better performance and attractive features. *Fourth,* operators can contemplate on exploiting Wi-Fi APs systematically. *Fifth,* researchers and technologists, based on the results obtained and future works proposed, may further study the existing wireless infrastructures and pin point possible performance bottlenecks, potential solutions, and adapt technologies suitable for local situations. *Last but not least,* it is possible that the insights obtained in this work-in-progress, and future supplementary, works may have some inputs for local policy improvements and business opportunities.

7   Conclusions and Future Works

This is a work-in-progress investigation towards a fully integrated and hybrid interworking architecture for mobile traffic offloading. The commercial-grade mobile devices and the performance of the network monitoring apps employed to collect data introduced some errors and skewness of the data which are taken care of right away.

Despite all, the results obtained in this work can be taken as lower bound indicators. Therefore, it can be concluded that the major spots of the city that are highly populated during the working hours are already covered with Wi-Fi APs that can be exploited for many purposes like content sharing, advertising, accident reporting, and mobile data traffic offloading, among others.

In the future, it's planned to continue this investigation in more detail and specificity as the output can be used for operators, policy makers, and business organizations, and researchers, alike. In addition, performance evaluation of a mobile user with different speeds can be extended for vehicular applications and services. It might be required to perform a thorough performance evaluation with time-of-day analysis to further understand the behavior and capability of Wi-Fi APs. The mobility and access behavior is also another dimension that can be pursued.

References

1. Wood, R.: Wireless network traffic worldwide: forecasts and analysis 2013–2018. Research Forecast Report, Analysys Mason Ltd., London, October 2013
2. Gabriel, C.: Wireless broadband alliance industry report 2013: global trends in public Wi-Fi. Technical report, Marvedis Rethink—Wireless Broadband Alliance, Singapore, November 2013
3. Jung, H.: Cisco visual networking index: global mobile data traffic forecast update 2010–2015. Technical report, Cisco Systems Inc., September 2011
4. Gass, R., Diot, C.: An experimental performance comparison of 3G and Wi-Fi. In: Krishnamurthy, A., Plattner, B. (eds.) PAM 2010. LNCS, vol. 6032, pp. 71–80. Springer, Heidelberg (2010). https://doi.org/10.1007/978-3-642-12334-4_8
5. Sommers, J., Barford, P.: Cell vs. WiFi: on the performance of metro area mobile connections. In: Proceedings of the 2012 Internet Measurement Conference, IMC 2012, Boston, Massachusetts, USA, 14–16 November 2012, pp. 301–314. ACM, New York (2012)
6. Mota, V.F.S., Macedo, D.F., Ghamri-Doudane, Y., Nogueira, J.M.S.: On the feasibility of WiFi offloading in urban areas: the Paris case study. In: IFIP Wireless Days, 2013 IFIP, Valencia, Spain, 13–15 November 2013. https://doi.org/10.1109/wd.2013.6686530
7. Lee, K., Lee, J., Yi, Y.: Mobile data offloading: how much can WiFi deliver? IEEE/ACM Trans. Netw. 21(2), 536–550 (2010)
8. Balasubramanian, A., Mahajan, R., Venkataramani, A.: Augmenting mobile 3G using WiFi. In: Proceedings of 8th International Conference on Mobile systems, applications, and services, MobiSys 2010, San Francisco, California, USA, 15–18 June 2010, pp. 209–222. ACM, New York (2010)
9. Jones, K., Liu, L.: What where Wi: an analysis of millions of Wi-Fi access points. IEEE International Conference on Portable Information Devices, pp. 1–4 (2007)
10. Berezin, M.E., Rousseau, F., Duda, A.: Citywide mobile internet access using dense urban WiFi coverage. In: Proceedings of the 1st Workshop on Urban Networking, UrbaNE 2012, Nice, France, 10 December 2012, pp. 31–36. ACM, New York (2012)
11. Afanasyev, M., Chen, T., Voelker, G.M., Snoeren, A.C.: Analysis of a mixed-use urban WiFi network: when metropolitan becomes neapolitan. In: Proceedings of the 8th ACM SIGCOMM Conference on Internet Measurement, IMC 2008, Vouliagmeni, Greece, 20–22 October 2008, pp. 85–98. ACM, New York (2008)
12. Lopez-Aguilera, E., Heusse, M., Rousseau, F., Duda, A., Casademont, J.: Performance of wireless LAN access methods in multicell environments. IEEE Global Telecommunications Conference, GLOBECOM 2006, San Francisco, CA, USA, 27 November – 1 December 2006. https://doi.org/10.1109/glocom.2006.782
13. Part 11: Wireless LAN Medium Access Control (MAC) and Physical Layer (PHY) Specifications. IEEE Std 802.11–2012, March 2012

A Finite-State Morphological Analyzer
for Wolaytta

Tewodros A. Gebreselassie[1](✉), Jonathan N. Washington[2],
Michael Gasser[3], and Baye Yimam[1]

[1] Addis Ababa University, Addis Ababa, Ethiopia
wolaytta.boditti@gmail.com
[2] Swarthmore College, Swarthmore, USA
jonathan.washington@swarthmore.edu
[3] Indiana University, Bloomington, USA
gasser@indiana.edu

Abstract. This paper presents the development of a free/open-source finite-state morphological transducer for Wolaytta, an Omotic language of Ethiopia, using the Helsinki Finite-State Transducer toolkit (HFST). Developing a full-fledged morphological analysis tool for an under-resourced language like Wolaytta is an important step towards developing further NLP (Natural Language Processing) applications. Morphological analyzers for highly inflectional languages are most efficiently developed using finite-state transducers. To develop the transducer, a lexicon of root words was obtained semi-automatically. The morphotactics of the language were implemented by hand in the lexc formalism, and morphophonological rules were implemented in the twol formalism. Evaluation of the transducer shows as it has decent coverage (over 80%) of forms in a large corpus and exhibits high precision (94.85%) and recall (94.11%) over a manually verified test set. To the best of our knowledge, this work is the first systematic and exhaustive implementation of the morphology of Wolaytta in a morphological transducer.

Keywords: Wolaytta language · Morphological analysis and generation
HFST · Apertium · NLP

1 Introduction

This paper describes the development of Free/Open-Source morphological analyzer and generator for Wolaytta, an Omotic language of Ethiopia with almost no computational resources. This tool was created as part of the research for developing a framework for exploiting cross-linguistic similarities in learning the morphology of under-resourced languages.

In language technology research, morphological analysis studies how the internal structure of words and word formation of a language can be modelled computationally. Word analysis involves breaking a word into its morphemes, the smallest forms paired with a particular meaning [1, 14]. The function of a morphological analyzer is to return a lemma and information about the morphology in a word. A morphological generator

© ICST Institute for Computer Sciences, Social Informatics and Telecommunications Engineering 2018
F. Mekuria et al. (Eds.): ICT4DA 2017, LNICST 244, pp. 14–23, 2018.
https://doi.org/10.1007/978-3-319-95153-9_2

does exactly the reverse of this; i.e., given a root word and grammatical information, a morphological generator will generate a particular form of a word [2]. Morphological analysis is a key component and a necessary step in nearly all natural language processing (NLP) applications for languages with rich morphology [2]. The output of morphological analysis can be used in many NLP applications, such as machine translation, machine-readable dictionaries, speech synthesis, speech recognition, lexicography, and spell checkers especially for morphologically complex languages [3].

In this work, we have considered the standard written Wolaytta text and used Helsinki Finite State Toolkit and tools from Apertium to build the morphological analyzer. All of the resources prepared for the development of the Wolaytta morphological transducer, including the lexicon, the morphotactics, the alternation rules, and the 'gold standard' morphologically analysed word list of 1,000 forms are all freely available online under an open-source license in Apertium's svn repository[1]. This paper is organized as follows. Section 2 briefly reviews the literature on morphological analysis generally and morphological analysers implemented in a similar way to the one described in this paper. Section 3 provides a brief overview of the Wolaytta language. The implementation of the morphological analyzer follows in Sect. 4. Section 5 then covers the evaluation and results. Finally, the paper concludes in Sect. 6 with some discussion of future research directions.

2 Literature Review

The importance of the availability of a morphological analyzer for NLP application development is reviewed by different researchers. Malladi and Mannem [19] stated that NLP for Hindi has suffered due to the lack of a high-coverage automatic morphological analyzer. Agglutinative languages such as Turkish, Finnish, and Hungarian require morphological analysis before further processing in NLP applications due to the complex morphology of the words [20]. In machine translation for highly inflectional (morphologically complex) and resource-limited languages, the presence of a morphological analyzer is crucial to reduce data sparseness and improve translation quality [2, 22]. It is with this reality that there exist fully functional morphological analyzers for languages like English, Finnish, French, etc.

Since Kimmo Koskenniemi developed the two-level morphology approach [15], several approaches have been attempted for developing morphological analyzers. The rule-based approach is based on a set of hand-crafted rules and a dictionary that contains roots, morphemes, and morphotactic information [14, 16, 17]. In this approach, the morphological analysis requires the existence of a well-defined set of rules to accommodate most of the words in the language. When a word is given as an input to the morphological analyzer and if the corresponding morphemes are missing in the dictionary, then the rule-based system fails [15].

---

[1] Available at: https://svn.code.sf.net/p/apertium/svn/incubator/apertium-wal/.

2.1 Related Work

The transducer for Wolaytta presented in this paper was developed using a rule-based approach, implemented using a Finite State Transducer (FST). As outlined in some of the sources below, the finite state methodology is sufficiently mature and well-developed for use in several areas of NLP. Other works overviewed show the application of finite-state transducers to other Afroasiatic languages.

Among languages of Ethiopia, there is some research on developing morphological analyzers, including for Amharic [2, 3, 21], Afan Oromo [2] and Tigrigna [2]. Amharic and Tigrigna are classified as Semitic languages, and Afan Oromo is classified as a Cushitic language. One of the most well-known of these is HornMorpho [2], which is accessible online. HornMorpho is a system for morphological processing of the most widely spoken Ethiopian languages—Amharic, Oromo, and Tigrinya—using finite state transducers. For each language, it has a lexicon of roots derived from dictionaries of each language. To evaluate the system, words from different parts of speech are selected randomly from each word list. The system shows 96% accuracy for Tigrinya verbs and 99% accuracy for Amharic verbs.

Washington et al. [9] describes the development of a Free/Open-Source finite-state morphological transducer for Kyrgyz using the Helsinki Finite-State Toolkit (HFST). The paper described issues in Kyrgyz morphology, the development of the tool, some linguistic issues encountered and how they were dealt with, and issues left to resolve. An evaluation is presented showing that the transducer has medium-level coverage, between 82% and 87% on two freely available corpora of Kyrgyz, and high precision and recall over a manually verified test set. In the other work using the same formalism, Washington et al. [23] describe the development of Free/Open-Source finite-state morphological transducers for three more Turkic languages—Kazakh, Tatar, and Kumyk—also using HFST. These transducers were all developed as part of the Apertium project, which is aimed at creating rule-based machine translation (RBMT) systems for lesser resourced languages. This paper describes how the development of a transducer for each subsequent closely-related language took less development time because of being able to reuse large portions of the morphotactic description from the first two transducers. An evaluation is presented shows that the transducers all have a reasonable coverage around 90% on freely available corpora of the languages, and high precision over a manually verified test set.

Yona and Wintner [18] describe HAMSAH (HAifaMorphological System for Analyzing Hebrew), a morphological processor for Modern Hebrew, based on finite-state linguistically motivated rules and a broad coverage lexicon. The set of rules comprehensively covers the morphological, morpho-phonological and orthographic phenomena that are observable in contemporary Hebrew texts. They show that reliance on finite-state technology facilitates the construction of a highly efficient and completely bidirectional system for analysis and generation.

3   Morphology of the Language

Wolaytta belongs to the Omotic language family, which is a branch of the Afroasiatic language phylum, and is spoken in the Wolaytta Zone and some other parts of the Southern Nations, Nationalities, and People's Region of Ethiopia [4]. Wolaytta has had a formal orthography since the 1940s, and is written in the Latin alphabet. A Bible was published in Wolaytta in 1981 [5].

Wolaytta is an agglutinative language and word forms can be generated from root words by adding suffixes. From a single root word, many word forms can be generated using derivational and inflectional morphemes. The order of added morphemes is governed by the morphotactic rules of the language. While suffixation is the most common word formation strategy in Wolaytta [6], compounding is also used [5].

In forming a word, adding one suffix to another, or "concatenative morphotactics", is an extremely productive element of Wolaytta's grammar [24]. This process of adding one suffix to another suffix can result in relatively long word forms, which often contain the amount of semantic information equivalent to a whole English phrase, clause or sentence. For example, "7imisissiis" is one word form in Wolaytta, which is equivalent to the expression in English "He caused someone to make someone else cause giving something to someone else". When we analyze this word, it consists of 7im-is-iss-iis give-CAUS.CAUS.-PF.3 M.SG. Due to this complex morphological structure, a single Wolaytta word can give rise to a very large number of parses.

The second word formation process in Wolaytta is compounding. Compounding is the process in which two or more lexemes combine into a single new word [6]. Although Wolaytta is very rich in compounds, compound morphemes are rare in Wolaytta and their formation process is irregular. As a result, it is difficult to determine the stem of compounds from which the words are made [5].

Wolaytta nouns are inflected for number, gender and case. According to Wakasa [4], common nouns in Wolaytta are morphologically divided into four subclasses, three of which are masculine and one of which is feminine. Place-name and personal nouns are inflected differently from common nouns. Numerals are morphologically divided into four subclasses. They inflect according to case, and concrete forms (singular and plural) of the common noun can be derived from them. Verbs in Wolaytta are inflected for person, number, gender, aspect and mood. Wolaytta has two genders (masculine and feminine), two numbers (singular and plural), three persons (first, second and third), and five cases (absolutive, oblique, nominative, interrogative, and vocative).

In terms of derivational processes, a common noun stem may be derived from a common noun stem or a verb stem by adding a suffix that has a particular function. In the same way, a verb stem may be derived from a common noun stem.

4   Implementation of the Morphological Analyzer

The modeling and implementation of the morphology is designed based on the popular Helsinki Finite State Toolkit (HFST), which is a free/open-Source reimplementation of the Xerox finite-state toolchain [9]. HFST provides a framework for compiling and applying linguistic descriptions with finite state methods and is used for efficient

Table 1. Words in their lexical and surface forms

Lexical form	Surface form
d-. -NOM.M.SG.	d-ées
wooss-. -PF.3 M.SG.	wooss-íis
m-. -PF.3 M.SG.	miss-íis
7im-.-CAUS.-CAUS.-PF.3 M.SG	7im-is- iss-íis

Table 2. Number of stems in each of the main categories

Part of speech	Number of stems	Example representation in lexc
Noun	4,628	LEXICON NounRoot aahotett:aahotett N-M-CMN-A ; ! "wid
Verb	2,609	LEXICON VerbRoot aac:aac V-IV ; ! "sprout"
Numeral	12	LEXICON NumberRoot iss:iss NUM-1 ; ! "1"
Pronoun	22	LEXICON Pronouns ta:ta PRONOUN-1-S ; ! "I/me"
Punctuation	16	LEXICON Punctuation %.%<sent%>:%. # ;
Adjectives	2,242	LEXICON Adjectives aammotida:aammotida ADJ ; ! "rotten,
Adverb	368	LEXICON Adjectives aayyee'ana:aayyee'ana ITJ ; !
Interjection	136	LEXICON Pronouns ta:ta PRONOUN-1-S ; ! "I/me"
Preposition	16	LEXICON Prepositions
Postposition	40	LEXICON POSTPOS %+yyo%<post%>:%>yyo CMN-To-All ; !
Connection	26	LEXICON Connection gishshaw:gishshaw CONN ; ! "because"
Nominalizer	21	LEXICON Connection %<nmlz%>%<sing%>%<masc%>%<abs%>:gaa;
Total	10,136	

language application development [9]. HFST has been used for creating morphological analyzers and spell checkers using a single open-source platform and supports extending and improving the descriptions with weights to accommodate the modeling of statistical information [11]. It implements both the *lexc* formalism for defining lexicons, and the *twol* and *xfst* formalisms for modeling morphophonological rules which describe what changes happen when morphemes are joined together.

FSTs are a computationally efficient, inherently bidirectional approach that distinguishes between the surface and lexical realizations of a given morpheme and attempts to establish a mapping between the two. It can be used for both analysis (converting from word form to morphological analysis) and generation (converting from morphological analysis to word form) [10, 13]. Table 1 below shows examples of lexical and surface form representations for sample Wolaytta words in the two-level morphology.

While building the Wolaytta morphological analyzer using HFST, the following information is used: a lexicon of Wolaytta words, morphotactics, and orthographic rules.

The lexicon is the list of stems and affixes together with basic information about them (Noun stem, Verb stem, etc.,). One of the challenges to develop natural language processing applications for languages like Wolaytta is the unavailability of digital resources. There are no available digital resources, like corpora, for Wolaytta. The Wolaytta lexicon was extracted semi-automatically from an unpublished Wolaytta-English bilingual dictionary and other printed reference books written for academic purposes. The data in Table 2 shows the part of speech, the number of stems in the lexicon of that part of speech, and an example of how the data is represented in the system.

Morphotactics is a model of morpheme ordering that explains which classes of morphemes can follow other classes of morphemes inside a word [10]. The lexicon and morphotactics are defined in the HFST-lexC compiler, which is a program that reads sets of morphemes and their morphotactic combinations in order to create a finite state transducer. Using HFST, morphophonology is mostly dealt with by assigning special segments in the morphotactics (lexc) which are used as the source, target, and/or part of the conditioning environment for twol rules [10]. In lexc, morphemes are arranged into named sets called sub-lexicons. As shown in Fig. 1, each entry of a sub-lexicon is a pair of finite possibly empty strings separated by ":" and associated with the name of a sub-lexicon called a continuation class.

```
LEXICON Root
          VerbRoot ;
LEXICON VerbRoot
          aac:aac V-IV ; ! "sprout"
LEXICON V-IV
          %<v%>%<iv%>:%> VERB-INFL ;
LEXICON VERB-INFL
          VERB-Imfr ;
LEXICON VERB-Imfr
          %<p3%>%<sing%>%<fem%>%<imfr%>:awsu # ;
```

Fig. 1. Example lexicons representing a single path, for the form *aacawsu*.

One of the challenging tasks is identifying the existing roots and suffixes of each word in all the word classes, since the available linguistic studies of the language are limited. For this language, the most useful study is that of Wakasa [4], which we used to categorize the collected lexicons from the dictionary into different classes based on their morphological characteristics.

Morphophonological and orthographic rules are spelling rules used to model the changes that occur in a word when two morphemes combine. The orthographic rules for the Wolaytta language in the HFST architecture are written in the HFST-TwolC formalism. HFST-TwolC rules are parallel constraints on symbol-Pair strings governing the realizations of lexical word forms as corresponding surface strings. HFST-TwolC is an accurate and efficient open-source two-level compiler. It compiles grammars of two level rules into sets of finite-state transducers. Identifying and writing the existing rules manually is a real difficulty for under-resourced languages like Wolaytta. Even when a resource such as Wakasa [4] exists, it may fail to express all relevant conditions. Some of the rules in the Wolaytta morphological analyzer are shown in Fig. 2.

```
1.    "change {V} to next vowel"
      %{V%}:Vy<=> _ :0* :Vy ;
      except _ :0* :Vy :Vow ;
      where Vy in Vow ;

2.    "degeminate consonant before -iss"
      Cx:0 <=> _ :Cx :0* :i :s :s ;
      Except    _ :Cx %{‼%}: ;
                _ :c ; ! avoid conflict with cc >sh
      where Cx in Cns ;

3.    "first c>s when cc >sh before -iss"
      c:s<=> _ c: :0* :i :s :s ;
      except _ c:0 ; ! avoid conflict with degemination, etc.

4.    "second c>h when cc >sh before -iss"
      c:h <=> c: _ :0* :i :s :s ;
```

Fig. 2. Example morphophonological/orthographic rules for Wolaytta in the twol formalism.

The symbol ! indicates comments; % is an escape character, and archiphonemes are in {}. Whenever there are exceptions, the archiphoneme %{‼%} (which is always deleted in the output) is used to block phonology from applying.

5   Analysis and Evaluation

As mentioned before, the system is implemented using Helsinki finite state tools. Morphotactic rules and possible morphemes are defined in the lexicon file. Alternation rules of Wolaytta verbs are defined and the rules are composed with the lexicon file in a HFST-twol file. The system works in two directions, between the lexical and surface levels.

We have prepared a Wolaytta sentence corpus from the Wolaytta-English bilingual dictionary. Identifying the existing Wolaytta-only sentences requires lots of manual work in line with the programs written to identify Wolaytta-only sentences. One of the difficulties is confusion with words that can also be English (E.g. "He" refers "This" in Wolaytta).

Table 3. Results: overall coverage

Total no. tokenized words in the corpus	38,479
% Recognized words	83.13
% Unrecognized words	16.87
Translation time	0.96 S

As listed in Table 3 above, 16.87% of words are not recognized by the Wolaytta morphological analyzer. Since most Wolaytta texts use the apostrophe character (U+0027) to represent the glottal stop instead of the more proper modifier letter apostrophe (U+02BC), most words with glottal stops are unrecognised. Among the top twenty unrecognized words, more than 75% are words with glottal stop characters. The remaining words fall into out-of-vocabulary words (mostly proper nouns) and noise. The lexicon is collected mostly from the Wolaytta-English dictionary. Adding more lexical entries collected from different domains to the system could further improve the coverage.

To evaluate the accuracy of the system, one thousand forms were chosen at random from a corpus of approximately 38K Wolaytta words. These forms were tokenised and hand-annotated, creating a gold standard. When compared against the output of the transducer, precision (the percentage of returned analyses that are correct) is 94.85% and recall (the percentage of correct analyses that are returned) is 94.11%.

6   Conclusions and Future Work

We described the construction of the first known morphological analyzer for Wolaytta using HFST and the Apertium framework. This morphological analyzer acts as a preliminary step to achieving relevant output for the applications like spell checking, text mining, text summarization, etc., by providing analyses of word forms. This morphological transducer can also easily be used to for developing a machine translation system for Wolaytta-English since our system is already incorporated into Apertium.

To develop a fully functional analyzer, the lexicon needs to be exhaustive and rich in morpho-syntactic information, and it is necessary to write additional phonological rules to cover all cases where they are needed. Our analyzer can handle inflectional and derivational morphology for native Wolaytta words, but so far not for loan words. In future work, analysis for other categories needs to be handled by adding exceptions for widely used loan words to existing rules. Moreover, we the working system is available on the web to anyone interested in further enhancing the analyzer or in need of a Wolaytta transducer for use in their own application development.

References

1. Allen, J.: Natural language understanding (1987)
2. Gasser, M.: HornMorpho: a system for morphological processing of Amharic, Oromo, and Tigrinya. In: Conference on Human Language Technology for Development, Alexandria, Egypt (2011)
3. Mulugeta, W., Gasser, M.: Learning morphological rules for Amharic verbs using inductive logic programming. Lang. Technol. Normalisation Less-Resourced Lang. **7** (2012)
4. Wakasa, M.: A descriptive study of the modern Wolaytta language. Unpublished Ph.D. thesis, University of Tokyo (2008)
5. Lamberti, M., Roberto, S.: The Wolaytta Language, vol. 6. Rudiger Koppe, Cologne (1997)
6. Lessa, L.: Development of stemming algorithm for Wolaytta text. Diss. aau (2003)
7. Bosch, S.E., Pretorius, L.: A finite-state approach to linguistic constraints in Zulu morphological analysis. Studia Orientalia Electronica **103**, 205–228 (2015)
8. Beesley, K.R., Karttunen, L.: Finite State Morphology. Center for the Study of Language and Information (2003)
9. Washington, J., Ipasov, M., Tyers, F.M.: A finite-State morphological transducer for Kyrgyz. In: LREC (2012)
10. Martin, J.H., Jurafsky, D.: Speech and Language Processing, International Edition 710 (2000)
11. Linden, K., Axelson, E., Hardwick, S., Silfverberg, M., Pirinen, T.: HFST—framework for compiling and applying morphologies. In: Mahlow, C., Pietrowski, M. (eds.) State of the Art in Computational Morphology. Communications in Computer and Information Science, vol. 100, pp. 67–85. Springer, Berlin Heidelberg (2011). https://doi.org/10.1007/978-3-642-23138-4_5
12. Lindén, K., Silfverberg, M., Pirinen, T.: Hfst tools for morphology—an efficient open-source package for construction of morphological analyzers. In: Mahlow, C., Pietrowski, M. (eds.) State of the Art in Computational Morphology. Communications in Computer and Information Science, vol. 41, pp. 28–47. Springer, Berlin Heidelberg (2009). https://doi.org/10.1007/978-3-642-04131-0_3
13. Karttunen, L.: Finite-state lexicon compiler. Technical report ISTL-NLTT-1993-04-02, Xerox Palo Alto Research Center, Palo Alto, California (1993)
14. Oflazer, K.: Two-level description of Turkish morphology. In: Proceedings of the Sixth Conference on European Chapter of the Association for Computational Linguistics, EACL 1993, p. 472. Association for Computational Linguistics, Stroudsburg (1993)
15. Koskenniemi, K.: A general computational model for word form recognition and production. In: Proceedings of the 10th International Conference on Computational Linguistics, pp. 178–181. Association for Computational Linguistics (1984)
16. Grac, M.: Yet another formalism for morphological paradigm. In: Recent Advances in Slavonic Natural Language Processing, RASLAN 2009, p. 9 (2009)
17. Oflazer, K., Kuruoz, I.: Tagging and morphological disambiguation of Turkish text. In: Proceedings of the Fourth Conference on Applied Natural Language Processing, ANLC 1994, pp. 144–149. Association for Computational Linguistics, Stroudsburg (1994)
18. Yona, S., Wintner, S.: A finite-state morphological grammar of Hebrew. Nat. Lang. Eng. **14**(02), 173–190 (2008)
19. Malladi, D.K., Mannem, P.: Context based statistical morphological analyzer and its effect on Hindi dependency parsing. In: Fourth Workshop on Statistical Parsing of Morphologically Rich Languages, vol. 12, p. 119 (2013)

20. Eray Yildiz, C., Bahadir Sahin, H., Mustafa Tolga Eren, O.: A morphology-aware network for morphological disambiguation (2016)
21. Amsalu, S., Gibbon, D.: Finite state morphology of Amharic. In: Proceedings of RANLP (2005)
22. Goldwater, S., McClosky, D. Improving statistical MT through morphological analysis. In: Proceedings of the Conference on Human Language Technology and Empirical Methods in Natural Language Processing, pp. 676–683. Association for Computational Linguistics (2005)
23. Washington, J., Salimzyanov, I., Tyers, F.M.: Finite-state morphological transducers for three Kypchak languages. In: Proceedings of LREC, pp. 3378–3385 (2014)
24. Beesley, K.R., Karttunen, L.: Finite-state non-concatenative morphotactics. In: Proceedings of the 38th Annual Meeting on Association for Computational Linguistics, pp. 191–198. Association for Computational Linguistics (2000)

Malaria Detection and Classification Using Machine Learning Algorithms

Yaecob Girmay Gezahegn[1(✉)], Yirga Hagos G. Medhin[2],
Eneyew Adugna Etsub[1], and Gereziher Niguse G. Tekele[2]

[1] Addis Ababa University, Addis Ababa, Ethiopia
yaecob.girmay@gmail.com, eneyew_a@yahoo.com
[2] Mekelle University, Mekelle, Ethiopia
yirgaatmail@gmail.com, gezubashay@gmail.com

Abstract. Malaria is one of the most infectious diseases, specifically in tropical areas where it affects millions of lives each year. Manual laboratory diagnosis of Malaria needs careful examination to distinguish infected and healthy Red Blood Cells (RBCs). However, it is time consuming, needs experience, and may face inaccurate lab results due to human errors. As a result, doctors and specialists are likely to provide improper prescriptions. With the current technological advancement, the whole diagnosis process can be automated. Hence, automating the process needs analysis of the infected blood smear images so as to provide reliable, objective result, rapid, accurate, low cost and easily interpretable outcome. In this paper comparison of conventional image segmentation techniques for extracting Malaria infected RBC are presented. In addition, Scale Invariant Feature Transform (SIFT) for extraction of features and Support Vector Machine (SVM) for classification are also discussed. SVM is used to classify the features which are extracted using SIFT. The overall performance measures of the experimentation are, accuracy (78.89%), sensitivity (80%) and specificity (76.67%). As the dataset used for training and testing is increased, the performance measures can also be increased. This technique facilitates and translates microscopy diagnosis of Malaria to a computer platform so that reliability of the treatment and lack of medical expertise can be solved wherever the technique is employed.

Keywords: Machine learning · Image segmentation · SIFT · SVM
Blood smear · Microscopic · Feature extraction

1 Introduction

Malaria is an endemic and most serious infectious disease next to tuberculosis throughout the world. Africa, Asia, South America, to some extent in the Middle East and Europe are affected by the disease [1]. Plasmodium species which affect humans are: Malariae, Ovale, Vivax, Falciparum and recently Knowlesi. The only species that is potentially fatal is Plasmodium Falciparum according to Center for Infectious Diseases (CDC) report [2, 4].

© ICST Institute for Computer Sciences, Social Informatics and Telecommunications Engineering 2018
F. Mekuria et al. (Eds.): ICT4DA 2017, LNICST 244, pp. 24–33, 2018.
https://doi.org/10.1007/978-3-319-95153-9_3

The distribution of Malaria in Ethiopia can be found in places where the elevation is less than 2300 m above sea level, as can be shown in Fig. 1. The transmission of Malaria is seasonal and hence reaches its peak from September to December following the rainy summer season [12].

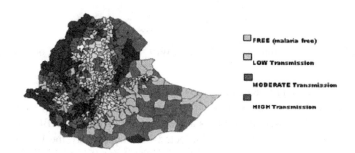

Fig. 1. Map of malaria strata in Ethiopia (©2014) [12].

The two widely known species of Plasmodium in Ethiopia are Falciparum (77%) and Vivax (22%). Relative frequency varies in time and space within a given geographical range. Plasmodium Malariae and Ovale are rare and less than 1%. 60% of the population lives in lowland areas where Malaria can easily spread. Out of the overall population more than 11 million (13%) is under high risk of the infectious disease.

The economic impact in the countries which are affected by Malaria is huge. According to World Health Organization (WHO), total funding for Malaria was estimated to be US$ 2.9 billion in 2015. Governments of endemic countries provided 32% of total funding. According to different studies, 40% of public health drug expenditure is allocated for Malaria, 30% to 50% of inpatient admissions and up to 60% of outpatient health clinic visits are due to Malaria [2, 3], not to mention the humanitarian and non-governmental organizations supporting in different ways.

The reasons for the death toll in the aforementioned regions are due to convenient tropical climate for the growth of the parasites, inadequate technology to combat the disease, illiteracy, and poor socio-economic conditions which make access difficult to health and prevention resources [3]. So, to prevent and eradicate Malaria by the help of technological applications, this paper tries to address image processing techniques and machine learning based identification and classification algorithms which facilitate the diagnosis process.

Mosquito consumes human blood by biting, sporozoites circulate in the blood stream and finally move to the liver where they multiply asexually for some time. In the liver merozoites are regenerated and then invade RBCs [4, 5]. Within RBC the parasite either grows until it reaches a mature form and breaks the cell to release more merozoites into the blood stream to conquer new RBCs or it may grow to reach asexual form named gametocyte and be taken by a mosquito to infect another person where it sexually regenerates to produce sporozoites [6].

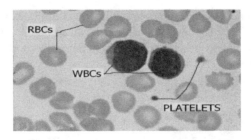

Fig. 2. Healthy thin blood film image with RBCs, WBCs and Platelets [9]. (Color figure online)

Conventionally, Malaria parasite diagnosis is done by visual detection and recognition of the parasite in a Giemsa (the widely used staining technique) stained sample of blood through a microscope. Blood is a combination of Plasma, RBC, White Blood Cells (WBCs), and Platelets [7]. In an infected blood, not only the blood cell components but also the parasites with the different life stages [8] can be detected.

WBCs, Platelets, Plasmodium species and artifacts are deeply stained and appear as dark blue-purplish whereas RBCs are less stained leaving a bright center (patch) with lightly colorized intensity, as shown in Fig. 2. Based on the variation of stain, which in turn tells us the intensity variation, the parasites can be analyzed. However, the quality of the stained image varies according to the available illumination used during acquisition. Malaria can also be diagnosed using Rapid Diagnosis Test (RDT) or Microscope. Microscopic diagnosis is the gold standard which requires special training and considerable expertise. It involves examination of Giemsa stained thick or thin blood film using a light microscope. The method is labor intensive, time consuming and accuracy depends on experience of experts at the field. Hence, automating the process is important to provide an accurate, reliable and objective result [10]. Furthermore, fast diagnostic method is essential for control and eradication of the disease once and for all. Here, an automatic diagnosing of Malaria, which uses image processing and machine learning algorithms has been presented in order to classify and detect the parasite species.

Table 1, depicts comparison of manual, RDT and Computerized diagnosis of Malaria. Using RDT the diagnosis can be performed in about 15–20 min and requires no special training, equipment or electricity. Detection sensitivities of RDTs are comparable to microscopic diagnosis for a larger number of parasite density. Nevertheless, they do not provide quantitative results. In addition, cost of RDT examination is higher than microscopy. On the other hand, computerized diagnosis can provide more consistent and objective results compared to manual microscopy. For instance, the time needed for examination using mobile devices is less than one minute [18], which implies the diagnosis can be done instantly. Generally, automated diagnosis can detect a large number of parasites per microliter, needs no special training and outperforms in both accuracy and computational time than the others.

The rest of the paper is organized as follows, Sect. 2 presents comparison of image segmentation techniques. Section 3 discusses feature extraction and classification using SIFT & SVM, and Sect. 4 addresses conclusion and future work.

Table 1. Comparisons of manual, RDT and computerized microscopy diagnosis requirements and specifications [14, 15].

	Microscopy (manual)	RDT	Computerized (automated)
Requirements	Electricity (optional)	None	Yes
	Special training	Basic training	Basic training
	Staining chemicals	None	Same + computer + camera
Time	∼60 min (subjective)	15–20 min	<1 min [18]
Cost	US $ 0.12-0.40	US$ 0.60–2.50	Similar to manual
Specifications			
Detection threshold	500 par/μl	∼100 par/μl	∼700 par/μl
Detection of all species	Yes	Some brands	Yes
Quantification	Yes	None	Yes
Species identification	Yes	None	Yes
Life-stage identification	Yes	None	Yes

2 Image Analysis

Analysis of images is the use of computer algorithms to extract some useful information [13]. One of the most critical tasks in image analysis is segmentation of images [11]. In this paper, segmentation and classification methods for malaria infected thin blood smear images are discussed. Clinical image processing can broadly be classified into (i) Macroscopic image analysis, and (ii) Microscopic image analysis [13].

Macroscopic analysis of images analyzes images of human organs such as heart, brain, eye, etc. Microscopic analysis of cells from blood, however, helps to understand the nature of cells, and if there is any parasite present, then it can be diagnosed by analyzing the cells [13]. The focus of the paper is microscopic analysis of blood smear images.

Segmentation of images can broadly be classified into deductive and inductive processing. Deductive processing is analyzing and segmenting of images from a higher level to a lower level which is computationally expensive. On the other hand, inductive technique defines object of interest with specific properties, it filters out objects which have unique parameters. Inductive techniques are computationally better than deductive, the details are depicted in Table 2. The reason being all deductive techniques need conversion of images to other image domains, removal of noise and artifacts, morphological processing, segmentation, post processing, feature extraction and classification. In conventional medical image analysis, different procedures are needed to filter

Table 2. Summary of deductive and inductive segmentation techniques

Main categories	Techniques	Advantages	Disadvantages
Deductive segmentation	K-means clustering, genetic algorithm, thresholding, otsu, harris corner detection	From higher level to lower level processing, have good sensitivity and image is processed step by step	Computationally expensive, sensitive to variation in illumination and it is mage specific
Inductive segmentation	Annular ring ratio (ARR) and modified ARR	No preprocessing, locates only stained components, insensitive to image variation, works with all images and provides accurate location of RBC	Computationally fast but accuracy wise a little bit lesser than deductive

out the RBCs from the rest of the image. Many papers on blood film images for Malaria diagnosis use different types of segmentation techniques for extraction of features and classification as shown in Table 2.

3   Detection of Malaria Parasite with the Help of Machine Learning Algorithms

With the help of Scale Invariant Feature Extraction (SIFT) and Support Vector Machine (SVM) it is possible to detect and classify images with some features into predefined categories or labels.

3.1   Feature Extraction of Images Using Scale Invariant Feature Transformation (SIFT)

This algorithm extracts features and descriptors from all the Gemisa stained images and then clusters using Hough transform. It enables the correct match for a key-point to be selected from a large database of other key-points. The algorithm is invariant to rotation, scale and translation and hence here it is applied to extract Malaria parasite infected RBC images which are deeply stained [16]. The four stages of SIFT have been employed in order to have a well feature extracted image (Fig. 7).

(a) **Scale-space Extrema Detection:-** helps to detect key points from an image by first applying difference of Gaussian at difference scale space and identifying the local minima or maxima of an image as is depicted in Fig. 5(a).

(b) **Key-point Localization:-** following the computation of the difference of Gaussian, each sample point is compared to its neighbor pixels in the current scale space as shown in Fig. 5(b). If the sampled point is maxima or minima then the sampled pixel is labeled as a key-point.

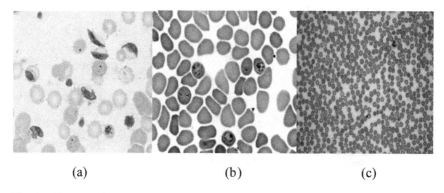

(a)	(b)	(c)

Fig. 3. Giemsa stained input images: (a) Falciparum, (b) Vivax and (c) Free blood cells.

Fig. 4. Flow diagram for diagnosing of malaria using machine learning algorithms.

(c) **Orientation Assignment:-** in order to make features invariant to rotation, orientation is assigned based on local image gradient directions to every feature.

(d) **Key-point Descriptor:-** lastly a descriptor is used at the selected scale (in our case 16 × 16 pixels) in the region around each key-point after an image's location, scale, and orientation to each key-point is known (Fig. 6).

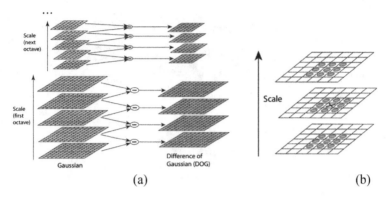

(a)   (b)

Fig. 5. (a) Repeatedly convolve and down sample by 2 to find difference-of-Gaussian of an image, (b) Computing the maxima or minima of the difference-of-Gaussian from its neighbors [16].

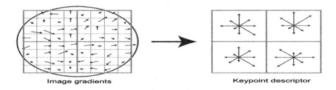

Fig. 6. A 2 × 2 image descriptor array computed from an 8 × 8 set of samples [16].

There are many fast feature detectors and descriptor extraction algorithms like Speed Up Robust Feature (SURF), Robust Independent Elementary Features (BRIEF) and Oriented Fast and Rotated BRIEF (ORB) in image processing but SIFT out performs well when it comes to preserving scale.

The input images are collected from nearby clinics and CDC [6, 19]. The 300 collected images (110 falciparum, 100 vivax and 90 are parasite free images) out of which 90 were used for testing purpose. Hence, each of the species and the parasite free images consists of 30 test images. Classification is done based on type of Plasmodium parasite species. Here, we have considered only parasite free and the two species of the parasite which are prevalent in Ethiopia. However, we are collecting (starting from image acquisition process) more images from the different regions of Ethiopia and we will be studying all the different species using deep learning in our future work. Having our own acquisition process helps us to collect a large number of images and mitigates noises and artifacts which might result due to uncontrolled environment during acquisition from other sources.

By applying SIFT to the input images, the descriptors are shown in Fig. 7(a) and (b). Images with Falciparum (a) and Vivax (b) are labeled with the key-points.

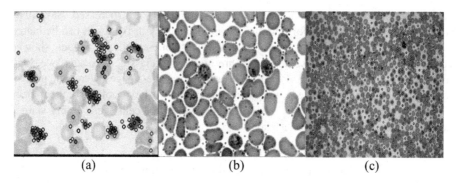

(a)   (b)   (c)

Fig. 7. (a) Image key-points of Falcipurum, (b) Image key-points of Vivax and (c) Free/clean of parasite image

3.2   Creating Bag of Features

Bag of features is an image processing algorithm derived from the well known document classification method known as Bag of Words Model (BoW). Bag of words classifies documents from a large vocabulary of words according to the number of occurrence of words. In a similar fashion, bag of features of images works by creating a vocabulary of image descriptors from the SIFT extracted descriptors.

3.3   Train and Classify Images Using SVM

SVM is a supervised machine learning algorithm that enables to classify new input images based on previously labeled or trained data. It estimates the optimal separating hyper-plane which maximizes the margin of the training data. SVM can use either linear-kernel for a small data set or Gaussian Radial Basic Function (RBF) if the data has large dimension. Since the data set that we have are images, then RBF is used [17].

RBF kernel is very dependent on parameters 'C' (penalty term for misclassification) and gamma, a parameter of a Gaussian that controls the shape. By varying gamma we can increase or decrease the variance. In order to have an optimized values of 'C' and gamma we used opencv's svm.train_auto method which finds the optimal 'C' and gamma values form the given data set. For detecting and classifying Malaria parasite, the features extracted data with SIFT are given to SVM as input for training.

In order to have a well-trained and classified data, Multi-class learning type of classifier is used. Hence, one-against-one method of classification is used to train the collected data into three labels (classes): such as Falciparum, Vivax and parasite free.

After the features are extracted and trained they can automatically classify a test image. If a test image is given to the algorithm, it can be compared with the database of trained images and the image is classified according to the category which is already trained (Falciparum, Vivax or parasite free), that is, the result of the new captured image can be an image that contains Falciparum, Vivax or parasite free. In this work, around 110 images for Falciparum and 100 Vivax, and 90 parasite free images are trained. So far, with a very limited training images, it is reached to a classification accuracy of approximately 78.89% with sensitivity of 80% and specificity of 76.67%. It can be concluded that as the number of training images are increased (say many hundreds of images are used for training) then the accuracy of the result can be better.

From Table 3, we can see that the sensitivity and specificity values showed acceptable results. However, some images are incorrectly classified, because we don't have enough data for training & testing. Furthermore, the images were not preprocessed, quality of the collected images vary because we have collected them from different sources, [6, 19]. We also noticed that parasite free cells were highly stained and hence they were wrongly classified.

Table 3. Performance measures of the experimentation

Type of component	Falciparum (%)	Vivax (%)	Parasite free (%)	Overall performance of SVM (%)
Sensitivity	83.33	76.67	80	80
Specificity	88.33	85	90	76.67
PPV	78.125	71.875	92.30	82.27
Accuracy	–	–	–	78.89

4   Conclusion

In this paper different conventional image processing techniques are compared in order to detect and classify Giemsa stained microscopic blood smear images of Malaria parasite. Conventional image processing techniques which are studied are preprocessing, filtering, segmenting, feature extraction and classification. We have also implemented SIFT and SVM based classification technique. We have learnt that if there is enough database of images of different species and stages of Malaria parasite, then parasites can be detected and classified with good quality by using machine learning algorithms such as SIFT and SVM.

In our future work we will be collecting a large dataset of Malaria images which include all the five species from the different regions of Ethiopia and employ deep-learning based approach in order to detect and classify the different species and their life stages.

References

1. WHO: Global report on antimalarial efficacy and drug resistance (2000–2010)
2. Korenromp, E., et al.: World malaria report. World Health Organization, Geneva, Technical report (2005)
3. Gallup, J., Sachs, J.: The economic burden of malaria. J. Trop. Med. **64**, 85–96 (2001)
4. National Centers for Disease Control Prevention: Laboratory identification of parasites of public health concern. Division of Parasitic Diseases. Accessed 4 Jan 2017
5. Coatney, G., et al.: The primate malarias. U.S. Department of Health, Education and Welfare (1971)
6. https://www.cdc.gov/malaria/about/biology/

7. Microsoft Corporation: Microsoft encarta encyclopedia (2002)
8. Sherman, I.W.: Malaria: parasite biology, pathogenesis and protection (1998)
9. Kareem, S., et al.: A novel method to count the red blood cells in thin blood films. In: IEEE International Symposium on Circuits and Systems (ISCAS), pp. 1021–1024 (2011)
10. Kareem, S., et al.: Automated malaria parasite detection in thin blood films: a hybrid illumination and color constancy insensitive, morphological approach. Applied DSP and VLSI Research Group, University of Westminster London, United Kingdom (2012)
11. Zhiming, T.: Research on graph theory based image segmentation and its embedded application, pp. 14–24. Dissertation of Shanghai Jiao Tong University, Shanghai (2007)
12. http://www.moh.gov.et/malaria
13. Acharya, T., Ray, A.K.: Image Processing Principles and Applications. Wiley, Hoboken (2005). Arizona State University, Tempe
14. WHO: New perspectives, malaria diagnosis. World Health Organization, Geneva, Technical report (2000)
15. Tek, F.B.: Computerized diagnosis of malaria. Ph.D. thesis, University of Westminster, September 2007
16. Lowe, D.G.: Distinctive image features from scale-invariant keypoints. Int. J. Comput. Vis. **60**(2), 91–110 (2004)
17. Cortes, C., Vapnik, V.: Support-vector networks. Mach. Learn. **20**, 273–297 (1995)
18. Kareem Reni, S.: Automated low-cost malaria detection system in thin blood slide images using mobile phones. Doctoral thesis, University of Westminster, March 2014
19. http://www.mu.edu.et/chs/

Intelligent Transport System in Ethiopia: Status and the Way Forward

Tezazu Bireda[(⊠)]

Addis Ababa Institute of Technology, Addis Ababa University,
Addis Ababa, Ethiopia
tezazubrs@yahoo.com

Abstract. Vehicular transportation systems are used extensively to transport people and goods which is detrimental for faster, reliable and cost effective socioeconomic activity. However, there are major challenges associated with accelerated utilization of such systems. These include threat to safety of life and property; pollutions; congestion triggered reduction of road network utilization; reduced cost effectiveness of vehicles; and increased waiting and travelling times of passengers. This paper briefly surveys the above problems in international and national context. It then assesses deficiency of conventional methods of mitigating the problems. Next it proposes introduction of intelligent transport system (ITS) in Ethiopia as a better and cross cutting solution to the above problems. The paper analyses and presents verifications of the hypothesis that if ITS is introduced, the nation would achieve better safety to life and property; less pollution; more efficient mobility traffic control and management; and better utilization of road networks and vehicles.

Keywords: Intelligent transport system · Mobility traffic · Pollution
Congestion · Safety · Utilization efficiency · Ethiopia

1 Introduction

Transportation of humans and goods have been playing important roles in people's daily lives and socioeconomic activities since civilization first formed and needed new means of reaching destinations [1]. Vehicular transportation eased and extended the living, working and entertainment environment people could reach in quicker, convenient and comfortable manner.

The mass production and affordability of vehicles resulted in a new era of modern life and as a consequence and perpetual reciprocation paved ways for modern town planning for efficient multifaceted services; construction of standardized road network infrastructure; use of essential standard traffic rules and signs; use of traffic control signalling systems; deployment of trained human power to drive, maintain, manage, monitor, control and enact laws; etc. all for the safe, cost effective, comfortable and smooth utilization of the vehicular transportation system.

Since the start of private, public and commercial transportation application of vehicles in late 19th century, the total world vehicle population in 2010 exceeded 1.015 billion 24 years after reaching 500 million in 1986 [2]. In 2011, the Organization for

© ICST Institute for Computer Sciences, Social Informatics and Telecommunications Engineering 2018
F. Mekuria et al. (Eds.): ICT4DA 2017, LNICST 244, pp. 34–45, 2018.
https://doi.org/10.1007/978-3-319-95153-9_4

Economic Co-operation and Development (OECD's) International Transport Forum forecasted that the number of cars worldwide would reach 2.5 billion by 2050. This justifies vehicles to be the most important land based transportation carrier that would also be anticipated to continue in the foreseeable future.

In line with this global trend, the total number of registered vehicles in Ethiopia in 2010 had been 377,943. Out of this 231,619 (61.3%) are cars and 4-wheel light vehicles; 44,847 (11.9%) are motorized 2- and 3-wheelers; 81,193 (21.5%) are heavy trucks and 20,284 (5.4%) are buses [3]. With the economic development being observed, the vehicle population in Ethiopia is expected to grow.

Apart from vehicles, a major integral part of a vehicular transportation system is mobility traffic control and management system. It may be termed conventional and modern. Its essence is to ensure the smooth, safe, reliable and faster arbitration in the utilization of the existing road network among vehicles, bicycles, trains, and pedestrians. The conventional system has inflexible traffic signalling time duration adjustment. It is also incapable of automatic synchronization of the traffic signalling systems at intersections distributed throughout a road network of a city. The modern one, however, is capable of both functions and more.

The windows of opportunities for improving mobility traffic with the conventional method are becoming more and more ineffective. This fact naturally leads to a paradigm shift into a modern method called intelligent transportation system (ITS). ITS is becoming attractive one reason being the ubiquities of modern wireless communication technologies with which it can be readily implemented.

The objective of this paper is to study the introduction of ITS for mobility traffic control and management in Ethiopia. The scope is limited to vehicular transportation system. Accordingly, in the paper, the global and national challenges of vehicular transportation systems will be briefly outlined first in Sect. 2. Second, the characteristics and the deficiency of the conventional approach of traffic control will be analyzed in Sect. 3. Next, ITS will be described and its prospects will be introduced. Finally, recommendation of ITS applications will be proposed and discussed for Ethiopia.

2 Challenges of Vehicular Transportation Systems

Challenges associated with increasing utilization of vehicular transportation system include issues of

- increased need of maintaining safety of life and property;
- congestion triggered delays, pronounced pollution, reduction of road utilization, inefficiency of vehicles, and discomfort of drivers, passengers and pedestrians;
- increased burden of rehabilitating existing road facilities and traffic control systems failing due to aging and vehicle related accidents;
- increased need of new road network and mobility traffic control systems;
- increased drain of hard-earned foreign currency for fuel.

One can, however, easily conclude that the benefits of vehicular transportation system outweigh their drawbacks significantly. However, governments and society should give significant attention to minimize the ever-increasing problems. These include loss of lives, injuries, damages to property as well as to increased operational and maintenance costs. Some highlights on some of the above problematic issues are briefly supported from literature as follows.

2.1 Safety Issues

The main causes of vehicular transportation related accidents may be attributed to inefficient mobility traffic management and control systems; poor road conditions and congestion; and driving skill deficiency and unacceptable behaviour of drivers. Other causes include the technical insufficiency of vehicles; bad weather; and lack of sufficient awareness of pedestrians about traffic rules and drivers' behaviour.

According to [4], road traffic accidents caused an estimated 1.24 million deaths worldwide in the year 2010. The risk of dying as a result of a road traffic accident is highest in the African Region (24.1 per 100,000 population), and lowest in the European Region (10.3 per 100,000). Adults aged between 15 and 44 years accounted for 59% of global road traffic deaths and 77% road deaths are among men.

The Ethiopian situation is such that in 2010 the reported number of road traffic fatalities had been 2,581 of which 76% involved males and 24% females. In the same year, the estimated economic loss due to road traffic crashes is at 0.8–1.0% of the GDP [3]. According to [7], Ethiopia loses about 500 million Br (equivalent to $25 million) and 3,000 lives each year from road accidents. About 80% of these losses are caused by drivers' faults and the remaining due to vehicle technical problems, low quality of roads and other causes. Existence of unreliable mobility traffic control and management system may also be one cause.

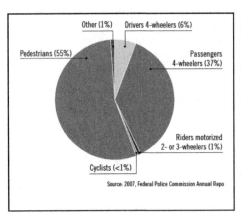

Fig. 1. Deaths by road user category [3]

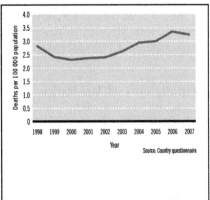

Fig. 2. Trends in road traffic deaths [3]

Organized data on traffic related deaths in Ethiopia in 2007 are depicted in Figs. 1 and 2 [3]. Figure 1 shows pedestrians are most victimized and Fig. 2 indicates the trend which is steadily increasing.

2.2   Environmental Pollution Issues

Transportation accounts for 23% of the world's greenhouse-gas emissions [5]. Congestion highly pronounces many forms of pollutions including over gas emissions, overheats and audible and vibration noises of overcrowded vehicles. Utilizing ITS as an effective mobility traffic control solution can significantly improve mobility and thereby reduce congestion.

2.3   Energy Exhaustion Issues

Some estimate, assuming current consumption rates, that current oil reserves could be completely depleted by the year 2050 [6]. One alternative solution, in the context of this paper, is to utilize systems that improve mobility as stated. When a vehicle moves at low speed, its efficiency reduces. Thus, mobility improvement would have the effect of preserving the existing oil resources from faster depletion.

2.4   Need of Improved Mobility Traffic Control and Management Systems

As the number of vehicles increases their monitoring and control would also grow. Repetitive stoppage of moving vehicles for long durations is mainly due to improper traffic light signalling times. This results in unnecessary fuel consumption, environmental pollution, increased delay, and reduction of productivity of people. As the number of vehicles grows, functioning of conventional mobility traffic control systems would not be suitable and cost effective. Accordingly, a modern way of mobility traffic control systems had been necessitated and implemented as witnessed in most developed nations such as the USA, Germany, and Japan to name a few.

2.5   Need of Rehabilitation of Existing and Expansion of New Road Networks

As population and economy of a nation grow, so does the mobility needs of more people and goods. To meet these needs, a first step would be optimizing all existing road networks, mobility control systems, and other facilities. This entails continuously servicing and maintaining them to their best status. This improves mobility while reducing congestion. If no more optimization is possible in response to increased vehicle population and congestion, the next step would be to construct additional roads. In addition, paradigm shifting from the conventional to the modern mobility traffic control and management systems with ITS would be effective.

2.6   Summarized Implications of the Above Issues Globally and for Ethiopia

The implications of the previous highlights can be summarized as follows. According to [8], if current transport related problems are left unaddressed with modern approach, the world might be continuing towards:

- 1.9 million road deaths annually worldwide by 2020, costing the world an estimated $100 billion each year.
- Close to 9,000 Megatons of global CO_2 emissions from transport vehicles will occur by 2030. This contributes significantly to climate change. Combined with other emissions, it would burden millions of people with health problems through air, water, soil and noise pollution; and
- 30% increase of traffic congestion by 2025 in some countries, costing society billions in fuel and overall economic penalties through time lost.

It could also be predicted that, considering the current level of development of the underdeveloped nations, Ethiopia would suffer in *its part* even worse than the summary implies.

2.7   Scope of Study of This Work

The servitude of vehicular transportation systems should be exploited in safer, cost effective, pollution free and efficient manner. This could be so if the too many problems stated in Sect. 2 are co-ordinately addressed. However, addressing these problems with a single approach and in only one discipline of study would be impossible.

This paper focuses only on mobility traffic control system as a cross cutting solution. It is supposed to address in some measure safety issues, operational and utilization efficiency of roads and vehicles, energy and environmental pollution, and mobility.

3   Mobility Traffic Control, Management and Its Status in Ethiopia

3.1   Overview of the Conventional Traffic Signal Control System

Some elements of the conventional system include traffic signalling lights, road side and on-the-road signs, weigh-in stations, and toll collection systems.

When the number of vehicles and pedestrians using existing road network is very low, the essence of traffic signalling would be minimal or not at all necessary. However, when the number of vehicles matches or outnumbers the required road network, then congestion would be prevalent. This distracts mobility of vehicles and pedestrians. The conventional system would be effective in this regard.

When very large number of vehicles and pedestrians as well as a large and complex road network is involved, the need for synchronization of multiple signalling systems becomes highly essential. For synchronized traffic control to be simple, sufficient and reliable data of mobility of vehicles, trains and pedestrians are necessary. It is with such conditions that the conventional method mostly becomes insufficient or even sometimes failing. This is mainly due to its major drawbacks some of which are:

- The traffic signalling time phases are usually constant for all times of the days. Some may be adjusted manually but may require study and many operators.

- The signalling systems at major road junctions are not automatically synchronized. This would bring congestion and its triggered problems.
- The conventional system has no automatic traffic related data detection and logging system that might be used to improve performance.

3.2 Status of Mobility Traffic Control and Management System in Ethiopia

The Ethiopian experience in using mobility traffic control and monitoring systems can be summarized as follows:

- A number of traffic signals are erected at critical road junctions.
- International traffic control signs have long been utilized for the same purpose.
- Some traffic police use walkie-talky to resolve traffic related problems.
- Most traffic polices control traffic related problems manually (when electrical operated signals are down or where there are no such systems).
- Some motor cycles are utilized to reach at abnormal traffic incident areas.
- Radar systems are used to limit vehicle speed in few intra-city movements.
- Attempt was tried on using GPS assisted navigation and guidance system built into vehicles in Addis Ababa city but no further development.
- GPS based fleet monitoring and controlling systems are being introduced in limited number by private companies.
- A toll based express way is constructed from Addis Ababa to Adama used to relive the highly-congested highway between the cities. The express way is equipped with fee charging station, monitor vehicles in road with CCTV, offer emergency service in case vehicles encountered problem or accidents, etc.
- The recently commissioned Light Rail Transit (LRT) in Addis Ababa introduced a relatively modern train vehicle traffic control system along its route.
- Public and private radio and TV broadcasts are being used to inform drivers and people about traffic updates.

The above facts imply that the current mobility traffic control and management system in Ethiopia is still conventional.

3.3 Analysis of the Conventional System

Already, too much congestion is being observed in arterial roads and junctions, particularly in Addis Ababa. This city is currently being renovated with the construction of new long and wide roads having a number of overpasses and underpasses as well as LRT railways. Similarly, new road networks are being constructed in other major cities. The population of vehicles, residents and passers-by in the cities are increasing. Though the expansion and renovation of the roads would improve the capacity of mobility, the outnumbering vehicles would exhaust this capacity soon to reinstate congestion.

Improvement of mobility in an existing road network may require a number of sequential or concurrent measures. This involves exploiting every possible window of opportunities. The first measure may be servicing and maintaining all roads and traffic control systems to their best status. Second is optimization of mobility and road utilization. This can be done through tuning of traffic control parameters, mainly signalling phase time durations of all traffic control signalling systems in the road network. Third, improving the synchronization of the various traffic control signalling systems at arterial roads may also be considered. The above measures would, however, have limits beyond which it becomes cost ineffective for further improvement. It may not at all even improve the mobility capacity of the road network.

The next higher measure in the conventional sense requires the expansion of road network infrastructure and allocation of land resource. These, however, are expensive. Furthermore, the more land is used for roads, the more congested towns become. Still worse is the usually observed lagging of the infrastructure deployment behind the increase rate of vehicles exacerbate the consequences of congestion. This leads naturally to a paradigm shift into the modern method called ITS, discussed next.

4   Intelligent Transport Systems (ITS)

4.1   What is ITS and Its Purpose?

ITS is the application of various technologies to the management of surface transportation systems in order to increase their efficiency and safety, whilst providing travellers with mobility options based on real-time information [9]. Another definition of ITS from Toyota [10] is as follows: "ITS are transport systems that use communications technologies to link people, roads, and vehicles with the aim of solving various traffic related issues such as preventing accidents, environmental measures, and energy conservation."

ITS helps reduce the time required to clear traffic incidents, the number of secondary accidents, queuing, congestion, fuel consumption and therefore air pollution. Efficiencies in traffic management are enhanced through techniques such as ramp metering to smooth peak traffic flows. Advanced traffic management systems along arterial roads, using computerized traffic signal systems, improve signal progression and synchronization - contributing further to the reduction of delays, fuel use and pollution [9].

The functional parts of ITS include: Traffic Management Systems, Traveller Information Systems, Public Transportation Systems, Vehicle Control and Safety Systems, Commercial Vehicle Operations, Emergency Management Systems, Vulnerable Individual Protection Systems, and Information Management Systems [1]. Many sub-systems are integrated into ITS. These include: CCTV cameras, variable message signs (VMS), vehicle detectors, highway advisory radio, ramp metering, telecommunications, management centers, automated vehicle identification systems, weigh-in-motion stations, and cashless (in-motion) toll collection system [9].

The development and implementation environment for ITS are plenty. It includes vehicular ad-hoc networks (VANET), vehicle to vehicle (V2 V) and vehicle to infrastructure (V2I) communication systems, wireless sensor networks, GPS and GPRS navigation and guidance systems, and cellular mobile network. It also includes sensors for vehicle and pedestrian detection, monitoring and security systems, as well as wireless technologies such as Wi-Fi, Bluetooth, and IR.

ITS contributes to all major transport policy objectives set by a nation. Many ITS applications are aimed at either optimizing the available supply of road infrastructure or reducing demand for it. The result of ITS technology is a more efficient and reliable road transport network that operates with a minimized effect on the environment. ITS also enables in both preventing accidents and mitigating their impacts.

A simplified description of the procedural steps in most ITS applications is [9]:

- **Data collection:** ITS is capable of capturing a range of roadway information from the number of vehicles passing a certain point. ITS can track the position of vehicles through, say, mobile phone or satellite.
- **Data transfer, processing and analysis:** ITS can communicate the data to central units. There, the data is aggregated and transformed into information used to determine future actions.
- **Informed decision-making:** The processed data can be applied in a number of ways to ensure the efficient operation of road networks. For e.g., a road operator may use ITS data for highway management; or a road user may alter his route from updated traffic data.

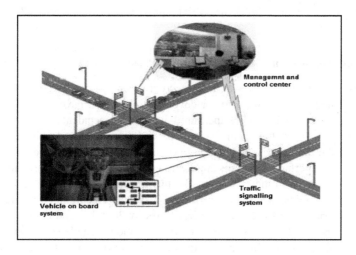

Fig. 3. Traffic management system [1]

Representing ITS with a single diagram would be too complex to accommodate in this short paper. However, the mobility traffic control and management function which is the core and foundation of ITS is illustrated in Fig. 3. above [1].

4.2   Benefits of ITS

With ITS in place, the following benefits may be obtained:

- Enables adaptive and real time control of mobility of vehicles and pedestrians that can minimize accidents, congestion, delays, and fatigue.
- Improved mobility results in improved efficiencies of vehicles and roads.

- Enables reduced road network needed than with conventional traffic control solutions for the same required mobility, safety, and energy efficiency. A fundamental debate exists between perceived needs to increase road supply and the increases in traffic flows obtainable by using existing capacities more intelligently [9].
- Drivers and passengers can get timely information on board of vehicles or from variable message boards as to which route to take that may be shorter and clearer.
- Easy detection and pinpointing of emergency.
- ITS platform enables communication of vehicles that help avoid accidents.
- Enables in-motion toll payment and weighting system that avoids stoppages.
- Getting information on nearest car parking plots.
- Integrated corridor management will entail highways, arterial roads and transit systems within a corridor to optimize people throughput within the corridor [9].
- ITS paves the way for "smart transport system" in which vehicles may be computer driven to move people and goods safer, faster and reliably.

Generally, successful ITS applications are to be found wherever there is significant road traffic. Precise priorities depend upon local circumstances, reflecting the structure of cities, relative distances, traffic densities and the balance of transport modes. All applications share common aims: increased safety, reduced emissions and improved traffic flows [9].

4.3 Global Applications Status and Future Prospect of ITS

ITS already exist and in many cases their successful applications are already deployed. They proved their worth in most major developed cities that have implemented such programs. Performance is readily measured in reduced accidents, reduced incident response times, reduced travel times, reduced emissions, reduced vehicle operating costs, increased traffic speeds, and increased on-time transit performance. For instance, in the Public Transportation Systems application of ITS in Sweden, a variable charging regime was introduced in the express public bus transport system. Charges were collected through automatic electronic fee collection system. Accordingly, this resulted in reductions of road traffic by 20–25%, travel times by 30–50%, and emissions by 10–14% [9]. ITS is being used as a cross cutting solution to address the multifaceted problems associated with vehicular and railways transportation systems. Some developing countries like Brazil, India and South Africa have also already deployed ITS [9]. Unfortunately, ITS technologies are not being used in anything like the scale and quantities that they need to be. Especially when one considers that such technologies are very cost-effective and cost-conservative by comparison with conventional solutions [8]. It is paradox that their utilization is slow, fragmented and uncoordinated.

A number of possible reasons may be enumerated for the slower adaptation of ITS. One reason may be that, developed nations have already invested too much on conventional mobility traffic control and management solutions to easily migrate to ITS. Another reason may be that there are already too many old model vehicles in operation that may need additional equipment to easily be integrated and utilize the advanced features of ITS. Still another reason may be lack of sufficient and consolidated international standard. Standards would have enabled users to easily decide and adopt or contextualize ITS technologies off the shelf. A final reason might be lack of proven universal business model to introduce ITS in the global market in full gear.

However, the ever-increasing problems not properly and intelligently handled by conventional solutions, is pushing many nations to migrate to ITS. This is witnessed by some nations whatever the cost but surely with un-matching benefits. The ubiquities and increased performance with reduced cost of the development environment for ITS is attracting nations to decide the deployment of ITS. Furthermore, another compelling condition to harness ITS is due to the advancement of modern vehicles. Most modern vehicles are coming with many sensors used to monitor, diagnose and guide each internal and external functioning of the vehicle. This enables them to be operated more easily, safely and reliably as well as maintained easily. These vehicles can be made to communicate among each other in V2V mode and with the road side infrastructure in V2I mode. This enables them to avoid collisions while at the same time operate at the maximum speed possible.

The built-in or the easy embedding of navigation, guidance, security and antitheft systems in them enables these cars to be easily controlled by human drivers and/or remote computer. The technology also helps easily pinpoint the exact time and location of incidents which is a requirement for smart transport system. Even old model cars can also use the blessings of ITS by adding into them the basic required hardware and software. A qualitative comparison of conventional and ITS based traffic signal control is tabulated below as extracted from observations in [11, 12] (Table 1).

Table 1. Comparison of conventional and ITS based traffic control systems

Comparison metrics	Conventional based traffic signal control systems	ITS based traffic signal control systems
Traffic signal timing	Fixed but operators may adjust them periodically	Adaptive that may account any time- of-a-day
Control scheme	Local, needing huge effort	Central configuration and control
Use of vehicular flow and speed detectors	Not used	May use detectors such as inductive loops and cameras
Synchronization of traffic signals at intersections	Done manually by operators periodically	Done adaptively by the system instantly to improve traffic
Vehicular traffic flow	Non steady, dominantly congested and saturated	Relatively steady, uncongested and faster
Informative-ness to drivers, passengers and pedestrians	Inflexible to update	Relatively flexible, adaptive and updated centrally
Accident (collision of vehicles and injuries)	Normal	Relatively reduced
Cost of implementation, operation, and maintenance	Normal	Relatively higher but worth the benefits it offers

5 Discussion on Prospects of ITS Applications in Ethiopia

The analyses described previously imply that modern mobility traffic control and management solutions for vehicular transportation system that use ITS would be more effective than the conventional. It is so, not only for the developed nations but also for Ethiopia.

There are a number of reasons for the need of introduction of ITS in Addis Ababa and other major cities of Ethiopia at the earliest possible. First, Ethiopia is currently a low income country whose 81% population still live in rural areas. Its road network and vehicle density can be said to be in their primitive stages. Addis Ababa and the other cities are currently being renovated and expanded almost anew with improved city master plans. This means that, a lot more road network would be constructed and this makes the process to consider ITS now or in the earliest possible.

Second, Ethiopia has about only half a million number of vehicles. This is a very small number compared with even other underdeveloped nations and only very few of them are modern. All newly imported and locally assembled brand new vehicles are increasing. Most of them are also expected to be modern with some ITS ready features so that they can be easily deployed in an ITS based control.

Third, there are already some resources and few expertise available in Ethiopia that serve as fertile ground. This enables to embark, develop and implement ITS which include:

- presence and expansive coverage of legacy to Long Term Evolution (LTE) mobile communication network
- existing conventional traffic signals that can possibly be integrated to the ITS system to be introduced
- presence of some experience with the Addis Ababa to Adama toll based express way corridor that is using some features of ITS
- the new Modjo-Hawassa express way being constructed is planned to have ITS elements including electronic toll collection (ETC) and CCTV systems
- existence of few expertise knowledge in ITS as well as in operating and utilizing this express way
- the recently deployed Light Rail Transit system with its own modern traffic control system and that can be integrated with the existing vehicular system.

Thus, rather than sticking to the relatively ineffective conventional way of mobility traffic control, it is recommended that ITS be incorporated in the master plans of Addis Ababa and other major cities. Their implementation can then be introduced at the early stage and in parallel with the execution of the master plans. It is expected that this would help optimize the utilization of the existing and newly introduced road networks than with conventional approach. It would also help curb accidents and pollution.

6 Conclusion

In Sect. 5, it has been attempted to justify the better merits of ITS over that of the conventional for mobility traffic control and management systems. Thus, if ITS is implemented in Ethiopia, as is done in many developed and few developing nations with reported successes of reduced accidents, reduced incident response times, reduced travel times, reduced emissions, reduced vehicle operating costs, increased traffic speeds, and increased on-time transit performance [9], then it would also do the same for Ethiopia.

This paper therefore strongly recommends that the issue of introduction of ITS be started in Ethiopia at the earliest possible. It is also proposed that discussion be held by all stakeholders through public- private-partnership approach. In this regards, establishment of a center of excellence on ITS composed of relevant disciplines and stakeholders might be necessary. This would help to fully understand, research, adapt and/or adopt its application to the Ethiopian context to exploit all benefits of ITS.

References

1. Huang, C.M., Chen, Y.S.: Telematics Communication Technologies and Vehicular Networks: Wireless Architectures and Applications. Information Science Reference, IGI Global, Hershey (2010)
2. World Vehicle Population Tops 1 Billion Units. http://wardsauto.com/ar/world_vehicle_population_110815
3. Violence and Injury Prevention: Country Profiles. Ethiopia. http://www.who.int/violence_injury_prevention/road_safety_status/country_profiles/en/
4. Global Status Report on Road Safety 2013: Supporting a Decade of Action. World Health Organization, Geneva, Switzerland (2013)
5. Number of Cars Worldwide Surpasses 1 Billion; Can the World Handle this Many Wheels? http://www.huffingtonpost.ca/2011/0823/car-population_n_934291.html
6. World Proven Reserves of Oil and Natural Gas, Most Recent Estimates, U.S. Energy Information Administration. http://en.wikipedia.org/wiki/World_energy_resources. Accessed 26 Mar 2015
7. Africa's Road Safety Challenges, International Road Federation (IRF), Addis Fortune, vol. 15, no. 776, 15 March 2015
8. The International Road Federation Vienna Manifesto on ITS: Smart Transport Policies for Sustainable Mobility. IRF, Geneva (2012)
9. IRF Bulletin Special Edition: Intelligent Transport Systems. International Road Federation (2008)
10. Toyota Intelligent Transport System. Toyota, UK (2012). https://www.youtube.com/watch?v=uwle3csyDac
11. Kotwal, A.R., Lee, S.J., Kim, Y.J.: Traffic signal systems: a review of current technology in the United States. Sci. Technol. 3(1), 33–41 (2013). https://doi.org/10.5923/j.scit.20130301.04
12. George, G.: Adaptive signal control technology: state of practice. Int. J. Sci. Res. Dev. (2016)

Survey on Indoor Positioning Techniques and Systems

Habib Mohammed Hussien$^{(\boxtimes)}$, Yalemzewed Negash Shiferaw,
and Negassa Basha Teshale

School of Electrical and Computer Engineering,
Addis Ababa Institute of Technology (AAiT), Addis Ababa University (AAU),
Addis Ababa, Ethiopia
habibmohammed2001@gmail.com, yalemzewdn@yahoo.com,
negasabasha4@gmail.com

Abstract. Navigating different devices and human beings in indoor scene has become very crucial for number of tasks specially in automated system. The efficiency of outdoor positioning has become excellent due to the development of GPS. However lots of mass market applications require very excellent positioning capabilities in almost every environments. As a result, indoor positioning has attracted the researchers attention and has been a focus of research during the past decades. This paper presents an overview of the four typical indoor localization schemes namely triangulation, trilateration, proximity and scene analysis are analyze and discussed. Moreover it gives a detailed survey of different positioning systems which are being both research-oriented solutions and commercial products and also attempts to classify the different systems into different groups based on the technology used. We categorized all 11 sighted wireless indoor positioning systems into 6 distinct technologies namely Infrared signals, radio frequency, ultrasound waves, vision-based analysis, electromagnetic waves, and audible sound and explains the measuring principles of each. These approaches are characterized and their key performance parameters are quantified individually. For a better understanding, these parameters are briefly compared in table form for each system so as to outline the trade-offs from the viewpoint of a user.

Keywords: Indoor positioning systems · Positioning techniques
Wireless positioning technology · Wireless localization

1 Introduction

An Indoor positioning system (IPS) is a continuous and real-time system which can decide the position of someone or something in a physical space (i.e. gymnasium, hospital, school, etc.) [1]. IPs has been widely researched study area for many years now. As a service, IPs has still not attain through global use as broadly compared to outdoor positioning services. Outdoor positioning is usually based on GPS satellite signals. In GPS [2], the location is approximated by computing the transit time of the signal from satellite to client device. When time and satellite position is known, the scheme can then compute the distance between user and satellite. In indoors, situation

© ICST Institute for Computer Sciences, Social Informatics and Telecommunications Engineering 2018
F. Mekuria et al. (Eds.): ICT4DA 2017, LNICST 244, pp. 46–55, 2018.
https://doi.org/10.1007/978-3-319-95153-9_5

is more complicated. Because GPS signals cannot penetrate through building walls good enough for accurate indoor positioning, other technologies has to be used or combined with the GPS system. Those other technologies include: WLAN, Bluetooth, Radio Frequency Identification (RFID) and more. Indoors is a very dynamic environment, with lot of moving people and in some places even obstacles tend to move a lot. There are some basic techniques and technologies used in indoor positioning. These include trilateration, triangulation (angle of arrival), RSS based positioning, time of arrival and fingerprinting. An overview of different existing technology options for the design of an positioning scheme As an example Infrared, ultrasound, RFID, WLAN, sensor networks, Bluetooth, UWB, vision analysis, magnetic signals and audible sound are explained in [1, 3]. Considering these key technologies, different localization systems have been formulated by different companies, higher institutions and research departments. This paper introduced and explained various research-oriented and commercially available indoor positioning systems. We also discussed the techniques and principles of these IPSs and made a comparison between them by considering a number of evaluation criterias such as cost, privacy and security, performance, complexity, robustness, user preferences, availability in commercial areas and drawbacks.

2   Survey on Wireless Indoor Positioning/Localization Techniques and Systems

There have been a number of surveys by different researchers about indoor positioning techniques and systems in the literature. This section describes literatures on indoor positioning, technologies, techniques and systems. Moreover various rating criterions are considered to examine the different indoor positioning systems for the services demanded by the users/required by the client.

2.1   Wireless Indoor Positioning Techniques

2.1.1   Triangulation

This algorithm is used find out the position of the target having the geometrical concepts of triangles and the target place can be estimated/computed by using the locations of three or more access points. Whenever the target devices receives the signals from one or more access points, the TOA, AOA and RSS of the signals will be utilized to estimate the distances between the target and the access points. The angle defines the estimated position of the target as illustrated in Fig. 1 below.

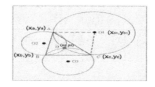

Fig. 1. Triangulation positioning techniques [3]

To calculate the value of the unknown nodes shown in Fig. 3 can be given as

$$\alpha = \angle AO_1C = 2\pi - 2\angle ADC$$

$$\left\{ \begin{array}{l} \sqrt{(x_{01} - x_a)^2 + (y_{01} - y_a)^2} = r_1 \\ \sqrt{(x_{01} - x_c)^2 + (y_{01} - y_c)^2} = r_1 \\ (x_a - x_c)^2 + (y_a - y_c)^2 = 2r_1 - 2r_1 \cos \alpha \end{array} \right\}$$

2.1.2 Trilateration

This approach [3, 4] determines the location of the target by measuring its distances from multiple reference points. The object in the field is located by creating a system which uses radio frequency signals. This RSS (radio frequency signal strength) is measured between the tagged object and the readers that are positioned in the field. Then the signal strength will be converted into a distance using the distance formula shown in Eqs. (1), (2) and (3) and plugged into a system known as trilateration. By using this approach we can determine the tagged object on the x, y plane (2D laateration) as well as x, y and z plane (3D lateration).

Fig. 2. 2D trilateration positioning techniques [3]

The equations for 2D trilateration [3] are as follows:

$$(x - x_1)^2 + (y - y_1)^2 = d_1^2 \tag{1}$$

$$(x - x_2)^2 + (y - y_2)^2 = d_2^2 \tag{2}$$

$$(x - x_3)^2 + (y - y_3)^2 = d_3^2 \tag{3}$$

The x and y coordinates are found using Cramer's rule [3].

$$x = \frac{\begin{vmatrix} (d_1^2 - d_2^2) - (x_1^2 - x_2^2) - (y_1^2 - y_2^2) & 2(y2 - y1) \\ (d_1^2 - d_3^2) - (x_1^2 - x_3^2) - (y_1^2 - y_3^2) & 2(y_3 - y_1) \end{vmatrix}}{\begin{vmatrix} 2(x_2 - x_1) & 2(y_2 - y_1) \\ 2(x_3 - x_1) & 2(y_3 - y_1) \end{vmatrix}} \tag{4}$$

$$y = \frac{\begin{vmatrix} 2(x_2 - x_1) & (d_1^2 - d_2^2) - (x_1^2 - x_2^2) - (y_1^2 - y_2^2) \\ 2(x_3 - x_1) & (d_1^2 - d_3^2) - (x_1^2 - x_3^2) - (y_1^2 - y_3^2) \end{vmatrix}}{\begin{vmatrix} 2(x_2 - x_1) & 2(y_2 - y_1) \\ 2(x_3 - x_1) & 2(y_3 - y_1) \end{vmatrix}} \tag{5}$$

The equations for 3D trilateration [3] are as follows:

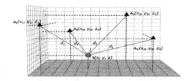

Fig. 3. 3D trilateration [3]

$$(x - x_1)^2 + (y - y_1)^2 + (z - z_1)^2 = d_1^2 \tag{6}$$

$$(x - x_2)^2 + (y - y_2)^2 + (z - z_2)^2 = d_2^2 \tag{7}$$

$$(x - x_3)^2 + (y - y_3)^2 + (z - z_3)^2 = d_3^2 \tag{8}$$

$$(x - x_4)^2 + (y - y_4)^2 + (z - z_4)^2 = d_{(9)}^2 \tag{9}$$

Now, the x, y and z components using Cramer's rule [3].

$$x = \frac{\begin{vmatrix} 2(d_1^2 - d_2^2) - (x_1^2 - x_2^2) - (y_1^2 - y_2^2) - (z_1^2 - z_2^2) & (2(y_2 - y_1)) & 2(z_2 - z_1) \\ 2(d_1^2 - d_3^2) - (x_1^2 - x_3^2) - (y_1^2 - y_3^2) - (z_1^2 - z_3^2) & (2(y_3 - y_1)) & 2(z_3 - z_1) \\ 2(d_1^2 - d_4^2) - (x_1^2 - x_4^2) - (y_1^2 - y_4^2) - (z_1^2 - z_4^2) & (2(y_4 - y_1)) & 2(z_4 - z_1) \end{vmatrix}}{\begin{vmatrix} 2(x_2 - x_1) & 2(y_2 - y_1) & 2(z_2 - z_1) \\ 2(x_3 - x_1) & 2(y_3 - y_1) & 2(z_3 - z_1) \\ 2(x_4 - x_1) & 2(y_4 - y_1) & 2(z_4 - z_1) \end{vmatrix}}$$

$$\tag{11}$$

$$y = \frac{\begin{vmatrix} 2(x_2 - x_1) & 2(d_1^2 - d_2^2) - (x_1^2 - x_2^2) - (y_1^2 - y_2^2) - (z_1^2 - z_2^2) & 2(z_2 - z_1) \\ 2(x_3 - x_1) & 2(d_1^2 - d_3^2) - (x_1^2 - x_3^2) - (y_1^2 - y_3^2) - (z_1^2 - z_3^2) & 2(z_3 - z_1) \\ 2(x_4 - x_1) & 2(d_1^2 - d_4^2) - (x_1^2 - x_4^2) - (y_1^2 - y_4^2) - (z_1^2 - z_4^2) & 2(z_4 - z_1) \end{vmatrix}}{\begin{vmatrix} 2(x_2 - x_1) & 2(y_2 - y_1) & 2(z_2 - z_1) \\ 2(x_3 - x_1) & 2(y_3 - y_1) & 2(z_3 - z_1) \\ 2(x_4 - x_1) & 2(y_4 - y_1) & 2(z_4 - z_1) \end{vmatrix}}$$

$$\tag{12}$$

$$z = \frac{\begin{array}{ccc} 2(x_2 - x_1) & 2(y_2 - y_1) & (d_1^2 - d_2^2) - (x_1^2 - x_2^2) - (y_1^2 - y_2^2) - (z_1^2 - z_2^2) \\ 2(x_3 - x_1) & 2(y_3 - y_1) & (d_1^2 - d_3^2) - (x_1^2 - x_3^2) - (y_1^2 - y_3^2) - (z_1^2 - z_3^2) \\ 2(x_4 - x_1) & 2(y_4 - y_1) & (d_1^2 - d_4^2) - (x_1^2 - x_4^2) - (y_1^2 - y_4^2) - (z_1^2 - z_4^2) \end{array}}{\begin{array}{ccc} 2(x_2 - x_1) & 2(y_2 - y_1) & 2(z_2 - z_1) \\ 2(x_3 - x_1) & 2(y_3 - y_1) & 2(z_3 - z_1) \\ 2(x_4 - x_1) & 2(y_4 - y_1) & 2(z_4 - z_1) \end{array}} \tag{13}$$

2.1.3 Scene Analysis

A principle of positioning approach in which first acquire/gather fingerprints of a scene and then determines an object position by matching with the information existing in the database [4]. The offline and online phases are the two phases of fingerprinting technique [5]. Strengths from access points are collected at reference points during the training phase, while in the tracking phase, user's surrounding access point signal strengths are compared/analyzed with the RP dataset collected in the 1st phase for matching.

2.1.4 Proximity

This approach investigates the location of an object with respect to a distinguished position by sensing its location [3]. Moreover, this approach requires a connection between the mobile and fixed node to track the target so that the tracked target is considered/assumed as in the proximity area.

2.2 Range Measurement Techniques

(1) *Received Signal Strength:* This scheme can achieve a maximum value when the gap between transmitter and receiver is smaller so as to investigate the distance. This scheme is used to locate the space/distance of the subscriber unit from other set of measurement units by using the attenuated output of emitted signal strength for calculating the signal loss.

(2) *Time of Arrival:* The propagation time of signal is approximately equal to the distance between the measurement units and the targeted object. A precise synchronization of all the transmitters and receivers and at least three measurement units are required to obtain 2D lateration.

(3) *Time Difference of Arrival:* This Technique estimates the relative position of the mobile transmitter by determining the difference of the signal arival time at number of measurement units. For example, 3 fixed receivers can give two TDOAs, which estimates position of the targeted object.

(4) *Phase of Arrival:* This technique estimates the distance of a target using the signal delay which is expressed as the fraction of signal wavelength. In this technique, the transmitters are needed to be placed at particular locations to perform the location of the target based on phase measurements.

(5) *Angle of Arrival:* Use antennae arrays at the receiver side to estimate the angle at which the transmitted signal impinges on the receiver by calculating TDOA at individual elements of the antennae array. It requires the measurement of at least two angles with direction oriented or array of antennas to estimate the 2D location of a target.

2.3 Criterias for Evaluating Wireless Indoor Positioning Systems

(1) *Privacy and Security: One of the evaluation criteria for a good IPS is its* security and privacy because both of them are very important [6] for Private as well as Social activities for controlling the positioning information and history. To improve privacy in IPS location as well as information should be controlled from the software or system architecture side [3].

(2) *Cost:* The most important factors which can determine the cost of a positioning system are money, time, space, weight and energy [3]. Installation and maintenance are related to time factor. Mobile units may have weight and tight space constraints. The final important factor of a system cost is energy.

(3) *Performance: For evaluating the performance of an IPSs* precision and accuracy are very important. The success probability of position localization with respect to predefined accuracy is precision. Accuracy is the average error distance [3]. Other performance parameters are calculated positioning delay of targeted object, measurement transformation of targeted object and scalability.

(4) *Fault Tolerance and Robustness: Even though* some equipments in the system are not working or have a dead battery energy, a robust IPS should able to operate and tolerable during the occurrence of faults in the system [3].

(5) *Complexity:* A good IPS is a system with optimum performance (accuracy), easily used software platforms and an existed infrastructure devices for the users [7]. The users device computational time for determining their position is another aspect which indicates complexity.

(6) *User Preference: A good* IPSs always assumes the clients' requirement of the targeted equipments, the infrastructures and the software. If the devices are lightweight, wireless, small, lower power consumption and computationally powerful, the system has a chance to be preferred by the user.

(7) *Commercially existed: From* the developed IPSs which are discussed in Sect. 2.4, some of them are existing in the market and others are still researching.

(8) *Limitations:* The medium which are used for position sensing is the fundamental limitations of IPSs. For example, WLAN technology can reuse the existing infrastructure. However, position sensing based on radio frequency has multiple-path and has a reflection effects which result in maximum error.

2.4 Types of Wireless Indoor Positioning Systems

2.4.1 Infrared (IR) Positioning Systems

Active Badge: This system is the first indoor localization systems developed by AT&T Cambridge. This system needs an IR technology to make location sensing so as to place persons in its desired area by computing the position of the badges using a unique IR transmitted signal [8]. One or more sensors should be fixed in a room to be detected by the IR signal, which are sent by a system so as to locate the device. The targeted active badges position data are forwarded to a central server for specifying the position. A room level accuracy is provided by the system and the signal can be affected by any light.

Firefly: This system is an IR based tracking scheme developed by Cybernet Corporation [9]. It uses IR technology that offers high accuracy about 3.0 mm. The system comprises tags, a tag controller of tags and one camera. The controller a tag is a small, lightweight and battery-powered which can be carried by a tracked person. An emitter which has been supported by controller of tags attached on different targeted parts and 3 cameras are installed on a 1 m bar to receive the IR signals and estimate 3D position. Even though, tags and tag controllers are small and easy to hold, they are not suitable/comfortable to be worn due to their cables. The coverage area is limited with in 7 m.

2.4.2   Ultra-Sound Positioning Systems

Active Bat: This scheme is developed by AT&T Cambridge and can offer 3D positioning for the tracked tags [10]. In this system ultrasonic technology receivers is required to compute the 3D location of the tag by multiple-lateration and triangulation. A tag frequently broadcasting pulse of ultrasound that will be catched by a matrix of receivers at an acknowledged position. The distance measurement is obtained by the ultrasonic signal TOA. The system acquires installing 720 receivers to the ceiling to cover a 1000 m^2 area. The system has 3 cm accuracy for 75 tracked tags.

Cricket: This system uses ultrasound system as infrastructure mounted on the walls/ceilings at acknowledged location and receiver are attaching on the individual targeted object [11] for using TOA method and triangulation technique to identify the targeted object. This approach offers privacy for the client by accomplishing all the location triangulation computation of targeted object so as to own its location information. This scheme offers 10 cm accuracy.

Sonitor: This system is developed by Sonitor Technologies Inc. for indoor positioning and tracking solution based on an ultrasound technology [12]. The system can offer location identification and tracking of peoples and equipments any-time and providing proximity positional information with room level accuracy due to the ultrasound signal (i.e. Ultrasound signal cannot penetrate walls and does not need LOS transmission). Thus the scheme is used for detecting and tracking hidden targets.

2.4.3   Radio Frequency (RF) Positioning Systems

(I) *WLAN:* These scheme/technology has been deployed in public areas (i.e. hospitals, train stations, universities, etc.). The followings are some of the WLAN technology based IPSs..

Radar: This system is suggested by a Microsoft research group as tracking method using WLAN infrastructure [13]. The system utilizes signaling strength and SNR with the triangulation. The Radar system can offer 2D information.

Compas: This system takes an advantages/merits of existing WLAN technology/infrastructures and digital compasses to give high and accurate services with considerable cost for a client holding a WLAN-based equipments [14]. Estimating/calculation the position is depend on the measurement of the signal strength from different APs. This scheme uses the fingerprint method determine/estimate the position of a client [14].

(II) *UWB:* The UWB offer higher accuracy because its [15] pulses have short duration (less than 1 nano seconds) and this pulses are used for filtering the reflected signals from the original signal. Ubisense is an UWB based scheme as discussed below.

Ubisense: This system is designed by AT&T Cambridge, which offers a real-time scheme [16]. In this system the triangulation technique is employed by taking advantages of both the TDOA AOA to provide flexible location sensing. This scheme cannot be affected by a complicated environment (i.e. walls, doors, etc.) [16]. The accuracy offered is about tens of centimeters.

2.4.4 Magnetic Positioning System

MotionStar Wireless: This system is designed by Ascension Technology Corporation, which is used to track the targeted object with a pulsed DC magnetic fields for locating sensors within 3 m area/coverage [17]. This scheme offers accurate motion tracker by the measurement of different sensors attached on the body of a person. The system tracks multiple targets (120 sensors) at a time in real time.

2.4.5 Vision-Based Positioning System

Easy Living: This system is vision based and developed by Microsoft research group [18]. Two cameras (stereo) attaching on the ceiling of a room is needed and the entire part of the room is covered by one camera. Two 3D cameras (real-time) can cover the measuring area and offer real-time visions (which can be used as an input for location estimations). Then the computer receives the photos from the cameras and process the raw data. After that Easy Living scheme creates a "person creation zone" just near to the entrance of the room (a place where the stereo module creates the vision instance of the person). Thus, when a person gets in to the room, the scheme tracks the motion of the person and publish the information of the person.

2.4.6 Audible Sound Positioning System

Beep: This system is an audible sound based technology and designed as a cheap 3D IPS method [19]. This scheme uses Triangulation technique with a standard 3D multiple lateration based on TOA.

3 Comparison of Wireless Indoor Positioning Systems

In this section, the aforementioned different existed IPSs are evaluated from the point of view of the client interest. IPSs are compared considering the evaluation criterias which has been discussed in Sect. 2.3 Table 1 shown below depicts evaluation and comparison results and thus results are important so as to to easily identify the best location methods.

Table 1. Comparison of IPSs based on security and privacy, cost, performance and commercial existence

IPSs with security	IPSs with expensive cost	IPSs with room level accuracy	IPSs which uses WLAN infrastructure	IPSs which are commercially available
Cricket	Firefly	Active Badge	Compass	Firefly
Beep	Activebat	Sonitor	Active Bat	Sonitor
	Ubisense		Senitor	Ubisense
				Easyliving

4 Conclusion

From this paper, readers can get a detailed understanding of the different existed IPSs, especially the 11 IPSs explained in this paper. The existing IPSs are classified into 6 categories based on the main technology used to sense the location. Moreover, the system architecture and working principles are presented. Eight have been proposed to so as to and compare the IPSs from the point of view of the client.

5 Recommendation

From this paper, we have seen that each technology used in position determination has its own drawbacks. None of them can fulfill the system demand. Therefore we recommend that instead of using a single medium to estimate the locations of the targets, It will be good combining some technologies so as to enhance the quality of services rather using a single technology. For instance WLAN and UWB. Where WLAN t cover large area and UWB can give highly accurate calculation.

References

1. Vossiek, M., Wiebking, L., Gulden, P., Wiehardt, J., Hoffmann, C., Heide, P.: Wireless local positioning. IEEE Microwave Mag. 4(4), 77–86 (2003)
2. Hofmann, B., Wellinhof, H., Lichtenegger, H.: GPS: Theory and Practice. Springer, Vienna (1997)
3. Jarvis, R., Mason, A., Thorn hill, K., Zhang, B.: Indoor Positioning System, 29 August 2011

4. di Flora, C., Ficco, M., Russo, S., Vecchio, V.: Indoor and outdoor location based services for portable wireless devices. In: Proceedings of 25th IEEE International Conference on Distributed Computing Systems Workshops (2005)
5. Aitenbichler, E., Mhlhuser, M.: An IR local positioning system for smart items and devices. In: Proceedings of 23rd IEEE International Conference on Distributed Computing Systems Workshops (IWSAWC03) (2003)
6. Smailagic, A., Kogan, D.: Location sensing and privacy in a contextaware computing environment. IEEE Wirel. Commun. **9**(5), 10–17 (2002)
7. Casas, R., Cuartielles, D., Marco, A., Gracia, H.J., Falc, J.L.: Hidden issues in deploying an indoor location system. **6**(2), 62–69 (2007)
8. Want, R., Hopper, A., Falcao, V., Gibbons, J.: The active badge location system. ACM Trans. Inf. Syst. **10**(1), 91–102 (1992)
9. Firefly Motion Tracking System User's guide (1999). http://www.gesturecentral.com/firefly/FireflyUserGuide.pdf
10. Active Bat website (2008). http://www.cl.cam.ac.uk/research/dtg/attarchive/bat/
11. Priyantha, N.B.: The cricket indoor location system. Ph.D. thesis, MIT (2005)
12. Sonitor System Website (2008). http://www.sonitor.com/
13. Ekahau (2008). http://www.ekahau.com/
14. King, T., Kopf, S., Haenselmann, T., Lubberger, C., Effelsberg, W.: COMPASS: a probabilistic indoor positioning system based on 802.11 and digital compasses. In: Proceedings of First ACM International Workshop on Wireless Network Testbeds, Experimental evaluation and Characterization (WiNTECH), Los Angeles, CA, USA, September 2006
15. Ingram, S.J., Harmer, D., Quinlan, M.: UltraWideBand indoor positioning systems and their use in emergencies. In: Proceedings of IEEE Conference on Position Location and Navigation Symposium, pp. 706–715, April 2004
16. Ubisense (2008). http://www.ubisense.net
17. MotionStar Wireless Website (2007). http://www.ascensiontech.com/products/motionstar wireless.php
18. Brumitt, B., Meyers, B., Krumm, J., Kern, A., Shafer, S.: EasyLiving: technologies for intelligent environments. In: Thomas, P., Gellersen, H.-W. (eds.) HUC 2000. LNCS, vol. 1927, pp. 12–29. Springer, Heidelberg (2000). https://doi.org/10.1007/3-540-39959-3_2
19. Lopes, C.V., Haghighat, A., Mandal, A., Givargis, T., Baldi, P.: Localization of off-the-shelf mobile devices using audible sound: architectures, protocols and performance assessment. ACM SIGMOBILE Mob. Comput. Commun. Rev. **10**(2), 38–50 (2006)

Comparative Study of the Performances of Peak-to-Average Power Ratio (PAPR) Reduction Techniques for Orthogonal Frequency Division Multiplexing (OFDM) Signals

Workineh Gebeye Abera[(✉)]

AAiT, School of Electrical and Computer Engineering, Addis Ababa University,
Addis Ababa, Ethiopia
workinehgebeye@gmail.com, workineh.gebeye@aait.edu.et

Abstract. In this paper, two distortionless PAPR reduction techniques, Selected Mapping (SLM) and Partial Transmit Sequences (PTS), are compared in terms of PAPR reduction capability and computational complexity for equal number of candidate OFDM symbols. Using MATLAB simulation, it is shown that SLM outperforms PTS in PAPR reduction capability. For small values of the number of subblock partitions, the overall computational complexity of PTS is less than SLM. However, the required PAPR reduction level may not be achieved using small values of number of subblock partitions. Hence, for large values of number of subblock partitions used in PTS, the overall computational complexity of PTS is greater than SLM. In that case, SLM outperforms PTS both in PAPR reduction capability and computational complexity.

Keywords: Orthogonal Frequency Division Multiplexing
Peak-to-Average Power Ratio · Selected Mapping · Partial Transmit Sequence

1 Introduction

International standards making use of OFDM for high-speed wireless communications are already established by IEEE 802.11, IEEE 802.16, IEEE 802.20, Digital Audio Broadcasting (DAB), and Digital Video Broadcasting (DVB) [1, 2]. An OFDM based system can be of interest for wireless applications because it provides greater immunity to multipath fading and impulse noise, and simplifies equalization process. All the desirable attributes of OFDM do not come for nothing, but at the expense of large envelope variation, which is often cited as the major drawback of OFDM and is usually quantified through the Peak-to-Average Power Ratio (PAPR). Such signal envelope or power variations can be difficult for practical High Power Amplifiers (HPAs) and Digital to Analog Convertors (DACs)/Analog to Digital Converters (ADCs) of the OFDM system to accommodate, resulting in either low power efficiency or signal distortion, including signal clips [1, 2]. The signal distortion in turn results in Bit Error Rate (BER) increase and Power Spectral Density (PSD) degradation. To avoid these

© ICST Institute for Computer Sciences, Social Informatics and Telecommunications Engineering 2018
F. Mekuria et al. (Eds.): ICT4DA 2017, LNICST 244, pp. 56–67, 2018.
https://doi.org/10.1007/978-3-319-95153-9_6

effects, the HPA can be made to work in its linear region with large back-off but this results in poor power efficiency. Similarly the DAC/ADC can be designed to accommodate the large dynamic range of the OFDM signal but this results in a reduced Signal to Noise Ratio (SNR), as the DAC/ADC already has significant amount of quantization noise. Thus, a better solution is to reduce the PAPR of the OFDM signal with some manipulation of the OFDM signal itself [1, 2].

Several researches have been done to the development of PAPR reduction schemes for OFDM signals. An overview of the various PAPR reduction schemes can be found in [1, 2]. In this paper, the performances of two distortionless PAPR reduction schemes are compared. The first technique is Selected Mapping (SLM), which was first presented in [3]. The second method is Partial Transmit Sequences (PTS), which was introduced for the first time in [4].

Muller and Huber in [5] compared the PAPR reduction capabilities of the two schemes making the number of IFFTs used in the transmitters of both schemes equal, in which case the number of candidate OFDM symbols may not be equal. It is shown that PTS has better PAPR reduction capability than SLM. The simulation results also show that the PAPR reduction capability of SLM increases with the number of candidate OFDM symbols D. This shows that the PAPR reduction capability of SLM is sensitive to the number of candidate OFDM symbols generated. Similarly, the PAPR reduction capability of PTS increases with the number of subblock partitions V. For a given number of phase rotation factors Q, the number of candidate OFDM symbols Q^V increases with V. This also shows that the PAPR reduction capability of PTS is sensitive to the number of candidate OFDM symbols. As a result, it is sensible to compare the PAPR reduction capabilities of the two schemes making the number of candidate OFDM symbols generated equal. That is why this comparison is chosen as one of the objectives of the paper.

Furthermore, the authors in [5] also stated that for equal number of transmitter IFFTs used in both schemes, PTS is more computationally complex than SLM. However, the work doesn't include computational complexity analysis and simulation results. In this paper, both the analysis and simulation are done.

Performance comparison of SLM & PTS and PAPR reduction techniques for OFDM signals are also done by the authors in [6, 7] respectively.

Hence, the objectives of this paper are

i. To compare the PAPR reduction capabilities of SLM and PTS for the same number of candidate OFDM symbols generated per given OFDM symbol intended for transmission.
ii. To compare the computational complexities of SLM and PTS for the same number of candidate OFDM symbols generated per given OFDM symbol intended for transmission.

In comparing SLM and PTS I have used an OFDM signal model such that for a given data vector $\mathbf{S}^\mu = \begin{bmatrix} S_0^\mu & S_1^\mu \cdots & S_{N-1}^\mu \end{bmatrix}^T$, a sequence of complex numbers drawn from a finite constellation (MPSK or MQAM), in the μth signaling interval, the baseband OFDM symbol $\left\{ s_{n/L}^\mu \right\}_{n=0}^{LN-1}$ is an oversampled IFFT output of $\mathbf{S}^\mu$. That is [8]

$$s^{\mu}_{n/L} = \frac{1}{\sqrt{N}} \sum_{k=0}^{N-1} S^{\mu}_k e^{j\frac{2\pi}{LN}kn}, n = 0, 1, \cdots, LN - 1$$

$$s^{\mu}_{n/L} = \frac{1}{\sqrt{N}} \left\{ \sum_{k=0}^{N/2-1} S^{\mu}_k e^{j\frac{2\pi}{LN}kn} + \sum_{k=LN-\frac{N}{2}}^{LN-1} S^{\mu}_{k-N(L-1)} e^{j\frac{2\pi}{LN}kn} \right\} \qquad (1)$$

$$s^{\mu}_{n/L} = IFFT\left\{ \sqrt{L}S^{\mu}_L \right\}$$

where N is the number of subcarriers, $L \geq 1$ is an integer and it is the oversampling factor, $IFFT\{\cdot\}$ is NL-point oversampled IFFT indexed by n/L, and $\mathbf{S}^{\mu}_L = \left[S^{\mu}_0 \cdots S^{\mu}_{\frac{N}{2}-1} \ 0 \cdots 0 \ S^{\mu}_{\frac{N}{2}} \cdots S^{\mu}_{N-1} \right]^T$ is the L times oversampled equivalent data vector generated by zero padding $\mathbf{S}^{\mu}$ with $N(L-1)$ zeros at its middle [8]. The baseband PAPR is defined as [8]

$$PAPR\left\{ s^{\mu}_{n/L} \right\} = \frac{\max_{n \in [0,LN)} \left| s^{\mu}_{n/L} \right|^2}{E\left\{ \left| s^{\mu}_{n/L} \right|^2 \right\}}, \qquad (2)$$

which is a random variable.

As the passband PAPR is roughly twice (3 dB higher than) the baseband PAPR, it is sufficient to consider only the PAPR of the baseband OFDM signal [8], pp. 22–23. In addition, the cyclic prefix of duration T_g, which is a repetition of part of the OFDM symbol, attached to the OFDM symbol to combat Inter-Symbol Interference (ISI) can be neglected for the purposes of PAPR analysis as the prefix will not produce a peak which is not already present in the OFDM symbol $s^{\mu}_{n/L}$. Theoretically, $PAPR\left\{ s^{\mu}_{n/L} \right\}$ approaches PAPR$\{s^{\mu}(t)\}$ as L becomes sufficiently large. However, it is has been shown in [9, 10] that when $L \geq 4$ the PAPR of $s^{\mu}_{n/L}$ approximates the PAPR of $s^{\mu}(t)$ and hence $L = 4$ is used in the simulation results of this paper.

The remaining part of the paper is arranged such that Sect. 2 presents the SLM and PTS PAPR reduction schemes. In Sect. 3, the computational complexity analysis of both schemes is presented. Section 4 provides comparative simulation results and discussions. Finally, the concluding remarks are provided in Sect. 5.

2   Selected Mapping and Partial Transmit Sequence

Selected Mapping (SLM): SLM is a distortionless PAPR reduction technique [3]. In the SLM technique, the transmitter generates a set of sufficiently different candidate data vectors, all representing the same information as the original data vector, for each data vector intended for transmission by rotating the phase of each data symbol and selects the candidate data vector with the lowest PAPR for transmission [3].

A set of D markedly different, distinct, pseudorandom but fixed phase rotation vectors [3, 10]

$$\mathbf{P}^{(d)} = \left[\mathbf{P}_0^{(d)} \mathbf{P}_1^{(d)} \cdots \mathbf{P}_{N-1}^{(d)} \right]^{\mathrm{T}}, \tag{3}$$

with $\mathrm{P}_k^{(d)} = e^{j\phi_k^{(d)}}, \phi_k^{(d)} \in [0, 2\pi), \mathrm{k} = 0, 1, \cdots, \mathrm{N} - 1, \mathrm{d} = 1, 2, \cdots, \mathrm{D}$ must be defined and available both at the transmitter and receiver. The data vector $\mathbf{S}^\mu$ is multiplied element-wise with each one of the D phase rotation vectors $\mathbf{P}^{(d)}$, resulting in a set of D different phase rotated data vectors $\mathbf{S}^{(\mu,d)}$ given by [3, 10]

$$S^{(\mu,d)} = S^\mu \circ \mathbf{P}^{(d)}. \tag{4}$$

Then, all the D data vectors are transformed into time domain to get D candidate OFDM symbols [3, 10]

$$s_{n/L}^{(\mu,d)} = \frac{1}{\sqrt{N}} \sum_{k=0}^{N-1} S_k^\mu P_k^{(d)} e^{j\frac{2\pi}{LN}kn}, n = 0, 1, \cdots, LN - 1$$
$$s_{n/L}^{(\mu,d)} = IFFT\left\{ \sqrt{L} S_L^{(\mu,d)} \right\} \tag{5}$$

Among the D candidate OFDM symbols, the transmitter selects the lowest PAPR sequence, $s_{n/L}^{(\mu,\bar{d})}$, for transmission where [3, 10]

$$\bar{d} = arg \min_{1 \le d \le D} PAPR\left\{ s_{n/L}^{(\mu,d)} \right\} \tag{6}$$

The SLM-OFDM transmitter is shown in Fig. 1.

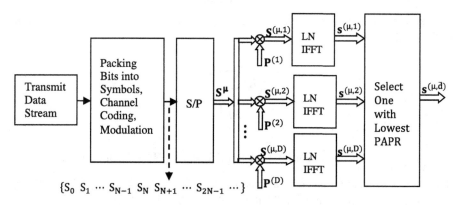

Fig. 1. Block diagram of SLM-OFDM transmitter.

It is assumed that the transmitter and the receiver have the D phase rotation vectors $\mathbf{P}^{(d)}$. However, in order to recover an OFDM symbol the receiver has to know which phase rotation vector $\mathbf{P}^{(\bar{d})}$ has actually been used by the transmitter. The simplest method is to transmit $\bar{d}$ as side information which requires $\log_2 D$ bits. As side information transmission decreases the information throughput, another method to determine $\bar{d}$ is the blind technique [11, 12] where it is determined based only on the received OFDM symbol and the known phase rotation vectors.

The original data vector $\mathbf{S}^\mu$ is recovered by multiplying the received data vector $\widetilde{\mathbf{S}}^\mu$ element-wise by $\mathbf{P}^{(\bar{d})} = \left[e^{-j\phi_0^{(d)}} \ e^{-j\phi_1^{(d)}} \ \cdots \ e^{-j\phi_{N-1}^{(d)}} \right]$. In the paper, it is assumed that the blind technique is used.

It is illustrated by simulation in [10] (p. 50 and 66) and [13] that for a given D, choosing $P_k^{(d)}, d = 1, 2, \ldots, D$ such that the corresponding $\phi_k^{(d)}$ are uniformly distributed in $[0, 2\pi)$, then the PAPR reduction capability of SLM is the same whether $P_k^{(d)}$ are chosen from set $\{\pm 1\}$ or $\{\pm 1, \pm j\}$. Note that $\mathbf{P}^{(d)}$ with elements $\{\pm 1\}$ is generated from a randomly generated binary data mapped onto BPSK symbols and hence number of bits per symbol m = 1. Similarly $\mathbf{P}^{(d)}$ with elements $\{\pm 1, \pm j\}$ is generated from a randomly generated binary data mapped onto QPSK symbols i.e. m = 2.

Partial Transmit Sequence (PTS): PTS is also a distortionless PAPR reduction technique [4]. In this technique the data vector $\mathbf{S}^\mu$ is partitioned into V pair-wise disjoint subblocks $\mathbf{S}^{(\mu,v)}, v = 1, 2, \ldots, V$. That is, data symbol positions in $\mathbf{S}^{(\mu,v)}$, which are already represented in another subblock are set to zero so that [4, 10]

$$S^\mu = \sum_{v=1}^{V} S^{(\mu,v)} \tag{7}$$

where $S^{(\mu,v)} = \left[S_0^{(\mu,v)} \ S_1^{(\mu,v)} \ \cdots \ S_{N-1}^{(\mu,v)} \right]^T$, such that $S_k^{(\mu,v)} = S_k^\mu$ or $0, k = 1, 2, \ldots, N - 1$.

The time domain representation of the subblocks can be generated using LN-point IFFT, i.e. [4, 8, 10]

$$s_{n/L}^{(\mu,v)} = \frac{1}{\sqrt{N}} \sum_{k=0}^{N-1} S_k^{(\mu,v)} e^{j\frac{2\pi}{LN}kn},$$

$$s_{n/L}^{(\mu,v)} = IFFT\left\{ \sqrt{L} S_L^{(\mu,v)} \right\} \tag{8}$$

Each $\left\{ s_{n/L}^{(\mu,v)} \right\}_{n=0}^{LN-1}$ is called Partial Transmit Sequence (PTS). Then each one of these PTSs are independently rotated by a phase rotation factor $b_d^{(\mu,v)} = e^{j\theta_d^{(\mu,v)}}, \theta_d^{(\mu,v)} \in [0, 2\pi)$ and then combined to form a candidate OFDM symbol, i.e. [4, 10]

$$s^{\mu}_{(n/L,d)} = \sum_{v=1}^{V} b_d^{(\mu,v)} . IFFT\left\{\sqrt{L}S_L^{(\mu,v)}\right\}, \tag{9}$$

where $d = 1, 2, \ldots, Q^V$ and Q is the number of phase rotation factors. The objective is to optimally combine the V PTSs to minimize the PAPR of the transmit OFDM symbol $\left\{s^{\mu}_{(n/L,\bar{d})}\right\}_{n=0}^{(LN-1)}$ by a suitable combination of the free phase rotation factors $\left\{b_d^{(\mu,v)}\right\}_{v=1}^{V}$. The $b_d^{(\mu,v)}$ may be chosen with a continuous valued phase rotation angle $\theta_d^{(\mu,v)}$, but more appropriate in practice is to restrict on a finite set of Q allowed phase angles to reduce the search complexity. Hence, we have Q^V possible combination of phase rotation factors where all of them need to be searched exhaustively to find one that results in minimum PAPR transmit OFDM symbol. In the paper, this method is used to find the optimum combination so that the best PAPR reduction capability of PTS can be achieved.

It is illustrated through simulation in [10], page 69, that the choice $b_d^{(\mu,v)} \in \{\pm1, \pm j\}$ gives better PAPR reduction capability than $b_d^{(\mu,v)} \in \{\pm1\}$.

There are three types of subblock partitioning schemes: adjacent, interleaved, and pseudo-random. It is shown in [10] (p. 67) and [14] that pseudo-random subblock partitioning scheme gives the best PAPR reduction and hence used in this paper. The PTS-OFDM transmitter is shown in Fig. 2.

The blind technique is used to determine the optimum phase factor combination $\left\{b_d^{(\mu,v)}\right\}_{v=1}^{V}$ at the receiver [12]. Assuming that the receiver knows the subblock partition scheme used by the transmitter, the received data vector is partitioned into subblocks. Then transmitted data block S^{μ} can be recovered by independently derotating each received subblock by $\left\{b_d^{(\mu,v)}\right\}^{*} = e^{-j\theta_d^{(\mu,v)}}$ and then combining them to get S^{μ} [10].

3   Computational Complexity Analysis of SLM and PTS

The computational complexity difference that may exist between SLM and PTS-OFDM systems mainly arises in the process of generating the candidate OFDM symbols and the subsequent selection of the symbol with the least PAPR.

For SLM, as it is shown in (4), ND complex multiplications are required to generate $S^{(\mu,d)}$, $d = 1, 2, \ldots, D$. Then, D length LN IFFTs are required to generate $s^{(\mu,d)}_{n/L}$. Each LN-point IFFT requires $(LN/2)\log_2(LN)$ complex multiplications and $LN\log_2(LN)$ complex additions [14, 15]. Finally, $\left|s^{\mu}_{n/L}\right|^2 = Re\left\{s^{\mu}_{n/L}\right\}^2 + Im\left\{s^{\mu}_{n/L}\right\}^2$ need to be calculated for each n in determining the PAPR which requires 2DLN real multiplications and DLN additions.

To generate the PTSs in (8), V length LN IFFTs are used. For pseudo-random subblock partitioning scheme this can be achieved at the expense of $V\frac{LN}{2}\log_2(LN)$ complex multiplications and $VLN\log_2(LN)$ complex additions. In generating the Q^V candidate OFDM symbols in (9), we need $Q^V VLN$ complex multiplications to create $b_d^{(\mu,v)}s_{n/L}^{(\mu,v)}$ which are combined through $Q^V(V-1)LN$ complex additions. Finally, to calculate the PAPR of $\left\{s_{(n/L,d)}^{\mu}\right\}_{n=1}^{LN}$, $d = 1, 2, \ldots, Q^V$, we need $2Q^V LN$ real multiplications and $Q^V LN$ real additions.

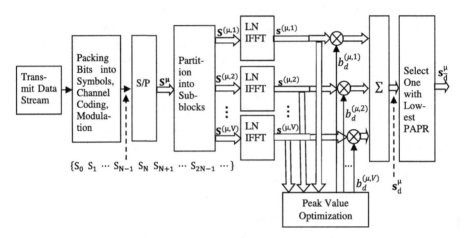

Fig. 2. Block diagram of PTS-OFDM transmitter.

Generally, a complex multiplication requires four real multiplications and two real additions. On the other hand, a complex addition requires two real additions. Hence, the total number of real additions A and multiplications M required for each scheme can be summarized as

$$A_{SLM} = DLN(3\log_2(LN) + 1) + 2ND \tag{10}$$

$$M_{SLM} = 2DLN(\log_2(LN) + 1) + 4ND \tag{11}$$

$$A_{PTS} = 3VLN\log_2(LN) + Q^V(4V - 1)LN \tag{12}$$

$$M_{PTS} = 2VLN\log_2(LN) + 2Q^V(2V + 1)LN \tag{13}$$

The computational complexity of PTS and SLM is quantified through a parameter f which is the number of addition instructions required for each multiplication operation. Therefore, the overall computational complexity of each scheme for $f = 4$ is

$$C_{SLM} = A_{SLM} + fM_{SLM}$$
$$C_{SLM} = [11LN \log_2(LN) + 9N(L+2)]D \qquad (14)$$

$$C_{PTS} = A_{PTS} + fM_{PTS}$$
$$C_{PTS} = 11VLN \log_2(LN) + LN(20V+7)Q^V. \qquad (15)$$

If the two schemes are made to have equal number of candidate OFDM symbols, i.e. $D = Q^V$, then Eq. (14) becomes.

$$C_{SLM} = [11LN \log_2(LN) + 9N(L+2)]Q^V. \qquad (16)$$

4 Comparative Simulation Results

This section presents comparative simulation results for PAPR reduction capability and computational complexity which are produced using MATLAB version 7.5. For the comparative PAPR reduction simulations, 10^5 randomly generated OFDM symbols each containing 128 QPSK modulated data symbols (subcarriers) are generated.

As stated in Sect. 1, the authors in [5] mentioned that for equal number of transmitter IFFTs used in SLM and PTS schemes, PTS is more computationally complex than SLM. However, the work doesn't include computational complexity analysis and simulation results. In this paper, the analysis, Eqs. (10)–(15), and the simulation (Fig. 3) are done. Figure 3 shows the plot of the ratio C_{PTS}/C_{SLM} in dB versus the number of subblock partitions V of the PTS scheme. The simulation was done for different number of subcarriers N, $L = 4, f = 4$, and the elements of the phase rotation vectors chosen from the set $\{\pm 1\}$ as a compromise for the large values of N, like N = 131,072 to decrease the long simulation time required had the set $\{\pm 1, \pm j\}$ been used. In the plots it can be seen that the ratio C_{PTS}/C_{SLM} increases with V, in fact the increment gets faster for large values of V. The plot clearly shows that the ratio C_{PTS}/C_{SLM} is always greater than 1 for all values of V. This in turn shows that the computational complexity of PTS is greater than SLM for all values of V, which is the cost to be paid for its better PAPR reduction capability.

Simulation results for comparisons in PAPR reduction capability and computational complexity for equal number of candidate OFDM symbols generated, i.e. $D = Q^V$, are shown in the following paragraphs. Hence, Fig. 4 shows a plot of the Complementary Cumulative Distribution Function (CCDF) of PAPR of PTS and SLM-OFDM signals for $D = Q^V$. For every OFDM symbol intended for transmission equal number of candidate OFDM symbols is generated in both techniques. In the simulation, pseudo-random subblock partition scheme is used to partition the data blocks in PTS.

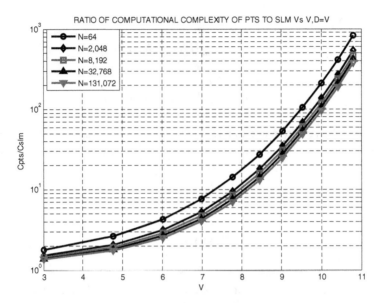

Fig. 3. Plot of ratio of computational complexity of PTS to SLM (C_PTS/C_SLM) versus number of subblock partitions V for L = 4, f = 4, equal number of IFFTs, D = V, and the elements of the of phase factor vectors chosen from the set {±1}.

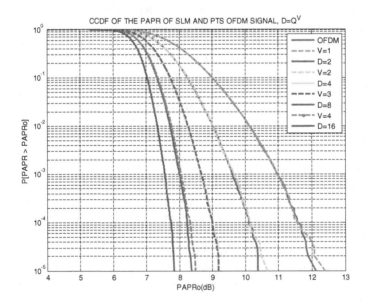

Fig. 4. CCDF of PAPR of SLM, PTS, and OFDM signal with, L = 4, the elements of the phase rotation vectors chosen from the set {1, −1}.

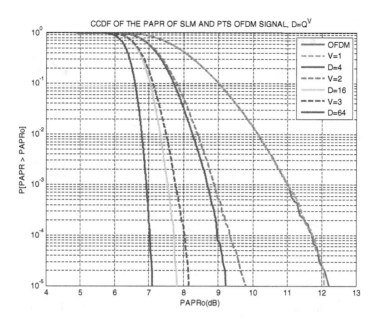

Fig. 5. CCDF of PAPR of SLM, PTS, and OFDM signal with L = 4, and the elements of the phase rotation vectors chosen from the set $\{\pm1, \pm j\}$.

As can be seen from the plot, at CCDF of 10^{-3} the PAPR difference is more than 1 dB when V = 1 for PTS and D = Q^V = 2 for SLM. In fact, this difference decreases as D = Q^V increases to 16. Therefore, the plot shows that SLM outperforms PTS in PAPR reduction capability for equal number of candidate OFDM symbols generated per given OFDM symbol in both schemes.

Figure 5 is a similar plot as Fig. 4, but in this case the elements of the phase rotation vectors are chosen from the set $\{\pm1, \pm j\}$. The plot illustrates the same result as Fig. 4.

It is shown above, Fig. 4, that for $D = Q^V$, SLM has a better PAPR reduction capability than PTS. Figure 6 shows comparative computational complexities of SLM and PTS for equal number of candidate OFDM symbols, i.e. D = Q^V. It shows the plot of the ratio C_{PTS}/C_{SLM} in dB versus the number of subblock partitions V. The simulation is done for different number of subcarriers N, L = 4, f = 4, and phase rotation factor set $\{\pm1\}$.

Though SLM has a better PAPR reduction capability than PTS, it is more computationally complex than PTS for small values of V, all values of V that make $C_{PTS}/C_{SLM} < 1$, and less computationally complex than PTS for large values of V, all values of V that make $C_{PTS}/C_{SLM} > 1$

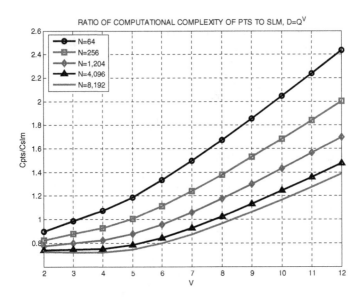

Fig. 6. Ratio of computational complexities of PTS to SLM (CPTS/CSLM) versus number of subblock partitions V for L = 4, f = 4, equal number of candidate OFDM symbols (D = Q^V), and the elements to the phase vectors chosen from the set $\{\pm 1\}$.

5 Conclusion

In this paper two distortionless PAPR reduction techniques, namely SLM and PTS, are compared for their PAPR reduction capability and computational complexity. Both schemes produce a number of candidate OFDM symbols per given OFDM symbol intended for transmission and then choose one, with the least PAPR, among them for transmission. In SLM, D length LN candidate OFDM symbols are generated using D parallel LN-point IFFTs, one for each candidate OFDM symbol. Whereas in PTS the candidate OFDM symbols are constructed from V PTSs and hence V LN-point IFFTs are required to generate the LN samples of each PTS. The receiver of each scheme uses one FFT, the same as the OFDM system without any PAPR reduction scheme, to detect the transmitted OFDM symbol from the received OFDM symbol. Hence, the additional system complexity in using the two PAPR reduction schemes is found in their transmitters.

In [5], the two schemes have been compared for equal number of IFFTs used in the transmitters of both schemes, and found that PTS has a better PAPR reduction capability than SLM. But the authors didn't do a thorough computational complexity comparison other than stating that PTS is more computationally complex than SLM. However, this comparison is done in this paper and hence it is found that for any number of subblock partitions V used in the PTS scheme, PTS is always more computationally complex than SLM.

In this work the two schemes are compared through simulation in terms of PAPR reduction capability and computational complexity for a given number of candidate

OFDM symbols generated per OFDM symbol in both schemes. Hence, it is shown through simulation that SLM outperforms PTS in PAPR reduction capability, which is illustrated in Fig. 3. When the number of subblock partitions V used in PTS are small, all values of V that result in $C_{PTS}/C_{SLM} < 1$, SLM is more computationally complex than PTS, which is the cost to be paid for its better PAPR reduction capability, which is illustrated in Fig. 4. Hence, if a PTS scheme using small number of subblock partitions V can achieve the required PAPR reduction, PTS is better than SLM; otherwise SLM is better than PTS. Whereas for relatively large number of subblock partitions V used in PTS, all values of V that make $C_{PTS}/C_{SLM} > 1$, PTS is more computationally complex than SLM, which is illustrated in Fig. 4. Therefore, SLM is better than PTS in both PAPR reduction capability and computational complexity for all values of V that result in $C_{PTS}/C_{SLM} > 1$.

References

1. Jiang, T., Wu, Y.: An overview: peak-to-average power ratio reduction techniques for OFDM signals. IEEE Trans. Broadcast. **54**(2), 257–268 (2008)
2. Han, S.H., Lee, J.H.: An overview of peak-to-average power ratio reduction techniques for multicarrier transmission. IEEE Wirel. Commun. **12**, 56–65 (2005)
3. Bäuml, R.W., Fisher, R.F.H., Huber, J.B.: Reducing the peak-to-average power ratio of multicarrier modulation by selected mapping. Electron. Lett. **32**(22), 2056–2057 (1996)
4. Müller, S.H., Huber, J.B.: OFDM with reduced peak-to-average power ratio by optimum combination of partial transmit sequences. IEEE Electron. Lett. **33**(5), 368–369 (1997)
5. Muller, S.H., Huber, J.B.: A comparison of peak power reduction schemes for OFDM. IEEE Global Telecommun. Conf. **1**, 1–5 (1997)
6. Hassan, Y., El-Tarhuni, M.: A comparison of SLM and PTS peak-to-average power ratio reduction schemes for OFDM systems. In: IEEE ICMSAO International Conference, April 2011
7. Ann, P.P., Jose, R.: Comparison of PAPR reduction techniques in OFDM systems. In: IEEE ICCES International Conference, October 2016
8. Abera, W.G.: Multicarrier Modulation with Low PAR: Applications to DSL and Wireless, Norwell. Kluwer Academic Publishers, Dordrecht (2002)
9. Ochiai, H., Imai, H.: On the distribution of the peak-to-average power ratio in OFDM signals. IEEE Trans. Commun. **49**, 282–289 (2001)
10. Workineh Gebeye: Comparative study of the performances of peak-to-average power ratio (PAPR) reduction techniques for orthogonal frequency division multiplexing (OFDM) Signals. Master of Science Thesis, Addis Ababa University, Faculty of Technology (2010)
11. Jayalath, A.D.S., Tellambura, C.: A blind SLM receiver for PAR-reduced OFDM. IEEE Veh. Technol. Conf. **1**, 219–222 (2002)
12. Jayalath, A.D.S., Tellambura, C.: SLM and PTS peak-power reduction of OFDM signals without side information. IEEE Trans. Wirel. Commun. **4**(5), 2006–2013 (2005)
13. Zhou, G.T., Peng, L.: Optimality condition for selected mapping in OFDM. IEEE Trans. Sig. Process. **54**(8), 3159–3165 (2006)
14. Kang, S.G., Kim, J.G., Joo, E.K.: A novel subblock partition scheme for partial transmit sequence OFDM. IEEE Trans. Broadcast. **45**(3), 333–338 (1999)
15. Cochran, W.T., et al.: What is the fast fourier transform? IEEE Trans. Audio Electroacoust. **55**(2), 45–55 (1967)

A Distributed Multi-hop Clustering Algorithm for Infrastructure-Less Vehicular Ad-Hoc Networks

Ahmed Alioua[1,3(✉)], Sidi-Mohammed Senouci[2], Samira Moussaoui[1],
Esubalew Alemneh[2], Med-Ahmed-Amine Derradji[3],
and Fella Benaziza[3]

[1] Computer Science Department, USTHB University, Algiers, Algeria
{aalioua, smoussaoui}@usthb.dz
[2] ISAT, DRIVE Labs, Burgundy University, Nevers, France
Sidi-Mohammed.Senouci@u-bourgogne.fr,
Esubalew_Jalew@etu.u-bourgogne.fr
[3] NTIC Faculty, Constantine 2 University, Constantine, Algeria
{ahmed.alioua, amine.derradji,
fella.benaziza}@univ-constantine2.dz

Abstract. Vehicular Ad-hoc Networks (VANETs) aim to improve travailing safety, comfort and efficiency via enabling communication between vehicles and between vehicles and infrastructure. Clustering is proposed as a promising technique to efficiently manage and deal with highly dynamic and dense features of vehicular topology. However, clustering generates a high number of control messages to manage and maintain the clustering structure. In this paper, we present our work that aims to facilitate the management of the disconnected infrastructure-less VANET areas by organizing the network topology using a distributed multi-hop clustering algorithm. The proposed algorithm is an enhanced version of the distributed version of LTE for V2X communications (LTE4V2X-D) [7] framework for the infrastructure-less VANET zone. We are able to improve the performance of LTE4V2X-D to better support clustering stability while decreasing clustering overhead. This is made possible due to a judicious choice of metrics for the selection of cluster heads and maintenance of clusters. Our algorithm uses a combination of three metrics, vehicle direction, velocity and position, in order to select a cluster-head that will have the longest lifetime in the cluster. The simulation comparison results of the proposed algorithm with LTE4V2X-D demonstrate the effectiveness of the novel enhanced clustering algorithm through the considerable improvement in the cluster stability and overhead.

Keywords: Infrastructure-less VANET · Distributed multi-hop clustering
Cluster stability

1 Introduction

Vehicular Ad-Hoc Network (VANET) enables mobile vehicles to communicate with each other in infrastructure-less mode through vehicle to vehicle (V2V) communication and with the road side infrastructure in infrastructure-based mode through vehicle to

© ICST Institute for Computer Sciences, Social Informatics and Telecommunications Engineering 2018
F. Mekuria et al. (Eds.): ICT4DA 2017, LNICST 244, pp. 68–81, 2018.
https://doi.org/10.1007/978-3-319-95153-9_7

infrastructure (V2I) communication. VANET is important to enhance traffic safety, comfort and efficiency. However, due to vehicles' high mobility and sparse topology, it is challenging to route the messages to their final destination in VANET and gain aforementioned benefits effectively and efficiently [1]. One of the most frequently used solutions to address this challenge is clustering. Clustering involves organizing a set of vehicles in smaller groups based on some predefined criteria like density, velocity, and geographical location. Clustering in VANET exhibits good scalability because it can provide a simple information management mechanism and improve communication efficiency [2]. In fact of this, various types of clustering algorithms have been proposed.

There are at least three phases in clustering algorithms. Neighborhood detection phase is the first phase in which vehicles in proximity are detected. This is possible because each vehicle broadcasts a periodic simple HELLO message containing its identifier, position and list of its neighbors. The next phase is cluster formation. In this phase, actual clusters are formed according to clustering algorithms and for each cluster, a cluster head (CH) is elected. The cluster head is a vehicle selected as a group leader or intra-cluster control server and has the responsibility of ensuring functionalities such as routing. The third phase, cluster maintenance phase, updates the cluster whenever there is any change in the structure of the cluster, due to the arrival of new vehicles, the exit of member vehicles or the transfer of the CH role to another vehicle in the cluster.

Clustering has got a lot of attentions in researches due to its many merits. Some of the literatures that deal with clustering are [1–5]. Clustering reduces network management, limits message broadcasting, allows hierarchical routing and network self-organization, reduces resource contention, facilitates scaling, etc. The difficulty of clusters management due to the high dynamic/dense topology and the overhead due to a large number of messages exchanged between vehicles for the maintenance of clusters represent the main challenges in clustering.

The reliability of any network depends largely on its ability to maintain a satisfactory level of stability. The adoption of clustering in the design of a vehicular network must take care of this problem given the highly dynamic nature of the topology of this type of network and the high mobility of the vehicles that characterizes it. Numerous researches have been carried out to meet this requirement and have proposed solutions that integrate the presence of base stations to ensure the maintenance of network stability through centralized management of clusters and CHs [4, 14]. As the focus of our study is the deployment of VANETs in areas with insufficient or no fixed infrastructure, centralization based on the use of roadside infrastructure is no longer considered. In our approach self-organization of the vehicles is possible by interconnecting vehicles using wireless technology especially IEEE 802.11p[1] that assists in forming a temporary and dynamic network without the help of pre-existing infrastructure, centralized administration or a fixed medium. That is in infrastructureless VANET each vehicle in the VANET network is a vehicle that acts as the sender,

---

[1] The IEEE 802.11p standard is an amendment to the IEEE802.11 standard that the IEEE Working Group (TGP: Task Group p) began developing in 2004 for wireless access in Intelligent Transport Systems. It defines the specifications of the MAC and PHY layers in the context of vehicular networks.

receiver, and router. In these conditions, the importance of maintaining the stability of the network becomes even more important.

Therefore, the solution we propose to address this challenge is to develop a distributed clustering protocol based on the choice of CHs that are as stable as possible. For this purpose, we have introduced election criteria for favoring the vehicle that will remain the longest time in its cluster. Our contribution relies on the distributed version of LTE for V2X communications [7] framework (we call it in this paper LTE4V2X-D protocol) for organizing the network. The new clustering protocol has five phases which can be mapped to the three general phases discussed above.

The rest of this paper is organized as follows. Section 2 describes background and motivation including a brief literature review. Section 3 presents the proposed clustering protocol. Simulation results are explained in Sect. 4. Finally, conclusion is drawn and future works are stated in Sect. 5.

2 Background and Motivation

2.1 Clustering in VANET

In clustering, the whole vehicular network is divided into groups (clusters) each one having a leader, known as CH. The cluster member vehicles transmit data to their respective CH and the CH performs aggregation/diffusion operations on this data. There are different ways of cluster formation and cluster head selection. Based on whether a central component is used or not, it can be centralized or distributed. In distributed approach cluster formation and CH selection is done by the vehicles themselves [7]. In centralized approach cluster formation and CH selection are performed at central component by roadside units [4]. Based on the number of hops separating a cluster head from its cluster member vehicles, clustering algorithms can be classified into two: 1-hop algorithm and k-hop algorithm. In a 1-hop algorithm, the distance between two member vehicles in a cluster does not exceed 2 hops so that the distance between the member vehicles and their associated CH is maintained at a single hop [8–10]. In k-hop algorithms, the CH can reach member vehicles of its most remote cluster by performing multiple jumps through intermediate member vehicles [11, 12]. Therefore, it is no longer required to maintain a direct connection with its associated vehicles. Various algorithms have been proposed for each clustering approach and each of them has its own advantages and disadvantages. There are many other ways to classify clustering mechanisms. For more details readers are advised to refer [1, 6].

2.2 LTE for V2X Communications -LTE4V2X

An innovative solution for a centralized organization of vehicular network using Fourth Generation Long Term Evolution (4G LTE) cellular network is proposed in [4]. In this paper, Rémy et al. come up with an idea of using LTE for centrally managing VANET clusters by observing widespread nature of the LTE network that has high potential to extend the coverage area of fixed infrastructure of a network through the use of eNodeB base stations to replace the Road Side Units (RSUs). LTE4V2X jointly uses both

802.11p and LTE technologies to provide an efficient means for periodically collecting data from vehicles and send them to a central server. The evaluation results of the proposed framework showed performance improvement over decentralized approach. As continuity of their work in [4], the authors have presented two extensions of the clustering protocol, LTE4V2X: a centralized version (we called it LTE4V2X-C) with one-hop for the areas covered by the fixed LTE-infrastructure, and a multi-hop distributed version (LTE4V2X-D) for areas not covered by the LTE- infrastructure [7]. Recently, in [5] Ucar et al. have proposed a hybrid architecture, called MaSC-LTE, combining IEEE 802.11p-based multi-hop clustering and 4G LTE, with the goal of achieving a high data packet delivery ratio and low delay while keeping the usage of the cellular architecture at a minimum level. In this method, CH selection is based on the relative mobility metric calculated as the average relative speed with respect to the neighboring vehicles and cluster connection with minimum overhead. This is achieved by introducing a direct connection to the neighbor that is already a head or a member of a cluster instead of connecting to the CH in multiple hops.

In this paper, we are particularly interested in the distributed multi-hop version of LTE4V2X-D based on V2V communications and dedicated for non-covered areas by the fixed network infrastructures. Despite its proven effectiveness, LTE4V2X-D has certain limitations because the method used elects the closest vehicle to the end of cluster segment as CH. This damages stability of the clusters as the vehicles moving at a high speed have a short life as CH. It also causes high control overhead due to the frequent execution of the CH election process. Moreover, the immediate disconnection of CH as soon as it leaves its cluster lets the cluster without coordinator during the whole re-election phase of a new CH, which can destabilize the whole structure. The last limitation we have observed is when a vehicle leaves a cluster, it is immediately disconnected from its CH and will not be assigned to any other cluster until the next maintenance cycle.

Therefore, starting from the limitations observed in the LTE4V2X-D algorithm, we propose a novel enhanced protocol that is able to overcome these limits and ensures a higher stability of the structure while reducing control overhead. In our method based on a fixed geographical division of the road segment, cluster head election is decided by vehicle's closeness to the beginning of the segment. This resolves most of the aforementioned problems. For the last limitation, if a member vehicle leaves its cluster, it remains connected to its CH until it synchronizes and gets integrated with its new CH in the new cluster.

3   A Distributed Multi-hop Clustering Algorithm for Infrastructure-Less VANET

This section presents our new distributed multi-hop clustering algorithm for the organization and management of vehicular networks in non-covered areas (infrastructure-less VANET). Architectures based on a fixed infrastructure like RSUs for V2I communications have many limitations. Firstly, the RSUs coverage area is very short and connectivity between a vehicle and an RSU is often intermittent. Moreover, deployment of infrastructure is expensive and the number of RSUs is often insufficient.

Our contribution involves the introduction of a distributed multi-hop protocol that depends mainly on V2V communications, enabling it to be implemented in an environment with poorly fixed infrastructure or where the infrastructure is absent at all. This is possible since each vehicle is equipped with an integrated unit called On Board Unit (OBU) with IEEE 802.11p interface which allows direct communication from vehicle to vehicle.

3.1   Basic Idea

The basic idea of our algorithm is inspired by the work LTE4V2X in [7]. This architecture uses a centralized one hop version (*i.e.,* LTE4V2X-C) based on cellular infrastructure in cases where there is LTE coverage and a distributed multihop extension (*i.e.,* LTE4V2X-D) is used in the areas where there is no LTE coverage for example in tunnels. LTE4V2X-D is based on the decentralized self-organizing protocol, Clustering Gathering Protocol (CGP) in [14]. A fixed geographical clusters topology is used to organize the network. The road is segmented into equal length segments and each segment representing a cluster, see Fig. 1.

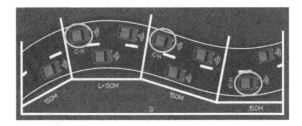

Fig. 1. The static equal road segments in our algorithm.

Even though the experimental coverage range of the IEEE 802.11p interface is about 300 m, we opted for segments of length 150 m to ensure the vehicle in the adjacent segments reach each other [7]. Note that CH is a vehicle closest to the beginning of each segment and with the slowest speed.

For correct functioning of our solution we assume that;

- In addition to OBU with IEE802.11p interface, each vehicle is equipped with Global Positioning System (GPS) which will indicate its position in real time,
- Traffic is constant on the road and a vehicle that breaks down is not taken into consideration, so the network remains reliable.

3.2   Algorithm Description

In our proposed distributed algorithm, all vehicles participate in the CH election and maintenance. The CH acts as a control server for all member vehicles in its cluster and will also manage intra-cluster and inter-cluster communications using a multi-hop method to route packets between different clusters. The algorithm implements the distributed clustering protocol in five phases. The first phase of this protocol is the initialization phase that will trigger the clustering algorithm. It will be followed by four periodic phases, the aim of which will be the formation of clusters, the election of the CHs, the maintenance of the clusters and finally the collection and routing phase, as illustrated in Fig. 2.

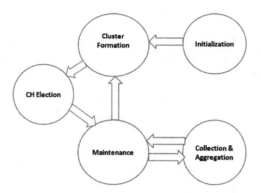

Fig. 2. Phases of the proposed algorithm.

During the initialization phase, each vehicle calculates its Floating Car Data (FCD), *i.e.*, its position, speed, and direction. This phase is carried out only once, when the protocol starts and allows the mobile vehicles to know their data information necessary for the proper operation of the following phases. The next phase, cluster formation phase, is executed in a distributed way and is ensured by all the vehicles. Each vehicle according to its position calculated from the GPS and the information provided by the road map can determine on which cluster it is located and therefore to which cluster it belongs. A cluster includes all vehicles that run in the same direction and are on the same segment.

After the cluster formation phase, each vehicle will run the CH election algorithm to determine a CH in each segment. A CH once elected will retain its status until it leaves its cluster. Distance, speed and direction are the metrics used for the choice of the best CH candidate. Based on these criteria, we determined a heuristic to calculate the weight of each vehicle to determine the best candidate to be CH. The travel time of a vehicle is represented by the ratio between the distance separating this vehicle from the end of its segment and its speed. The distance is determined by the position of the vehicle inside its cluster. The travel time for i^{th} vehicle ($T_{Traveling}(i)$) is therefore calculated as follows:

$$T_{Traveling}(i) = \frac{Distance(position(i), Segment\_End)}{Speed(i)} \quad (1)$$

At the beginning of CH election, each vehicle will potentially broadcast a CH_ANNOUNCE (CH status) message after observing a wait time. This timeout represents the back-off time plus the time required for sending a packet from one end of the cluster to the other, called sending time (T_S) [7]. As one tries to determine the vehicle that has the highest traveling time of its segment it is to say the vehicle having the smallest back-off time. Therefore, the back-off time of vehicle i ($T_{bac-koff}(i)$) is equal to the inverse of the segment travel time and it is given by the following formula:

$$T_{back-off}(i) = \frac{Speed\ (i)}{Distance\ (position\ (i), Segment\_End)} \qquad (2)$$

The application of this back-off time calculation formula will determine which vehicle is the most likely to be CH. The sending time of a message from one end to the other of the segment is obtained by the following formula:

$$T_s(i) = \frac{Length\ of\ Segment}{Packet\_Sending\_Speed(i)} \qquad (3)$$

The waiting time required for a vehicle i to transmit its message CH_ANNOUNCE is obtained by adding the back-off time and the time of routing a message from one end of the segment to the other:

$$T_{waiting}(i) = T_{back-off}(i) + T_s^{-1}(i) \qquad (4)$$

Each vehicle will calculate its back-off time using formula (2), and then wait for a certain calculated time in formula (4) before sending a CH_ANNOUNCE message. If a vehicle receives a message CH_ANNOUNCE then it will have to cancel the sending of its own message and considers that the source vehicle of the message is a better candidate than him to be CH. Thus, the vehicle that receives no message will be elected CH because it was the first to send its message CH_ANNOUNCE because having the smallest back-off time is due to the fact that it has the smallest weight. Finally, the newly elected CH broadcasts to all the vehicles of the segment to inform them that it is the new CH. The algorithm for the election of CH is summarized below:

```
Initially all vehiclesare considered cluster members.
For Each vehicle i do
    Calculate the back-off time
    Wait for the expiration of a certain delay (T_waiting)
    If a message CH_ANNOUNCE_j is received then
        Cancel sending CH_ANNOUNCE_i (do nothing)
        Otherwise, Log in as CH and Distribute a message CH_ANNOUNCE in
    the cluster
    End if
End For
```

The maintenance of clusters is a crucial phase in order to guarantee the stability of the clustering structure, which is very important due to the highly dynamic nature of the VANETs. The objective of this phase is to maintain connectivity between the clusters in spite of the changes that may occur, because of the arrival or departure of a vehicle, through periodic checks. A new vehicle arrives and indicates its presence in the new cluster by broadcasting a HELLO_MEMBER message (the message contains its ID, its IP, as well as its POSITION). This message will enable the vehicle to ask the CH to integrate it into its cluster. Receiving a CH_ANNOUNCE message will indicate that the message is part of the cluster. The newly arrived vehicle will then update its cluster ID. The CH will also update the data concerning its member clusters. Finally, an updating of the topology packet is carried out by the CH and diffused accordingly during the periodic operations. If the new vehicle does not receive a message CH_ANNOUNCE for the duration of one cycle, the vehicle that has just arrived automatically becomes the cluster-head. This CH status of the newly arrived vehicle is justified by the fact that it is at the beginning of the segment thus meeting the criterion of the election of the CH which stipulates that it is the vehicle furthest from the end of the segment that constitutes the best candidacy to play the role of CH. Algorithm for integration of a new vehicle is summarized next:

```
As long as the number of new unassigned vehicles remaining > 0 do
        Broadcast of a HELLO_MEMBER message by the newly arrived vehicle
        Wait for a CH_ANNOUNCE message to be received.
        If the new vehicle has received a message CH_ANNOUNCE then
        The vehicle sends its coordinates to the CH.
        The CH integrates the new vehicle into its list.
        The new vehicle updates the information in its new cluster
        End if
        If the new vehicle does not receive any message then
            The new vehicle is elected as the CH of the new cluster
        End if
End As long as
```

The departure of a vehicle can seriously disrupt the stability of a cluster especially if the vehicle is a CH. If a vehicle crosses the boundary of its segment, its CH will be able to detect its departure by comparing its new position with the boundaries of the segment. However, the vehicle always remains connected to the CH of its old cluster until it is integrated into a new cluster. This choice has been made so that even if the vehicle has left the segment it always remains in the coverage area of the CH of its former segment. This approach has double advantage of overcoming the problem of changing the topology inherent in the VANETs and of avoiding an early loss of information which will affect the reliability of the network. This mechanism is largely inspired by the concept of seamless handover in cellular networks. Once the vehicle is connected to its new CH, it will be removed from the member list of its old CH during the periodic checks step in the next cycle. During the periodic operations step, the new CH will update the topology packet and distribute it accordingly. In the event that the vehicle that is about to leave the segment is CH, it must first start the phase of electing a new CH from its cluster vehicles to ensure polling before disconnecting. A lapse of time is observed to guarantee the continuity of the service during which the old CH transmits the data packets collected during its mandate to the new CH. High level algorithm for the departure of a vehicle is described below:

```
As long as the vehicle is no longer part of the segment
        If the outgoing vehicle is CH then
            Start CH election phase
            Perform data transfer
        Disconnect from the old cluster.
        Else
            Disconnect from the old cluster.
            Delete the vehicle from the CH list of the old cluster
        End if
    End As long as
```

After the initialization phase, periodic checks are carried out at all times in order to maintain a stable structure and ensure the longest possible lifetime at the CH. The objective of this phase is to initiate different operations and functions of the algorithm with each change in the topology of the network.

During the last phase, data collection and aggregation phase, each CH receives information about its cluster vehicles and their data. Once collected, they are aggregated, compressed and possibly routed to the next CH in the case of a collection application.

```
For every second
    For each segment_i Make
            Initiate cluster maintenance
    End For
End For
```

Since the proposed protocol is based on distributed approach, routing and dissemination of data in the network will be done without the intervention of any fixed infrastructure component in a self-organized manner and under the supervision of CHs. Thus, the routing and dissemination of the data in our protocol are done in two ways, intra-cluster routing orchestrated by the CH and an inter-cluster routing from CH to CH. In intra-cluster routing, communication is made through the CH that provides coordination between its member vehicles. In inter-cluster routing, communication between clusters for the dissemination of information across the network is made between CHs. Each CH after having collected the information from its member clusters, aggregates them and transmits to the CH of the neighboring cluster, and so on.

3.3 Description of Some Packets Used by Our Algorithm

Different packets are used by our protocol during the different phases of its execution. *Vehicle Identification packet* contains the vehicle identifier, IPV4 address, direction, position, speed and collected data. The vehicle transmits this packet periodically to its CH to allow maintenance operations to keep the network structure up-to-date. *Cluster ID packet* identifies each cluster by cluster identifier, the CH, the number of vehicles in the cluster at particular time, the dimensions of the cluster (width and height), list of vehicles and their data. These data are compressed using an algorithm to decrease its volumes. *Notification packet*, on the other hand, is used to report accident alerts, blocked roads or incidents that require notification of the situation. In this case, the notification message is broadcasted to all vehicles or to only those which will be concerned with respect to the position, the zone and the time of the event. *Network topology packet* contains all the cluster information, the cluster member vehicles as well as the data scattered in the network that each CH needs to know to fulfill its mission. An example of network topology packets is shown in Fig. 3.

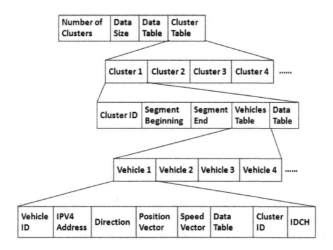

Fig. 3. Example of network topology packet.

4   Simulations Results

In order to evaluate the proposed clustering protocol, we have used discrete event network simulator ns-3 [15] for network simulation and the traffic simulator SUMO [16] to generate traffic mobility traces. The main propose of the simulation is to evaluate the stability and efficiency of our clustering algorithm/protocol in term of control overhead, cluster-head lifetime and re-election while comparing the performance with that of LTE4V2X-D.

For the simulation model, we use Open Street Map [17] to simulate an infrastructure-less road segment from Constantine city, Algeria deployed on 1200 × 1200 m area, as illustrated in Fig. 4. The road is divided into equal segments of 150 m each. The vehicle density is 20 vehicles and they communicate only using V2V multi-hop communication through IEEE 802.11p based interface. The transmission range of the IEEE 802.11p based interface is up to 300 m. The vehicle velocity is between 10 and 30 m\s. The simulation time is 180 s and the packet generation rate is 6 packets per second. The duration of the initiation phase is 2 s and the duration of each cycle is 3 s.

The performance metrics we used are:

- *Cluster-head lifetime*: is the elapsed time between the election of a cluster-head and the time when it leaves the cluster. It represents the cluster stability.

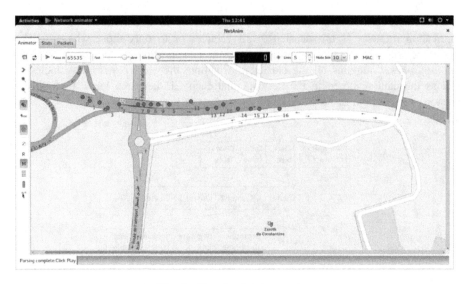

Fig. 4. The simulated scenario.

- *Control overhead message*: it represents the number of control messages used for the clustering procedure.
- *Number of cluster-head re-election*: it represents the number of CH election during a period of time.

In the evaluation results illustrated in Fig. 5, the average CH lifetime in our clustering algorithm for a different number of vehicles is depicted and compared with that of LTE4V2X-D.

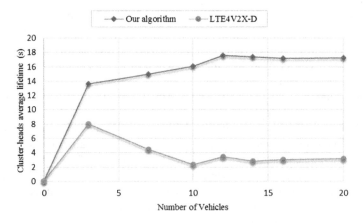

Fig. 5. Impact of vehicles number on the cluster-head lifetime.

It can be seen from Fig. 5 that the CH average lifetime of our clustering algorithm increases regularly with the increase of vehicles number before stabilizing. Contrarily, in LTE4V2X-D the cluster head average lifetime decreases with the increase of the number of vehicles. Moreover, our enhanced algorithm largely overcome LTE4V2X-D in term of the cluster-head average lifetime and can ensure a better stability for the clustering structure and thus for the whole network. This can be justified by the use of good CH election metrics that involves selection of the vehicle nearest to the beginning of the road segment and that has a slow speed. Exactly, the inverse of LTE4V2X-D that elects a vehicle which is nearest to the end of road segment (cluster) and that has the fastest speed use as cluster-head. Our algorithm CH election metrics can ensure good cluster stability via enhancing the cluster-head traverse time (lifetime).

The evaluation figure in Fig. 6 compares the clustering overhead of our clustering algorithm with that of LTE4V2X-D for a different number of vehicles.

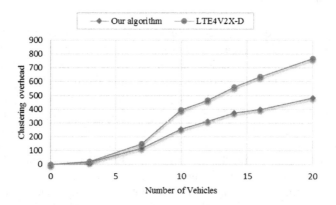

Fig. 6. Clustering overhead versus vehicle number.

The comparison results in Fig. 6, show that the number of messages exchanged in our protocol is clearly lower than LTE4V2X-D and this demonstrates the efficiency of our algorithm in reducing the clustering overhead. This is due to the stability of the clustering structure and the longer CH lifetime as the election is triggered only when it is needed. Therefore, our algorithm decreases the number of CHs re-elections and thus the clustering messages exchanged.

Figure 7 illustrates the comparison of the performance of our enhanced clustering algorithm with LTE4V2X-D in term of cluster-head re-election number for a different number of vehicles.

As we can clearly see from the comparison result above, the performance of our enhanced algorithm is largely better than LTE4V2X-D and can reduce three times the cluster-head re-election number. This can be justified again by the long lifetime of the CH in our algorithm compared to that in LTE4V2X-D.

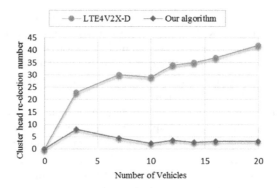

Fig. 7. Cluster head re-election number versus vehicle number.

5 Conclusion

In this paper, we have presented an enhancement of the multi-hop distributed clustering algorithm (LTE4V2X-D) in [7] to better support clustering stability and reduce overhead messages. The analysis carried out on the LTE4V2X-D protocol showed its limitations in terms of maintaining the stability of vehicular network and reducing the overhead, which are two decisive criteria for evaluating the effectiveness of a clustering protocol. On the basis of these limitations, we formulated proposals that were the basis of our solution. We have defined and introduced new metrics for the election of the cluster-head so that the choice is made for the one with the longest service lifetime, thus ensuring more stability for the network. The other outcome of our algorithm is a reduction of the overhead by reducing the number of cluster-head re-election. The protocol, which has taken advantage of the concept of seamless handover, also reduces the rate of packet loss and reduce the risk of a change in topology by providing a connectivity delay for an unexpected cluster-head change. The simulation comparing results of our algorithm with that of LTE4V2X-D, demonstrates the effectiveness of our enhanced clustering algorithm in term of two of the most important clustering metrics: cluster stability and overhead.

As future work, we plan to extend our algorithm for dealing with network partitioning problem and exploit its logic for a dissemination and collection application in infrastructure-less Vehicular Delay Tolerant Network (VDTN).

References

1. Bali, R.S., Kumar, N., Rodrigues, J.J.: Clustering in vehicular ad hoc networks: taxonomy, challenges and solutions. Veh. Commun. **1**, 134–152 (2014)
2. Chen, Y., Fang, M., Shi, S., Guo, W., Zheng, X.: Distributed multi-hop clustering algorithm for VANETs based on neighborhood follow. EURASIP J. Wirel. Commun. Netw. **2015**, 98 (2015)

3. Basagni, S.: Distributed clustering algorithm for ad-hoc networks. In: Proceedings of the International Symposium on Parallel Architectures, Algorithms, and Networks (I-SPAN) (1999)
4. Remy, G., Senouci, S., Jan, F., Gourhant, Y.: LTE4V2X: LTE for a centralized VANET organization. In: 2011 IEEE Global Telecommunications Conference - GLOBECOM 2011 (2011)
5. Ucar, S., Ergen, S.C., Ozkasap, O.: Multihop-cluster-based IEEE 802.11p and LTE hybrid architecture for VANET safety message dissemination. IEEE Trans. Veh. Technol. **65**, 2621–2636 (2016)
6. Sucasas, V., Radwan, A., Marques, H., Rodriguez, J., Vahid, S., Tafazolli, R.: A survey on clustering techniques for cooperative wireless networks. Ad Hoc Netw. **47**, 53–81 (2016)
7. Remy, G., Senouci, S.-M., Jan, F., Gourhant, Y.: LTE4V2X—Collection, dissemination and multi-hop forwarding. In: 2012 IEEE International Conference on Communications (ICC) (2012)
8. Corson, M.S., Ephremides, A.: A distributed routing algorithm for mobile wireless networks. Wirel. Netw. **1**, 61–81 (1995)
9. Lin, C., Gerla, M.: Adaptive clustering for mobile wireless networks. IEEE J. Sel. Areas Commun. **15**, 1265–1275 (1997)
10. Kwon, T.J., Gerla, M., Varma, V., Barton, M., Hsing, T.: Efficient flooding with passive clustering - an overhead-free selective forward mechanism for ad hoc/sensor networks. Proc. IEEE **91**, 1210–1220 (2003)
11. Chen, G., Nocetti, F., Gonzalez, J., Stojmenovic, I.: Connectivity based k-hop clustering in wireless networks. In: Proceedings of the 35th Annual Hawaii International Conference on System Sciences, pp. 2450–2459 (2002)
12. Amis, A.D., Prakash, R., Vuong, T.H., Huynh, D.T.: Max-min d-cluster formation in wireless ad hoc networks. In: Proceedings of the Nineteenth Annual Joint Conference of the IEEE Computer and Communications Societies, vol. 1, pp. 32–41 (2000)
13. Benslimane, A., Taleb, T., Sivaraj, R.: Dynamic clustering-based adaptive mobile gateway management in integrated VANET—3G heterogeneous wireless networks. IEEE J. Sel. Areas Commun. **29**, 559–570 (2011)
14. Salhi, I., Cherif, M., Senouci, S.M.: A new architecture for data collection in vehicular networks. In: IEEE International Conference, pp. 1–6 (2009)
15. Network Simulator 3 (ns-3). http://www.nsnam.org/
16. Simulation of Urban Mobility (SUMO). http://sumo-sim.org/
17. Open Street Map. https://www.openstreetmap.org/

Radar Human Gait Signal Analysis Using Short Time Fourier Transform

Negasa B. Teshale$^{(\boxtimes)}$, Dinkisa A. Bulti, and Habib M. Hussien

School of Electrical and Computer Engineering Addis Ababa,
Addis Ababa, Ethiopia
negasabasha4@gmail.com, dinqiisa@gmail.com,
habibmohammed2001@gmail.com

Abstract. Human gait detection and identification by using radar signal is one of the recent subject of increased research area in signal processing. It has been indicated human gait information/signal is highly unusual which can be used for human detection and identification from one person to another. Most previous works related to this area extraction of features from the pace of pedestrians is only depending on the motions rhythm signal analysis and synthesis. Then Fourier transform and more recently time-frequency transforms are used to analyze the time shift/delay and identify the different parts of the human body playing part during the human movement. The analysis of the time/frequency shift usually needs to observe the process by taking a bit long time, at least long enough to get the gait signal cycle. However, the presence of several people simultaneously in the radar field of sight could involve interferences. Hence, in this paper we have been trying to use one of a powerful tool short time Fourier transform for the analysis of time-varying signals among the time frequency methods to extract some feature of human gait.

Keywords: Time frequency analysis · Radar signal · Matlab

1 Introduction

This work introduces radar signal analysis which retrieved from a number human gait movement signals. Unlike the analysis of the movement of rigid bodies within the context of conventional autonomous target recognition, the analysis of human gait signal exhibits substantially a bit more difficulties because the individual portion of the human body experience different signal movements that change over time/frequency results in a dynamically alternating the wave of the target which in turn produces a high perplexed time–frequency (TF) construction of the radar signals that determine the target movement via time [1–3].

While the analysis of human gait has been studied in a deep way by the various fields for different application starting from the last few decades [3]. Some recent research works attempts to generalizing the frame work of human gait from radar signals are relatively more recent [4]. Here also we try recognize/identify the response human gait signal information from radar spectrum signal of various human scenarios

© ICST Institute for Computer Sciences, Social Informatics and Telecommunications Engineering 2018
F. Mekuria et al. (Eds.): ICT4DA 2017, LNICST 244, pp. 82–88, 2018.
https://doi.org/10.1007/978-3-319-95153-9_8

like walking and running and so on using different extracting techniques of signal processing method for individuals are different [4].

2   Related Work

Human gait is composed of very complicated body structures and reflects radar signals with time shift modulations that shows data about pedestrian movement has various dynamic behavior. The overall frequency shift signal of a human movement, including breathing and heartbeat, which includes the biometric radar signals, has get substantial concern in the time of some courses [4]. Recognizing this signal using time-frequency representations (TFRs) are an efficient tool for non-stationary signal classification of human gait analysis has typically been performed with joint time-frequency signal techniques [5]. The scatter diagrams of stride and appendage/torso ratio vs. velocity are also taken as gait signature and a linear classifier is built to identify gender and human presence [7].

Furthermore, the extraction of data from the nature of the motion of human being using time shift radar echo signals are represented by their time-frequency signatures in the most of previous related works. The time-frequency classifier used in this paper follows the work in which no specific feature is extracted, but rather the entire time-frequency representation is used.

The human gait model is the starting point for human signal performance description. Dealing with the relationship between the different body components at the time of movement; factors that gives us gait signal distinct can easily be identified from the experiment data analysis. The basic significant human gait parameters of radar dependent behavior controlling are velocity profile and radar x-section.

Consider an individual is walking at a constant velocity, V wrt an initial point in a certain direction. Another assumption is we may segment the body into m rigid body portions. Each of the body parts including the torso have a velocity profile, $V_m(t)$ that can be expressed as a summation of sinusoidal signals in the form of equation [9]:

$$V_m(t) = v + A \cdot \{k_{m1} + \sin(\omega_c t + p_m) + k_{m2} \cdot \cos(\omega_c t + p_m) + k_{m3} \cdot \sin(2\omega_c t + p_m) + k_{m4} \cdot \cos(2\omega_c t + p_m)\}$$

Where, $k_{m1}, ---, k_{m4}$ and $p_m\{0 \leq p_m \leq \pi$ are constants that characterize each of the body components.

3   Radar

A simple experimental radar generates continuously a sinusoidal wave signal which can operate in the frequency ranges of 50 Hz. This continuous wave radar is like the hand-held machines applied by police to determine the speed of moving vehicles. As mentioned above human beings are complex target due to having many complexly arranged elements during movement of body components in motion along different trajectories with various speeds. It's always make even more complex human kinematic modeling when we consider extreme excess of different human motions, which all have radically different kinematics, such as running, walking, jumping, swimming, slithering creeping, or playing ball and so on. Even within the same type of movement, such as running as an example, by handling something load or running in a ring, as opposed to linear, trajectory can change the kinematics. In this work, we confine our coverage particularly by assuming human walking, which is the most common human motion.

3.1   Human Motion Identification Using Radar

CW radars employ continuous sinusoidal signal wave-forms, expressed as $\cos(2\pi f_0 t)$. Transmitting and receiving the frequency spectrum of the radar echo from stationary body will be considered when frequency in Hz is at f_0. The frequency shift during echoes or radar signals from non-stationary bodies represented as fd in Hz, which is called Doppler frequency as depicted in the Fig. 1 below. Hence, by determining continuous wave radar signals frequency shifts or differences, radar signals vary in the same manner of perfect target radial velocity. Because of the continuous nature of CW emission, range measurement is not possible without some modifications to the radar operations and waveforms

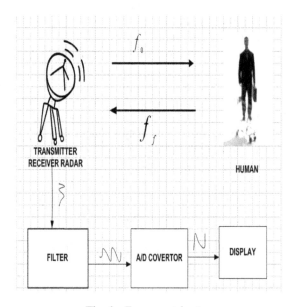

Fig. 1. Expermental setup

The bandwidth of our experimental radar signal ranges about 50 Hz. From this simple diagram the person told stay in front of the radar at about 50 m distance for few seconds. Then, s/he begins walking in relation to the radar at unvarying rate. This experiment is done in a 2 m wide and 50 m long corridor. A time counter indicate that many people takes 12–14 s finish about 15 m.

3.2 Requirements of CW Radar for Human Movement Characterization

Unlike, the optical system of human gait signal analysis continuous wave radar signals do not need light signal to take information/signature from human movement which can be used as identification even though the signal are needs to analyzed and synthesized from different parts of the body [12, 13].

It has indicates that human movement signature is different and can help for recognition. Though the performance is more challenging by radar transceiver signals, previous studies also proved that radar signature can discole information on the human's behave or manner of acting.

Another very important requirement of this CW radar is when someone moves, the various parts of his/her body (heads, torso, arms, legs) have a especial movement that develops feature of Doppler signatures. Finally as the nature of the Doppler spectrum is mostly periodic, a time Doppler variation analysis permits to extract features of the human gait easily by using time frequency representation analysis techniques.

4 Time Frequency Representation

The analysis of non-stationary signals are mostly existed in many field practical application areas, like speech signal processing, earthquake excitations, medical instrument, electromyography, radar, sonar, and machine vibration signals. Nonstationary signal models account for possible time variations of statistical functions and spectral characteristics of signals. Understanding these variations is important because they are often indicative of the underlying processes that generate the signal. The main purpose of this special session is to include research work on theory, methods, and applications of non-stationary signal models.

Accordingly, a fundamental role has been played in the growth of Time-Frequency (TF) methods, which makes a virtual representation of the spectral behaviors of the informatios/data. Some TF methods include the Fractional Fourier Transform (frft), Short-time Fourier Transform (STFT), the Wavelet Transform (WT), the Wigner-Ville Distribution (WVD), and Hilbert Transform.

4.1 Short Time Fourier Transform (STFT)

The STFT assumed as a method that breaks up non-stationary signal into many small constitute manageable signal segments, which can be considered to be locally stationary, and implements traditional FFT for signal build up analysis [5, 12].

The STFT of a signal $s_t(\tau)$ is obtained by convolving the two signals to gather, $h(\tau)$, centered at τ, to produce a modified signal.

$$S_t(\omega) = \frac{1}{2\pi} \int\limits_{-\infty}^{\infty} e^{-j\omega\tau} s(\tau) h(\tau - t) d\tau$$

The energy density signal at time τ:

$$p(t, \omega) = |s_t(\omega)|^2 = \left| \frac{1}{2\pi} \int\limits_{-\infty}^{\infty} e^{-j\omega\tau} s(\tau) h(\tau - t) d\tau \right|^2$$

The main shortcoming of signal analysis method STFT is the resolution tradeoff between time and frequency. Resolutions in time and frequency will be determined by the width of window h(τ). A large window width gives high resolution in the frequency domain, but less resolution in the time domain.

The other limitation of STFT is with regard to its computation is somehow expensive, but ways of accelerating it by avoiding redundant calculations are available. These drawbacks however, STFT is an ideal tool various aspects, the most vital being its nature of best spectrogram structure, which is consistent with its regarding frequency spectra, which makes spectrum visualization better.

5   Evaluation and Discussion

– Human gait analysis by time-frequency algorithm.
– Received signal analysis according to the setup shown below.
– The signal extracted during stationary state is very small as relative to the signal during movement. This is due to:
  • The unidirectional antenna helps to decrease the direct signal from transmitter to receiver.
  • The experiment was processed in a corridor where potential reflectors from a faraway (Fig. 2).

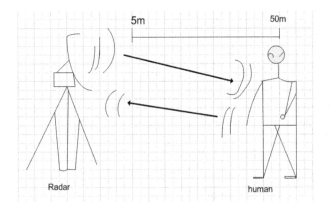

Fig. 2. Practical experiment setup during record

- As we can see from the waveform when the person is moving toward the radar is different from moving away, when the movement is lose by to the radar the signal is very strong.

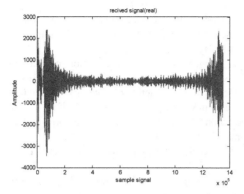

- Gait feature extraction from radar signal using different frequency signal analysis method are shown below.

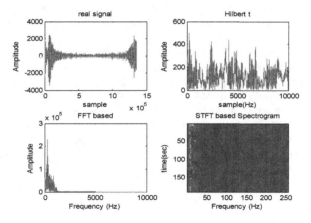

6   Conclusion

All techniques signal analysis method good at detecting a single elements of signal but no techniques whether it's traditional or new paradigms can able to detect and identify and provide all the best results for all cases. When the moving part is not clearly not known it's a great to choose which signal analysis techniques affords the better result. From this paper work, someone could find a lot of signal analysis and syntheses methods that can utilize to analyze non-stationary and stationary data's has been discussed in detail. The betterment and drowbacks of each method of time-frequency analysis has pointed out, and the practical application of these techniques in the extracting information from human gait radar signal have been highlighted especially using STFT.

References

1. Balazia, M., Plataniotis, K.N.: Human gait recognition from motion capture data in signature poses. IET Biom. **6**(2), 129–137 (2017)
2. Anderson, M.G.: Design of multiple frequency continuous wave radar hardware and micro-Doppler based detection and classification algorithms, Ph.D. dissertation, University of Texas at Austin, May 2008
3. Chi, W., Wang, J., Meng, M.Q.H.: A gait recognition method for human following in service robots. IEEE Trans. Syst. Man Cybern. Syst. **PP**(99) (2017)
4. Hornsteiner, C., Detlefsen, J.: Extraction of features related to human gait using a continuous wave radar. In: German Microwave Conference (2008)
5. Chen, V.C.: Detection and analysis of human motion by radar. In: 2008 IEEE Radar Conference, Rome, pp. 1–4 (2008)
6. Brandwood, D.: Fourier Transforms in Radar and Signal Processing. Artech house, inc., London (2003)
7. Gurbuz, Z., Melvin, L., Williams, B.: Detection and identification of human targets in radar data. In: Proceedings of the SPIE, vol. 6567 (2007)
8. Ding, M., Fan, G.: Multilayer joint gait-pose manifolds for human gait motion modeling. IEEE Trans. Cybern. **45**(11), 2413–2424 (2015)
9. Ma, H., Liao, W.H.: Human gait modeling and analysis using a semi-Markov process with ground reaction forces. IEEE Trans. Neural Syst. Rehabil. Eng. **25**(6), 597–607 (2017)
10. Mahafza, B.R.: Radar Signal Analysis and Processing Using MATLAB. CRC Press, Boca Raton (2008)
11. Geisheimer, J., Marshal, W., Greneker, E.: A CW radar for gait analysis. In: IEEE Conference on Signals, Systems and Computers, vol. 1, pp. 834–838 (2001)
12. Ram, S., Li, Y., Lin, A., Ling, H.: Doppler-based detection and tracking of humans in indoor environment. J. Franklin Inst. **345**, 679–699 (2008)
13. Seifert, A.K., Zoubir, A.M., Amin, M.G.: Radar-based human gait recognition in cane-assisted walks. In: 2017 IEEE Radar Conference (RadarConf), Seattle, WA (2017)
14. Badiezadeh, A., Ayatollahi, F., Ghaeminia, M.H., Shokouhi, S.B.: Human gait recognition using Dual-Tree Complex Wavelet Transform. In: 2017 Iranian Conference on Electrical Engineering (ICEE), Tehran, pp. 461–466 (2017)

Classification of Mammograms Using Convolutional Neural Network Based Feature Extraction

Taye Girma Debelee[1,3(✉)], Mohammadreza Amirian[1], Achim Ibenthal[2],
Günther Palm[1], and Friedhelm Schwenker[1]

[1] Institute of Neural Information Processing, Ulm University, 89069 Ulm, Germany
{taye.debelee,mohammadreza.amirian,guenther.palm,
friedhelm.schwenker}@uni-ulm.de, tayegirma@gmail.com
[2] Adama Science and Technology University, Adama, Ethiopia
ibenthal@gmx.net
[3] Addis Abeba Science and Technology University, Addis Abeba, Ethiopia

Abstract. Breast cancer is the most common cause of death among women in the entire world and the second cause of death after lung cancer. The use of automatic breast cancer detection and classification might possibly enhance the survival rate of the patients through starting early treatment. In this paper, the convolutional Neural Networks (CNN) based feature extraction method is proposed. The features dimensionality was reduced using Principal Component Analysis (PCA). The reduced features are given to the K-Nearest Neighbors (KNN) to classify mammograms as normal or abnormal using 10-fold cross-validation. The experimental result of the proposed approach performed on Mammography Image Analysis Society (MIAS) and Digital Database for Screening Mammography (DDSM) datasets were found to be promising compared to previous studies in the area of image processing, artificial intelligence and CNN with an accuracy of 98.75% and 98.90% on MIAS and DDSM dataset respectively.

Keywords: Breast cancer · Mammogram · CNN
K-nearest neighbour · Feature extraction

1 Introduction

Breast cancer is one of the most prevalent types of cancer and the second cause of death among women [1,15,17,20,21]. In the USA breast cancer has been proven to be the second cause of death for women after lung cancer [1,19,21,30]. There are two severity of abnormalities associated with breast cancer cells: benign and malignant. The benign ones are cancerous cells that do not grow to neighboring tissues of the breast from where they originated and are no risk to life. The malignant ones, however, are cancerous cells that multiply to other parts of surrounding breast tissues from point of their origin and need to be treated as

© ICST Institute for Computer Sciences, Social Informatics and Telecommunications Engineering 2018
F. Mekuria et al. (Eds.): ICT4DA 2017, LNICST 244, pp. 89–98, 2018.
https://doi.org/10.1007/978-3-319-95153-9_9

early as possible. Oliver explained the most common class of abnormalities that can indicate breast cancer [2,12]. The abnormality class includes geometrical asymmetries between left and right breast, normal architectural distortions of the breast tissue, presence of calcifications in the breast, and presence of masses. Breast cancer mass is a localized swelling or lump that appears to exist as benign or malignant in the breast [2,12].

According to the recent review made by Palazuelos et al. [20], breast cancer incidence rate has increased by 20% since 2008 and it is the most frequent diagnosed cancer. However, a study has shown that there is a decrease in mortality rate by 14% [20]. The reasons for decrease in mortality rate include: (a) improvement made on medical imaging technology for better visualization [18], and (b) the start of better treatment plan especially in developed countries [20] and (c) Computer Aided Detection and/Diagnosis (CAD). The CAD in turn enhanced the efficiency of radiologists and eased early detection of the breast abnormalities which indeed increased the survival rate of the patients through starting early treatment [21]. However, building CAD system using machine learning algorithm is not an easy task [5]. A set of features that well discriminate images from abnormal and normal must be extracted to build a well performing machine learning algorithms [5]. As cited in [5], X. Liu and J. Tang have explained how handcrafted method was used as a means of feature gathering and selection for mass lesion classification. But it is time consuming and also dependent on experts' knowledge.

As an alternative, deep learning became a choice to learn discriminant features directly from the data itself without special design of feature detectors [5]. CNN is one among many to become popular in the area of large size image processing. Based on the review made in [5,22], the success of CNN is proved to be promising in shape recognition, mass lesion classification using texture features and video recognition.

2   Convolutional Neural Networks

Convolutional Neural Networks are a biologically inspired variants of ordinary Neural Networks like multilayer perceptrons (MLP) which reduces the computational time and translational invariance [5,26]. Its major components are convolutional layer, pooling layer, normalization layer and fully connected layer [5,26]. And so far three different attempts are made to gain improvement in CNN architecture and achieve better accuracy [22]. In [28] using smaller window size and stride were made possible. In [27] training and testing the CNN over the whole image at multiple scales is achieved. As a result of smaller convolutional filters, authors in [22] have increased the depth of the convNet through increasing convolutional layers, and among them convNet with 16 and 19 layers achieved the best performance. The architectural overview of CNN is indicated in Fig. 1 and its detail can be found in [31] and Sect. 2.1 of [22]. Figure 1 depicts the basic CNN architecture where two convolutional and two pooling layers are stacked one after the other and then applied to the original images. In this architecture the extracted features are given to the fully connected layers as input to make classification. However, in our case the extracted features are fed to KNN after dimensionality reduction. The convolutional layer is responsible to create the feature mapping from the original image, and as indicated in Fig. 1, four feature maps are generated after convolutional operation. The convolutional operation is followed by the down-sampling operation using max-pooling layer to avoid non-maximal values which in turn reduces the computation to the subsequent upper layers [26, 29].

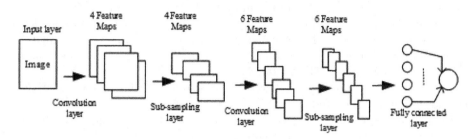

Fig. 1. Basic layers (convolutional, pooling, fully-connected) build CNN architecture from [26]. Convolutional layer is followed by pooling for down-sampling and in between, rectified linear unit (ReLU) is used with element wise activation function like $max(0, x)$ without changing the size of the volume [22].

3   Related Work

There are many proposed and implemented approaches related to classification of mammograms using different techniques on MIAS and DDSM datasets. However, in this paper an attempt is made to briefly show the current state-of-the-arts in the area of image processing techniques, artificial intelligence technique and CNN.

In [4], the pixel-based approach is proposed to classify the mammograms taken from MIAS database as tumor and non-tumor. The computed Gabor feature pool from the mammograms are given to the support vector machine (SVM) classifier and obtained an accuracy of 80%.

In [10], a Particle Swarm Optimized Wavelet Neural Network (PSOWNN) for classification and Laws Texture Energy measures for feature extraction are proposed. A privately collected 216 mammograms are used for the experiment. Features are extracted from region of interest (ROI) after segmentation. The aim of the paper is to classify mammograms as normal or abnormal and the proposed approach achieved an accuracy of 93.68%, sensitivity of 94.14%, specificity of 92.10% and area under the receiver operating characteristic curve(AUC) of 0.968.

In [9], a GLCM texture features extracted from MIAS database are used in the proposed method. These features are given to Radial Basis Function Neural Network(RBFNN) as an input to classify the mammograms as normal or abnormal. The method achieved an accuracy of 93.98%.

In [8], 100 mammograms from MIAS database are used in their experiment to classify the mammograms as normal, benign and malignant. Before ANN classifier, the median filter and seeded region growing algorithm are applied to mammograms to remove noise and artifacts. The rough-set theory based feature selection algorithm is applied to the extracted 16 texture properties so as to reduce the number of features to 5. And using these features, the ANN classifier achieved a sensitivity of 98.6%, specificity of 89.3% and accuracy of 96%.

The mammograms from MIAS database is used in [7] as source image dataset during classification of mammograms as normal and cancerous. The mammograms are first enhanced and noise removal technique has been applied before extracting the wavelet coefficients using generalized Gaussian density model. Two classifiers are used in this paper and the accuracy achieved by Neural Network with a Bayesian Back Propagation(NNBBP) algorithm is 97.08% and 95.42% by Artificial Neuro-Fuzzy Inference system (ANFIS).

In [6], high-level and middle-level features are extracted from images in DDSM database using pre-trained CNN model at two different layers. The aim of the paper is to classify the breast mass as bengin and malignant using SVM as a classifier, which achieved an accuracy of 96.7%.

In [5], the performance of classifying mammography mass lesion as benign and malignant has been increased from 0.787 to 0.822 in terms of area under ROC. The features are extracted from the BCDR database, particularly BCDR-F03, using the pre-trained CNN model and given as input to SVM classifier. In this paper, data augmentation operation like flipping and rotation are applied to the original images to achieve balanced dataset for each class.

4   Materials and Methods

4.1   Dataset

The proposed approach is applied on benchmark databases that many researchers have used in previous breast cancer image analysis. The two databases are DDSM [13] and MIAS [14,16]. There are 322 images in the MIAS database with information that include character of background tissue, class of abnormalities, severity of abnormality, central coordinate of abnormality, and radius of circle enclosing abnormality [11].

The images used were 112 abnormal and 208 normal from MIAS database. DDSM database contains 2620 cases and 43 volumes with images taken in MLO and craniocaudal(CC) views. Similar number of images were used from DDSM database.

4.2   Preprocessing

Preprocessing stage plays an important role in many image processing application. To reduce the impact of dark parts in the borders of the mammograms, cropping was performed. This stage also removes the background and artifacts

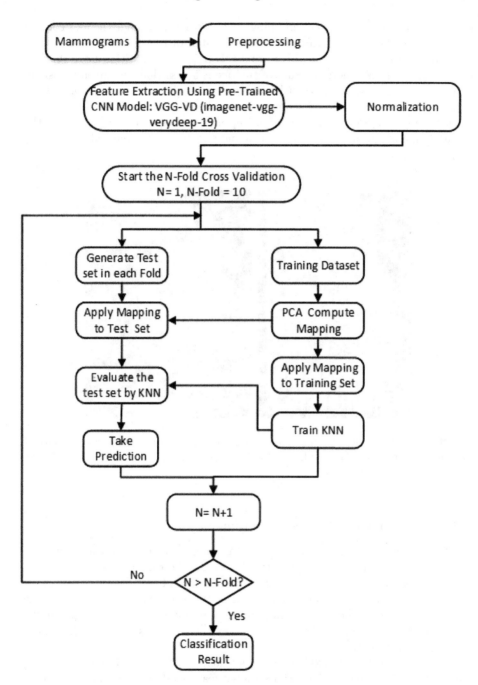

Fig. 2. Framework of the proposed approach. Mammograms from MIAS and DDSM is preprocessed and features are extracted using the pre-trained CNN model and normalized. Finally PCA is used for features dimensionality reduction inside 10 fold cross validation to train and evaluate the performance of KNN

on the original images [10]. For cropping, an algorithm that finds the first column in the left of the mammograms in which the sum of the pixels is greater than the threshold value is written. Then from this point the algorithm finds the first column in the right where the sum of the pixels is less than the given threshold value. The same cropping algorithm is applied to all mammograms used from MIAS and DDSM databases. Then, image enhancement, noise removal, image scaling and histogram equalization are applied to improve the quality of the original mammograms. In Fig. 3, the original and contrast enhanced image after cropping is given.

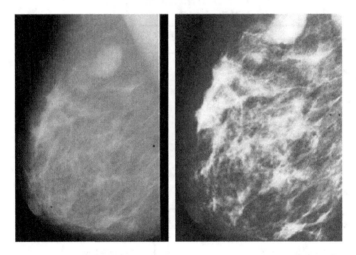

Fig. 3. Abnormal original image-MIAS (mdb015.pgm) (left), cropped and contrast ehnanced image (right) from [14]

4.3   Feature Extraction and Selection

The major steps in CAD system are preprocessing, segmentation, feature extraction, feature selection and classification. Even so, the role of feature extraction and selection are very significant on the performance of any classifier. After Preprocessing and image segmentation, set of features are required for each image that well represents the normal and abnormal mammograms. In this paper the pre-trained CNN model in [22] is used to extract features from the dataset of MIAS [3] and DDSM.

Once the features are extracted, classification can be performed as the next step without feature selection. All extracted features don't mean always important for better classification accuracy [23]. Feature selection is a search method that can be used to generate the subset of features [24]. It reduces the redundant features and computational cost [23,24]. For this purpose, PCA is used in dimensionality reduction.

4.4 Classification

Classification is one of the major decision making step of image recognition to separate mammogram whether cancerous or not. Among many of the classifiers, Naive Bayes (NB), Support Vector Machine (SVM), K-Nearest Neighbor (KNN) and Artificial Neural Networks (ANN), etc. are already introduced. In this paper KNN is used as a classifier with an aim of separating the mammograms as normal and abnormal.

KNN is one of the simplest and most important non-parameter algorithms among the supervised learning algorithms. It memorizes the training set and then predicts the label of any new instance based on the labels of its closest neighbors in the training data set. The classification performance of KNN classifier is evaluated based on accuracy as indicated in Eq. 1 [6,24].

5 Result and Discussion

The experiment was done to evaluate the performance of KNN with K value of 3 on MIAS and DDSM databases. The feature vectors extracted is given as input to the KNN classifier after PCS dimensionality reduction and trained using 10-fold cross-validation. The performance of a classifier was evaluated using accuracy, sensitivity and specificity as evaluation parameter. Given True Positive(TP), True Negative(TN), False Negative(FN) and False Positive(FP), the accuracy, sensitivity and specificity can be defined as:

$$Accuracy = \frac{TP + TN}{TP + FN + FP + TN} \qquad (1)$$

$$sensitivity = \frac{TP}{TP + FN} \qquad (2)$$

$$specificity = \frac{TN}{TN + FP} \qquad (3)$$

The experimental result shows that KNN has scored a higher performance in terms of classification accuracy. The classification accuracy of KNN was 98.75% and 98.90% for MIAS and DDSM databases respectively. The 2D visualization of the data points after KNN is given in Fig. 4. It shows the classification boundary with misclassified data points. The data points near the boundary lines were checked to which image groups they belong to confirm that they are well classified or misclassified. The result of this study was also compared with previous research outputs as indicated in Table 1 and this study scored a better classification accuracy, sensitivity and specificity. The comparison was conducted in terms of time required to build the model during training and testing, and the result indicates that, for both datasets, computational time is insignificant.

The feature vector after dimensionality reduction is also given to RBF and SVM. The performance of both classifiers were evaluated in terms of sensitivity, specificity and accuracy. They achieved better performance compared to the state-of-the-art.

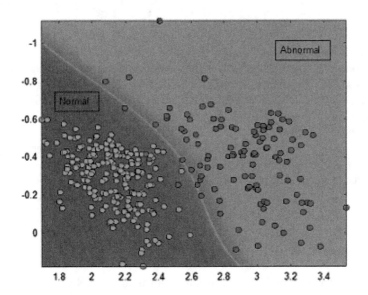

Fig. 4. 2D visual observation of the data points and the decision boundary of a polynomial of degree 3. The red data points represent data points from abnormal mammograms and yellow represents data points from normal mammograms (Color figure online)

Table 1. Comparison of proposed approach with previous studies

Author, year	Dataset	Accuracy(%)/ AUC	Features	Classifier
J. Torrents-Barrena et al. 2014	MIAS	80.00	Gabor	SVM
Y. A. Reyad and M. A. Berbar 2014	DDSM	98.63	Statistical and LBP	SVM
W. Xie et al. 2016	MIAS, DDSM	96.02,95.73	-	ELM
A. Alqoud and M. A. Jaffar 2016	MIAS	95.97	Gabor	ANN
A. Alqoud and M. A. Jaffar 2016	MIAS	96.82	LBP	ANN
A. Alqoud and M. A. Jaffar 2016	MIAS	98.72	Gabor and LBP	ANN
J. Dheeba et al. 2016	Private dataset	93.68	-	PSOWNN
Mellisa Pratiwi et al. 2015	MIAS	93.98	Texture	RBFNN
W. Peng et al. 2016	MIAS	96.00	Texture	ANN
Hela Mahersia et al. 2016	MIAS	97.08,95.42	-	NNBBP, ANFIS
Zhicheng Jiao et al. 2016	DDSM	96.70	CNN based features	SVM
John Arevalo et al. 2016	BCDR	-/0.822	CNN based features	SVM
Proposed approach	MIAS, DDSM	98.75,98.90	CNN based features	KNN

6   Conclusion

In this paper, a CNN based feature extraction method was proposed. The experiment was done to evaluate the distinguishing power of the features using KNN classifier. From the experimental result shown in previous section, the CNN based Feature Extraction technique for automatic breast cancer detection and classification is possible even without segmentation for region of interests. The results achieved in this study for the two popular datasets, MIAS and DDSM are promising and encourage for further improvement with better segmentation algorithm.

References

1. American Cancer Society: Breast Cancer Facts and Figures 2015–2016. http://www.cancer.org/acs/groups/content/@research/documents/document/acspc-046381.pdf
2. Sampat, M.P., Markey, M.K., Bovik, A.C.: Computer-aided detection and diagnosis in mammography. In: Handbook of Image and Video Processing. Elsevier Academic Press, San Francisco (2005)
3. Vedaldi, A., Lenc, K.: MatConvNet-convolutional neural networks for MATLAB. In: Proceedings of the 23rd ACM International Conference on Multimedia, Brisbane, Australia, pp. 689–692 (2015)
4. Torrents-Barrena, J., Puig, D., Ferre, M., Melendez, J., Diez-Presa, L., Arenas, M., Marti, J.: Breast masses identification through pixel-based texture classification. In: Fujita, H., Hara, T., Muramatsu, C. (eds.) IWDM 2014. LNCS, vol. 8539, pp. 581–588. Springer, Cham (2014). https://doi.org/10.1007/978-3-319-07887-8_81
5. Arevalo, J., González, F.A., Ramos-Pollán, R., Oliveira, J.L., Lopez, M.A.G.: Representation learning for mammography mass lesion classification with convolutional neural networks. Comput. Methods Programs Biomed. **127**, 248–257 (2016)
6. Jiao, Z., Gao, X., Wang, Y., Li, J.: A deep feature based framework for breast masses classification. Neurocomputing **197**, 221–231 (2016)
7. Mahersia, H., Boulehmi, H., Hamrouni, K.: Development of intelligent systems based on Bayesian regularization network and neuro-fuzzy models for mass detection in mammograms: a comparative analysis. Comput. Methods Programs Biomed. **126**, 46–62 (2016)
8. Peng, W., Mayorga, R.V., Hussein, E.M.A.: An automated confirmatory system for analysisof mammograms. Comput. Methods Programs Biomed. **125**, 134–144 (2016)
9. Pratiwi, M., Alexander, Harefa, J., Nandai, S.: Mammograms classification using gray-level co-occurrence matrix and radial basis function neural network. Procedia Comput. Sci. **59**, 83–91 (2015)
10. Dheeba, J., Albert Singh, N., Tamil Selvi, S.: Computer-aided detection of breast cancer on mammograms: a swarm intelligence optimized wavelet neural network approach. J. Biomed. Inform. **49**, 45–52 (2014)
11. Pereira, E.T., Eleutério, S.P., Marques de Carvalho, J.: Local binary patterns applied to breast cancer classification in mammographies. RITA. **21**(2), 32–46 (2014)
12. Mammographic Image Analysis: Signs of Diseases. http://www.mammoimage.org/signs-of-disease/
13. University of South Florida Digital Mammography. http://marathon.csee.usf.edu/Mammography/Database.html
14. The mini-MIAS database of mammograms. http://peipa.essex.ac.uk/info/mias.html
15. Kanadam, K.P., Chereddy, S.R.: Mammogram classification using sparse-ROI: a novel representation to arbitrary shaped masses. Expert Syst. Appl. **57**, 204–213 (2016)
16. Dong, M., Lu, X., Ma, Y., Guo, Y., Ma, Y., Wang, K.: An efficient approach for automated mass segmentation and classification in mammograms. J. Digit. Imaging **28**(5), 613–625 (2015)
17. Rouhi, R., Jafari, M.: Classification of benign and malignant breast tumors based on hybrid level set segmentation. Expert Syst. Appl. **46**, 45–59 (2016)

18. Prasad, S.N., Houserkova, D.: The role of various modalities in breast imaging. Biomed. Pap. Med. Fac. Univ. Palacky Olomouc Czech Repub. **151**(2), 209–218 (2007)

19. Tirona, M.T.: Breast cancer screening update. Am. Fam. Physician **87**(2), 274–278 (2011)

20. Palazuelos, G., Trujillo, S., Romero, J.: Breast tomosynthesis: the new age of mammography. Rev. Colomb. Radiol. **25**(2), 3926–3933 (2014)

21. Dubey, R.B., Hanmandlu, M., Gupta, S.K.: A comparison of two methods for the segmentation of masses in the digital mammograms. Comput. Med. Imaging Graph. **34**, 185–191 (2010)

22. Simonyan, K., Zisserman, A.: Very deep convolutional networks for large-scale image recognition. CoRR abs/1409.1556(2014)

23. Xie, W., Li, Y., Ma, Y.: Breast mass classification in digital mammography based on extreme learning machine. Neurocomputing **173**, 930–941 (2016)

24. Rouhi, R., Jafari, M., Kasaei, S., Keshavrzian, P.: Benign and malignant breast tumor classification based on region growing and CNN segmentation. Expert Syst. Appl. **42**, 990–1002 (2015)

25. Shalev-Shwartz, S., Ben-David, S.: Understanding Machine Learning: From Theory to Algorithms. Cambridge University Press, New York (2014)

26. Convolutional Neural Networks (LeNet). http://deeplearning.net/tutorial/lenet.html

27. Howard, A.G.: Some improvements on deep convolutional neural network based image classification. CoRR abs/1312.5402(2014)

28. Zeiler, M.D., Fergus, R.: Visualizing and understanding convolutional networks. CoRR abs/1311.2901 (2014)

29. Convolutional Neural Networks for Visual Recognition. http://cs231n.github.io/convolutional-networks/

30. Bonafede, M.M., Kalra, V.B., Miller, J.D., Fajardo, L.L.: Value analysis of digital breast tomosynthesis for breast cancer screening in a commercially-insured US population. ClinicoEconom. Outcomes Res. **7**, 53–63 (2015)

31. Krizhevsky, A., Sutskever, I., Hinton, G.E.: ImageNet classification with deep convolutional neural networks. Adv. Neural Inf. Process. Syst. **25**, 1097–1105 (2012)

Exploring the Use of Global Positioning System (GPS) for Identifying Customer Location in M-Commerce Adoption in Developing Countries

Patrick Kanyi Wamuyu[(✉)]

United States International University-Africa, Nairobi, Kenya
kanyiwamuyu@yahoo.com, pwamuyu@usiu.ac.ke

Abstract. M-commerce in Kenya has seen tremendous growth over the last few years due to the availability of mobile payments, mobile internet access, and expansion of mobile banking systems. A critical factor to the success of m-commerce is timely delivery of purchased items to the customers' premises. Timely delivery is highly dependent on the courier's ability to locate the buyer's physical location. To do this, the courier requires a reliable physical addressing system. However, like most developing countries, Kenya lacks a National Addressing System to provide properly registered physical identity of buildings, streets, and roads. The study explored the use of GPS in identifying customer's location as an alternative to named physical addresses. This paper describes the study design and discusses the findings concerning the use of GPS tracking application among six retailers and thirty customers. The study reveals that geolocation can substitute physical addresses in m-commerce home deliveries.

Keywords: M-commerce · Kenya · GPS · National Addressing System
Geolocation

1 Introduction

The Communications Authority of Kenya [1] indicates that during the fourth quarter of 2016/2017 (January–March, 2017) a total of 290.5 million mobile commerce transactions were completed, in which goods and services valued at Kenya Shillings 627.4 billion were merchandised. The success of m-commerce in Kenya could be attributed to the country's high mobile phone penetration level of 86.2% [1] and the availability of affordable mobile internet technologies for home users [2]. Kenya is also a world leader in mobile money, mobile payments, and other related mobile financial transactions. This has been attributed to "population demographic characteristics and the cultural practices of the Kenyan people which over the years demanded person-to-person money transmittals" [3, p. 15]. M-commerce is defined as any transaction involving the transfer of ownership or rights to use goods and services which is initiated and completed using mobile access to computer-mediated networks [4]. Other studies define mobile commerce as any transaction with a monetary value that is conducted via a mobile telecommunications network [5], while [6] describes mobile

© ICST Institute for Computer Sciences, Social Informatics and Telecommunications Engineering 2018
F. Mekuria et al. (Eds.): ICT4DA 2017, LNICST 244, pp. 99–111, 2018.
https://doi.org/10.1007/978-3-319-95153-9_10

commerce as buying and selling of goods and services, using wireless hand-held devices. There are many mobile commerce services and applications which include mobile banking, mobile marketing, mobile entertainment, mobile information services and mobile shopping [5]. This study focus is on physical delivery of customer's purchases from the business premises or collection point to the buyer's premises or selected drop-off point. Therefore, the study's mobile commerce application is mobile shopping [5].

A critical factor to the success of m-commerce is the timely delivery of the purchased items to the buyer's residence rather than the retailer's drop-off points. Timely delivery is highly dependent on the courier's ability to locate the buyer's physical location. To do this, the courier requires a reliable physical addressing system. However, like most developing countries, Kenya lacks a National Addressing System to provide properly registered physical identity of buildings (homes or business), streets and roads. One of the major benefits of using mobile commerce is the greater convenience [3] the user enjoys including fast on-demand delivery services, cheaper prices, and instant gratification. Thus, the customer expects the items ordered to be delivered immediately to the address they have specified without having to step out of their home or office. Most m-commerce firms do not hire in-house couriers but engage courier services from an external courier company. The Last mile delivery in Kenya is hampered by lack of registered physical addresses of the customers' physical location. Lack of registered physical addresses negatively affects the on-demand delivery services particularly with the popular food and groceries deliveries.

The main purpose of this study is to evaluate the viability of using GPS to provide an m-commerce customer geolocation as a substitute to a physical address for the last mile home deliveries. The study used an open-source GPS tracking application for identification of a customer's physical location as an addressing system for quick delivery of Liquefied Petroleum Gas (LPG). Specifically, the study was guided by the following objectives:

(a) Analyze the impact of lack of physical addressing systems on the last mile mobile commerce on-demand deliveries;
(b) Analyze the use of GPS based geolocation as an alternative to physical addressing systems in facilitating the last mile mobile commerce on-demand deliveries.
(c) Compare mobile GPS based geolocation with desktop computer IP based geolocation as an alternative to physical addressing systems in facilitating the last mile mobile commerce on-demand deliveries.

The paper explores how the use of GPS based geolocation services as an addressing system in environments where physical addressing system is not in place and how these services can be applied to enhance the m-commerce customer shopping delivery experience. The next section has the study background. Section 3 describes the study research approach; Sect. 4 gives the analysis and findings while Sect. 5 has the discussions and conclusions of the study. Section 5 also gives a reflection on the success of the study, the study conclusion and directions for further research.

2 Background

M-commerce is the extension of e-commerce to wireless mediums. There are many different examples of m-commerce services in Kenya today which includes ticketing, gaming, banking, retailing and payments. Many e-commerce retailers are still struggling with the best way to approach m-commerce as a medium of their business transactions. Use of mobile websites and mobile apps continue to compete with the traditional good old websites. The retailers' main objective is to provide the customer who is using a mobile device to make their purchases a good mobile experience, as though they were in a physical shop. To make shopping experiences hassle-free for their customers' convenience and the choice of shopping anytime, anywhere, some online retailers such as Jumia [7] use a combination of the three (mobile app, mobile website and a traditional desktop website). Jumia [7] indicates that over the last one year (2015/2016) 32% of their customers used the tradition desktop website, 17% accessed their services using a downloaded Jumia mobile app while 51% used their mobile responsive website. In the African continent, KPMG [8] and Jumia [7] ranks South Africa, Egypt and Morocco higher than Kenya in their use of m-commerce services. However, Kenya is ranked highly globally in the adoption of mobile money transfers. Kenya's poor ranking on the adoption of m-commerce could be attributed to the absence of reliable, low-cost delivery services, coupled with the lack of a National Addressing System to provide properly registered physical identity of the customers' premises or selected drop-off points. These two factors are significant for reliable, timely and profitable m-commerce deliveries.

Some challenges associated with the fruitful use of m-commerce by individuals have been highlighted in literature to include complicated checkout and payment process, the high cost of delivery, security concerns and small phone screens. For the challenges relating to small phone screens, the checkout and payment processes can easily be solved through better application designs and dynamically designed sites and specialist apps to support the users' shopping experiences. Security concerns are a multifaceted problem which includes users' experience, application and device security and devices' operation environment. The problems associated with high cost of delivery have been mitigated through the use of third-party courier services, and E-tail focused logistics service providers globally [9, 10]. In contrast, little has been written regarding alternatives to identifying an m-commerce customer's physical location in developing countries where there are no formal physical addressing systems.

The challenge of identifying physical location of the customer in the absence of a standard named physical address is very exhausting particularly in areas which are densely populated and with no house numbers or even street names. Studies have shown that delivery challenges related to inadequate physical addressing systems are a significant barrier to the uptake of online shopping [11, 12]. The Communications Authority of Kenya [1] has identified the absence of reliable, low-cost delivery services as one of the key factors hindering the development of online shopping in Kenya. A local courier company YUM, which offers a food delivery service in Nairobi, has indicated that lack of physical addressing systems is an obstacle to making deliveries to their new customers within the promised time [13]. YUM's director of operations indicated that their couriers have challenges in "navigating the less familiar neigh-borhoods of Nairobi" [13]. To alleviate the last mile courier delivery service, the Chairman of the Kenya Courier Industry Association suggested the government to "roll out a national and regional physical addressing system" [14]. The Chairman also indicated that appropriation and use of the "Google Maps may help, but they are not precise" [14]. The online shoppers desire faster deliveries and the retailers are also keen on having a frictionless delivery process. Therefore, this study posits that lack of low-cost last mile delivery services is attributable to the absence of a reliable physical addressing system for stress-free identification of the customers' premises or selected drop-off points.

The Chairman of the Kenya Courier Industry Association opined that a combination of the physical addressing and mobile applications that provide an online shopper's geolocation make a perfect recipe to solve the problem associated with lack of a physical address system [14]. To help in increasing efficiency in deliveries and to decrease the delivery time, geolocation services can be used in determining the geographical location of an m-commerce shopper. There are two types of geolocation techniques, one based on the user handset and the other based on the network. The mobile phone handset based geolocation technique uses the GPS system to determine a user's location. The second technique uses the replicas of signals from the same handset at different base stations which are then combined to determine a user's location [15]. GPS-based positioning is reliable and accurate for outdoor situations [15] which is a requirement in successful m-commerce home and office deliveries. With GPS assisted geolocation identification, it would be easy to identify a customer's physical location much easier and with good accuracy. Another advantage of using GPS is that it allows tracking by both the cus-tomer and the retailer. The tracking feature allows the customer to know the location of the purchased items during the delivery process.

Geolocation refers to the determination of the geographical position of an object using Global Positioning System-based systems [16]. It is a technology which utilizes data obtained from an individual's computing device to describe the user's actual physical location [17]. GPS can be used on any modern mobile phones which is GPS-capable as well as on GPS-specific devices [16]. Information obtained using geolocation technology could be utilized for Georeferencing, Geocoding or Geotagging [17]. These three technologies are essential to facilitating identification of a customer's home address. Geocoding is the process of converting addresses (like "Soweto, Kayole Mwisho, Bus Terminus") into geographic coordinates while reverse geocoding is the process of converting geographic coordinates into a human-readable address. Geo-tagging is the process of adding geographical identification metadata to an object while georeferencing is the determining of objects physical location in relation to a coordi-nate system [17].

To assist in identification and tracking of an m-commerce delivery, use of user-device geolocation technique would be the most appropriate. User-device geolo-cation technique is also referred as the "Active geolocation." Active geolocation uses technologies such as GPS, Wi-Fi positioning, and mobile applications and can be used for real-time tracking and provide high levels of accuracy [16, 18]. User-device geolocation technique raises privacy and security issues as a compromised active geolocation system can lead to people being tracked in real time. Location data can also be analyzed for patterns or other variables to reveal private information [16]. A GPS enabled device can obtain location-based information in real time over the internet with a relatively high degree of accuracy. GPS works through the use of satellites. Groups of GPS satellites commonly referred to as arrays transmit information to GPS enabled devices. The information can be broadly described as information pertaining to the location of the satellite in orbit and the time the transmission was sent. The receiver then calculates its position by timing the various signals sent by any of the satellites in the array [16, 18].

Similar to the Kenyan case, United Arab Emirates (UAE) lacks a national physical address system. The country has over the years tried some technologies in addressing this problem with the first successful attempt being the completion of phase one of Dubai Municipality's Geo Address System (Gas) in 2013. However, the UAE based Fetchr [19] uses its proprietary Fetchr App which utilizes the GPS coordinates from a consumer's phone to allow local retailers and e-commerce firms to more accurately track down customers for easier home and office deliveries. Successful use of the Fetchr App is an indication that it is possible to use customers' mobile phones to identify their location and to achieve m-commerce deliveries successfully.

OkHi [20] a Nairobi based startup is hoping to solve Kenya's problem of not having a physical addressing system by facilitating people to log the details of where they live using their phones and combining a GPS data point with a photo of their house's front door. The OkHi App works by allowing users to upload an image of their exterior front door or home and locating it on the GPS system. The company then uses the OkHi App to make an OkHi address. OkHi users can then share their OkHi address using WhatsApp, SMS or email so that other users can use the addresses to locate their friends or families or even markets and physical landmarks.

Cost is a significant factor influencing adoption of ICT among micro and small enterprises [21, 22]. The study participants are small-scale retailers operating within marginalized communities. This means that the retailers may not be in a position to invest in a commercial GPS tracking application such as Fletchr. Their businesses are also categorized as Jua Kali or informal businesses. The informal nature of these business makes it hard for retailers to borrow or save enough money for them to acquire commercially available GPS applications. Thus, the study proposes to evaluate the use of an open-source GPS tracking app among the retailers and customers from marginalized communities where there are no named roads or notable landmarks which can be used to guide an m-commerce delivery courier.

3   Research Approach

The study utilized mixed methods theoretical premise in two phases. The first phase was a qualitative study using semi-structured interviews while the second phase was an experiment using an open-source GPS tracking application. A mixed method design was considered most appropriate as the study focus was exploring whether GPS could facilitate physical delivery of customer's purchases from the retailer's premises, even when the customer's residence has no known physical address.

The study population was purposely selected based on the study objectives. Three areas were chosen as the study sites. The study sites selected were residential areas within Nairobi Embakasi area and included Kayole, Mihang'o and Mowlem. The study areas were purposely selected because they lack registered physical identity of either the homes, businesses or the streets.

The study sample was the LPG retailers within the selected study sites and their customers. The retailers selected were expected to be offering the "*Cooking GAS Sales and Delivery Service*," as usually advertised in some of the retailers' outlets. This is usually an indication that a retailer is providing courier services to deliver the LPG to their customers' doorstep within a specified duration after the customer requests a refill. From each of the study site, two retailers were randomly selected and tasked with the task of assisting the study with five of their customers. The customers were expected to be willing to participate in the study voluntarily. Thirty customers were randomly selected.

This being an exploratory study, qualitative data was collected through open-ended face-to-face semi-structured interviews and supported by observations during the initial phase. Patton's [23] qualitative interviewing strategies was used in developing the structure of the open-ended interview and the interview guide. Although all the participants were asked the same basic questions which were prepared in advance, the exact wordings and sequence of questions were determined in the course of the interviews. Participants were also assured that any data collected for the study would be anonymized. The interviews lasted between 10–15 min. The interviews were conducted mainly to identify the participants' characteristics and to ensure the homogeneity of the study sample. The participants were expected to be using a GPS enabled phone and had to have some basic digital and media literacy skills.

During the second phase of the study, the participants' phones were installed with the open-source GPS tracking application. The customers and the retailers were offered basic training on how to use the application and on issues relating to information systems' security and ethical use of the application. The data were collected over a period of two months with the defined objective of testing whether the retailer or the courier, with the assistance of the GPS tracking application, was able to reach the customer's doorstep within a specified duration after the customer sends an SMS text requesting a refill.

4   Analysis and Findings

The study had six participating retailers, two from each study site. Each retailer was to work with five of their clients. Hence the study had thirty-six participants. All the participants were randomly selected.

A total of seventy-eight LPG refill requests were made by the study participants as presented in Fig. 1. The LPG refill requests were distributed unevenly among the study sites.

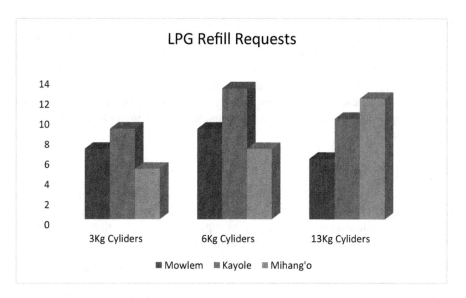

Fig. 1. Successful LPG refill requests

4.1 Without GPS Tracking

The customer would call for a refill give directions to their residence using some existing physical features. The courier would then try to navigate the residential area to find the desired location. In some instances, the courier took a long time to trace the location and sometimes would even be forced to call the customer for further guidance. The customer could also be waiting at a particular location to escort the courier the rest of the distance to their home.

One retailer had such experience and gave this example, *"I was given a call to deliver a 13 kg LPG cylinder one morning, the caller gave direction as, 'kuja Kayole mwisho, shukua chochoro nyuma ya Paradise Pub, tembea kindogo, upande wako wa kushoto kunja nahio njia, kuna mahali utaona plot ya green, nitakuwa na kungoja hapo nnje.'* (come to Kayole bus terminus, take the path behind the Paradise Pub, take a few steps, take a left turn and follow the path, you should find an apartment painted in green color, I will be waiting for you outside the building) *When I went there, I saw that there were several apartments painted in green color. When I called the customer, I realized that I had walked for a longer distance before taking the left turn and had to go back as I had taken to the wrong direction. Sometimes the customers do not give me the instructions that are explicit enough"*. Though with good intentions, the retailer was not able to deliver the LPG and the customer was forced to meet him and to walk with him half of the journey. All the six study participating retailers had such similar experiences.

For most of the customers from Mihang'o, there was no specific land mark to use when giving directions and most of them were forced to walk to the LPG store and then take a motorbike ride back to their residence with the courier. A number of customers who had this experience explained that "*it is faster for me to come here, and guide the courier to my home, rather than having him waste time trying to locate my residence*".

Waiting for a refill at home when the courier has nothing to direct him to the specific residence may result to delayed deliveries and could also be expensive as the courier may keep on calling for direction and distance clarifications in order to make sure that they are heading to the right location. The selected study sites are characterized by unplanned and informal developments, narrow and unmarked streets and no major landmarks.

4.2   With GPS Tracking

Two parameters were essential to the study. Identification of a client's physical location (residence) and the customer is in a position to track the delivery by monitoring the courier's movement. A few considerations were put in place during the selection of the GPS tracking application. The application should allow the participants to:

i. Decide when to share their location and with whom by opting when to switch on and off the localization function.
ii. Receive automatic notifications when the courier departs the LPG stall and when he arrives at a customer's residence.
iii. Share their location continuously with the couriers and see the courier's movement in real-time.
iv. Only use a username and a phone number to connect to the application. This is to ensure that the application does not connect to the participants' social networking sites such as the Facebook or Google accounts automatically.
v. To broadcast their location to the courier while appearing offline to other contacts.

When the customer needed a refill, they would initialize the GPS enhanced LPG delivery procedure and successful delivery should be accomplished efficiently and in a timely manner.

i. The customer makes sure that the GPS tracking application is running.
ii. Chooses to share their location.
iii. Sends an SMS text to the retailer for a refill.
iv. The retailer receives the request and prepares for the delivery.
v. The retailer using the application identifies the location of the customer and departs to deliver the refill to the customer's residence.
vi. The customer is notified of the courier departure.
vii. The customer could opt to monitor the courier's movement real-time.
viii. The customer is notified when the courier arrives at their residence.
ix. The customer collects the refill, pays the retailer and can stop broadcasting their location or just chose to appear offline to the retailer.

The GPS tracking App was able to detect the customer's location, and to generate complete and accurate addresses of the customer. Using the application GPS functionalities, the GPS tracking facilitated accurate and efficient deliveries. This resulted in greater customer and retailer satisfaction. One customer indicated that "*mimi ni lituma tu ujumbe mfupi kwa muuzaji wa gesi ya kupikia, baada ya muda mfupi alikuwa mlangoni*" (I just sent an SMS to the LPG retailer, in a short while, he was at my door). Therefore, all that the customer needed was to send an SMS text, and he did not need to give directions or fear that the courier will not deliver the refill in time. One of the studies participating retailer who did not have the means to offer the delivery services but relied on hiring the motorcycle operators commonly known as *boda boda* indicated that "*it is now possible to track in real-time the bodaboda rider movement to the customer's premises*".

The study participants had positive feedback on the success of using the GPS to facilitate their m-commerce transactions while using their mobile GPS application. The research study tested the use of the GPS geolocation using desktop applications.

4.3   Using IP Based Geolocation

Grounded on the study results, geolocation is a viable and versatile solution to facilitate last mile on-demand deliveries. It eliminates the problems encountered by the couriers during the m-commerce deliveries by offering an alternative to physical addressing systems. The study third objective was to compare mobile GPS based geolocation with desktop computer IP based geolocation as an alternative to physical addressing systems in facilitating the last mile mobile commerce on-demand deliveries. The goal of doing this comparison is because GPS based geolocation is normally accurate while IP based geolocation of most of the desktop devices is mostly an approximation location of the host and it is depending on which database is being used. The accuracy for IP based geolocation for a particular location in a city range between from 50% to 75% [24].

Using the experimental design, the study designed and implemented by integrating geolocation capabilities to a food delivery e-commerce application. The geolocation capabilities were supported by use of the Google Maps API. The application had the capabilities to automatically and dynamically generate users' physical address and multi-device compatibility. The application was expected to work on both the desktop and mobile devices. The Google Maps API proved invaluable to the application as it was used in the translation of customer location information into address information through reverse geocoding as well as distance and route calculations through the Google Maps API distance and route services respectively. The e-commerce application required constant internet connection and the users' devices had to have location services enabled.

4.4   Comparing Mobile GPS Geolocation to the IP Based Geolocation

To compare the accuracy of the two geolocation services, a total of 80 online transactions were carried out using the study's e-commerce application. Forty transactions were completed using mobile device while the other forty transactions were placed at the exact same location using desktop device. A predetermined address within the location provided the control data which was used to evaluate the accuracy of the address generated. The desktop device shared location information through IP geolocation and the mobile device shared location information through GPS geolocation.

The geolocation address generated by the two distinct devices was then compared to the predetermined control addresses to determine their accuracy. Identification of the customer location was considered to be accurate when the physical location address was the same as the application generated location. The distance between the two points was recorded as the distance offset.

The results showed that only 45% of the IP Geolocation generated location addresses were within ten meters of the physical location, while 25% of the IP generated addresses were more than one kilometer away from the actual physical location. Results for the orders placed using mobile GPS, 92.5% of the geolocation addresses generated were within ten meters of the physical location, while 5% of the generated addresses were more than one fifty meters away from the actual physical location.

5   Discussions and Conclusions

Today's m-commerce shoppers expect more from their package delivery experience. For there to be successful of adoption of mobile commerce in Kenya, reliable, timely and cost-effective delivery of any m-commerce purchases is paramount. Studies have suggested that reliable, safe and timely delivery is important to online buyers [25–27]. A study by the European Commission [28] indicates that problems associated with the delivery services prevent people from buying online. The study participating retailers stated that, in the past, they have relied on phone conversations to make their deliveries. The retailers' motorbike couriers are usually paid per the number of kilometers to and from the customer's premises. This has always resulted in increased delivery complexities and costs if the courier is not able to find the customer's residence. The GPS tracking application introduced to the retailers and their customers in the study facilitated accurate and efficient LPG home deliveries. This resulted in greater m-commerce transactions user satisfaction. In many developing countries, lack of a National Addressing System to provide properly registered physical identity of residential and business premises, roads and streets and postal regions acts as a barrier to adoption of m-commerce. From the study, use of GPS tracking application eliminated the problem by helping in the identification of the desired delivery location. Therefore, integrating GPS platforms in the m-commerce applications could enhance successful delivery of customers' items to their premises and hence improve the uptake of m-commerce in developing countries. The experiment helps to make a case for GPS integration into the m-commerce delivery processes. The customer location data could also be used for other m-commerce strategies in today's age of the big data. The study also shows that there are opportunities to leverage the GPS to facilitate m-commerce where there are no defined physical addresses.

There are security issues [29], privacy risks [30] and ethical concerns [31] linked to the use of the GPS Tracking Applications. However, most manufacturers of GPS systems are employing encryption technologies to make GPS tracking safer. For successful m-commerce adoption, [32] strongly suggest that businesses should address the users' security and privacy concerns. As opposed to trust which has a direct positive effect on intention to use m-commerce, perceived risk has a negative effect [33]. Over the years, the retailers seemed to have built a strong business relationship with their customers. This made it possible for the customers to trust the retailers and to participate in the study. During the entire study period, the participants were willing to share their location information using the open source GPS tracking application. Therefore, measures had to be taken to protect the participants' privacy. This was achieved by ensuring that the study team adhered to research ethics and regulations provided by the study team's University. Other measures taken included limiting data access to only appropriate parties and offering digital literacy skills on responsible use of GPS, cyber-safety, and cyber-ethics.

The study wanted to find out the impact of lack of physical addressing systems on the last mile m-commerce on-demand deliveries. Park and Regan [34] indicate that one significant factor that draws customers towards online shopping is the ability to shop online and have goods delivered to their door step. The study results indicate that lack of physical addressing system negatively impacts the development of m-commerce in Kenya. Online shoppers expect timely and reliable deliveries [25]. The study established that without a well-defined method of identifying the m-commerce customer's location, the time taken to deliver an item is increased. This results in high costs and unpredictability in the last mile delivery services. The study participants associated these challenges with the lack of a physical addressing system for their neighborhood.

The study shows that GPS based geolocation could be used as an alternative to physical addressing systems in facilitating the last mile mobile commerce on-demand deliveries in Kenya. Suggestions have been made by the Communication Authority of Kenya [35], that considerations should be given to the use of mobile devices, and specifically the GPS technology to form the basis of an address system. The study affirms this suggestion and posits that GPS should be used as an alternative to the physical address system. From the study, the results have shown that GPS applications can be used to accurately detect a customer's location and to generate the customer's address. The GPS based geolocation produced more accurate and consistent customer location address compared to the IP based geolocation. This suggest that the there is a need for the developers of desktop hardware to consider integrating the GPS hardware in the desktop devices for the platforms to offer better geolocation services.

Even though the study sites represent classical urban areas in developing and the experiment was successfully conducted, the study has some limitations. One limitation of this study is the comparatively small number of retailers and customers used in the study investigation. The second limitation is the use of an open-source GPS tracking application whose parameters the study did not have the power to contextualize.

To establish the trustworthiness of this study's results, respondent validation was done using a retailer and a consumer from each of the three study sites for member checking [36] as recommended when doing qualitative studies.

References

1. Communications Authority of Kenya: Quarterly Sector Statistics Report Fourth Quarter for the Financial Year 2016/2017 (January–March 2017), June 2017. http://ca.go.ke/images/downloads/STATISTICS/SECTORSTATISTICSREPORTQ3FY2016-2017.pdf. Accessed 17 Mar 2017
2. Wamuyu, P.K.: The impact of information and communication technology adoption and diffusion on technology entrepreneurship in developing countries: the case of Kenya. Inf. Technol. Dev. **21**(2), 253–280 (2015)
3. Wamuyu, P.K.: The role of contextual factors in the uptake and continuance of mobile money usage in Kenya. Electron. J. Inf. Syst. Dev. Ctries. **64**(4), 1–19 (2015)
4. Müller-Veerse, F.: Mobile Commerce Report, World Wide Web, 9 February 2000. http://www.dad.be/library/pdf/durlacher1.pdf. Accessed 17 Mar 2017
5. Tiwari, R., Buse, S., Herstatt, C.: From electronic to mobile commerce: opportunities through technology convergence for business services. Asia Pac. Tech. Monit. **23**(5), 38–45 (2006)
6. United Nations Conference on Trade and Development (UNCTAD): E-Commerce and Development Report 2002, United Nations, New York and Geneva (2002). http://r0.unctad.org/ecommerce/ecommerce_en/edr02_en.htm
7. Jumia (2017). http://www.modernmom.co.ke/2017/04/white-paper-2017-trends-from-kenyan.html
8. KPMG: Payments Developments in Africa, vol. 1. KPMG, Cape Town (2015)
9. PWC: eCommerce in India, Accelerating growth, PricewaterhouseCoopers (2015). http://www.pwc.in/assets/pdfs/publications/2015/ecommerce-in-india-accelerating-growth.pdf
10. KPMG: Impact of E-commerce on Employment in India (2016). https://assets.kpmg.com/content/dam/kpmg/in/pdf/2016/12/impact-of-ecommerce-on-employment-in-india.pdf
11. Hawk, S.: A comparison of B2C e-commerce in developing countries. Electron. Commer. Res. **4**, 181–199 (2004)
12. Lawrence, J.E., Tar, U.A.: Barriers to E-commerce in developing countries. Inf. Soc. Justice **3**(1), 23–35 (2010)
13. Nelson, K.G.: App aims to fill critical need for physical addresses in Nairobi (2016). http://www.humanosphere.org/basics/2016/01/app-aims-to-fill-critical-need-for-physical-addresses-in-nairobi/
14. CIO East Africa: Physical Addressing will Boost E-commerce in Kenya, 25 February 2016. https://www.cio.co.ke/blogs/physical-addressing-will-boost-e-commerce-in-kenya/
15. Papadimitriou, G.I., Pomportsis, A.S., Nicopolitidis, P., Obaidat, M.S.: Wireless Networks. Wiley, Hoboken (2003)
16. Holdener III, A.T.: HTML5 Geolocation. O'Reilly Media Inc., Sebastopol (2011)
17. ISACA: Geolocation: Risk, Issues and Strategies. ISACA, Rolling Meadows (2011)
18. Donnet, B.: IP Geolocation Databases: Unreliable?. Fonds National de la Recherche Scientifique, Bruxelles (2011)
19. Fetchr. https://fetchr.us/. Accessed 17 Mar 2017
20. OkHi. http://www.okhi.com/ Accessed 17 Mar 2017
21. Wamuyu, P.K.: Use of cloud computing services in micro and small enterprises: a fit perspective. Int. J. Inf. Syst. Proj. Manag. **5**(2), 59–81 (2017)
22. Wamuyu, P.K., Maharaj, M.: Factors influencing successful use of mobile technologies to facilitate ecommerce in small enterprises: the case of Kenya. Afr. J. Inf. Syst. **3**(2), 47–71 (2011)
23. Patton, M.Q.: Qualitative Research. Wiley, Hoboken (2005)

24. Where is Geolocation of an IP Address? https://www.iplocation.net/. Accessed 17 Mar 2017
25. Turban, E., King, D., Lee, J.K., Liang, T.P., Turban, D.C.: Electronic Commerce: A Managerial and Social Networks Perspective. Springer, Cham (2015). https://doi.org/10.1007/978-3-319-10091-3
26. Ziaullah, M., Yi, F., Akhter, S.N.: E-loyalty: the influence of product quality and delivery services on E-trust and E-satisfaction in China. Int. J. Adv. Res. Technol. **3**(10), 20–31 (2014)
27. Handoko, L.P.: The effect of product quality and delivery service on online customer satisfaction in Zalora Indonesia. J. EMBA **4**(1), 1189–1199 (2016)
28. Eurobarometer: Consumer Attitudes Towards Cross-border Trade and Consumer Protection. European Commission, Brussels (2013)
29. Barcena, M.B., Wueest, C., Lau, H.: How Safe is Your Quantified Self?. Symantech, Mountain View (2014)
30. Cooney, M.: How do mobile location services threaten users? Network World, Paragraph 5, 5 June 2014. https://www.networkworld.com/article/2360206/mobile-security/how-do-mobile-location-services-threaten-users.html. Accessed 17 Mar 2017
31. Michael, K., McNamee, A., Michael, M.G.: The emerging ethics of humancentric GPS tracking and monitoring. In: Proceedings of the International Conference on Mobile Business, Copenhagen, Denmark, 25–27 July 2006
32. Friedman, B., Khan, P.H., Howe, D.C.: Trust online. Commun. ACM **43**(12), 34–40 (2000)
33. Vasileiadis, A.: Security concerns and trust in the adoption of M-commerce. Soc. Technol. **4**(1), 179–191 (2014)
34. Park, M., Regan, A.: Issues in Emerging Home Delivery Operations. University of California, California (2005)
35. Communications Authority of Kenya: White Paper on Facilitation And Adoption of E-commerce via the Postal/Courier Networks. Communications Authority of Kenya, Nairobi (2016)
36. Angen, M.J.: Evaluating interpretive inquiry: reviewing the validity debate and opening the dialogue. Qual. Health Res. **10**(3), 378–395 (2000)

Developing Knowledge Based Recommender System for Tourist Attraction Area Selection in Ethiopia: A Case Based Reasoning Approach

Tamir Anteneh Alemu[(✉)], Alemu Kumilachew Tegegne,
and Adane Nega Tarekegn

Faculty of Computing Bahir Dar Institute of Technology,
Bahir Dar University, Bahir Dar, Ethiopia
tamirat.1216@gmail.com, alemupilatose@gmail.com,
nega2002@gmail.com

Abstract. A knowledge based recommender reasons about the fit between a user's need and the features of available products and it uses knowledge about users and products to pursue knowledge based approach to generate a recommendation, reasoning about what products/services meet the user's requirements. Providing an effective service in the Tourism sector of Ethiopia is critical to attract more foreign and local tourists. However, there are major problems that need immediate solution. First, the difficulty of getting fast, reliable, and consistent expert advice in the sector that is suitable to each visitor's characteristics and capabilities. Second, inadequacy of the number of experienced experts and consulting individuals who can give advice on tourism issues in the country. Therefore, this paper aims to design a recommender system for tourist attraction area and visiting time selection that can assist experts and tourists to make timely decisions that helps them to get fast and consistent advisory service so that visitors can identify tourist attraction areas that have the highest potential of success/satisfaction and that match their personal characteristics. For the development of case based recommender system, essential knowledge was acquired through semi-structured interview and document analysis. Domain experts and visitors were interviewed to elicit the required knowledge about the selection process of attraction area. The acquired knowledge was modeled using hierarchical tree structure and it was represented using feature value case representation. At the end, jCOLIBRI programming tool was used to implement the system. The main data source (case base) used to develop case based recommender system for tourist attraction area selection is previous tourist cases collected from national tour operation and ministry of culture and tourism. As a retrieval algorithm, nearest neighbor retrieval algorithm is used to measure the similarity of new case (query) with cases in the case base. Accordingly, if there is a similarity between the new case and the existing case, the system assigns the solution (recommended attraction area and visiting time) of previous case as a solution to new case. To decide the applicability of the prototype system in the domain area, the system has been evaluated by involving domain experts and visitors through visual interaction using the criteria of easiness to use, time

© ICST Institute for Computer Sciences, Social Informatics and Telecommunications Engineering 2018
F. Mekuria et al. (Eds.): ICT4DA 2017, LNICST 244, pp. 112–128, 2018.
https://doi.org/10.1007/978-3-319-95153-9_11

efficiency, applicability in the domain area and providing correct recommendation. Based on prototype user acceptance testing, the average performance of the system is 80% and 82% by domain experts and visitors respectively. The performance of the system is also measured using the standard measure of relevance (IR system) recall, precision and accuracy measures, where the system registers 83% recall, 61% precision and 85.4% accuracy.

Keywords: Recommender system · Case based reasoning
Tourism in Ethiopia

1 Introduction

Nowadays it is very important for people to be supported in their decisions, due to the exponential increase of the available information. This exponential growth of information creates information overload. However, the term is defined, there cannot be many people who have not experienced the feeling of having too much information which uses up too much of their time, causing them to feel stressed which, in turn, affects their decision-making. i.e. people may tend to be reluctant in making decision or they may leads to wrong decision [1].

Recommender systems have proven to be an important response to such a problem by providing users with more proactive and personalized information services. It usually track user's behavior and collect [19]. Recommender systems attempt to reduce information overload and retain customers by selecting a subset of items from a universal set based on user preferences. Case based recommender system is a part of knowledge based recommender system that exploits case based reasoning to generate personalized recommendations for exploiting the knowledge contained in past recommendation cases [2].

Tourism is one of the largest and rapidly growing industries in the world, and is even considered by the UN World tourism Organization as the biggest industry in the world when related and complementary industries are taken into consideration. Ethiopia has immense tourism potential owing to its natural, historical and cultural endowments and the flow of tourists in the country becomes increasing from time to time [6]. But there are a number of problems in Ethiopian Tourism faced by Experts in the sector and tourists alike. the problems faced by experts in the sector are lack of appropriate, relevant and understandable information that they need to give advice and guidance to their clients.

As stated by [3], advice is one of the most important problems of the tourism sector because the sector also uses traditional advisory system of tourists. Tourists tend to lose money by making the wrong choices of areas to visit and the wrong time based on their characteristics or location of the area or income level of the tourist. The main problem in Ethiopian tourism sector advice system is, the advising services given are not fast. Because of this, it takes long time to get the required tourist attraction areas and permissions to visit. Difficulty of getting appropriate advice is a critical issue for tourists since knowing the right tourist attraction area is a key factor and also knowing the right time to visit in is another factor to consider to new tourists [7]. Therefore, this study aims to design a recommender system that helps visitors to get fast and consistent advisory service so that visitors can identify tourist attraction areas that have the highest potential of success/satisfaction and that match their personal characteristics.

1.1 The Comparison of Case Based and Rule Based Reasoning

A case typically represents the description of a problem situation together with the experiences gathered during the solution of the problem situation. It may also contain other items such as the effects of the solution applied or a justification for the solution and explanation or be enriched by an administrative part (including e.g., a case number) [13]. A case-based reasoning (CBR) system is a problem solver that uses the recall of examples as the fundamental problem-solving process. It also contains a number of different knowledge containers like the case base, the vocabulary in which cases are described, the similarity measure used to compare cases, and, if necessary, the knowledge needed to transform recalled solutions. Case-based reasoning relates to a reasoning process based on recalling a related previous experience (a memory of stored cases recording specific prior episodes) rather than reasoning based on generalized rules It can also means using old experiences to understand and solve new problems. In case-based reasoning, a reasoner remembers a previous situation similar to the current one and uses that to solve the new problem [4].

Conceptually case based reasoning (CBR) is commonly described by the CBR-cycle. This cycle comprises four activities [8].

a. RETRIEVE the most similar case or cases.
b. REUSE the information and knowledge in that case to solve the problem.
c. REVISE the proposed solution.
d. RETAIN the parts of this experience likely to be useful for future problem solving.

In CBR, nearest-neighbor retrieval technique is used to measure similarity between the source case and the case which we are searching. The similarity of the problem (target) case to a case in the case-library for each case attribute is determined. This measure may be multiplied by a weighting factor. Then the sum of the similarity of all attributes is calculated to provide a measure of the similarity of the case in the case-base to that of the target case [9].

Similarity $(T, S) = \sum f(Ti, Si) \times Wi,$
Where:

T- Target case
S- Source case
i - An individual attribute from 1 to n
f- Similarity function for attribute i
W- Weight of attribute i.

The similarity of the problem (target) case to a case in the case-library for each case attribute is determined. It is possible to use the unification mechanism directly as matching operation to retrieve similar cases [10].

Rule based reasoning: Symbolic rules are one of the most popular knowledge representation and reasoning methods. Their popularity stems mainly from their naturalness, which facilitates comprehension of the represented knowledge.

The basic form of a rule is the following:

If <conditions>
Then <conclusion>

Where <conditions> represents the conditions of a rule, whereas <conclusion> represents its conclusion. The conditions of a rule are connected between each other with logical connectives such as AND, OR, NOT etc., thus forming a logical function. When sufficient conditions of a rule are satisfied, the conclusion is derived and the rule is said to fire (or trigger). Rules represent general knowledge regarding a domain [11].

Rules are suitable to represent general knowledge, whereas cases are suitable for representing specific situations. Rules in a rule based system have the abilities to represent experiential knowledge acquired from experts in a direct fashion. Cases are capable of representing specific historical knowledge. The problem here is that it is difficult to acquire complete and perfect knowledge in a complex domain. Cases are natural and easy to obtain. They can be collected from the historical record, repair logs or other sources [11]. CBR uses partial matching to draw a conclusion. If some of the given problem descriptions match with a given case, then the case is applicable to the proposed solution. It also tries to handle novel problems by referring previously solved cases. Rule based reasoning uses perfect matching to apply a rule for a given problem.

2 Problem Description

As stated [3], advice is one of the most important problems of the tourism sector because the sector also uses traditional advisory system of tourists (i.e. today internet has been connected to people more in the world of tourism, amusement, and economics and as a trend huge number of travel firms provides online services and these services are provided by individual sectors. there are many travel packages existing from different websites to almost all the places over the world. A customer finds it very difficult to search for the best package as he/she has to browse multiple websites, contact many travel agents and etc. which is a tedious process and is time consuming. And these traditional nature of the existing advisory system make it interesting to undertake the study. Lack of access to appropriate information is encountered by Ministry of Culture and Tourism due to the fact that information system is not developed to enable proper collection, organization and dissemination in the sector. n addition, there is no integration or collaboration among different experts that are found in different tourism sectors to develop an organized guidance to new tourists because collection of ideas from different tourists is important to develop well defined and organized guidelines to the tourists. For instance, one expert may have awareness about natural tourist attraction areas but have no more idea about historical tourist attraction areas, etc. These shows experts advice is limited only with the one which is most familiar with them [12]. In the context of visiting, the wise words of the oracle emphasize that success depends on ensuring that your visiting strategy fits your personal characteristics

[7]. Even though all visitors are trying to get satisfaction, each one comes from a diverse background and has different needs and capabilities. It follows that specific visiting vehicles and methods are suitable for certain types of visitors.

According to the interview made with Ministry of Culture and Tourism develop-ment promotion expert, tourists have a few factors to consider, when looking for the right place to visit such as age, nationality, gender, travel frequency, attraction pref-erence and current income level. The expert further comments that due to lack of knowledgeable domain experts to give appropriate advice in Ministry of Culture and Tourism, visitors are confused about where to visit, which route they should follow, and which tourist attraction area is best to them to be satisfied/successful in their recreational program. In developing countries, like Ethiopia, the availability of specialists/experts who can provide an effective service in the tourism sector is also a problem in many small towns and villages and case based recommender systems can prove to be indispensable in such conditions.

3   Related Works

Even though we are often making choices without sufficient personal experience of the alternatives that are available to us in different circumstances, in our everyday life, we sometimes rely on recommendations from other people either by word of mouth, recommendation letters or on movie and book reviews to select from the huge amount of Information that is available in different places but this suggestion is not enough in this digital age [5].

One of the related works is "An Automated University Admission Recommender System for Secondary School Students" by Fong and Biuk-Aghai [14]. Admission and placement of students is based on the perspective of Universities who knows little about the incoming student background but not based on the perspective of high schools who knows the detail of their students. There is value in extending the uni-versity admission process to include secondary schools [14].

In this work, the author proposes a novel design of a recommender system that can provide recommendations about which universities a student should apply to, taking not only the student's secondary school scores but also other factors such as back-ground interest and special skill into account. In the summary of the author, education systems which do not have a standardized open exam for university admissions face the challenges of matching the right secondary school students with the right universities and field of studies and the ways that they should enter. This implies some manual processes are needed and web based recommendation system is very important for decision making. To do that, the author applied a hybrid data mining model to implement a recommender system prototype and analyze different data from secondary schools.

In addition to that, a work entitled "Recommender system for higher education" has been done to discuss the process of developing recommender system for educational institutions. The system is web based application that guides students for decision making based on their personal test. Information about course, curriculum research and facilities in the field of education is important to be available on the web. Clear information about educational activities with description enables students, partners and people to choice more efficiently and scientifically to make right decision [15]. The author concludes that, we can make beneficial use of artificial intelligence techniques like database design and selection, content based recommendations, user profiling, integrating groups of users with similar interests and integrating the domain knowledge and expertise. Hybrid recommendation system approach is important in educational institutions [15].

The paper [6], also tried to discus about course recommendation using data mining techniques called association rule. According to the author, students often need guidance in choosing adequate courses to complete their academic degrees. Course recommender systems have been suggested in the literature as a tool to help students make informed course selections. Students who join higher education degrees are faced with two main challenges: a myriad of courses or field of studies from which to choose, and a lack of knowledge about which courses or field of studies are relevant to follow and in what sequence. Mostly, it is according to their friends and colleagues' manual recommendations that the majorities of them choose their field 40 of study and register for it. It would be useful to help students in finding courses of interest by the intermediary of web based recommender system [16].

The main focus of the authors was on the effectiveness of the incorporation of data mining in course recommendation. The system is based on the following collaborative filtering algorithms: user-based and item-based. According to the author, the system can predict the usefulness of courses to a particular student based on other users' course ratings. To get accurate recommendations, one must evaluate as many courses as possible. Based on the evaluation results, the author suggests C4.5 as the best algorithm for course recommendation. The system cannot predict recommendations for students who have not taken any courses at the University. Generally, there are many recommender systems developed globally and few attempts have been done locally on the area of recommender system in different sectors.

To conclude, several studies have been developed in recommender systems to the solution of a particular problem. Although, most of the recommender system doesn't provide explanation facility on the specified domain area, in this study an attempt is made to design a case based recommender system for tourist attraction area selection that can provide recommendation for visitors about the recommended attraction area with the appropriate time period and also give explanation facility about it.

4 Methodology of the Study

The following methodologies have been used in the course of this study to achieve the above stated research objective.

A. Data source

The main data source used for this study was domain Experts working at MoCT (Ministry of Culture and Tourism) and NTO (National Tour Operation) as well as previously solved cases which are available in the aforementioned organizations. The Researcher's selects these organizations since they use traditional advisory system of tourists and the traditional nature of the Existing advisory system makes it interesting to undertake the study.

B. Data collection Methods

To collect the required domain knowledge, both primary and secondary data collection methods have been employed. As primary sources, Tourism experts from MoCT & NTO and tourists from different tourism sectors have been interviewed. In addition, relevant literature from all possible sources including journal articles, tourism related websites, manuals especially on Ethiopian tourism, and guidelines has been reviewed. To acquire the required tacit knowledge from the selected domain expert, the researcher has employed semi-structured interview technique which focuses on the concept, procedures, and guidelines as well experience which domain expert used while advising in tourists. The researcher's selects semi-structured interview technique because it allows the interviewer to change the order of the questions and add new question based on the participant response.

C. Sampling Techniques

The researchers used Purposive sampling technique to select domain experts for knowledge acquisition and to collect previous tourist cases archived in Ethiopian ministry of culture and tourism. The selection criteria of domain experts for the study are based on the expertise, educational qualification level, year of experience and their immediate position. A total of six experts are selected from sector and they have been interviewed accordingly. These experts are consulted throughout the research work to evaluate the correctness of the acquired knowledge and to verify the cases acquired from the previous visitors cases.

D. Knowledge (Case) Representation

After the knowledge is acquired, the next task is knowledge (case) representation. Although there are various knowledge representation methods, like relational database knowledge representation, feature-value case representation, predicate based representation and soft computing knowledge representation methods have their own advantages and disadvantages. But for this research the researcher used feature-value case representation. The reason for representing the cases using feature-value representation is that this approach supports nearest neighbor retrieval algorithm and it represents cases in an easy way [17]. This approach also uses old experiences to understand and solve new problems. It also reuses its solutions and lessons learned for future use. In addition, it represents cases in an easy way by using attribute and value pair representation [18]. The algorithms used to calculate the similarity of cases in a case base representation for this research are nearest neighbor retrieval algorithm. The similarity function of nearest neighbor retrieval algorithm involves in computing the similarity between the stored cases in the case base and the new query. After that, it selects the most similar stored cases to the query.

In the process of case based recommender system development, Knowledge representation is one of the basic steps. It refers to the formalism, both syntax and semantics, used to store knowledge in the architecture. It is also the process of interpreting domain knowledge into computer understandable form using various knowledge representation techniques. The object of a knowledge representation is to express knowledge in a computer tractable form, so that it can be used to enable our AI agents to perform well [18]. The common Knowledge representation techniques include semantic network, logics, rules, case base and frames. Among these, the researchers use case based representation method for this research.

E. Development Tools

To develop a recommender system there are various programming tools which are available both freely and commercially. Among this SWI-prolog, myCBR, and jCO-LIBRI are the most widely used and known frameworks for teaching and academic research purpose. All of the aforementioned tools have their own capabilities and limitations.

According to [20], jCOLIBRI framework has the following features. Therefore for this research the researcher used jCOLIBRI framework due to the following unique capabilities of the tool.

- jCOLIBRI supports the full CBR cycles (Retrieval, Reuse, Revise and Retain).
- jCOLIBRI is extensible, reusable, different types of users and different purposes (development, research and/or teaching), compatible with commercial applications and, supporting different types of CBR systems, since it is just a.jar file suitable for web applications.
- It is suitable for developing large scale applications.
- jCOLIBRI works well in external database.

F. Testing/Evaluation

Once the prototype is developed, the functionality and user acceptance of the system should be tested. The evaluation processes focus on system's user acceptance of the prototype and the performance of the system. User acceptance measurements are concerned with issues how well the system addresses the needs of the user, whereas performance measurement determine if the system perform the required task successfully. In addition to this, the standard measures of relevance (performance of the system) in the information retrieval (precision, and recall) have been used to evaluate the performance of the prototype.

The researcher tested user acceptance of the system by involving evaluators using visual interaction methods together with questionnaire. System evaluators were interacting with it by using appropriate cases. That is, sample cases has been selected purposely and then evaluators from the domain area were interacting with the system by taking a sample of test cases then, an experiment was conducted to know how new cases are matched with the cases from the case base using case similarity measurement. Each case are selected purposively and used to test the performance of the prototype. Based on that, they evaluate the performance of the system by using close ended questions. Recall and precision value of the system have been calculated based on its retrieval results.

5 Knowledge Modeling/Model Development

According to [21], Knowledge modeling is very significant for knowing the operational means in the development process of a knowledge-based system. It is also a vital stage of the knowledge engineering process. It can provide a means to easily understand the source of knowledge, the inputs and outputs of knowledge, and the designation of other parameters.

Although, there are various conceptual modeling techniques, for this study hierarchical tree structure is used to model how tourist attraction area selection is performed. The reason for using this one as modeling technique is, it easily model concepts and clearly explains the concepts in the problem area. It models the knowledge in the hierarchical manner. This model starts from the main concept at the highest level of the hierarchy and other sub concepts that can affect or affected by the highest level concept put next to down ward in the hierarchy (Fig. 1).

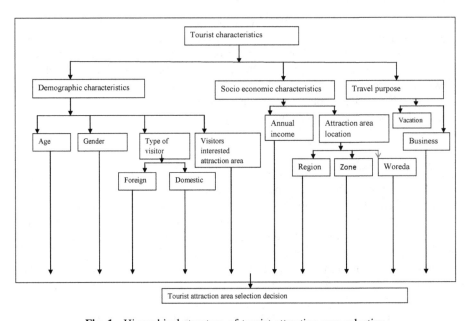

Fig. 1. Hierarchical structure of tourist attraction area selection

6 Factors that Affects the Selection of Tourist Attraction Area Decision

Everyone can be specifically differentiated on various parameters in tourist attraction area selection decision. The major factors that influence attraction area selection decisions are on the tourist's demographic characteristics such as Gender, and Age, type of tourist (nationality) and socio-economic factors such as Annual Income, and location of attraction area or environment.

7 Architectural Design of CBR System for Tourist Attraction Area Selection

As the new query (problem) is entered, the prototype of the system matches the new case with the solved case in the case base of the system by using similarity measurement. If relevant cases are found within the case base, then the prototype system ranks the relevant retrieved cases based on their local similarity. After that, the prototype by itself proposes a solution.

The proposed solution can be derived directly from a retrieved case that matches exactly or partially to the problem of the new case. Partially match of retrieved cases means some attribute values of the existing case and new cases (query) are the same and some attribute values are different. Using the proposed solutions directly may have a risk because some attribute values may need editing (changing) based on different conditions. As a result the user of the system should have made an adaptation on the proposed solution having differences between the proposed case and the new case. In addition to adaptation, case contradictions are revised if there are situations where previous visitor's cases attribute values are not similar with the new case (query) attribute values. There is no similarity between the existing case and new case means there are no previous stored cases having similarity with the new case (query) in all attribute values. Therefore if there is no similarity between the existing and new case, the proposed solution cannot give recommendation to new cases. So during this time, this new case or problem of visitor can be revised and stored in the case base. Finally, the revised solution or stored cases is retained in the case base for problem solving in the next time.

Building of case based recommender system was started by collecting previously solved cases (i.e. previous visitor's cases) from NTO & MoCT consisting of recorded data of visitors who are successful or satisfied in their recreational program. Since previously solved cases contains missing values and unnecessary information for this research, it need further processing in order to avoid such a problem and remove unnecessary attributes for tourist attraction area selection process. After processing of cases and selecting the most significant attributes, assigning weight and important parameters for each attribute was the next task which was performed.

For the selection of important attributes that influence the recommendation of best tourist attraction area and visiting time, the researcher used data mining attribute selection algorithm called attribute selection algorithm. The reason for using attribute selection mechanism is since all attributes are not equally important to recommend tourist attraction areas and suitable visiting time to new visitors.

Once the case based recommender system is developed, users/tourists can use the system easily to choose their attraction areas based on the recommendation given by the system in order to retrieve the best cases that can match with their query. When users/visitors enter their query/case description through the user interface window, the system searches the best matching cases from the case base and retains the possible solution. If there is exact matching between the query and previous cases in the case base, the system recommends the most matched attraction area and visiting time for visitors. If the similarity between query and existing case is approximate, the proposed solution needs modification (adoption of solution) to fit the new case (query). At the end, the best modified solution should be stored into the case base for future use. The case base updates incrementally when the system learns from new case used by visitors (Figs. 2 and 3).

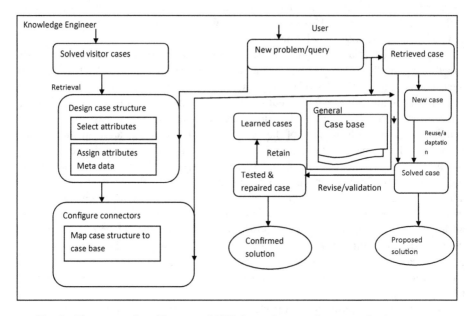

Fig. 2. The proposed architecture of CBR in tourist attraction area selection process

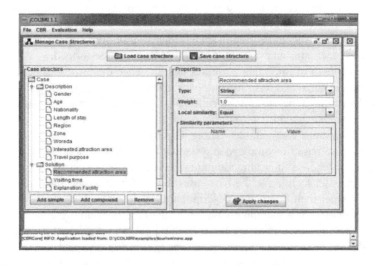

Fig. 3. Case structure defining and similarity

As it is shown above, the case structure of this research contains, nine descriptions attributes which consists of descriptions of the problem needed. And there are three solutions attribute to make sound decision by the system. Solution attribute is assigned to the new case (visitor) after they supply the value of all description attributes and measuring the similarity between the existing case attribute value and new case attribute value. For this research the solution attributes include recommended attraction area, recommended visiting time, and explanation facility about the recommended attraction area (Fig. 4).

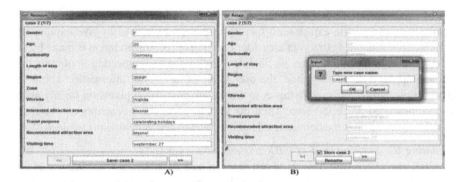

Fig. 4. Revision and retain tasks

8 Deploy the Case Based Recommender System

After defining and configuring all the necessary steps required in designing case based recommender system using the programming tool JCOLIBRI, new case (query) entry application for new tourists is the next step as shown in the prototype bellow.

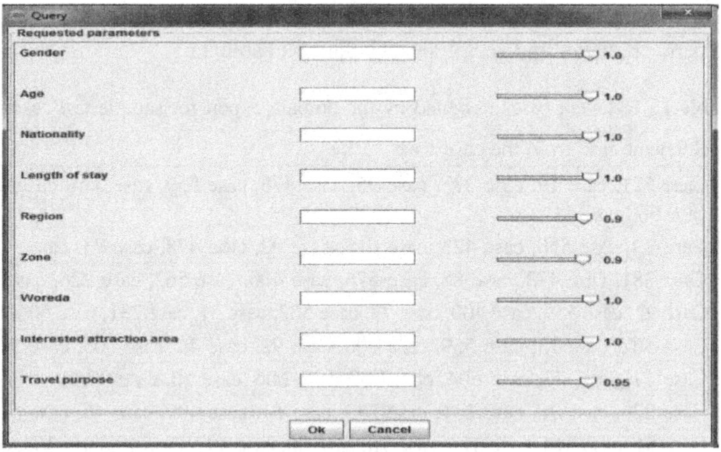

Fig. 5. Windows for case entry in to the case bas

As indicated in Fig. 5 query window, visitors are expected to enter the query to each requested parameters or attributes in the space provided. After entering the query, at the bottom of the screen they will see the results of similar previous visitor cases and the recommended attraction areas, recommended visiting time, and explanation facility about the attraction areas on the execution log. For example in "Nationality" box visitors are required the query of their ethnic group as Ethiopian, Germany, Italy, Spain etc.

9　Explanation Facility

One of the more interesting features of knowledge based systems is their ability to explain themselves. The explanation facility in this study is used to give explanation about the recommended attraction area after decision or recommendation is made by the system. Once the system reaches its final decision on the recommendation of attraction area and appropriate visiting time, the user may not have brief information about the recommended attraction area. In this case the system provides explanation facility about the recommended attraction area. Then the system gives more descriptions about the attraction areas such as the definitions, location, type of accommodations while visiting.

Validating the Performance of CBR System
The CBR engine has a built-in set of test cases in their case library. Effective use of this feature can facilitate the validation process by minimizing the involvement of domain experts in the process. Retrieval of previously stored cases to solve new problems is the first step in any CBR application. Retrieval of similar cases to the new case from previously solved cases is followed by the reuse of similar solutions.

The CBR retrieval test is designed to evaluate the correctness of the retrieval function. To conduct the retrieval testing, for each test case the relevant visitors' cases from the case base should be identified. For identification of relevant cases, test cases are given to the domain expert in order to assign possible relevant cases from the case base to each of the test cases. The domain expert uses the recommendation value and solution attributes of the tourist cases as the main concept to assign the relevant case to the test cases. After the identification of the relevant cases to the test cases by the domain expert, precision and recall are calculated (Table 1).

Table 1. Relevant cases assigned by the domain expert for sample test cases

Test case	Relevant case from the case base
Case 364	Case 521, case 19, case 273, case 95, case 476, case 559, case 314, case 603, case 66, case 44
Case 277	Case 29, case 550, case 423, case 615, case 92, case 478, case 73, case
Case 472	Case 381, case 473, case 88, case 576, case 400, case 562, case 226, case 12
Case 44	Case 92, case 559, case 400, case 73, case 562, case 51, case 231, case 606, case 17
Case 556	Case 562, case 73, case 559, case 400, case 92, case 44, case 605, case 500
Case 600	Case 17, case, 43, case 604, case 605, case 606, case 20, case 99,
Case 12	Case 226, case 78, case 231, case 233, case 51, case 499, case 46, case 519
Case 311	Case 51, case 314, case 312, case 78, case 66, case 497, case 19, case 364, case 13, case 607, case 2

Once the relevant cases are identified and assigned to the test cases the next step is calculating the recall and precision value of the retrieval performance of the CBR system with a threshold interval. As indicated in the research of [22], there is no standard threshold for the degree of similarity that has been used for retrieving relevant cases in CBR. Different CBR researchers use different case similarity threshold. For this study, the threshold level of [1.0, 0.8) is adopted. This means cases with global similarity score greater than 80% are retrieved.

As shown in Table 2, the average recall and precision results were registered as 82% and 61% respectively which is a promising result and indicates that retrieval was done properly. For every test case more than average is registered for both recall and precision. But, precision is lower compared to the average recall. This is because of the tradeoff between precision and recall and small number of cases.

Table 2. Performance measurement of the system using precision and recall

Test case	Recall	Precision
Case 364	0.7	0.71
Case 277	1.0	0.5
Case 472	0.87	0.57
Case 44	0.77	0.64
Case 556	0.87	0.57
Case 600	1.0	0.5
Case 12	0.87	0.57
Case 311	0.63	0.78
Average	0.82	0.61

User Acceptance Testing

User acceptance testing is the process of ensuring that whether the system satisfies the requirements of its end-users or not. This performed in real circumstances at National Tour Operation specifically with Tourism Experts and visitors. During testing the user acceptance, the applicability of the prototype is evaluated by potential users of the system. Potential users of the system are tourism experts and visitors. Case based reasoning system user acceptance evaluation method allows users, (domain expert and visitors) to directly interact with the system and evaluate the performance of the case based system from the users' point of view. User acceptance testing helps to ensure the performance of the prototype by assessing the feedback acquired from the domain expert and visitors towards the developed prototype system. In order to evaluate the user acceptance of the developed prototype system, the researcher used questionnaire adapted from Ethiopia, (2002). To achieve the ambition of user acceptance evaluation of the prototype system, fourteen visitors and eight domain experts from NTO who were participating in different tourism sectors in the country were purposely selected For the ease of analyzing the performance of the system based on user's feedback, the researcher assigned numeric values to the five options as follows: Excellent = 5, V. good = 4, Good = 3, fair = 2 and poor = 1 for of the criteria's (Table 3).

Table 3. Evaluation questions for user acceptance testing

Question No	Evaluation criteria
Question 1	Easy to use of the recommender system Interaction?
Question 2	Is the system efficient in time system
Question 3	Is the user interface interactive
Question 4	Adequacy and clarity of decision support free physicians from boring routine tasks
Question 5	Relevancy of the retrieved case in the decision making
Question 6	Fitness of the final solution to the new case understand for new users
Question 7	Does the explanation facility give brief description about the recommended attraction area description about the recommended attraction area visitors case simplicity and understandability of the system
Question 8	Rate the significance of the system in the domain area ate and useful
Question 9	Relevancy of attributes in representing visitors case

As it is shown in Table 4, below the average value of each questionnaire is calculated using the sum of values of Excellent, V. good, good, fair and poor. As indicated in Table 4, 21.4% of the respondents rated the easiness of the recommender system as good, and 64.2% of them rate as very good and the remaining 14.2% rated as excellent. In case of efficiency of the system in terms of time, 57.14% of the respondents were rated as very good, and the remaining 42.85% of them rated as excellent. Regarding to the interactivity of the prototype, 85.71% of the respondents rated as very good and the remaining 14.28% of them rated as excellent. In the case of adequacy and clarity of the system, 28.57% of the respondents rated as good, 50% of them rated as very good and the remaining 21.42% of the respondents rated as excellent. In the same way, 92.85% of the respondents rate the applicability of the prototype in their domain area as excellent and the remaining 7.14% of the respondent's rate as very good. Generally, it was found that most evaluators have positive feedback about recommender system. The average performance of the system according to the evaluation results filled by the domain experts is 4.2 out of 5 or 82% which shows a promising result and users are satisfied with the recommender.

Table 4. Performance evaluation by visitor

Question number	Excellent	V. good	Good	Fair	Poor	Average
1	2	9	3	–	–	3.9
2	6	8	–	–	–	4.4
3	2	12	–	–	–	4.1
4	3	7	4	–	–	3.9
5	3	9	2	–	–	4.0
6	4	7	3	–	–	4.0
7	1	8	5	–	–	3.7
8	1	13	–	–	–	4.9
9	3	11	–	–	–	4.2
	Average					4.1

10 Testing and Evaluation

Evaluation is an important issue for every system. The purpose of the evaluation process is to get the end user's views on the significance or usefulness of the system. The evaluation and testing issue of the system answers the question "To what extent the recommender system gives acceptable and accurate recommendation and explanation facility service to tourists/visitors?" To answer this question, system performance testing and user acceptance testing methods are used. In this study, both system performance testing and user acceptance testing have been done for the prototype recommender system. In measuring the performance (accuracy) of the system, the CBR modules are validated. The accuracy of CBR module is calculated as 85.4%. In addition to accuracy, user acceptance evaluation of the prototype system has been calculated as 82%. The researchers faced some challenges during the study which limits the recommender system to register a better performance for recommending tourist attraction area. These are discussed as follows: The tacit knowledge elicited from the domain experts, the explicit knowledge acquired from documented sources and cases collected from the different tourist cases were in the form of paper printed format. During the system development process, it was difficult for the researchers to convert all the needed knowledge into the electronically recorded format because it needs a lot of data preprocessing and this task was also tough. The performance of the prototype system depends directly on the quality of the knowledge acquired from domain experts. However, knowledge elicitation from domain experts was the most difficult task due to the fact that, tacit knowledge is difficult to transfer to another in written format.

11 Conclusion and Future Work

As studies shown that, the advising services given on the area of tourism in Ethiopia is in its infant stage. There are various factors that affect the tourism sector to be in its infant stage. Among these, shortage of skilled man power in the area, lack of guide line or criteria to assign visitors in different attraction area, absence of experts that can provides consistency advising service, and lack awareness on the side of visitors about the purpose of advising systems In this paper a recommender system that can provide possible recommendation system for visitors has been developed. The system is evaluated using different evaluation methods and achieved 85.4% of an average performance. The relevant attributes used for this research were collected from the previous tourist cases from NTO and MoCT. These attributes are not sufficient for the selection of attraction area and visiting time decision. So, the researcher further recommends expanding this work by adding other important attributes such as housing preference, level of education, marital status, and purchasing habits by making a direct survey of successful visitors.

References

1. Edmunds, A., Morris, A.: The problem of information overload in business organizations. Department of Information Science, Southborough University (2000)
2. Burke, R.: Hybrid web recommender systems. In: Brusilovsky, P., Kobsa, A., Nejdl, W. (eds.) The Adaptive Web. LNCS, vol. 4321, pp. 377–408. Springer, Heidelberg (2007). https://doi.org/10.1007/978-3-540-72079-9_12
3. Culture and Tourism Office: Tourism Development Strategy, Addis Ababa, Ethiopia (2011)
4. Ethiopia T.: Application of Case-Based Reasoning for Amharic Legal Precedent Retrieval: A Case Study with the Ethiopian Labor Law. Addis Ababa University, Ethiopia (2002)
5. Lorenzi, F., Ricci, F.: Case-based recommender systems: a unifying view. In: Mobasher, B., Anand, S.S. (eds.) ITWP 2003. LNCS (LNAI), vol. 3169, pp. 89–113. Springer, Heidelberg (2005). https://doi.org/10.1007/11577935_5
6. Mehiret, Y.: Tourism certification as a tool for promoting sustainability in the Ethiopian tourism industry. Addis Ababa University, Addis Ababa, Ethiopia (2011)
7. Ministry of Culture and Tourism: Manuals of Ethiopian tourism guide, Addis Ababa, Ethiopia (2012)
8. Main, J., et al.: A tutorial on case based reasoning. In: Pal, S.K., Dillon, T.S., Yeung, D.S. (eds.) Soft Computing in Case Based Reasoning, pp. 1–28. Springer, London (2001). https://doi.org/10.1007/978-1-4471-0687-6_1
9. Shimazu, H.: ExpertClerk: a conversational case-based reasoning tool for developing salesclerk agents in E-commerce webshops. Artif. Intell. Rev. **18**(3–4), 223–244 (2002)
10. Bergmann, R.: Introduction to case-based reasoning. Department of Computer Science University of Kaiserslautern (1998)
11. Prentza, J., Hatzilygeroudi, I.: Categorizing approaches combining rule-based and case-based reasoning. Department of Computer Engineering and Informatics, School of Engineering, University of Patras (2007)
12. United Nations World Tourism Commission: Tourism Highlights. 2007 Edition (2007)
13. Aamodt, A., Plaza, E.: Case-based reasoning: foundational issues, methodological variations, and system approaches. AI Commun. **7**(1), 39–59 (1994)
14. Fong, S., Biuk-Aghai, R.: An automated admission recommender system for secondary school student. In: The 6th International Conference on Information Technology and Application (2009)
15. Satyanarayana, K., Rajagoplan, S.P.: Recommender system for educational institutions. Asian J. Inf. Technol. **6**, 964–969 (2007)
16. Bendakir, N., Aïmeur, E.: Using association rules for course recommendation. Am. Assoc. Artif. Intell. (2006)
17. Salem, A.B.M., et al.: A case base experts system for diagnosis of heart disease. Int. J. Artif. Intell. Mach. Learn. **5**(1), 33–39 (2005)
18. Bergmann, R., et al.: A representation in case based reasoning. Knowl. Eng. Rev. **20**, 1–4 (2005)
19. Burke, R.: Knowledge based recommender systems. University of California, Irvine (2006)
20. Recio, J.A., et al.: jCOLIBRI 1.0 in a nutshell. A software tool for designing CBR systems (2002)
21. Sagheb-Tehrani, M., et al.: A Conceptual model of knowledge elicitation, college of business. Technology and Communication, p. 2 (2009)
22. Getachew, W.: Application of case-based reasoning for anxiety disorder diagnosis, Addis Ababa University, Ethiopia (2012)

A Corpus for Amharic-English Speech Translation: The Case of Tourism Domain

Michael Melese Woldeyohannis[1(✉)], Laurent Besacier[2], and Million Meshesha[1]

[1] Addis Ababa University, Addis Ababa, Ethiopia
{michael.melesele,million.meshesha}@aau.edu.et
[2] LIG Laboratory, UJF, BP53, 38041 Grenoble Cedex 9, France
laurent.besacier@imag.fr

Abstract. Speech translation research for the major languages like English, Japanese and Spanish has been conducted since the 1980's. But no attempt were made in speech translation to/from the under-resourced language like Amharic. These activities suffered from the lack of Amharic speech and Amharic-English text corpus suited for the development of speech translation between the two languages. In this paper, therefore, an attempt has been made to collect, translate and record speech data from resourced language (English) to under-resourced language (Amharic) taking a Basic Traveler Expression Corpus (BTEC) as domain. Since there is no any Amharic text and speech corpus readily available for speech translation purposes, first, 7.43 h of Amharic read-speech has been prepared from 8,112 sentences, and second, 19,972 parallel Amharic-English corpus has been prepared taking tourism as an application domain. The Amharic speech data is recorded using smartphone based application tool, LIG-Aikuma under a normal working environment. With the availability of such standard speech and text corpus, researcher will find a ground to further explore speech translation to/from under resourced languages.

Keywords: Amharic speech corpus · Basic traveller expression corpus
Amharic-English corpus

1 Introduction

Speech is the most natural form of communication in an increasingly globalized world economy, national security and humanitarian service [1]. Alongside this, computers with the ability to understand speech spoken in different languages greatly contribute for the development of man-machine interfaces [2]. This can be extended through different digital platforms such as radio, mobile, TV, CD and others.

1.1 Speech Translation

Research in speech translation for technological supported major languages like English, European languages (like French and Spanish) and Asian languages

© ICST Institute for Computer Sciences, Social Informatics and Telecommunications Engineering 2018
F. Mekuria et al. (Eds.): ICT4DA 2017, LNICST 244, pp. 129–139, 2018.
https://doi.org/10.1007/978-3-319-95153-9_12

(like Japanese and Chinese) has been conducted since the 1983s by NEC Corporation [3]. The advancement of speech translation captivates the communication between people who do not share the same language.

The state-of-the-art speech translation system can be seen as a cascade of three major components [4]; Automatic Speech Recognition (ASR), Statistical Machine Translation (SMT) and Text-To-Speech (TTS) synthesis. ASR is the process by which a machine identifies spoken words, by means of talking to computer, and having it correctly understand what the speaker is saying [5]. Beside ASR, SMT deals with mapping of sentences from one source language into another target language using a model projected from parallel corpora automatically [6]. Finally, TTS system converts the text data into synthesized speech [7].

As one main component of speech translation, Amharic ASR started in 2001. As discussed in Melese et al. [8], several attempts have been made for Amharic ASR using different methods and techniques to solve a different issues encountered during speech recognition. Besides ASR, preliminary experiments on English-Amharic machine translation has been conducted using phonemic transcription on the Amharic corpus and encouraging result were found [9].

As a last component of speech translation, a number of TTS research have been attempted using a number of techniques and methods as discussed by Anberbir [10]. Among these, concatenative, cepstral, formant and a syllable based speech synthesizers were the main methods and techniques applied.

However, all the above researches conducted using different domain data, methods and techniques. Beside this, dataset used in the above research not available, in addition to the difficulty to evaluate the advancement of research in speech technology for local languages. As a result, these activities suffer from the lack of unavailability of Amharic-English text and Amharic speech corpus. Thus, collecting, preparing a text and speech corpus for the development of Amharic-English speech translation system alleviates the problem of data inadequecy.

1.2   The Need for Speech Translation in Tourism Domain

Tourism involves the direct contact between people and cultures, becoming pleasing sustainable economic development and serving as an alternative source of foreign exchange for the country like Ethiopia [11]. According to the official site of the Ethiopian Embassy in the USA [12], Ethiopia has much to offer for international tourists. The historic root comprises of ancient and medieval cities including world heritages, which is registered as Ethiopian tourist attraction by UNESCO.

Moreover, The 2015 United Nations World Tourism [13] and the World Bank[1] report indicate that, a total of 864,000 non-resident tourists come to Ethiopia to visit different locations; out of more than 1 billion international tourists. Since the year 2010 until 2015, the number of tourist increase every year on average by 13.9%.

---

[1] http://data.worldbank.org/indicator/ST.INT.ARVL.

As a result, Walta Information Center[2], citing Ethiopia Ministry of Culture and Tourism, noted that the country has secured about 3.3 billion dollar in the 2016/17 fiscal year from more than 886,000 international tourists. The revenue was collected from various tourist attraction sites across the country, majority of the tourists were from USA, England, Germany, France and Italy and they don't speak any of the Ethiopian languages. These tourists speak foreign languages hindering them to communicate in local languages with tourist guides.

Hence, language barrier is a major problem for today's global communication. Beside this, tourist express their idea using different languages, majority of the tourist can speak and communicate in English to exchange information about tourist attractions. As a result, they look for an alternate option that lets them to communicate with the environment. Thus, speech translation system is one of the best technology used to fill the communication gap between the people who speak different languages.

However, under-resourced languages such as Amharic, suffer from having a text and speech corpus to support speech translation technology. Therefore, the main aim of this paper is to develop Amharic speech corpus and construct Amharic-English parallel text corpus for speech translation in the tourism domain taking basic traveler expression as a domain. Accordingly, moving one step further by collecting resource for under-resourced language helps in overcoming language barriers in today's global communication.

2 Amharic Language

Ethiopia has 89 different languages which are registered in the country with up to 200 different spoken dialects [14]. Among these languages, Amharic is the official working language of government of Ethiopia, and some regional states, such as Addis Ababa, Amhara, Diredawa and Southern Nations, Nationalities and People (SNNP). As Semitic language Amharic is a derived from Ge'ez with the second largest speaker in the world next to Arabic. The name Amharic (አማርኛ-amarəñña) comes from the district of Amhara (አማራ) in northern Ethiopia, which is thought to be the historic center of the language [15]. Moreover, the language Amharic is used in governmental administration, public media and mass communication (television, radio, literature, entertainment, etc.), and national commerce.

According to Language of the world [15], the number of Amharic speaker is more than 25 million with up to 22 million native speakers. The majority of Amharic speakers found in Ethiopia even though there are also speakers in a number of other countries, particularly Italy, Canada, the USA and Sweden.

In the following section a review of Amharic writing system and its phonetics is given in view of preparing speech and text corpus for the development of Amharic-English speech translation.

---

[2] http://www.waltainfo.com/news/detail/32016.

2.1 Amharic Writing System

Amharic characters represent a consonant vowel (CV) sequence and the basic shape of each character is determined by the consonant, which is modified for the vowel. Unlike other Semitic languages, such as Arabic and Hebrew, modern Amharic script has inherited its writing system from Ge'ez (**ግእዝ**) /gə'əzə/. Amharic script uses a grapheme based writing system called fidel /fidälə/ which is written and read from left to right being the classical and ecclesiastical language of Ethiopia.

Amharic writing system is categorized into four distinct categories consisting of 276 different symbols [16]; 231 core characters, 20 labiovelar symbols, 18 labialized consonants and 7 labiodental characters. The first category possess 33 primary characters each representing a consonant having 7 orders (ə/**ህ**/, u/**ሁ**/,i/**ሂ**/, a/**ሃ**/, e/**ሄ**/, ʔ/**ህ**/, o/**ሆ**/) in form to indicate the vowel which follows the consonant to represent CV syllables.

Likewise, labiovelar symbols contains 4 (**ቀ**/k'/, **ሀ**/h/, **ከ**/k/ and **ገ**/g/) characters with 5 orders (^{w}ə, ^{w}i, ^{w}a, ^{w}e and ^{w}) that generates 20 distinct symbols. Similarly, labiodental category possess 1 character (**ቭ**/v/) with 7 order like core characters and only appears in modern loan words borrowed from foreign languages like **ቪዛ**/viza/. There are also labialized 18 characters; for instance, **ሏ**/l^{w}a/, **ሟ**/m^{w}a /, **ሯ**/r^{w}a / and **ሷ**/s^{w}a / that are used in Amharic writing system.

In Amharic writing, all the 276 distinct symbols are indispensable due to their distinct orthographic representation. However, for cascading components of speech translation, we mainly deal with distinct sound in speech recognition and orthographic representation for machine translation.

Thus, among the given character set, different graphemes that generate the same sound has normalized to minimize sounds and words modelled in speech recognition and machine translation respectively. Table 1 presents variants of Amharic graphemes that has been normalized into common graphemes.

Table 1. Amharic characters normalization (adopted and modified from [8])

Variants	Count	Normalized
ሀ, ሐ, ኀ and **ኸ**	4	**ሀ**
አ and **ዐ**	2	**አ**
ሠ and	2	**ሰ**
ጸ and **ፀ**	2	**ጸ**

Among the given 33 core character set, graphemes with multiple variants have to be normalized into their orders to generate equivalent graphemes as shown in Table 1. The selection of graphemes is made based on the usage of most characters frequency in Amharic writing system. Thus, as a result of normalizing the seven orders of (**ሀ, ሐ, ኀ, ኸ**) to **ሀ**/h/, (**አ, ዐ**) to **አ**/ʔ/, (**ሠ, ሰ**) to **ሰ**/s/, (**ጸ, ፀ**) to **ጸ**/ts'/ there is a great reduction in one-to-many, many-to-one and many-to-many model of the cascading component of speech translation.

2.2 Amharic Phonetics

The Amharic phoneme inventory is comprised of 38 phones, 31 consonants and 7 vowels which handles a complete set of sound for Amharic language [17]. Consonants are classified into three categories; manner of articulation, place of articulation, and voicing method [16]. The manner of articulation refers to the interaction of speech organs such as the tongue, lips, and palate when making a speech sound. Similarly, place of articulation indicate where the air flow is blocked in the mouth in order to create sound. Voicing determine whether the sound in query is pronounced while the vocal folds are vibrating or not. Table 2 depicts a complete set of Amharic consonant with respect to their manner of articulation, voicing, and place of articulation.

Table 2. Amharic consonants categories.

Manner of articulation	Voicing	Place of articulation				
		labial	dental	palatal	velar	glottal
Stop	voiceless	ጥ	ት	ች	h	አ
	voiced	ብ	ድ	ጅ	ግ	
	glottalized	ጰ	ጥ	ጭ	ቅ	
	rounded				ኵ ጕ ቈ	
Fricatives	voiceless	ፍ	ስ	ሽ		ህ
	voiced		ዝ	ዥ		
	glottalized		ጸ			
	rounded					ኍ
Nasals			ም	ን	ኝ	
Liquids	Voiced		ል ር			
Semi-vowel		ው			ይ	

Based on the manner of articulation, Amharic sound consist of stops, fricatives, nasals, liquids, and semi-vowels sound whereas taking place of articulation, labial, dental, palatal, velar and glottal sound. Voicing consist of voiced, voiceless, glottalized and rounded type sound.

Beside the consonant, Amharic has a seven-term vowel system (እ[ə], ኡ[u], ኢ[i], አ[a], ኤ[e], እ[ʔ] and ኦ[o]) that are categorized as rounded (ኡ[u] and ኦ[o]) and unrounded (እ[ə], ኢ[i], አ[a], ኤ[e] and እ[ʔ])). .

Likewise, Amharic vowels are categorized according to the place of articulation which includes horizontal movement of tongue such as front, center and back and vertical movement of tongue such as high, middle and low as depicted in Fig. 1. The place of articulation of the Amharic vowel እ[ə] is middle and center, ኡ[u] back and high, ኢ[i] front and high, አ[a] center and low, ኤ[e] front and middle, እ[ʔ] center and high while ኦ[o] is back and middle based on the movement of the tongue in mouth.

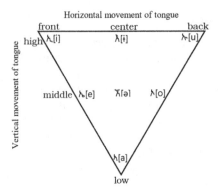

Fig. 1. Category of Amharic vowels in terms of articulation

3   Corpus Preparation

Though speech and text corpora are one of the fundamental resources for any speech translation system; Collecting and preparing standardized and annotated corpora is a challenging and expensive task [14]. This is especially true when working with under-resourced languages like Amharic; under-resourced language require innovative data collection methodologies since there is a lack of language resources that suffers from devising text and speech corpora in digital format. Beside these, due to inaccessibility of standardized digital corpora in tourism and other domains, a text corpus is acquired from resourced and technologically supported languages. Accordingly, parallel English-Arabic text corpus was acquired from BTEC 2009 which is made available through International Workshop on Spoken Language Translation (IWSLT) [18]. In this corpus preparation, currency, time, date, numbers and location have been translated as it is. Moreover, one English sentence is translated in to multiple equivalent Amharic sentence taking the most common expression used in Amharic document as shown in Table 3.

English sentence "I have to catch a plane for Los Angeles early tomorrow morning" is translated in to four different sentence due to equivalence of meaning "የሚበረውን" with "የሚሄደውን" and "መያዝ" with "ላይ መሳፈር" as underlined in Table 3 without considering grapheme variation.

Similarly un-normalized data leads to possible multiple translation for Amharic equivalent even with a single graphemes change. If we take English sentence "I'll take my son to the zoo" and the equivalent translation "ልጇን ዛሬ ወደ እንስሳት መንከባከቢያ ዕወሥደዋለሁ", there are $2^5(32)$ possible way of writing for a single English sentence as a result of using the graphemes አ or ዐ to እ, ስ or ሥ to ስ and ኀ to ሀ to ሃ in the word "እንስሳት" and "ዕወሥደዋለሁ". Thus, normalizing these graphemes to common writing system results to one translation equivalent than 32.

This corpus consists of 28,084 sentences in basic traveller expression domain of which 19,972 is to be used for machine translation and the remaining 8,112

Table 3. One-to-many translation of English to Amharic sentence.

English Sentence	Possible Amharic translation
I have to catch a plane for Los Angeles early tomorrow morning.	ነገ ጠዋት ወደ ሎስአንጀለስ የሚሄደውን አውሮፕላን መያዝ አለብኝ ።
	ነገ ጠዋት ወደ ሎስአንጀለስ የሚበረውን አውሮፕላን መያዝ አለብኝ ።
	ነገ ጠዋት ወደ ሎስአንጀለስ የሚሄደውን አውሮፕላን ላይ መሳፈር አለብኝ ።
	ነገ ጠዋት ወደ ሎስአንጀለስ የሚበረውን አውሮፕላን ላይ መሳፈር አለብኝ ።
Can I cook by myself ?	እራሴ ምግብ ማብሰል እችላለሁ ?
	እራሴ ምግብ ማዘጋጀት እችላለሁ ?
	እኔ ራሴ ምግብ ማብሰል እችላለሁ ?
	እኔ ራሴ ምግብ ማዘጋጀት እችላለሁ ?
Which floor is the kitchen appliances department ?	የኩሽና እቃዎች ያሉበት ስንተኛው ወለል ላይ ነው ?
	የኩሽና እቃዎች ያሉበት የትኛው ወለል ላይ ነው ?
	የኩሽና እቃዎች ያለት የትኛው ወለል ላይ ነው ?
	የኩሽና እቃዎች ያለት ስንተኛው ወለል ላይ ነው ?

used for Amharic speech recognition. Section 3.1 discuss the Amharic-English machine translation corpus while Sect. 3.2 discuss the Amharic speech corpus as part of cascading components.

3.1 Amharic-English Text Corpus

Parallel text corpus is required for designing machine translation system. Accordingly, from a parallel English-Arabic corpus, the English part is translated to Amharic to prepare a parallel Amharic-English BTEC corpus using a bilingual speaker linguistic expert. After translation, the Amharic data have been transcribed into Unicode; then, to keep the dataset consistent, the text corpus has been further preprocessed, such as typing errors are corrected, abbreviations have been expanded, numbers have been textually transcribed and concatenated words have been separated. Table 4 presents the distribution of parallel Amharic-English sentence prepared for machine translation.

Table 4. Amharic-English machine translation corpus distribution

	Sentence	Token	Type	
			Unnormalized	Normalized
Amharic	19,972	109,528	20,210	19,014
English	19,972	152,918	8,389	7,357

In addition to this, the translated text corpus collected has been normalized to their orders for consistency of Amharic and English sentences in the data[3].

---

[3] Normalization in Amharic refers to converting the common graphemes of writing to one while in English it represent lowering the case.

This results in vocabulary size reduction. However, the reduction is minimal due to the use of domain specific text corpus. During translation of English to Amharic, multiple words in English are translated into limited Amharic words, which decrease the number of words in Amharic as compared to the size of words in English as reflected in Table 3. This is due to the morphological richness of Amharic than English.

The Amharic corpus has a word length ranging from 1 to 40 (average of 5 to 6) while, the English corpus consists of 1 to 63 (average of 7 to 8) words per sentence. Figure 2 presents distribution of Amharic and English sentence length against the frequency. Figure 2 presents distribution of Amharic and English sentences interms of frequency of occurence of sentence length (words per sentence)

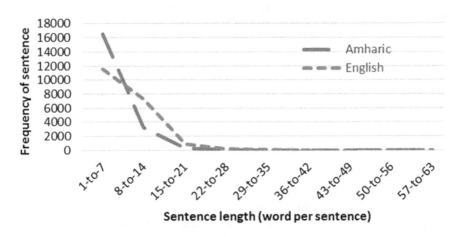

Fig. 2. Distribution of length vs frequency of Amharic-English sentences

Figure 2 depicts that, around 82% of Amharic and 58% of English corpus tend to fall below word length of 8 per sentence, which is below the average due to the domain restriction for English language. Whereas for Amharic, there is no standard average sentence length to the knowledge of the researcher.

Beside sentence length, the Amharic machine translation corpus has 0.71% of Amharic words occurred more than 100 times and 62.7% of Amharic words occurred only once. Similarly, the English data has 44.2% words with frequency of one and 2.9% frequent words more than 100 time occurence.

In general, fact Fig. 2 we found, as the frequency of the sentence increases the sentence length decreases for both languages and the rate of decrease is at an increasing rate for Amharic and at a decreasing rate for English.

3.2   Amharic Speech Corpus

As discussed by Davel [19], traditional methods of data collection is not convenient, consistent and usually time taking particularly for collecting large amount of data compared to handheld device like mobile phones. Beside this, mobile and handheld devices are becoming increasingly available and sharply decreasing cost even for the developing country to collect speech data. Thus, for our typically under-resourced conditions, we opted to incorporate a smartphone based application called LIG-Aikuma [20] to facilitate the speech data collection process under normal office environment. Aikuma does not rely on internet connection to perform audio data collection, but does require that text prompts be loaded on the device manually. The main reason for using LIG-Aikuma is due to its ease of use and an open-source tool that runs on Android platform.

The researcher explained the purpose of the research and instructed to start the recording when they are ready to read in the absence of the researcher. The speech data is collected from eight native Amharic speakers (4 male and 4 female) with different age range for a total of 8112 sentences. Table 5 presents the distribution of the utterance per age and gender of the speaker. The speakers read the Amharic parts of Amharic-English aligned sentence with the possibility to record over again the sentence anytime they mispronounced the sentence. The speech data have been recorded with a length ranging from 1 to 28 word length (average of 4 to 5 words) per sentence. A total of 7.43 h read speech corpus ranging from 1,020 ms to 14,633 ms with an average speech time of 3,297 ms was collected. The distribution of speech length across sentence is presented as depicted in Fig. 3.

Table 5. Age and gender distribution of Amharic speech corpus.

	Age and Gender			
	Male		Female	
	18–30	31–50	18–30	31–50
Number of utterance	1,000	1,112	1,000	1,000
	1,000	1,000	1,000	1,000
Total	2,000	2,112	2,000	2,000

As we can see from Fig. 3, 98.54% of the speech data fall below 7 s. Moreover, the speech data corpus consist of 8112 sentences (37,288 tokens) of 4,168 types. In addition to this, 1.2% of Amharic words occurred more than 100 times.

On the contrary, 42.4% of Amharic words occurred once from ASR data. BTEC developed as a wide-coverage, consistent corpus containing basic travel expressions in technologically supported language, for the purpose of providing basic data for the development of high quality speech translation systems.

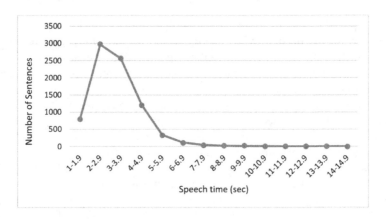

Fig. 3. Distribution of Amharic speech dataset

4   Concluding Remarks

Under-resourced language, like Amharic needs to be supported by technology, like speech translation. To this end, standardized corpus preparation is a must to use it as a test bed to control and evaluate the progress of the research in the area of speech translation. Attempts in this area from under-resourced languages like Amharic, is particularly, not yet started. To ease speech translation from under-resourced language (Amharic) to resourced language (English) text and speech corpus have been developed by translating traveller expression corpus.

Accordingly we have constructed a 19,972 Amharic-English parallel corpus for machine translation and a 7.43 h read-speech corpus from 8112 sentences in tourism domain from widely covered, consistent and technologically supported English language. Thus, the corpus we developed will be used for Amharic-English speech translation by means of cascading components, which is our immediate research direction.

References

1. Gao, Y., Gu, L., Zhou, B.: Speech-to-Speech Translation. World Scientific, Singapore (2007)
2. Honda, M.: Human speech production mechanisms, NTT Commun. Sci. Lab. **1**(2), 24–29 (2003)
3. Karematsu, A., Morimoto, T.: Automatic Speech Translation: Fundamental Technology for Future Cross-Language Communication, vol. 11. Gordon and Breach Publishers, Philadelphia (1996)
4. Gao, Y., Gu, L., Zhou, B., Sarikaya, R., Afify, M., Kuo, H.-K., Zhu, W., Deng, Y., Prosser, C., Zhang, W., Besacier, L.: IBM mastor: multilingual automatic speech-to-speech translator. In: Proceedings of 2006 IEEE International Conference Acoustics Speech Signal Processing, vol. 5, p. 5, December 2006
5. Jurafsky, D., Martin, J.H.: An Introduction to Natural Language Processing, Computational Linguistics, and Speech Recognition, Second edn. Pearson

6. Philipp, K.: Statistical Machine Translation. Cambridge University Press, Cambridge (2009)
7. Lemmetty, S.: Review of Speech Synthesis Technology. Helsinki University of Technology, Helsinki (1999)
8. Woldeyohannis, M.M., Besacier, L., Meshesha, M.: Amharic speech recognition for speech translation. In: JEP-TALN-RECITAL 2016. Paris, France, vol. 11, p. 114 (2016)
9. Teshome, M.G., Besacier, L., Taye, G., Teferi, D.: Phoneme-based English-Amharic statistical machine translation. Presented at the AFRICON, 2015, Addis Ababa, Ethiopia, pp. 1–5 (2015)
10. Anberbir, T., Takara, T.: Development of an Amharic text-to-speech system using cepstral method. In: Proceedings of the EACL 2009 Workshop on Language Technologies for African Languages (AfLaT 2009), Athens, Greece, pp. 46-52 (2009)
11. Ethiopia: A Preferred Location for Foreign Direct Investment in Africa, Ethiopian Investment Commision (2014). http://www.investethiopia.gov.et/images/pdf/Investment_Brochure_to_Ethiopia.pdf
12. Ethiopian Embassy: Investing in ethiopia: Briefing for tour operators. http://www.ethiopianembassy.org/PDF/InvestingTourism.pdf. Accessed 10 Aug 2017
13. UNWTO: World Tourism Organization annual report 2015. Technical report, United Nation, Madrid, Spain (2016)
14. Simons, G.F., Fennig, C.D.: Ethnologue: Languages of the World. SIL, Dallas (2017)
15. Teklehaimanot, T.: Ethiopian Languages. http://www.ethiopiantreasures.co.uk/pages/language.htm. Accessed 10 Aug 2017
16. Abate, S.T., Menzel, W., Taflla, B.: An Amharic speech corpus for large vocabulary continuous speech recognition. In: Proceedings of the XVth International Conference of Ethiopian Studies, Hamburg, Germany (2005)
17. Yimam, B.: Yeamarigna sewasew (Amharic version). Addis Ababa, Ethiopia, EMPDA (1986)
18. Fondazione Bruno Kessler: International Workshop on Spoken Language Translation, Paris, France, pp. 2–3 (2010)
19. Davel, M.H., Badenhorst, J., Basson, W.D., De Wet, F., Barnard, E., De Waal, A., De Vries, N.J.: A smartphone-based ASR data collection tool for under-resourced languages, vol. 56, pp. 119–131 (2014)
20. Blachon, D., Gauthier, E., Besacier, L., Kouarata, G.-N., Adda-Decker, M., Rialland, A.: Parallel speech collection for under-resourced language studies using the Lig-Aikuma mobile device app. In: SLTU (2016)

Experimenting Statistical Machine Translation for Ethiopic Semitic Languages: The Case of Amharic-Tigrigna

Michael Melese Woldeyohannis[(⊠)] and Million Meshesha

Addis Ababa University, Addis Ababa, Ethiopia
{michael.melese,million.meshesha}@aau.edu.et

Abstract. In this research an attempt have been made to experiment on Amharic-Tigrigna machine translation for promoting information sharing. Since there is no Amharic-Tigrigna parallel text corpus, we prepared a parallel text corpus for Amharic-Tigrigna machine translation system from religious domain specifically from bible. Consequently, the data preparation involves sentence alignment, sentence splitting, tokenization, normalization of Amharic-Tigrigna parallel corpora and then splitting the dataset into training, tuning and testing data. Then, Amharic-Tigrigna translation model have been constructed using training data and further tuned for better translation. Finally, given target language model, the Amharic-Tigrigna translation system generates a target output with reference to translation model using word and morpheme as a unit. The result we found from the experiment is promising to design Amharic-Tigrigna machine translation system between resource deficient languages. We are now working on post-editing to enhance the performance of the bi-lingual Amharic-Tigrigna translator.

Keywords: Under-resourced language · Amharic-Tigrigna
Semitic language · Machine translation

1 Introduction

Computers with the ability to understand human language contribute greatly to the development of more natural man-machine interfaces through better processing speeds and storage capacity [1]. Beside this, the advancement of ICT and the rise of the internet as a means of communication led to an ever increasing demand for Natural Language Processing (NLP). Among these applications, Machine translation (MT) is one, which refers to a process by which computer software is used to translate a text from one language to another [2]. The ideal aim of machine translation systems is to produce the best possible translation with minimal human intervention. Translation is not just word-for-word substitution rather it is a complex task that the meaning of source must be fully restored in the target holding grammar, syntax and semantics of the languages [3].

© ICST Institute for Computer Sciences, Social Informatics and Telecommunications Engineering 2018
F. Mekuria et al. (Eds.): ICT4DA 2017, LNICST 244, pp. 140–149, 2018.
https://doi.org/10.1007/978-3-319-95153-9_13

Moreover, a translator must interpret and analyze all of the elements in the text and know how each word may influence another; this requires an extensive expertise as well as familiarity with source and target languages. For these, machine translation can follow rule-based, example-based, statistical-based or else machine learning approach. In this work statistical machine translation (SMT) have been applied.

According to world language [4], there are around 7,097 known living languages in the world and most of them are under resourced, Especially the African languages which contribute around 30% (2139) of the world language highly grieve from the lack of sufficient NLP resources. This is specially true for Ethiopic languages such as Amharic, Tigrigna and Afaan-Oromo among others.

Ethiopia being multilingual and multinational country, its constitution decrees that each nation, nationality and people has the right to speak, write and develop its own language. However, a lot of written documents, brochures, text books, magazines, advertisements and the web that are being produced in Amharic language than other. These would result in unbalanced production and distribution of material in different languages as an official and working language of Ethiopia.

Thus, to bridge the gap there is a need to develop a system that translate materials and documents into multiple languages, thereby ensuring effective information and knowledge sharing among the public at large as much as possible. In this paper an attempt is made to design a bi-directional statistical machine translation for semitic Amharic-Tigrigna language.

2   Ethiopic Language

Ethiopia has 89 languages which are officially registered in the country with up to 200 different spoken dialects [4–6]. Among these languages, this study consider semitic languages specifically Amharic and Tigrigna. This is because Amharic and Tigrigna are the second and the third widely spoken semitic languages in the world, next to Arabic. Unlike other Semitic languages, such as Arabic and Hebrew, both Amharic and Tigrigna uses a grapheme based writing system called fidel /fidälə/ which is written and read from left to right derived from Ge'ez /gə'əzə/ [7,8]. The majority of Amharic and Tigrigna speakers found in Ethiopia even though there are also speakers in a number of other countries, particularly Eritrea, Italy, Israel, Canada, the USA and Sweden.

The name Amharic (አማርኛ-amarəñña) comes from the district of Amhara (አማራ) region in northern Ethiopia, which is thought to be the historic center of the language being the official working language of the government of Ethiopia and some regional state such as Addis Ababa, Amhara and Southern Nations, Nationalities and People (SNNP). Whereas, Tigrinya (ትግርኛ/tigriñña/) is one of the language spoken by the Tigray people and serves as a working language of Tigray regional state of Ethiopia; it is also widely spoken in central Eritrea as an official languages.

Amharic language is spoken by more than 25 million with up to 22 million native speakers while Tigrigna has more than 7 million with up to 4 million native speakers [4]. The following section discuss a review of Amharic and Tigrigna writing system in a view of preparing parallel text corpus for the development of Amharic-Tigrigna statistical machine translation system.

2.1 Amharic Writing System

Amharic symbols are categorized into four groups consisting of 276 distinct symbols [9,10]; core characters, labiovelar, labialized and labiodental. The detail category is presented in Table 1.

Table 1. Distribution of Amharic character set

Category	Character set	Order	Total
Core characters	33	7	231
Labiovelar	4	5	20
Labialized	18	1	18
Labiodental	1	7	7
Total			276

As shown in Table 1 Amharic has a total of 231 distinct core characters, 20 labiovelar symbols, 18 labialized consonants and 7 labiodental. The first category possess 33 primary characters each representing a consonant having 7 orders in form to indicate the vowel which follows the consonant to represent CV syllables. In the same way, labiodental category contains a character ቭ/v/ with 7 order borrowed from foreign languages and appears only in modern loan words like ቪዛ/viza/. Similarly, the labiovelar category contains 4 (ቀ/k'/, ኀ/h/, ከ/k/ and ገ/g/) characters with 5 orders that generates 20 distinct symbols. Furthermore, there are 18 labialized characters; for instance, ሏ/ lʷa/, ሟ/mʷa/, ሯ/rʷa/ and ሷ/sʷa/.

In Amharic writing, all the 276 distinct symbols are indispensable due to their distinct orthographic representation. In the machine translation task, we mainly deal with distinct words rather than with orthographic representation; Table 2 presents graphemes that have been normalized into common graphemes.

Table 2. List of normalized Amharic graphemes

Graphemes variants	Graphemes count	Equivalent graphemes	Normalized graphemes
ሀ, ሐ, ኀ, and ኸ	4	/h/	ሀ/h/
አ and ዐ	2	/?/	አ/?/
ሠ and ሰ	2	/s/	ሰ/s/
ጸ and ፀ	2	/ ts'/	ጸ/ts'/

Thus, among the given character set, different graphemes that generates same word have been normalized. Among the given 33 core character set, graphemes with multiple variants have to be normalized into their sixth order along with derivatives to generate equivalent graphemes as shown in Table 2. The selection of graphemes is made based on the usage of character in Amharic document. Thus, as a result of normalizing the seven orders of (ሀ, ሐ, ኀ, ኸ) to ሀ/h/, (ኣ, ዐ) to አ/?/, (ሠ, ሰ) to ሰ/s/, (ጸ, ፀ) to ጸ/ts'/ there is a great reduction in one-to-many, many-to-one and many-to-many modelling for machine translation task.

2.2 Tigrigna Writing System

Tigrigna symbols are grouped into three different categories; consisting of 249 distinct symbol [6]; these are core characters, labiovelar and labiodental. The detail category of distinct symbols used in Tigrigna writing systems is presented in Table 3.

Table 3. Distribution of Tigrigna character set

Category	Character set	Order	Total
Core characters	31	7	217
Labiovelar	5	5	25
Labiodental	1	7	7
Total			249

Tigrigna has a total of 217 distinct core characters, 25 labiovelar symbols and 7 labiodental. The first category possess 31 primary characters each representing a consonant having 7 orders in form to indicate the vowel which follows the consonant to represent CV syllables. Whereas the second category contribute 5 labiovelar character with each representing five order. In the third category, like Amharic, Tigrigna possess one labiodental character with an order of 7.

Unlike Amharic writing system, all the 249 distinct Tigrigna symbols are indispensable due to their distinct orthographic representation and sound without overlapping. Unlike the Amharic script writing, Tigrigna does not require normalization as they do not provide the same meaning using different graphemes.

3   Data Preparation

One of the most fundamental resources for any statistical machine translation system is to have a parallel corpora. Collecting standardized and annotated corpora is one of the most challenging and expensive task [11]. This is specially true when working with under resourced languages. Unlike English, European languages (like French and Spanish) and Asian languages (like Japanese and Chinese) Amharic and Tigrigna can be considered as an under-resourced and technologically less supported languages that suffers from devising digital corpora.

For this research project, bible has been selected as a domain. The selection is made due to the existence of comparable Amharic-Tigrigna corpus and complex nature of expression it contains.

Data collected from web cannot be used directly for statistical machine translation. Thus, the corpus collected from web has been aligned to create parallel Amharic-Tigrigna sentence. Then, the corpus has been normalized, cleaned and segmented accordingly for both language. Finally, verified by linguist to have Amharic-Tigrigna parallel corpora. Beside this, all typing errors are corrected and further filtering done to overcome the problem that may arise as a result of one-to-many, many-to-one and many-to-many relationship due to orthographic variation that generates the same meaning.

This may be due to unnormalized, typing error and uncleaned text in the sentence. Hence, to normalize, clean the corpus and align at the sentence level after identifying the sentence boundary using Perl[1] and Python[2] as a programming languages.

The phrase based translation between the concepts in the source and target sentence greatly affect the statistical machine translation experiment. Figure 1 presents a sample one-to-one, one-to-many, many-to-one and many-to-many word level translation for Amharic-Tigrigna language.

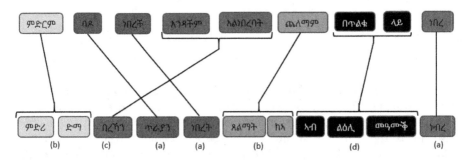

Fig. 1. Word correspondence between Amharic and Tigrigna (a) one-to-one, (b) one-to-many, (c) many-to-one and (d) many-to-many word translation mapping

Let us take a sample Amharic sentence "ምድርም ባዶ ነበረች አንዳችም አልነበረባትም ጨለማም በጥልቁ ላይ ነበr" and its equivalent Tigrigna translation "ምድሪ ድማ በረኻን ጥራያን ነበረት ጸልማት ከአ አብ ልዕሊ መዓሙ-ቅ ነበረ". Before applying normalization, the Amharic word "አንዳችም" and "አልነበረባትም" has 2 variants አ and ዐ. This results in 4 (2^n where n is number character variant) possible combination in a given sentence of the of same meaning.

Similarly, Tigrigna sentence translation of "ምሽት ኮነ ብጊሓትውን ኮነ ሳልሰይቲ መዓልቲ" has a

---

[1] Available at https://www.perl.org.
[2] Available at https://www.python.org.

total of 64 Amharic "*ማታም ሆነ ጥዋትም ሆነ ሦስተኛ ቀን*" sentence as a result one grapheme variation. Among this, 16 of them generated from **ሆ** variants whereas 4 from **ሦ** and **ስ** variants. Table 4 present sample unnormalized Tigrigna-Amharic sentence translation.

Table 4. Amharic-Tigrigna unnormalized translation

Tigrigna	Amharic
ም ድሪ ድማ በረኻን	*ምድርም ባዶ ነበረች አንዳችም አልነበረባትም ጨለማም በጥልቁ ላይ ነበረ*
ጥራያን ነበረት ጸልማት	*ምድርም ባዶ ነበረች አንዳችም ዐልነበረባትም ጨለማም በጥልቁ ላይ ነበረ*
ከአ አብ ልዕሊ መዓሙቕ	*ምድርም ባዶ ነበረች ዐንዳችም አልነበረባትም ጨለማም በጥልቁ ላይ ነበረ*
ነበረ	*ምድርም ባዶ ነበረች ዐንዳችም ዐልነበረባትም ጨለማም በጥልቁ ላይ ነበረ*
	ይሁዳም ባያት ጊዜ ጋለሞታን መሰለችው ፊትዋን ተሸፍና ነበረና
	ይሑዳም ባያት ጊዜ ጋለሞታን መሰለችው ፊትዋን ተሸፍና ነበረና
ይኑዳ ምስ ረአያ ገጻ ሸፊና	*ይኑዳም ባያት ጊዜ ጋለሞታን መሰለችው ፊትዋን ተሸፍና ነበረና*
ነበረት እም አመንዝራ	*ይኹዳም ባያት ጊዜ ጋለሞታን መሰለችው ፊትዋን ተሸፍና ነበረና*
መሰለቶ	*ይሁዳም ባያት ጊዜ ጋለሞታን መሠለችው ፊትዋን ተሸፍና ነበረና*
	ይሑዳም ባያት ጊዜ ጋለሞታን መሠለችው ፊትዋን ተሸፍና ነበረና
	ይኑዳም ባያት ጊዜ ጋለሞታን መሠለችው ፊትዋን ተሸፍና ነበረና
	ይኹዳም ባያት ጊዜ ጋለሞታን መሠለችው ፊትዋን ተሸፍና ነበረና

Thus, more than 25,000 Amharic and Tigrigna sentences have been extracted from web in religious domain specifically bible. Then, the corpus were aligned to create a parallel corpora to fit the need of statistical machine translation with word and morpheme as a unit.

The Amharic corpus contains 25,470 sentences consisting of 355,993 tokens (64,259 types) with an average of 14 words per sentence. Similarly, Tigrigna corpus consist of 25,470 sentences consisting of 396,565 tokens (61,175 types) with an average of 16 words per sentence. Table 6 presents detail training, development, testing and language model data used for statistical machine translation

Table 5. Distribution of data per unit for Amharic-Tigrigna SMT

	Units	Amharic			Tigrigna		
		Sentence	Token	Type	Sentence	Token	Type
Training	Word	25,470	335,993	64,259	25,470	396,565	61,175
	Morpheme	25,470	541,425	23,809	25,470	561,057	30,138
Development	Word	500	7,362	3,374	500	8,917	3,015
	Morpheme	500	11,922	2,784	500	12,602	2,828
Testing	Word	1,000	13,845	6,042	1,000	16,300	5,439
	Morpheme	1,000	22,468	4,625	1,000	23,881	4,708
Language model	Word	36,989	679,716	112,511	62,335	1,089,435	109,988
	Morpheme	36,989	2,175,853	34,894	62,335	2,999,627	49,636

against the unit used for each language for words and morphemes parallel corpus (Table 5).

Beside the parallel corpus, we prepared a separate language model for both languages. The language model consists of 36,989 sentences (697,716 tokens of 112,511 types) for Amharic languages and 62,335 sentences (1,089,435 tokens of 109,988 types) for Tigrigna language at word level.

Similarly for the morpheme-based translation; the training, development, testing and language model data have been segmented into sub-word unit using corpus-based, language independent and unsupervised segmentation for both Amharic and Tigrigna language using morfessor 2.0[3] [12]. Figure 2 depicts the distribution of Amharic-Tigrigna training sentences used for word-based and morpheme-based translation.

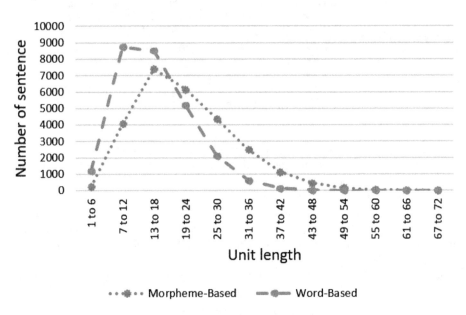

Fig. 2. Distribution of Amharic-Tigrigna sentence at word and morpheme levels

As we can see from Fig. 2, 67.8% of the parallel Amharic-Tigrigna machine translation data fall below 20 words per sentence. In addition to this, 6.7% of Amharic-Tigrigna sentence occurred more than 37 words per sentence.

4   Experiment

Both Amharic and Tigrigna are morphologically rich and complex languages; therefore, conducting the experiment through word and morpheme units

---

[3] The unit obtained with Morfessor segmentation is referred here as morpheme without any linguistic definition of morpheme.

are important. Towards putting the architecture inplace, a word and morpheme based translation have been conducted. For these we prepared a word-word, word-morpheme, morpheme-word and morpheme-based, word-based and morpheme-morpheme Amharic-Tigrigna and Tigrigna-Amharic parallel data. In addition to this, for each experiment, a word and morpheme based language model has been prepared for target language using tri-gram language model.

Once we prepared the parallel corpus for training, tuning and testing; Subsequently, the prepared parallel training data is aligned statistically by using multi-threaded giza (MGIZA). Then we trained the model using Moses and further tuned the model using the tuning data prepared for parallel corpus to create a translation model. A total of 8 models have been constructed taking word and morpheme as a unit of model. This includes, word-word, word-morpheme, morpheme-word and morpheme-morpheme for both Amharic-Tigrigna and Tigrigna-Amharic machine translation.

Once the translation model is ready for word and morpheme based translation, test data is prepared for evaluating the prototype. For this, 1000 sentences have been selected for word and morpheme based evaluation from the same domain. Then, the performance of each translation model have been tested at a sentence level using Bilinguale Evaluation Understudy (BLEU). Table 6 depicts the result obtained from machine translation with respect to each unit of translation.

Table 6. Distribution of data per unit for Amharic-Tigrigna SMT

Units			Target			
			Amharic		Tigrigna	
			Word	Morpheme	Word	Morpheme
Source	Amharic	Word			8.25	9.11
		Morpheme			9.09	13.49
	Tigrigna	Word	6.65	10.71		
		Morpheme	5.81	12.93		

Accordingly, the prototype have been evaluated using the same units (word-word and morpheme-morpheme) and different units (morpheme-word and word-morpheme). The word-word unit based translation correctly translated with BLEU score of 6.65 and 8.25 from Tigrigna-Amharic and Amharic-Tigrigna respectively. In addition, using morpheme as a unit for Amharic and Tigrigna, Amharic-Tigrigna resulted 13.49 while Tigrigna-Amharic scores 12.93 BLEU score.

On the contrary, a BLEU score of 5.81 for Tigrigna-Amharic and 9.11 for Amharic-Tigrigna have been achieved using word unit for Amharic and morpheme unit for Tigrigna. Moreover, using morph unit for Amharic and word unit for Tigrigna, 10.71 for Tigrigna-Amharic and 9.09 BLEU score for Amharic-Tigrigna have been achieved. Figure 3 presents summary of BLEU score registered for bilingual Amharic-Tigrigna statistical machine translation for each unit combination.

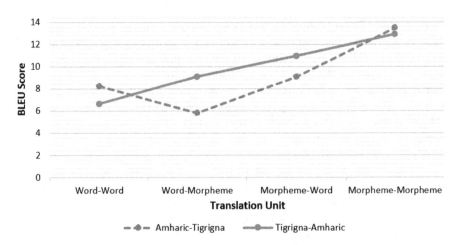

Fig. 3. Experimental result for bilingual Amharic-Tigrigna machine translation

Moreover, the performance of target side segmentation registered better result of translation than that of source side segmentation. The performance improvement in the target morpheme is as a result of minimizing morphological variation introduced in translation of the test set.

5   Concluding Remarks

In this research an attempt is made to design a bilingual machine translation for Amharic-Tigrigna. To conduct this study a total of 27,470 parallel Amharic and Tigrigna sentences have been selected from religious domain bible. The selected corpus have been preprocessed and analyzed morphologically using morfessor. Beside this, word and morpheme are used as translation unit with a sentence pair of maximum 80 words or morphemes per sentence selected after removing punctuation that should not be translated such as exclamation mark and colon.

Finally, the result obtained in this research is promising and serve as a proof that it is possible to have a SMT system for implementing a translation system for a pair of local languages. Experimental result shows that morpheme-based Amharic-Tigrigna translation outperforms word-based translation with a performance improvement by 4.24%. Beside this, SMT system may miss the real meaning of the source information since it depends on the size of corpus used for training. Had it been further analyzed beside morphological analysis, by combining with example based translation it would even give a better result than the current output. Hence, it is our next research direction to is to integrate example based with SMT system and further work on post-editing to enhance the performance of translator.

Acknowledgement. We would like to thank Ethiopia Ministry of Communication and Information Technology (MCIT) for funding to collect parallel text corpus and conduct an experiement for a bilingual Amharic-Tigrigna statistical machine translation research project.

References

1. Nakamura, S.: Overcoming the language barrier with speech translation technology. Sci. Technol. Trends Q. Rev. **31**, 35–48 (2009)
2. What is machine translation, SYSTRAN: we speak your industry's language. http://www.systran.co.uk/systran/corporate-profile/translation-technology/what-is-machine-translation
3. Martínez, L.G.: Human Translation Versus Machine Translation and Full Post-editing of Raw Machine Translation Output. Dublin City University, Dublin (2003)
4. Simons, G.F., Fennig, C.D.: Ethnologue: Languages of the World, 20th edn. SIL, Dallas (2017)
5. Zekaria, S.: Summary and Statistical Report of the 2007 Population and Housing Census. Central Statistical Agency, Addis Ababa (2008)
6. Ager, S.: Omniglot, the online Encyclopedia of writing systems and languages
7. Hudson, G.: The world's major languages: Amharic. In: The World's Major Languages, 2nd edn, pp. 594–614. Routledge, Oxon/New York (2009)
8. Abyssinica dictionary: Amharic, the official language of Ethiopia (2015)
9. Teferra, S., Menzel, W., Tafila, B.: An Amharic speech corpus for large vocabulary continuous speech recognition. In: Proceedings of the XVth International Conference of Ethiopian Studies, Hamburg, Germany (2005)
10. Woldeyohannis, M.M., Besacier, L., Meshesha, M.: A corpus for Amharic-English speech translation: the case of tourism domain. In: Mekuria, F., Nigussie, E.E., Dargie, W., Edward, M., Tegegne, T., et al. (eds.) ICT4DA 2017. LNICST, vol. 244, pp. 129–139. Springer, Cham (2018)
11. Besacier, L., Le, V.-B., Boitet, C., Berment, V.: ASR and translation for under-resourced languages, Grenoble cedex 9, France
12. Creutz, M., Lagus, K.: Unsupervised discovery of morphemes. In: Proceedings of the Workshop on Morphological and Phonological Learning of ACL-02, pp. 21–30, Philadelphia, Pennsylvania (2002)

Synchronized Video and Motion Capture Dataset and Quantitative Evaluation of Vision Based Skeleton Tracking Methods for Robotic Action Imitation

Selamawet Atnafu[1]([⊠]) and Conci Nicola[2]

[1] Bahir Dar Institute of Technology, Bahir Dar, Ethiopia
wselame7@gmail.com
[2] University of Trento, Trento, Italy
conci@disi.unitn.it

Abstract. Marker-less skeleton tracking methods are being widely used for applications such as computer animation, human action recognition, human robot collaboration and humanoid robot motion control. Regarding robot motion control, using the humanoid's 3D camera and a robust and accurate tracking algorithm, vision based tracking could be a wise solution. In this paper we quantitatively evaluate two vision based marker-less skeleton tracking algorithms (the first, Igalia's Skeltrack skeleton tracking and the second, an adaptable and customizable method which combines color and depth information from the Kinect.) and perform comparative analysis on upper body tracking results. We have generated a common dataset of human motions by synchronizing an XSENS 3D Motion Capture System, which is used as a ground truth data and a video recording from a 3D sensor device. The dataset, could also be used to evaluate other full body skeleton tracking algorithms. In addition, sets of evaluation metrics are presented.

Keywords: Joint angle · Accuracy · Tracking ability · Human motion dataset
3D camera · Ground truth

1 Introduction

The intention of making humanoid robots perform human like motions, which needs the development of easy and simple motion control approaches, has attracted the attention of many researchers [5]. Rather than using very complicated motion planning techniques, learning by demonstration, which combines motion capture and control systems, has being considered as an efficient and intuitive way to control the motion of humanoid robots and to teach them how to perform human like motions [5]. The first task in the process of learning by imitation is to have a robust and accurate motion capture system. Even if a number of marker-less skeleton tracking algorithms, which are convenient for this purpose, have been being proposed for years, there needs a way to quantitatively evaluate the performance of each method. Most of the evaluation schemas provide qualitative results due to lack of a common human motion dataset with a ground truth data [11]. The earliest efforts to collect synchronized motion

© ICST Institute for Computer Sciences, Social Informatics and Telecommunications Engineering 2018
F. Mekuria et al. (Eds.): ICT4DA 2017, LNICST 244, pp. 150–158, 2018.
https://doi.org/10.1007/978-3-319-95153-9_14

capture and ground truth data have been used to analyze only 2D tracking methods [14]. Others also have tried to provide their synchronized dataset available to the public but some lack joint level ground truth information [15] and others do not provide calibration information [16]. HumanEva is the most recent and complete dataset which is made available to the public [11]. Since the subjects wore natural closing, on to which markers are attached, the accuracy of the ground truth data is reduced due to the movement of the markers [11]. In this work, two marker-less skeleton tracking methods are evaluated quantitatively. The two methods are chosen because they showed good tracking performances and are open sources which make them accessible for investigation. Both algorithms take input data from a 3D camera. RGB-D is a vision based method that takes depth and color information from the camera and outputs 3D location of human skeleton without requiring unnatural initialization poses [2]. It has two iterations, each one performing pixel-wise labeling, body part proposal and kinematic tree search steps. It doesn't involve any pre-processing of the input data [2]. While Skeltrack takes a buffer containing the depth image. From the depth image in the buffer a search for extreme points is performed [4]. Starting from those points the position for other joints is computed using heuristics and mathematics [4].

Skeltrack is implemented to track only upper body joints while, RGB-D has full body skeleton extraction ability [2, 4]. In this paper we are focused only on the upper body skeleton tracking. A common dataset of human motions is generated which is used as a ground truth data. Evaluation metrics and comparative results are presented here.

2   Related Works

Motion capture has been considered as a way for imitation learning of a robot from humans doing some motion in human-robot interaction/collaboration applications [5].

Marker based solutions, which are the most available real-time motion tracking methods in the market, are being used for most motion capture applications. In the work of Ott [6] and Shon [7] markers are attached to the body to get the measure of body position which is used by the tracking algorithm. Even though marker based systems provide a good tracking results, they are expensive and need the user to wear such a suit or a marker every time a person interacts with a robot which makes it inconvenient to use and difficult to maintain.

Also, the accuracy of joint positions depends on the precise placement of the markers [13]. Marker-less, Vision based methods on the other hand, are usually simple and do not need additional arrangements [13]. The research about this approach, would lead to one big step towards autonomous on line learning movements [8]. Before the introduction of low cost depth cameras, image based techniques have been used widely. But generally they have a drawback of segmenting foreground from background. Due to this they are effective for stationary camera and static backgrounds [2].

The advent of low cost depth sensors has initiated the study of depth-based methods to be considered as the latest tracking solutions. Real time and reliable pose estimation results, which are also robust to occlusions, have been found from tracking systems using multiple depth sensors [9]. But since our task is to use the data collected by the depth sensor on the robot's head, they are not very much convenient. Monocular kinect based approaches by Shotton [1], OPenNI/Nite and Microsoft Solutions Microsoft Kinect SDK and Microsoft Kinect for windows are the recent and mostly used skeleton tracking solutions. Even though they show good performances, the source code is closed and do not let us do further researching and modifications.

In this study the most recent motion tracking solutions [2, 4] are explored to discover opportunities that push the performance of these methods towards accurate, stable and robust enough, with regard to joint position and joint angle calculations, to be used for robotic motion imitation applications.

3   Experimental Method

After exploring the two algorithms in detail, comparative experiment is done to see the performances quantitatively. Since a common dataset of human motions is required, we have recorded data from both the camera and from the sensor suit, which is considered as a ground truth data, by synchronizing the recordings in time. A small Asus Pro Live Xtion depth sensor is used to record a video data. The ground truth data is captured using the MVN motion capture suit. It consists of inertial sensors which are used to measure translation and orientation of body segments [12]. Although in our analysis we have only consider upper body motions, a full body tracking configuration is chosen to make the dataset useful for other researches. Then we have tested both on a common set of actions by extracting joint positions and joint angles.

The 3D camera was placed at a height of 1.8 m at a distance of one up to two and half meters from the subjects. Two subjects are participated to collect the motion dataset. It was necessary to take body measurements for the calibration of the MVN Moven Motion capture system. Table 1 shows the body segment dimension measures taken for each subject.

Table 1. Body dimensions for the two subjects

Body segment	Body segment measure (cm)	
	Subject 1	Subject 2
Body height	150	172
Shoe size	23	27
Arm span	142	161
Knee height	40	51
Hip height	70	82

We have implemented a Motion Sensor Suit Receiver which uses a UDP network streaming protocol. We have also implemented a software synchronization to start and stop both recordings simultaneously. Every recording has a length of 30–40 s. Both recordings from the camera and the suit are compressed as binary files and dumped on to the Hard Disk which helps to reduce the size of the files and save memory space. A synchronized play back code is also implemented here.

3.1   Synchronized Video and Motion Capture Dataset

In our dataset we have tried to include a wide variety of poses to show the performances of the algorithms in different cases. HumanEvaII provides a complex sequence of action, walking along an elliptical path, jogging and body balancing, which involve a full body motion [11]. Instead in our dataset even though complex sequence of actions is included, we have mainly focused on simple upper body motions which involve hand movements. We started from simple set of upper body motions that involve hand and head movements. Hands stretched to the sides, hands up, hands close to the body, waving one hand and both hands are some of the cases to mention. We took captures of poses with the subjects facing the camera from the side and turning to the back to evaluate the performances of the methods in unusual body positions. We have also included complex motions, such as walking, rotating the whole upper body part to the left and to the right with legs fixed, one hand pointing up and the other down and others. Each pose is repeated two times to insure that a backup is taken. In total we have collected 120 different sets of motion captures.

3.2   Data Processing

The two algorithms are made to run on the recorded binary data, which contains 3D information and camera intrinsic parameters for the calibration purpose, and the outputs are saved as text files. The files contain the 3D locations, given as x, y, z position, of each upper body joint. The data is then imported into Matlab for further processing and analysis. The joint positions are given relative to the global coordinate system of the Xtion sensor. While for the suit, during the calibration step, the global coordinate frame is fixed at the right heel point of the subject (Fig. 1).

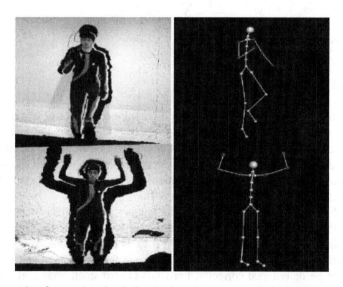

Fig. 1. A snapshot from point cloud play back and reconstructed skeleton from the recorded motion capture data

All the segment positions are computed with respect to this reference frame. Due to the different coordinate systems we did the comparison of the skeleton outputs based on the joint angle measures. From the 3D position of each joint, we have calculated joint angles using Matlab functions. Tracking of elbow and shoulder angles for both right and left side are computed and are plotted with respect to time.

$$\theta = atan2(norm(cross(vec_1, vec_2)), dot(vec_1, vec_2)) \tag{1}$$

3.3   Evaluation Metrics

Robustness of each method is calculated as the rate of detection of a joint or a body part over all frames of a recorded stream. We have used an $L - 1$ norm distance metric to compute joint angle errors and we presented joint angle error plots with respect to time. A list of average joint errors is also included to determine the accuracy of the methods with respect to joint angles we got from the suit. We did a statistical analysis on the joint angle error distribution and precision values are used to explain the tracking ability. Standard error of the mean is used as a way to measure the precision of each set of motions. This parameter measures how close the angle errors are distributed to the average joint angle error. The tracking ability is represented as precision values. It is calculated as:

$$SEM = \frac{SD}{\sqrt{N}} \tag{2}$$

Where, SD is the standard deviation which is computed as

$$SD^2 = \frac{1}{N-1} \sum_{i=1}^{N} (X_i - X_{mean})^2 \tag{3}$$

Where, N is the total number of frames.

4   Results and Discussion

Elbow and Shoulder joint angles for both hands are plotted with respect to time. In each of the plots below, elbow and shoulder joint angles together with angle deviations from the ground truth are listed. For both methods, Shoulder joint angles are better estimated than elbow angles. In addition, the plots illustrate the results in detail to give quantitative explanations. The tables list average joint angle errors for each joint for a video stream with 30–40 s length (Figs. 3, 4, 6 and 7).

In Fig. 2 joint angles are plotted for the subject performing two hands waving motion. This is the pose where the two methods show better performances and give slightly smaller joint angle errors. The reason for this is that for the skeltrack the pose allows detecting all the extreme points (the head and the two hands) and if so, all the rest joints can be determined correctly. For RGB-D also small body parts, hands and elbow points which have lesser chance of being detected, are further from the larger body part (the torso) and hence are detected correctly.

Fig. 2. Figure showing waving the two hands motion

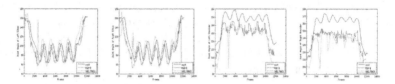

Fig. 3. Joint angle plot for waving the two hands

Fig. 4. A sequence of motions, Y pose, hands down, T pose, hands up, hands down

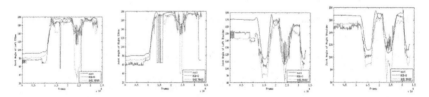

Fig. 5. Joint angle plot for a sequence of motions; Y pose, hands down, T pose, hands up, hands down

Fig. 6. Sequence of motions while turning to the back

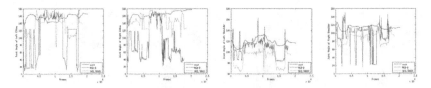

Fig. 7. Joint angle plot while turning to the back

In the second sequence of actions, Fig. 5, due to hands down and hands up poses, joint angle errors are increased for both methods.

The Tables 2 and 3, show that RGB-D gives lesser joint angle error and hence it is a more accurate tracking algorithm than Igalia's Skeltrack. But this works for the subject performing actions facing to the camera. For un-natural poses like, turning to the back and to the sides, RGB-D fails to estimate the pose. Here Skeltrack performance is better. This can be shown from Table 4.

Table 2. Joint angle estimation for two hands waving motion

Joint	Average angle error		Precision	
	RGB-D	Skeltrack	RGB-D	Skeltrack
Left elbow	13.1	18.08	1.99	1.18
Right elbow	18.85	20.63	1.84	1.61
Left shoulder	14.65	18.31	0.45	0.41
Right shoulder	19.29	26.42	0.8	0.54

Table 3. Joint angle estimation for a subject performing a sequence of actions; Y pose, hands down, T pose, hands up, hands down

Joint	Average angle error		Precision	
	RGB-D	Skeltrack	RGB-D	Skeltrack
Left elbow	14.52	18.48	1.17	0.79
Right elbow	10.42	21.26	1.2	0.81
Left shoulder	15.25	20.15	0.81	0.35
Right shoulder	15.75	15.42	2.04	0.52

In all the cases precision values for Skeltrack are lower than RGB-D. This clearly indicates that Skeltrack has better tracking ability. In the source codes RGB-D has no tracking implemented in to it. Each new frame is detected and the pose is estimated without the prior information from the previous frame.

Table 4. Joint angle estimations for the sequence of actions while turning to the back

Joint	Average angle error		Precision	
	RGB-D	Skeltrack	RGB-D	Skeltrack
Left elbow	54.45	31.61	3.44	2.03
Right elbow	73.29	18.96	2.69	1.18
Left shoulder	29.69	15.16	0.88	0.54
Right shoulder	27.64	26.22	2.04	0.52

5 Conclusion

In this paper we have generated a human motion dataset which can be used to quantitatively evaluate skeleton tracking methods. A 3D Asus Xtion camera to record the video and MVN sensor suit to collect the ground truth data are involved in the experiment. A quantitative evaluation scheme is also introduced. Finally two open source tracking algorithms are tested for the application of upper body robot action imitation task. The results demonstrate, RGB-D gives better angle estimations for a variety of poses but for those where the body is facing the camera. We observed a total failure of detection and pose estimation for unusual poses like turning to the side and to the back.

Regarding the tracking ability, skeltrack gives better results than RGB-D producing smooth and stable joint angles.

On average both have shown an angle error of 10–20° which make them hard to use directly for the robot motion control application. By incorporating a tracking algorithm in to the RGB-D method and by compensating the angle error, good results would be found. In the case of Skeltrack, incorporating markers (Inertial Sensors) at the extreme points would improve the accuracy and hence would produce good tracking results.

References

1. Shotton, J., Fitzgibbon, A., Cook, M., Sharp, T., Finocchio, M., Moore, R., Kipman, A., Blake, A.: Real time human pose recognition in parts from single depth images. In: CVPR. Microsoft Research Cambridge and Xbox Incubation (2011)
2. Buys, K., Cagniart, C., Baksheev, A., De Laet, T., De Schutter, J., Pantofaru, C.: An adaptable system for RGB-D based human body detection and pose estimation. J. Vis. Commun. Image Represent. **25**, 39–52 (2014)
3. Baak, A., Müller, M., Bharaj, G., Seidel, H.P., Theobalt, C.: A data-driven approach for real-time full body pose reconstruction from a depth camera. In: Fossati, A., Gall, J., Grabner, H., Ren, X., Konolige, K. (eds.) Consumer Depth Cameras for Computer Vision. Advances in Computer Vision and Pattern Recognition (ACVPR), pp. 70–98. Springer, London (2013). https://doi.org/10.1007/978-1-4471-4640-7_5
4. Joaquim, R.: IgaliaSkeltrack

5. Luo, R.C., Shih, B.H., Lin, T.W: Real time human motion imitation of anthropomorphic dual arm robot based on cartesian impedance control
6. Ott, C., Lee, D., Nakamura, Y.: Motion capture based human motion recognition and imitation by direct marker control
7. Shon, P., Keith, G., Rao, P.N.: Robotic imitation from human motion capture using Gaussian processes
8. Azad, P., Ude, A., Asfour, T., Dillmann, R.: Stereo-based markerless human motion capture for humanoid robot systems. In: IEEE (2007)
9. Zhang, L., Sturm, J., Cremers, D., Lee, D.: Real-time human motion tracking using multiple depth cameras
10. The point cloud documentation. http://pointclouds.org/
11. Sigal, L., Balan, A.O., Black, M.J.: HumanEva: Synchronized Video and Motion Capture Dataset and Baseline Algorithm for Evaluation of Articulated Human Motion
12. MVN Sensor suit Manual
13. Ong, A., Harris, I.S., Hamill, J.: The efficacy of a video-based marker-less tracking system for gait analysis. Comput. Methods Biomech. Biomed. Eng. **20**, 1089–1095 (2017)
14. Wang, P., Rehg, J.M.: A modular approach to the analysis and evaluation of particle filters for tracking. In: IEEE Conference on Computer Vision and Pattern Recognition (CVPR), vol. 1, pp. 790–797 (2006)
15. Gross, R., Shi, J.: The CMU motion of body (MoBo) database. Robotics Institute, Carnegie Mellon University, Technical report CMU-RI-TR-01-18 (2001)
16. CMU motion capture database. http://mocap.cs.cmu.edu/

Ethiopian Public Universities' Web Site Usability

Worku Kelemework[(✉)] and Abinew Ali

Faculty of Computing, Bahir Dar University, Bahir Dar, Ethiopia
workukelem@gmail.com, abinewaliayele@gmail.com

Abstract. Usability is the vital aspect of any system for having quality products. There are various models for testing usability. The objective of the study is to assess the applicability of the USE (Usefulness (Usability), Satisfaction, Ease of use, and Ease of learning) model for Ethiopian Universities' web site context. The USE model is evaluated using PLS-SEM method. The study uses three university web sites to test the model. The result found is encouraging. It has found that usability is affected by 53.3% jointly by the considered usability factors. Independently, usability is influenced by user satisfaction, ease of use, and ease of learning by 53.1%, 20.1%, and 6.1% respectively. Based on the result found, user satisfaction is the major determinant for web site usability and the "USE" model is convenient to study web site usability of Ethiopian universities.

Keywords: "USE" · Web site usability · User satisfaction · Ease of use
Ease of learning · PLS-SEM

1 Introduction

The concept of usability is defined by different scholars in a similar manner with a little bit difference. According to Jafari and Sheehan (2002) cited in [13], usability is defined as the extent to which a system supports its users in completing their tasks efficiently, effectively and satisfactory. Usability on the web, may be extended to include ideas like speed, clarity, intuitiveness of navigation, ease of use, readability and personalization.

Usability refers to terms such as ease of use and ease of learning that implied providing users with systems requiring minimum cognitive and physical effort to accomplish users' needs and expectations (Sindhuja and Surajith (2009) cited in [11]).

In the view of ISO cited in [12], usability is "the extent to which a product can be used by specified users to achieve specific field goals with effectiveness, efficiency, and satisfaction in a specified context of use". Usability can also viewed as "a set of attributes[1]" that collectively assess the usability of a product/website.

---

[1] Attribute, factor, construct, latent variable, usability aspect, usability dimension refer the same concept.

© ICST Institute for Computer Sciences, Social Informatics and Telecommunications Engineering 2018
F. Mekuria et al. (Eds.): ICT4DA 2017, LNICST 244, pp. 159–171, 2018.
https://doi.org/10.1007/978-3-319-95153-9_15

The Institute of Electrical and Electronics Engineers (IEEE) also defines usability as "the ease with which a user can learn to operate, prepare inputs for, and interpret outputs of a system or component" IEEE cited in [12].

Usability specifies how easily an object is used. The object can be anything; that is, a machine, process, software application, tool, book or website. Anything, with which a person can interact, should be usable. In case of software applications and websites, usability has been stated as the simplest way by which an average person can use the software or website to achieve certain goals [9].

This research focused on the applicability of the "USE" model. The method concentrates on the attributes of usability; namely, Usefulness (Usability), Satisfaction (User satisfaction), Ease of use, and ease of learning. For assessing "USE" usability method, three university web sites are taken into consideration [1, 2, 5].

The study answers the questions: Whether usability is determined by user satisfaction, ease of use, and ease of learning, and by the combined effect of user satisfaction, ease of use, and ease of learning.

2 Materials and Methods

2.1 Structural Equation Modeling

Structural Equation Modeling (SEM) is a multivariate technique combining aspects of multiple regression (examining dependence relationships) and factor analysis (representing unmeasured concepts-factors with multiple variables) to estimate a series of interrelated dependence relationships simultaneously [8]. SEM is a more powerful multivariate analysis technique that creates greater flexibility that researchers have with the interplay of theory and data ([14] citing Chin 1998). Data analysis using SEM procedures can incorporate both unobserved (latent) and observed variables, but the former data analysis methods (linear regression, ANOVA, MANOVA) are based on observed measurements only [8].

[15] has noted that there are two sub-models in a structural equation model; the inner model and the outer model. The inner model specifies the relationships between the independent and dependent latent variables and the outer model specifies the relationships between the latent variables and their observed indicators. In SEM, a variable is either exogenous or endogenous. An exogenous variable has path arrows pointing outwards and none leading to it. Meanwhile, an endogenous variable has at least one path leading to it and represents the effects of other variable(s). The SEM model showing the inner Vs outer models and exogenous and endogenous latent variables is indicated below in Fig. 1.

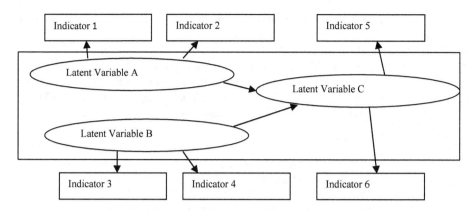

Fig. 1. Inner vs. outer model in SEM

Note: In Fig. 1, elements found inside the box are called inner or structural model; out of the box it is called outer or measurement model.

Partial Least Square-Structural Equation Modeling (PLS-SEM). According to [15], PLS is useful for structural equation modeling in applied research projects even when there are limited participants. PLS is a soft modeling approach to SEM with no assumptions about data distribution. PLS-SEM has been deployed in many fields including behavioral sciences and information system. In this study, among the different approaches of SEM (Covariance based, competent based and variance based), the analysis of variance based approach of the PLS-SEM is used using the SmartPls software.

2.2   The Model

The model is based on [10] usability questionnaire and it is called "USE". "USE" stands for usefulness (usability), satisfaction (user satisfaction), ease of use, and ease of learning. Each of the attributes are described by items or indicators. There are 25 indicators that explain the latent variables (independent and dependent). Respondents are asked to rate each indicator using five point Lickert scale (Strongly disagree, Disagree, Neutral, Agree, Strongly agree). The indicators or items for each attribute or latent variable are indicated below.

Usability items

1. The web site helps me to be more effective (U1)
2. The web site helps me to be more productive (U2)
3. The web site is useful (U3)
4. The web site gives me more control over the activities in my life (U4)
5. The web site saves me time when I use it (U5)
6. The web site meets my needs (U6)
7. The web site does everything I would expect it to do (U7)

Ease of use items

1. The web site is easy to use (eu1)
2. The web site is user friendly (eu2)

3. The web site requires the fewest steps possible to accomplish what I want to do with it (eu3)
4. Using the web site is effortless (eu4)
5. I can use the web site without written instructions (eu5)
6. I don't notice any inconsistencies when I use the web site (eu6)
7. I can recover from mistakes quickly and easily when using the web site (eu7)
8. I can use the web site successfully every time (eu8)

Ease of Learning items

1. I learned to use the web site quickly (el1)
2. I easily remember how to use the web site (el2)
3. The web site is easy to learn to use it (el3)
4. I quickly became skillful with the web site to use it (el4)

User Satisfaction items

1. I am satisfied with the web site (s1)
2. I would recommend the web site to a friend (s2)
3. The web site is enjoyable to use (s3)
4. The web site works the way I want it to work (s4)
5. The web site is wonderful (s5)
6. I feel I need to use the web site (s6)

The following diagram (Fig. 2) shows model of this study, which shows usability and its determinants (ease of use, ease of learning, and user satisfaction) and indicators of each latent variable.

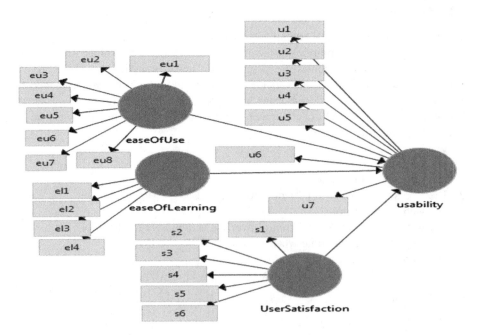

Fig. 2. The study model

2.3   The Data

In accordance with [15], the number of arrows pointing at a latent variable in the model determines, the number of samples to be taken. For a model having 8 arrows pointing at a latent variable in the model, a minimum of 84 samples are required. Since, increasing the sample size increases the model performance, more samples have been taken.

The experiment is done with four categories of data. The first experiment is using Addis Ababa University (AAU) Web site data, the second one is using Bahir Dar University (BDU) web site data, the third experiment is by using Gondar University (GU) web site data, and the final experiment is by merging data collected from the three universities.

The data is collected from undergraduate graduating class students. The reason is that graduating class students have better experience of using their university's web site. The assessment of "USE" method is based on this data collected using questionnaire.

The total data amounts to 541 from 3637 population. 212 data is collected from Addis Ababa University (1344 population), 160 samples are taken from Bahir Dar University (1173 population), and 169 data is collected from Gondar University (1120 population).

3   Results

3.1   Inner Model Coefficients

Path coefficients are numbers on the arrows connected from the independent latent variables (ease of use, ease of learning, user satisfaction) to the dependent latent variable (usability). Refer Fig. 2. Table 1 below shows such results.

Table 1. Inner model path coefficients

	Usability				
	AAU	BDU	GU	All	Average
UserSatisfaction	0.541	0.412	0.608	0.564	0.531
easeOfLearning	0.101	0.110	−0.016	0.047	0.061
easeOfUse	0.209	0.272	0.142	0.181	0.201

In Table 1, AAU means Addis Ababa University, BDU means Bahir Dar University, GU means Gondar University. and All represents all the 3 universities data combined together.

Positive numbers indicate that positive impact on usability. Only ease of learning has inverse relationship in Gondar University data. In all the data categories, user satisfaction is the highest, ease of use is the second and ease of learning with the least path coefficient result.

Based on the result, user satisfaction is the major determinant for usability, ease of use is the second determinant, and finally ease of learning.

Table 2 shows T statistics values, which tests the significance of the path coefficients obtained above in Table 1. T statistics value greater than 1.96 at 0.05 confidence interval indicates the value has significant impact [4]. Thus, on average, user satisfaction and ease of use have significant impact on usability. Whereas, ease of learning is not significant determinant for web site usability.

Table 2. Inner model coefficients significance test

	T statistics				
	AAU	BDU	GU	All	Average
UserSatisfaction → usability	8.0	5.0	6.2	12.7	8.0
easeOfLearning → usability	1.8	1.1	0.1	1.00	1.0
easeOfUse → usability	2.6	2.7	1.4	3.54	2.5

3.2 Outer Model Coefficients

Outer model or measurement model shows indicator reliability to measure the indicated latent variable. They show the paths from a factor to its representative indicator variables (refer Fig. 2). The coefficients are said to be outer loadings, which reflects contribution of the indicator to the latent variable. The square of the coefficients gives the reliability of the indicator. For a well-fitted reflective model, path loadings should be above 0.70 (Henseler et al. 2012 cited in [4]). On the other hand, if outer loading of an indicator is greater than 0.50, it is sufficient [6].

Each indicator's outer loading is greater than 0.5. Some values with less than 0.5 outer loading result are shown in Table 3 below (shaded ones). Based on Table 3, eu4 and eu5 are slightly below 0.5 on average. Others are above 0.5 on average.

Table 3. Outer loading of indicators

	AAU	BDU	GU	All	Average
eu4	0.585	0.461	0.289	0.461	0.449
eu5	0.611	0.507	0.247	0.448	0.453
eu6	0.618	0.578	0.293	0.521	0.503
u5	0.766	0.258	0.76	0.512	0.574

When the significance is tested, all outer loading value is significant on average which portrays that the indicators are representative.

3.3 Measurement or Outer Model Fit

In Fig. 2, arrows go from the factor (ease of use, ease of learning, user satisfaction and usability) to the indicator variables, determines the values of the measured and representative indicator variables. The model fit of this can be done using Composite Reliability, Cronbach's Alpha, Average variance extracted (AVE), The Fornell–Larcker Discriminant Validity criterion, the Standardized Root Mean Square Residual (SRMR), and Heterotrait-Monotrait Ratio (HTMT). The result found is presented below in the following sections.

Composite Reliability. Composite reliability is a test of convergent validity in a reflective model. The result of composite reliability is depicted as follows in Table 4.

Table 4. Composite reliability

	Composite reliability			
	AAU	BDU	GU	All
UserSatisfaction	0.934	0.900	0.904	0.921
easeOfLearning	0.908	0.891	0.881	0.894
easeOfUse	0.879	0.830	0.767	0.835
Usability	0.901	0.869	0.909	0.883

Composite reliabilities should be equal to or greater than 0.6 as indicated by Chin 1998; Höck and Ringle 2006 cited in [4]. Based on this, the result indicates that indicators explain the latent variables well.

The significance test for composite reliability is shown below in Table 5. Since all the values are greater than 1.96, composite reliability is significant.

Table 5. Significance test for composite reliability

	T statistics			
	AAU	BDU	GU	All
UserSatisfaction	121.339	61.202	65.343	154.070
easeOfLearning	69.405	49.251	32.157	96.691
easeOfUse	61.991	41.243	10.953	65.801
Usability	66.682	42.342	73.138	58.609

Cronbach's Alpha. Cronbach's alpha addresses the question of whether the indicators for latent variables display convergent validity and hence display reliability. The result of this study is shown below in Table 6.

Table 6. Cronbach's alpha

	Cronbach's alpha			
	AAU	BDU	GU	All
UserSatisfaction	0.915	0.866	0.872	0.896
easeOfLearning	0.866	0.839	0.824	0.844
easeOfUse	0.843	0.771	0.716	0.783
Usability	0.869	0.818	0.882	0.843

The same cut off applies like composite reliability. So, the indicators are representatives of the latent variables.

Table 7, here under shows T statistics for Cronbach's Alpha. All values are greater than 1.96, which shows Cronbach Alpha values are significant at 0.05 confidence interval.

Table 7. Significance test for Cronbach's alpha

	T statistics			
	AAU	BDU	GU	All
UserSatisfaction	85.167	39.241	42.648	104.983
easeOfLearning	41.259	28.465	26.246	55.554
easeOfUse	40.748	26.343	15.354	47.086
Usability	43.733	24.916	49.968	62.631

Average Variance Extracted (AVE). AVE may be used as a test of both convergent and divergent validity. AVE reflects the average communality for each latent factor in a reflective model. In an adequate model, AVE should be greater than 0.5 (Chin 1998; Höck and Ringle 2006 cited in [4]).

Table 8 shows AVE is better for the 4 latent variables; whereas, slightly below the cut off for ease of use.

Table 8. Average variance extracted

	Average variance extracted			
	AAU	BDU	GU	All
UserSatisfaction	0.703	0.602	0.612	0.660
easeOfLearning	0.713	0.673	0.650	0.680
easeOfUse	0.479	0.386	0.321	0.396
Usability	0.572	0.504	0.593	0.526

Table 9 shows T statistics for AVE. Based on the result, all values are significant.

Table 9. Significance test for AVE

	T statistics			
	AAU	BDU	GU	All
UserSatisfaction	27.6	16.0	16.8	36.5
easeOfLearning	22.6	16.8	14.1	32.1
easeOfUse	15.2	12.8	7.3	19.8
Usability	15.2	12.7	17.2	14.7

The Fornell–Larcker Discriminant Validity Criterion. The Fornell-Larcker criterion table shows the square root of AVE appears in the diagonal cells and correlations appear below it. Therefore, in absolute value terms, if the top number (which is the square root of AVE) in any factor column is higher (which is the case in this study) than the numbers (correlations) below it, there is discriminant validity. Table 10 below shows the result in this study.

Table 10. The Fornell-Larcker discriminant validity

	UserSatisfaction	easeOfLearning	easeOfUse	Usability
	Average	Average	Average	Average
UserSatisfaction	0.802			
easeOfLearning	0.589	0.823		
easeOfUse	0.683	0.680	0.627	
Usability	0.705	0.508	0.604	0.740

The Standardized Root Mean Square Residual (SRMR). SRMR is a measure of approximate fit of the researcher's model. It measures the difference between the observed correlation matrix and the model-implied correlation matrix. By convention, a model has good fit when SRMR is less than 0.08 [7].

For this study, SRMR values are 0.064 for AAU data, 0.077 for BDU data, 0.213 for GU data, and 0.063 for All data combined together. Based on the cut off (0.08), all the models are good except the result for Gondar University data. The significance test result is indicated below in Table 11.

Table 11. Significance test for the standardized root mean square residual

	T statistics			
	AAU	BDU	GU	All
Saturated model	17.1	14.9	13.5	33.4
Estimated model	23.5	23.2	12.7	19.6

Table 11 shows significance result. All T value is above 1.96. Hence, the model is appropriate.

Heterotrait-Monotrait Ratio (HTMT). Henseler et al. 2015 cited in [4] suggest that if the HTMT value is below 0.90, discriminant validity has been established between a given pair of reflective constructs. Clark and Watson use the more strict cutoff of, which is 0.85 [3]. Based on the cut offs, the result of the study shows discriminant validity is established as indicated in Table 12 below.

Table 12. Heterotrait-Monotrait ratio

	User satisfaction	easeOfLearning	easeOfUse
	Average	Average	Average
easeOfLearning	0.625		
easeOfUse	0.700	0.775	
Usability	0.750	0.525	0.625

The significance is high as indicated below on Table 13.

Table 13. Significance test for Heterotrait-Monotrait ratio

	T statistics			
	AAU	BDU	GU	All
easeOfLearning → UserSatisfaction	11.1	13.5	7.3	17.7
easeOfUse → UserSatisfaction	28.4	16.9	9.7	26.0
easeOfUse → easeOfLearning	18.9	11.8	12.4	24.2
usability → UserSatisfaction	24.1	14.6	14.3	33.8
usability → easeOfLearning	10.8	7.70	4.55	12.0
usability → easeOfUse	17.6	11.4	7.6	18.6

3.4 Goodness of Fit for the Structural Model

Structural fit is examined only after measurement fit is shown to be acceptable. In this study, the measurement or outer model is accepted. Hence, the inner model is assessed. The structural or inner model consists of the factors and the arrows that connect one factor to another (in this context ease of use to usability, ease of learning to usability and user satisfaction to usability). R-square and R-square adjusted shows goodness of the structural model.

R-square and R-square Adjusted. R-square, also called the coefficient of determination, is the overall effect size measure for the structural model.

Table 14. R-square and R-square adjusted

	R square					R square adjusted				
	AAU	BDU	GU	All	Average	AAU	BDU	GU	All	Average
Usability	0.603	0.506	0.486	0.535	0.533	0.597	0.506	0.477	0.532	0.528

As shown in Table 14, R-square value for AAU data is 0.603, meaning that about 60.3% of the variance in usability is explained by the model; that is, jointly by user satisfaction, ease of learning and ease of use; 50.06% for BDU data, 48.6% for GU data, 53.5% for all the data, and 53.3% on average.

Note that adding predictors to a PLS-SEM model tends to increase R^2, even if the added predictors have only trivial correlation with the endogenous variable. To penalize for such a bias, adjusted R^2 may be used [4]. Hence, Smaller R^2 values are shown in R^2 adjusted than original R^2 values as indicated in Table 14.

Chin 1998: 323; Höck and Ringle 2006 cited in [4] describes results above the cutoffs 0.67, 0.33 and 0.19 to be "substantial", "moderate" and "weak" respectively. The R-square here would be considered to be of moderate strength or effect. Based on this, both R-square and R-square adjusted have moderate effect in this study.

The significance of R-square and R-square adjusted are shown by Table 15.

Table 15. Significance test for R-square and R-square adjusted

	T statistics R-square				T statistics R-square adjusted			
	AAU	BDU	GU	All	AAU	BDU	GU	All
Usability	13.0	8.3	7.8	16.6	12.6	8.0	7.5	16.4

The result shows, R-square value obtained is significant. Hence, we can say that usability is significantly affected by ease of use, ease of learning, and user satisfaction.

4 Discussion

The result found is good. The USE model can be applied for studying web site usability. The model considers three latent variables to measure usability. These are: ease of use, ease of learning, and user satisfaction. Each of the latent variable is represented by indicators. Indicators reflect the reality of the latent variables. Usability is also represented by its own indicators. Throughout the course of this study, the importance of indicators representation for its own latent variable is seen and the importance of each latent variable has been studied.

The study experiment is carried out in 4 dataset categories: AAU data, BDU data, GU data, and All data. The total data is amounted to 541. The model is appropriate based on model fit results found. So, it is legitimate to discuss the results found and come up with conclusions and recommendations.

The indicators represent the latent variables well but the representation of three indicators for Gondar university data is not significant. These are ease of use 4, 5, and 6. These three indicators are items of ease of use. The variables or indicators are: ease of use 4 (Using the web site is effortless), ease of use 5 (I can use the web site without written instructions), and ease of use 5 (I don't notice any inconsistencies when I use the web site). This result occurred only for Gondar university data. The other one is the impact of usability 5 is not significant for Bahir Dar University data. This indicator is: The web site saves me time when I use it. When the average is considered from the four experiments the indicators are better representative of the latent variables.

Based on the experiments, it is found that the three latent variables have positive effect on usability. One exceptional result is ease of learning negatively related to usability in Gondar university's data.

Though the result indicates positive relationship, ease of learning has no significant impact on usability. User satisfaction and ease of use has significant impact on usability. Here again, Gondar University data shows insignificant impact of ease of use for usability. User satisfaction resulted higher relationship with usability followed by ease of use and ease of learning. The combined effect of all the three latent variables (ease of use, ease of learning, and user satisfaction) on usability is significant.

The following recommendations are forwarded that are thought to improve the result and discover different aspects.

In this study 25 indictors are used to represent factors or latent variables. Additional indicators may be employed for factor representation. Even different indicators for the same construct can be employed and the effect can be tested.

In this study, three aspects of usability has been studied. Other factors like memorability, efficiency, error, etc. can be included for usability study.

The path model used in this study is from the latent variables (ease of use, ease of learning, user satisfaction) to usability. Other path models can be used and the effect can be seen to test usability.

The model used can be seen by increasing the number of data and the number of universities in order to improve the result.

This study is done on educational web site. The study can be extended to assess usability model based on different types of web sites like: e-commerce web sites, government web sites, etc.

The model can also be tested on software products other than web sites. The products can be web applications or desktop applications like registrar systems, financial systems, human resource systems, etc.

The method employed for this study is PLS-SEM. Different methods can be used for testing the model, like: PLS regression, CB-SEM.

The questionnaire used in this study is 5 point licker scale (strongly agree, agree, neutral, disagree, strongly disagree); specially, for the indicator variables. Seven point licker scale (strongly agree, somewhat agree, agree, neutral, somewhat disagree, disagree, strongly disagree) can also be tried to test the model.

5   Conclusion

Usability is at the heart of any product for continuous improvement. Different methods are available for usability measurement. The one which is assessed in this study is USE model for usability. Based on the results found the following conclusions are made.

- The assessment of model indicated that the structural equation model used is appropriate.
- It is found that the selected indicators based on USE model are better representatives of the factors of usability or latent variables (ease of use, ease of learning, user satisfaction).
- Usability is highly determined by user satisfaction. The contribution of user satisfaction is 53.1% on average. Hence, user satisfaction is the major determinant for usability.
- Ease of use has 20.1% impact on usability and this impact is significant. The result shows ease of use of web sites is the second important factor for maximizing usability of web sites.
- Even though ease of learning has 6.1% contribution on usability on average, the effect is not significant. This does not mean that ease of learning has nothing to do with web site usability. Ease of learning has some effect but it is less than other factors and not significant enough.

- The combined effect of ease of use, ease of learning, and user satisfaction on usability is significant. The result based on R-square indicated that usability is expressed by the three factors by 53.3%. The result shows the three factors have paramount importance but still there are other remaining factors that can maximize usability of web sites.
- Using the result benchmark we can conclude that USE model can be applied for evaluating university web sites usability in particular and any web site in general.

Acknowledgement. The first thank goes to our God. Next, we would like to express our gratitude to the School of Research and Post graduate Office of Bahir Dar Institute of Technology, Bahir Dar University, for funding this research. The helpful comments of our friends contribute to have best quality questionnaire; specially, we thank Dr. Abate Shiferaw and Mr. Mekonnen Wagaw.

References

1. AAiT: Addis Ababa Institute of Technology. http://www.aait.edu.et
2. BiT: Bahir Dar Institute of Technology. http://bit.bdu.edu.et
3. Clark, A., Watson, D.: Constructing validity: basic issues in objective scale development. Psychol. Assess. **7**, 309–319 (1995)
4. Garson, D.: Partial Least Squires: Regression and Structural Equation Models. Statistical Associates Publishing, Asheboro (2016)
5. GU: University of Gondar. http://www.uog.edu.et/en
6. Hair, J.F., Hult, G.T.M., Ringle, C.M., Sarstedt, M.: A Primer on Partial Least Squares Structural Equation Modeling (PLS-SEM). Sage, Thousand Oaks (2014)
7. Hu, L., Bentler, P.: Fit indices in covariance structure modeling: sensitivity to underparameterized model misspecification. Psychol. Methods **3**, 424–453 (1998)
8. Kripanont, N.: Examining a technology acceptance model of internet usage by academics with in Thai Business Schools. Ph.D. dissertation, Victoria University, Melbourne, Australia (2007)
9. Kumar, M., Yadav, D., Singh, J.: Usability testing for web application. Int. J. Electr. Electron. Comput. Sci. Eng. **2**, 82–84 (2015)
10. Lund, A.M.: Measuring usability with the USE questionnaire. STC Usability SIG Newsl. **8**, 2 (2001)
11. Mentes, A., Turan, A.: Assessing the usability of university websites: an empirical study on Namik Kemal University. TOJET: Turk. Online J. Educ. Technol. **11**, 61–69 (2012)
12. Mustafa, S.: Is an accessible website a more usable one? Senior Honors thesis, Carnegie Mellon University, Pennsylvania (2014)
13. Rezaeean, A., Bairamzadeh, S., Bolhari, A.: The importance of website innovation on students' satisfaction of university websites. World Appl. Sci. J. **18**, 1023–1029 (2012)
14. Saneifard, R.: Exploring factors affecting mobile commence B2C adoption in Iran. M.Sc. thesis, Lulea University of Technology, Sweden (2009)
15. Wong, K.: Partial Least Squares Structural Equation Modeling (PLS-SEM) techniques using SmartPLS. Mark. Bull. **24**, 1–32 (2013). (Technical Note)

Comparative Analysis of Moving Object Detection Algorithms

Habib Mohammed Hussien[1]([✉]), Sultan Feisso Meko[2],
and Negassa Basha Teshale[1]

[1] School of Electrical and Computer Engineering,
Addis Ababa Institute of Technology (AAiT), Addis Ababa University (AAU),
Addis Ababa, Ethiopia
habibmohammed2001@gmail.com, negasabasha4@gmail.com
[2] Addis Ababa Science and Technology University (AASTU),
Addis Ababa, Ethiopia
sultanfeisso@gmail.com

Abstract. Moving object detection plays a key role in surveillance systems, vehicle and robot guidance, regardless of it is a very troublesome task. Detecting as well as tracking objects in the video so as to distinguish motion features has been rising as a concerning research/study area in image processing/computer vision fields. One of the current demanding study area in computer/machine vision domain are humans and vehicles motion video surveillance system in a dynamic environment. It is considered as a big challenge for researchers to design a good detection technique which is computationally efficient and consuming less time. Moving object detection algorithms must be fast, reliable and vigorous to make video surveillance systems so as to avoid terrorism, crime and etc. This paper presents comparison of different detection schemes for segmenting/ detecting moving objects from the background environment. The algorithms are adequate for adapting to dynamic scene condition, removing shadowing, and distinguishing/identifying removed objects both in complex indoor and outdoor. These algorithms are frame/temporal differencing (FD), simple adaptive background subtraction (BS), Mixture of Gaussian Model (MoG) and approximate median filter. These algorithms are appropriate for real time surveillance applications and each of them have their own advantages and drawbacks.

Keywords: Surveillance system · Object detection · Segmentation
Temporal differencing · Gaussian mode · Approximate median filtering

1 Introduction

In computer vision/image processing the focus of research that tries to explore, admire and monitor objects over a succession photographs is Video surveillance system. Object detection and/or monitoring are the most essential and challenging duties in bunches of vision system comparable to surveillance, automobile and self-reliant robot navigation. There have been various studies about motion detection, tracking, classification and activity analysis in the lit. Due to dynamic scene in natural scenes like abrupt illumination and change of climate, motions repetitiveness that cause clutter

© ICST Institute for Computer Sciences, Social Informatics and Telecommunications Engineering 2018
F. Mekuria et al. (Eds.): ICT4DA 2017, LNICST 244, pp. 172–181, 2018.
https://doi.org/10.1007/978-3-319-95153-9_16

(tree leaves moving in blowing wind), motion detection is a troublesome issue to process constantly. Numerous algorithms for detecting objects have been developed in surveillance system. The making/attaining of best surveillance acquires fast, reliable/constant, powerful and versatile algorithm for detecting and tracking moving objects. Identifying/distinguishing object movements from a video sequence is a key and critical task in numerous computer/machine vision applications. This paper exhibits a comparative analysis of 4 types of motion detection algorithms for monitoring outdoor and indoor scenes/environments. These methods are frame/temporal differencing, Background subtraction, Mixture of Gaussian Model and approximate median filtering. At last these four algorithms are compared and assessed.

2   Survey of Moving Object Detection Methods

Identifying the moving pixels (foreground) from the environment (background) is very significant and troublesome. The initial step of a surveillance systems is detecting foreground objects and this step requires efficient algorithm so as to develop reliable, robust and fast system. This paper explores the four key algorithms (background subtraction, frame differencing, approximate median filter and adaptive online Gaussian mixture model) for detecting objects and analyze and test their differences as well as their performances as discussed in the following sections.

2.1   Frame Differencing (FD)

This scheme detects moving regions/pixels by pixel-by-pixel difference of consecutive (2 or 3) frames. FD is very good at adapting the scene changes dynamically but cannot detect whole applicable pixels as well as stopped objects in the scene.

According to Lipton et al. [1], a two-frame differencing scheme can estimate the foreground pixels if the Eq. 1.1 satisfies as follows. A pixel $I_t(x, y)$ can be classified as foreground if the difference between $I_t(x, y)$ and $I_{t-1}(x, y)$ is larger than I_{th}

$$|I_t(x, y) - I_{t-1}(x, y)| > I_{th} \tag{1.1}$$

On the other hand the shortcoming of two frame differencing solved using three frame differencing [2] as illustrated by Collins et al. [3]. Let $I_t(x, y)$ denotes the intensity/gray-level value at position (x) and at time instance n of video image sequence $I(x, y)$ in the range [0, 255]. The two- temporal differencing pixel is moving if it meets the following rule:

$$|I_t(x, y) - I_{t-1}(x, y)| > T_h \tag{1.2}$$

Equation 1.2 cannot detect some of the pixels inside the object even if the object moves due to the uniform color regions. The threshold, T_h, is initially set to a predetermined value and later can be updated as follows:

$$Th_{t+1} = \begin{cases} \alpha * Th_t(x,y) + (1-\alpha)(\gamma * |I_t(x,y) - I_{t-1}(x,y)|), (x,y) \in B_g \\ Th_t(x,y), |(x,y) \in F_g \end{cases} \quad (1.3)$$

If α (updating parameter) set to 0, the background holds the image I_{t-1} and this value becomes similar to two-frame temporal differencing. FD algorithm can detect only the exterior pixels and left the interior pixels which results in holes. The FD methods, initially subtract the current pixel from the past/previous one. Then, the value has compared with a particular threshold. Finally, if the result is larger than the assigned value, then the pixel pertains/belongs to the foreground/detected, otherwise, it pertains to the background/not detected. The FD detection technique is described below.

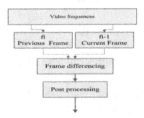

Fig. 1. Block diagram for frame differencing algorithm

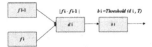

Fig. 2. Temporal differencing algorithm

2.2 Adaptive Mixture of Gaussian Model (MoG)

A dynamic model that can genuinely deal with change of lights, motions repetition, clutter, adding or avoiding objects from the environment and slow motion objects are proposed by Stauffer and Grimson [4]. Since a unimodal model could not manage noise of image acquisition, change of light and etc. for a specific pixel at a time, they used a MoG to denote each pixel in the model [4, 7]. In this model, the values of an individual pixel over time is considered as a "pixel process" and the present history of individual pixel {X1, ..., Xt} is modeled by Gaussian mixture model or K. The probability of looking present pixel value then becomes:

$$P(X_t) = \sum_{i,t}^{k} \omega_{i,t} * \eta(X_i, \mu_{i,t}, \sum_{i,t}) \quad (1.4)$$

Where $w_{i,t}$ is an estimated weight of the ith Gaussian $G_{i,t}$ at time t, $\mu_{i,t}$ is mean value of $G_{i,t}$ and $\sum_{i,t}$ is the covariance matrix of $G_{i,t}$.

The Gaussian probability density function can be:

$$\eta(X_t, \mu, \textstyle\sum) = \left\{ \frac{1}{(2\prod)^{\frac{n}{2}}|\sum|^{\frac{1}{2}}} e^{\frac{-1}{2}(X_t-\mu_t)^T \sum^{-1}(x_t-\mu_t)} \right\} \tag{1.5}$$

The value of K is decided by using the existed memory as well as power calculation/computation. Moreover, the covariance matrix for efficient computation, is described in Eq. 1.6 below, which assumes a unique (red, green and blue) color components which have similar variance.

$$\sum_{k,t} = \alpha_k^2 I \tag{1.6}$$

There are certain procedures for detecting foreground pixels. Initially, K distributions are initialized with defined mean, large variance and minimum prior weight. Then sequence, type and RGB vector of the image will be estimated/determined against K till match is available. Matching is defined as a pixel value in the range $\gamma = 2.5$ standard deviation. Next, the existing weights of K distributions will be updated as follows:

$$\omega_{k,t} = (1 - \alpha)\omega_{k,t-1} + \alpha(M_{k,t}) \tag{1.7}$$

Where
α is the learning rate,
$M_{k,t}$ is 1 for the matching Gaussian and 0 for the remaining distributions.
After this step the existing weights of the distributions are normalized and the matching Gaussian are updated as follows for the new observation:

$$\mu_t = (1 - \rho)\mu_{t-1} + \rho(X_t) \tag{1.8}$$

$$\sigma_t^2 = (1 - \rho)\sigma_{t-1}^2 + \rho(X_t - \mu_t)^T(X_t - \mu_t) \tag{1.9}$$

Where

$$\rho = \sigma\eta(X_t|\mu_k - \sigma_k) \tag{1.10}$$

If no match is found, the Gaussian distribution with the least probability is replaced with a new distribution. Then the first B distributions are chosen as the background model, where B = arg min$_b$ and T is the minimum portion of the pixel data that should be accounted.

$$B = \arg \min_b \left(\sum \sum_{k=1}^{b} \omega_k > T \right) \tag{1.11}$$

If T is very small, the background is unimodal. Accumulated pixels define the background Gaussian distribution whereas scattered pixels are classified as foreground.

When the new frame incomes at times t + 1, a match test is made for each pixel if the Mahalanobis distance is

$$sqrt((X_{t+1} - \mu_{i,t})^T \sum_{i,t}^{-1} (X_{t+1}. - \mu_{i,t})) < k\sigma_{i,t} \tag{1.12}$$

Where k is a constant threshold equal to 2.5.
Then, two cases can occur:

$$\omega_{i,t+1} = (1 - \alpha)\omega_{i,t} + \alpha \tag{1.13}$$

Where α is a certain constant learning rate

$$\mu_{i,t+1} = (1 - \rho)\mu_{i,t} + \rho.X_{t+1} \tag{1.14}$$

$$\sigma_{i,t+1}^2 = (1 - \rho)\sigma_{i,t}^2 + \rho(X_{t+1} - \mu_{i,t+1}).(X_{t+1} - \mu_{i,t-1})^T \tag{1.15}$$

Where

$$\rho = \alpha.\eta(X_{t+1}, \mu_t, \sum_t) \tag{1.16}$$

For the unmatched component, μ and $\sum$ are unchanged, only the weight is replaced by:

$$\omega_{j,t+1} = (1 - \alpha)\omega_{j,t} \tag{1.17}$$

Once the parameters maintenance is made, foreground detection can be made and so on [5, 6].

2.3   Background Subtraction (BS)

A Scheme used for object detection in motionless scenes/environment is BS [6]. BS is performed by subtraction of current/present and reference/background frame to detect moving parts/regions. The pixel difference larger than the threshold is assumed as foreground/detected. After creating a detection pixels map, some morphological post processing (dilation/expanding, erosion/shrinking, and closing) are performed so as to minimize noise and enhancing the detected/foreground regions. The background is updated with new images over time to adapt a changing environment.

The simple type of BS method was presented by Heikkila and Silven as shown in Eq. 1.18 below. A pixel at location (x, y) in the present/current image I_t is marked as foreground if

$$|I_t(x,y) - B_t(x,y)| > T \tag{1.18}$$

is fulfilled where T is a threshold. To update B_T, we use an Infinite Impulse Response (IIR) filter as below:

$$B_{t+1} = \alpha I_t + (1 - \alpha)B_t \qquad (1.19)$$

BS scheme is too much sensitive to change of dynamic scenes but performs well at extracting moving parts regardless of detecting stooped objects. BS algorithm is partially motivated by the research exhibited in [3] as follows.

Let $I_t(x, y)$ denotes intensity value at pixel location (x, y) and image sequence $I(x, y)$ in the range [0, 255]. Let $B_g(x, y)$ be background intensity value for pixel location (x, y) determined over time from video images $I_0(x, y)$ through $I_{t-1}(x, y)$. As BS method indicates, a pixel at location (x, y) in the present/current video image belongs to foreground/detected if it fulfills

$$|I_t(x, y) - B_g(x, y) > T_h| \qquad (1.20)$$

BS provides the most complete features of data. This scheme is successful for lots of surveillance scenarios where objects moving endlessly and the background is visible. The block diagram of BS is shown below.

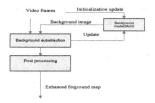

Fig. 3. Block diagram for background subtraction

BS detection algorithm can be described as below.

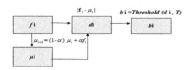

Fig. 4. Background subtraction algorithm

Foreground (region of motion) will be attained, if the difference is larger than thresh.

$$|I(x, y) - Bg(x, y)| > thresh \qquad (1.21)$$

Initially, Bg is the first frame and threshold can be initialized automatically using global techniques. For foreground pixels, FG,

$$Fg(x, y) = \begin{cases} 1, & \text{for } fr\_diff(x, y) > thresh \\ 0, & otherwise \end{cases} \tag{1.22}$$

Where

$$Bg_{t+1}(x, y) = \begin{cases} \alpha * Bg(x, y) + (I - \alpha) * I_t(x, y) \in BG \\ Bg(x, y), (x, y) \in FG \end{cases} \tag{1.23}$$

$$thresh = \begin{cases} thresh & \text{for } (x, y) \in FG \\ \alpha * thresh + (1 - \alpha)(\gamma * (fr\_diff(x, y))) & \text{for } (x, y) \in BG \end{cases} \tag{1.24}$$

From the above equations background and threshold are selectively update at each new frame for non-moving pixels α = rate of adaptation, γ = local temporal average.

2.4   Approximated Median Filter Method

A recursive filter for evaluating an image pixels median is proposed by McFarlane and Schofield [8]. In this scheme the running estimate of median is augmented by 1 if the input pixel is larger than the estimate and decremented by 1 if it is lesser than the estimate. This estimate ultimately converges to median and the median filtering buffers the leading N frames of the video input. then the background frame is calculated from buffered frame and the foreground/detected pixel can be obtained by subtracting the background from the current frame as indicated in Eqs. 1.25 and 1.26 below.

$$F_r > B_g \rightarrow \sum_{n-1.1}^{l,m} B_g(l, m) + 1 \tag{1.25}$$

$$F_r < B_g \rightarrow \sum_{n-1.1}^{l,m} B_g(l, m) - 1 \tag{1.26}$$

Side effects: It did not provide same results in all conditions. But, it needs minimum memory.

2.5   Thresholding

Gray scale image can be obtained from binary image by applying thresholding. A binary image composed of 2 colors, black (zero) or white (one). A careful selection of threshold value is required so as to separate the object from the background. Mathematically thresholding can be expressed as follows.

$$f(x, y) = \begin{cases} 1 & ('255') & f(x, y) > T_h \\ 0 & ('0') & f(x, y) < T_h \end{cases} \tag{1.27}$$

Where T = Threshold value
Any point of (x, y) for which $fr(x, y) \geq thresh$ is called an object point: otherwise, it is a background point. In other words, the thresholded image $ga(x, y)$ is defined a

$$g_a(x,y) = \begin{cases} 1 & if \quad fr(x,y) \geq thresh \\ 0 & if \quad fr(x,y) \leq thresh \end{cases} \tag{1.28}$$

2.6   Post Processing

The outputs of from above algorithms for foreground detection contains noise and therefore are not suitable for extra processing unless post processing is applied, to directly enhance the quality of the segmentation mask.

2.6.1   Morphological Operations (MO)

MO can be erosion/removing, dilation/adding, and hit/miss or cascaded form of them [10]. MO is applied on images with either 0 or 1 pixel values. Erosion scheme is used to shrink extra white noise pixels as well as diminish, the edges using a mask of the same size as shown in Fig. 5. Dilation is used to expand/enlarge the binary objects as shown Fig. 5 below.

Fig. 5. Results of erosion, (a) detected object, (b) structuring element, (c) erosion output.

From the above results we can see that post processing (morphological operations) can remove noises.

Fig. 6. Results of dilation, (a) output after erosion, (b) structuring element, (c) output after dilation

3   Experimental Results and Discussion

3.1   Graphical User Interface (GUI) Design

The GUI enabled us to start, stop and show the program and its results. During the moment the starting button is clicked the system will be running and the selected program will be called to carry out the computations till the stopping button is clicked and the output can be performed as detection.

Fig. 7. GUI layout design

3.2 Comparison of Different Detection Algorithms Result

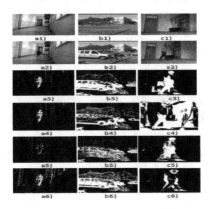

Fig. 8. Outputs of different algorithms, ((a1), (b1), and (c1)) are background images, ((a2), (b2), and (c2)) are video inputs, (a3), (b3), and (c3) are approximate median filter outputs, ((a4), (b4) and (c4)) are background subtraction outputs, ((a5), (b5) and (c5)) are mixture of Gaussian outputs, ((a6), (b6) and (c6)) are frame differencing outputs

3.3 Morphological Operations Detection Results

As shown in Fig. 9 below results are obtained after applying MO. MO take its input by combining the structuring element together with binary images by using a set operators.

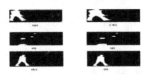

Fig. 9. Morphological operations detection results

4   Conclusions

This paper presents a widespread review of visual surveillance systems describing its phases of object detection. Various approaches of detection and their representation have been explained and compared. Object detection techniques like background subtraction, frame differencing, mixture of Gaussian and approximate median filter are briefly described and a comparative study is also presented. The above four moving object detection methods have compared based on their basic principles, computational time, accuracy and drawbacks are also described.

References

1. Lipton, A.J., Fujiyoshi, H., Patil, R.S.: Moving target classification and tracking from real-time video. In: Proceedings of Workshop Applications of Computer Vision, pp. 129–136 (1998)
2. Wang, L., Hu, W., Tan, T.: Recent developments in human motion analysis. Pattern Recogn. **36**(3), 585–601 (2003)
3. Collins, R.T., et al.: A system for video surveillance and monitoring: VSAM final report. Technical report CMU-RI-TR-00-12, Robotics Institute, Carnegie Mellon University, May 2000
4. Stauffer, C., Grimson, W.: Adaptive background mixture models for real-time tracking. In: Proceedings of the IEEE Computer Society Conference on Computer Vision and Pattern Recognition, pp. 246–252 (1999)
5. Horprasert, T., Haritaoglu, I., Wren, C., Harwood, D., Davis, L., Entland, A.: Real-time 3D motion capture. In: Workshop on Perceptual User Interfaces (PUI 1998), San Francisco, California, November 1998, pp. 87–90 (1998)
6. Atev, S., Masoud, O., Papanikolopoulos, N.: Practical mixtures of Gaussians with brightness monitoring. In: IEEE Conference on Intelligent Transportation Systems, Proceedings (ITS 2004), 423–428 (2004)
7. Zang, Q., Klette, R.: Parameter analysis for mixture of Gaussians. CITR Technical Report 188, Auckland University (2006)
8. McFarlane, N., Schofield, C.: Segmentation and tracking of piglets in images. Mach. Vis. Appl. **8**(3), 187–193 (1995)
9. Haritaoglu, I., Harwood, D., Davis, L.S.: W4: who? When? Where? What? A real-time system for detecting and tracking people. In: Proceedings of 3rd Face and Gesture Recognition Conference, pp. 222–227 (1998)
10. Heijden, F.: Image Based Measurement Systems: Object Recognition and Parameter Estimation. Wiley, Hoboken (1996)

Multiple Antenna (MA) for Cognitive Radio Based Wireless Mesh Networks (CRWMNs): Spectrum Sensing (SS)

Mulugeta Atlabachew[1](✉), Jordi Casademont[2],
and Yalemzewd Negash[1]

[1] Addis Ababa University, Addis Ababa, Ethiopia
mulugetaatlabachew@yahoo.com,
yalemzewd.negash@aait.edu.et
[2] UPC, BarcelonaTech, Barcelona, Spain
jordi.casademont@entel.upc.edu

Abstract. The concept of cognitive radio (CR) rings a big paradigm shift to the wireless communication domain. Extending this concept in to wireless mesh networks (WMN) results a CRWMN which alleviates the pragmatic spectrum congestion in the ISM bands. The assimilation of MAs technology in to CRWMN brings an astonishing system performance improvement. The use of MAs in WMN improves system capacity and reliability, increases coverage area and spectrum usage efficiency; and result in lower power consumption, better interference cancellation, efficient spectrum sensing, and spectrum sharing. In spite of the significant advantages, the use of multiple antennas has considerable limitations. In this paper, we investigate the challenges, opportunities, and the possible research directions that the cognitive radio network (CRN) in general and the CRWMN in particular experience while incorporating MAs to the system and its effect on spectrum sensing.

Keywords: Multiple antennas · Beamfoming · WMN · CRN
CRWMN · Spectrum sensing

1 Introduction

Capacity, flexibility, reliability and security are the most pressing problems of the current wireless networks. In these respect, WMN is a superior networking paradigm with huge network capacity and reliability gains. WMN is a better network paradigm because it is a dynamically self-organized and self-configured, with the nodes in the network automatically establishing and maintaining mesh connectivity among themselves.

The design of WMNs has evolved from single-radio single-channel architecture to single-radio multi-channel architecture then to multi-radio multi-channel (MRMC) architecture to bring considerable capacity gain, but connectivity and interference still remains being the most critical challenges for the WMN. These problems can be alleviated by availing additional bandwidth. The ideal solution for these problems is to add cognition flavor to the conventional WMNs architecture, i.e. to help conventional

F. Mekuria et al. (Eds.): ICT4DA 2017, LNICST 244, pp. 182–192, 2018.
https://doi.org/10.1007/978-3-319-95153-9_17

WMNs evolve to CRWMN. CRWMN is a marriage of WMN and CR technology where the active players of the WMN are equipped with CR technology. The integration of CR in to the WMNs brings many advantages, among others reduced spectrum scarcity, increased network, integration of heterogeneous wireless access networks [1–6].

In this paper we are interested to explore the impacts of MAs in terms of capacity gain and, SS on CRN in general and to the CRWMN in particular. Therefore, the challenges, opportunities, and future directions of MAs technology for CRWMN are investigated in detail.

2 Multiple Antenna (MA) Technology

The use of MAs has three fundamental benefits:- array gain, diversity gain and multiplexing gain. Multiple small antenna elements can be arranged in space and interconnected to produce a more directive radiation pattern which is called array gain. Spatial diversity (SD) and spatial multiplexing (SM) gains are obtained by taking advantage of the spatial signature and sending a replica of the same message by all the elements to reduce BER (SD gain), and by sending different messages concurrently (SM gain) [8, 11].

2.1 Array Gain

Array antenna technology is a more practical way of producing highly directive radiation pattern and it brings the following advantages: narrow beams, low side lobes, steerable beams, tracking multiple targets, it can be conformed to surface, and it scans/steers electronically. In [11], a reference antenna which is located at the origin radiates an electromagnetic field with far field components that are proportional to $F_0 = I_0 \frac{e^{-jkr}}{r} f(\theta, \varphi)$, Where: I_0 is complex amplitude, $f(\theta, \varphi)$ is the radiation pattern, r is the distance of observation, and k is the wave number which is equal to $2\pi/\lambda$. For an N number of identical radiating elements placed in parallel to each other within a volume of radius a, which is much smaller than the distance r (a/r < < 1). The far field components of the ith antenna element, whose position vector with respect to the origin $\bar{r}_i$ is proportional to

$$F_i = I_i \frac{e^{-jk R_i}}{R_i} f(\theta_i, \varphi_i), \quad \text{where } R_i = |r - r_i| = \sqrt{(x - x_i)^2 + (y - y_i)^2 + (z - z_i)^2}$$

The far field due to all of the antenna elements by using superposition principle becomes [8, 11]

$$S(\theta, \varphi) = I_0 \frac{e^{-jkr}}{r} f(\theta, \varphi) \sum_{i=1}^{N} \frac{I_i}{I_0} e^{j\psi_i(\theta, \varphi)} = F_0 AF(\theta, \varphi), \quad \text{Where} \quad AF(\theta, \varphi) = \sum_{i=1}^{N} \frac{I_i}{I_0}$$

$e^{j\psi_i(\theta, \varphi)}$ is array factor, $\psi_i(\theta, \varphi) = 2\pi d_i/\lambda$, Where d_i is the projection of $\bar{r}_i$ on $\bar{r}$, and λ is wave length.

Consider uniform linear antenna (ULA) with N number of elements and uniform distance of separation d with phase $\psi_i(\theta, \varphi) = (i-1)kd \cos \theta$, and the exciting current $I_i = I_0 e^{-j\beta_i}$ at the ith element the array factor expression could be rewrite as

$$AF(\theta) = \sum_{i=1}^{N} e^{j(i-1)(kd \cos \theta - \beta)}$$

Using Taylor Series and trigonometric identity, we can have a closed form expression for the array factor expression which is given by [7–11]

$$AF(\theta) = e^{j(N-1)\frac{\xi}{2}} \frac{\sin(N\xi/2)}{\sin(\xi/2)}$$

Where $\xi = kd \cos \theta - \beta$ and β is the current phase reference, and it is periodical for $\xi = 0, \pm 2\pi, \ldots$

The effect of varying array parameters on the radiation pattern of ULA which holds true for other variants of array antenna is presented both in rectangular and polar plot using simulation in Fig. 1. The simulations show that increased number of array element results narrower beam, increased number of side lobes and nulls; increased distance of separation results in a narrower beam but it is obtained at the cost of antenna size, and excitation phase has no effect on the beam width but it controls the direction of the beam.

2.2   Spatial Multiplexing (SM) and Spatial Diversity (SD) Gains

A system which uses MAs at transmitter (TX) and receiver (RX), known as Multiple-Input Multiple-Output (MIMO) system, is a promising way to augment data rate for the same spectrum and power. The MAs in MIMO systems can be used to achieve diversity and/or multiplexing gains. In SM there is a linear increase in channel capacity with the minimum number of transmit (N) and receive (M) antennas. MIMO systems can be grouped into two groups based on the channel state information (CSI). The first group requires CSI at the receiver, but not at the transmitter. The second group requires CSI both at the transmitter and the receiver ends (beamforming). In MIMO systems, beamforming separates the MIMO channel into parallel independent sub-channels. When the best sub-channel is used, the technique is called single beamforming, and when more than one sub-channel is used it is called multiple beamforming. The output of a MIMO channel is modeled by [12–14].

$Y = HX + n$, Where X is the transmitted signal, H channel transition matrix and n is additive Gaussian noise.

The capacity of MIMO channel is an extension of SISO (single input single output) channel capacity to a matrix form which is given by

$$C = \max_{p(x)} I(X, Y)$$

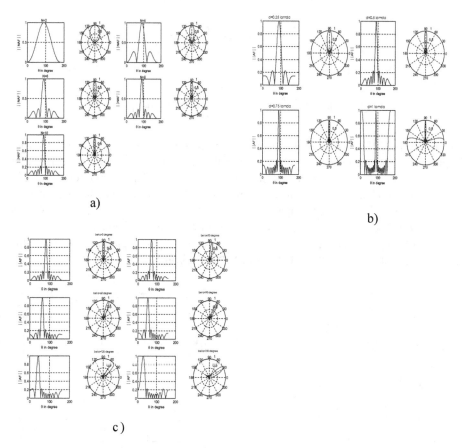

a)

b)

c)

Fig. 1. The effect of varying (a) number of array elements for $\beta = 0^0$ and d = 0.5λ, (b) distance of separation for $\beta = 0^0$ and n = 10, (c) excitation phase between adjacent elements, d = 0.5λ on the radiation pattern.

The maximization of I(X,Y) for full channel state information (CSI) only at the receiver with uniform power allocation yields the capacity expression

$$C = w \log_2 \det(I_m + \frac{P}{N\delta^2} Q),$$

Where Q = HH*, for M < N and H * H for M $\geq$ N, P it the total transmitted power, w is the bandwidth.

Using singular value decomposition (SVD) we can write H as $H = UDV^*$. Where D is M × N diagonal matrix, U and V are M × M and N × N unitary matrices respectively. For M × N matrix H, the rank is at most equals to m = min(M,N). This implies that there are at most m non-zero eigenvalues. The capacity expression then reduces to [12]

$$C = w \sum_{i=1}^{r} \log_2(1 + \frac{p_{ri}}{\delta^2}) = w \log_2 \prod_{i=1}^{r} (1 + \frac{\lambda_i P}{n_T \delta^2}), \quad p_{ri} = \frac{\lambda_i P}{n_T}.$$

Whereas SISO's channel capacity is given by

$$C = w \log(1 + \frac{P}{\delta^2}|h|^2), \text{ where } |h|^2 \text{ is the path gain.}$$

Therefore, MIMO's channel capacity can be interpreted as the sum of the channel capacities of the sub-channels with channel path gain λ_i, i = 1,2,...r. i.e. we can have a maximum of min(M,N) independent paths through which independent information can be sent. If the channel coefficients are random variables, the above channel capacity expressions give instantaneous capacity values and the ergodic channel capacity becomes $C = E[w \log_2 \det(I_m + \frac{P}{N\delta^2} Q)]$, Where E is an expectation operator.

The simulations shown below in Fig. 2 show the capacity gain observed for different SNR values for MISO, SIMO, and MIMO system.

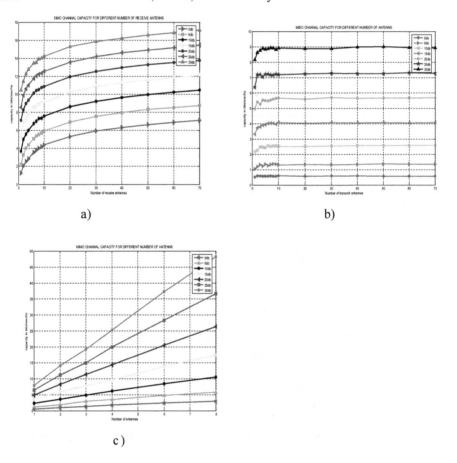

Fig. 2. (a) Capacity of receive diversity for different SNR values, (b) Capacity of transmit diversity for different SNR values, (c) Capacity of MIMO channel for different SNR values

3   Impact of MAs on the Capacity of CRNs and WMNs

In the wireless domain the impact of MAs on network performance is astonishingly immense. Now we shall examine the influence of MAs on the performance of CRNs in general and on the CRWMN in particular.

In [15], the upper and lower bound capacity for MAs based CRs have been developed. In [16], the authors analyzed the sum throughput of an underlay multiuser CR system with MA base stations operating either in the multiple access channel (MAC) or broadcast channel (BC) mode where both the users are equipped with MAs. In the model, there are N (primary) and n (secondary) users with their base stations having M and m antennas, respectively. For primary BC network with a set of interference power constraints on the primary, the maximum throughput of the secondary MAC grows as $\frac{m}{N+1}\log n$ and for primary MAC it grows as $\frac{m}{M+1}\log n$. For the secondary BC they have shown that the throughput can grow as $m\log\log n$ in the presence of primary BC or MAC, thus the growth rate of the throughput is unaffected by the presence of the primary system.

In [17], they have shown that directional antenna (MA) improves the performance of WMNs in contrast to the omnidirectional antenna. It is also observed that increasing the number of antennas and decreasing the beam width increases the capacity of the WMN. Moreover, in [18] it is shown that there is a capacity gain by using directional antennas (MA) in random adhoc network both at the transmitter and receiver. In [19], it is also shown that using directional antennas in MRMC WMN improves the throughputs by up to 231% and reduces packet delay drastically compared to omni-directional MRMC WMN. In [20], the advantages of smart antennas to the WMNs are explored and it is noted that the use of smart antennas enhances the capacity of WMNs.

4   Spectrum Sensing (SS) Using MA for CRWMNs

SS in CR is a process of detecting the primary transmitter. Sensing time, system complexity, and probability of false alarm, detection and miss detection can be used to evaluate the performance of different SS techniques. The most common SS methods for CRNs are Likelihood Ratio Test (LRT), Matched Filter (MF), Energy Detection (ED), and Cyclo-Stationary feature Detection (CSD) and Eigenvalue based Detection (EVD).

In different literatures the use of MAs for spectrum detection has been explored and found to be a promising candidate in the spectrum detection process of CRNs. In addition to the conventional benefits of MAs, a CR equipped with MAs shows better detection performances and shorter sensing time than single antenna CR systems. Therefore, we have explored different literatures on the use of MAs in CRNs as follows.

In [21], the authors proposed a SS algorithm using MAs receiver. It is a statistical covariance based spectrum detection algorithm which compensate for the noise level uncertainty at the detector. Generally, they have extended the covariance-based detector for MAs receiver, they have derived the decision variable distribution for the case of signal in noise, and they have investigated the noise uncertainty impact to the detector's performance and gave guidelines on how to control the detection probability in case of noise uncertainty.

In [22], the authors presented SS using MAs where the noise and the PU signal are assumed to be independent complex zero-mean Gaussian random signals. They have made performance comparison for Rayleigh fading and AWGN channel. They have considered Generalized Likelihood Ratio (GLR) detectors for three different cases when: channel gains are unknown (GLRD1), channel gains and PU variance are unknown (GLRD2), and channel gains, PU and noise variances are unknown (blind GLR detector). Increasing the SNR, number of antennas, and number of samples improves the performance of all spectrum detectors. They have also shown that the optimal detector can outperform the GLR detectors provided that the optimal detector knows the noise variance accurately. Moreover, it is shown that the GLR detectors are more robust to the noise uncertainty than the optimal detector and ED, and in fact under noise variance mismatch, the optimal detector performs similar to the GLRD1, and the blind GLRD performs slightly better than the GLRD1. When the PU signal is not a Gaussian signal, the performance of the proposed detectors, i.e., blind detector and GLRD1, are acceptable, and the blind detector performs like and even slightly better that the CSD based detector. Generally, the proposed GLR detectors perform better than the ED and almost identical to the optimal detector under noise variance mismatch but it is complex than ED.

In [23], the authors studied the performance of ED using MAs at the CR receivers. They have considered two MA processing methods and analyzed their detection performance. They have derived closed form expressions for the probabilities of detection and false alarm maximum ratio, and selection processing. They have shown that using MAs for SS improves the probability of detection. Moreover, from the two MAs processing techniques maximum ratio processing performs better than the selection processing. For a finite number of signal samples, and in the presence of unknown parameters, the GLRT is optimal in detecting the PU.

In [24], the authors investigated the PU signal detection performance in an OFDM based primary and secondary networks where the secondary user (SU) receiver is equipped with MAs. The square low combining scheme in ED based MAs SS resulted in higher probability of PU detection even at low SNR, and increasing number of symbols increases the detection performance with higher sensing time. Generally, increasing the ratio of symbol period of the primary to the secondary subcarriers makes the probability of detection to decline, and the performance of PU signal detection using MAs is much more better than single antenna ED based OFDM CRN.

In [25], the authors proposed an ED SS which is a parallel, multi-resolution SS technique that uses MAs for the CR users. It has reduced the SS time in a significant way with respect to the serial, fixed-resolution technique, first by sensing the system bandwidth using a coarse resolution and then by performing fine resolution sensing over a small range of frequencies which eliminates sensing the entire system bandwidth at the maximum resolution. It is shown that increasing number of antennas decreases the sensing time approximately by a factor of the number of antennas on the receiver, whereas it is observed that number of antennas and the total number of blocks to be sensed at a fine resolution (α) are inversely related. For the number of points in FFT (N), they have revealed that sensing time decreases almost linearly with N until a point at which it begins to increase (N = 4), which is the optimum number of points for the FFT.

In [26], the authors proposed MA based SS using the GLRT paradigm that make use of eigenvalues of the sample covariance matrix of the received signal vector. By making different assumptions on the availability of the white noise power value at the CR receiver, they have derived two algorithms that do not require prior knowledge of the primary signals which outperform the conventional ED with or without noise power uncertainty. The proposed algorithms are computationally complex but it has shorter sensing time for a given probability of detection and false alarm.

In [27], the authors proposed a suboptimal MAs detector under unknown noise which does not require obtaining the eigenvalues of the spatial correlation matrix. The performance of the proposed detector is better than many EVDs. However, its performance degrades when the noise variance is not uniform across the antenna elements. They proposed another MAs detector based on GLR which performs better for two antennas.

In [28], the authors proposed an affordable CSD based spectrum sensor using smart antenna which is less computationally complex in relative to the conventional SCD spectrum detector but not the ED. It is assumed that the SUs have limited priori knowledge of the PUs' signal characteristics. They have used an adaptive beamforming algorithm for the proposed SS, and it is called the adaptive cross-self-coherent-restoral (ACS) algorithm. They have proposed a universal spectrum sensor that uses ACS algorithm to extract the desired signal from the antenna array measurement and able to decide whether the spectrum is occupied by the PU or by the SU or vacant which is not possible for ED.

In [29], the authors studied the effect of secondary receiver antenna correlation on the performance of ED based SS using MAs. They have derived the detection and false-alarm probabilities, and have shown that the presence of antenna correlation decreases the performance of the spectrum detector by increasing the false-alarm probability, however they have also shown that even if the antenna correlation degrades the performance of the spectrum detection, it can be compensated by increasing the number of antennas of the secondary receiver.

In [30], the authors proposed spectrum detection technique that overcomes the noise uncertainty problem observed in ED while maintaining its advantages using MAs receiver. The proposed spectrum detection method is based on eigenvalues of the covariance matrix of the received signal. It is the ratio of the maximum eigenvalue to the minimum eigenvalue that is used to detect the signal existence. Based on random matrix theories (RMT), they have quantized the ratio and find the threshold. In general, the method can be used for various sensing applications without knowledge of the signal, the channel and noise power.

In [31], the authors proposed a simple non-iterative GLRT sensing algorithm which is obtained based on a fast-fading signal model, offers the best performance in all systems under considerations, including slow-fading channels, fast-fading channels,

MIMO systems, and OFDMA systems. For a small number of signal samples, non-iterative GLRT sensing algorithm significantly outperforms several state-of-the-art SS methods in the presence of noise uncertainty. Its complexity is very small in relative to the computational complexity of the iterative GLRT sensing algorithms.

5   Opportunities, Limitations, and Research Directions on the Use of MA for CRWMN

The use of MAs significantly improves the node capacity and reliability, and in terms of SS MA brings many advantages such as shorter sensing time, robustness to noise uncertainty, better probability of detection, and reduced probability of false alarm. The limitations and possible research directions can be summarized as follows:-

- It is still critically challenging to come up with a low cost reconfigurable, multi-band, and wideband MA systems which can better suit the basic nature of CRWMN.
- So far there is no literature on capacity analysis of MA based CRWMNs. To observe the capacity gain due to MAs in CRWMNs, it is important to make capacity analysis.
- Designing less computational complex SS system using MAs could be a new direction.
- Lack of comprehensive study on MAs based SS in terms of sensing time, robustness to noise uncertainty, increased number of antennas and samples, impact of antenna correlation, computational complexity, and noise variance mismatch.
- There is no single study that evaluates the impact of SS on the performance of the different types of wireless networks.
- Investigating suitable SS technique which better ensemble the unique nature of CRWMNs. Therefore, investigation of suitable MA based SS is mandatory.

6   Conclusion

In this paper one of the basic elements of CRN that is SS, is well explored being associated with MA system. Generally speaking, the use of MA has many advantages like network capacity improvement and connection reliability among others. Besides, the use of MA in SS could bring magnificent advantages to the CRN by providing shorter sensing time, better probability of detection, and lower probability of false alarm. For these reasons, MA based SS particularly GLRT detector (non-iterative) is a promising candidate for CRWMN.

References

1. Ian, X.W.: Wireless mesh networks (WMNs). IEEE Commun. Mag. 43(9) (2005)
2. Tao, H.Z., Gian, I.C.: CogMesh: a cluster-based cognitive radio network. In: 2007 2nd IEEE International Symposium on New Frontiers in Dynamic Spectrum Access Networks, Dublin, Ireland (2007)

3. Anusha, V.S.: Enhancement of wireless mesh network using cognitive radio's. Eur. J. Appl. Sci. **7**(3), 108–113 (2015)
4. Almasaeid, H.M.: Spectrum allocation algorithms for cognitive radio mesh networks. Ph.D. dissertation, Iowa State University (2011)
5. Zhao, Y., Wu, J., Lu, S.: Throughput maximization in cognitive radio based wireless mesh networks. In: 2011 - MILCOM 2011 Military Communications Conference Conference, Baltimore, MD, USA (2011)
6. Mehdi, L.D., Mohamad, Z.D.: A scalable decentralized MAC scheduling for cognitive wireless mesh network. In: The 7th Advanced International Conference on Telecommunications, AICT (2011)
7. Carr, J.: Practical Antenna Handbook, 2nd ed., 574 p. McGraw-Hill (1998)
8. Warren, L.S.: Gray: Antenna Theory and Design, 2nd edn. Wiley, New York (1998)
9. Lo, S.W.: Antenna Handbook: Theory, Application, and Design. Van Nostrand Reinhold, New York (1988)
10. Proakis, J.G. (ed.): Wiley Encyclopedia of Telecommunications, vol. 1. Wiley, New Jersey (2003)
11. Balanis, C.A.: Antenna Theory, Analysis and Design, 2nd edn. Wiley, New York (1997)
12. Lozano, N.J.: Transmit diversity vs. spatial multiplexing in modern MIMO systems. IEEE Trans. Wireless Commun. **9**(1), 186–197 (2010)
13. Goldsmith, A.: Wireless Communication. Cambridge University Press, Cambridge (2005)
14. Zheng, D.T.: Diversity and multiplexing: a fundamental tradeoff in multiple-antenna channels. IEEE Trans. Inf. Theory **49**(5), 1073–1096 (2003)
15. Sridharan, S., Vishwanath, S.: On the capacity of a class of MIMO cognitive radios. IEEE J. Sel. Top. Sig. Process. **2**(1), 103–117 (2008)
16. Li, Y., Nosratinia, A.: Capacity limits of multiuser multiantenna cognitive networks. IEEE Trans. Inf. Theory **58**(7), 4493–4508 (2012)
17. Zhang, J., Jia, X.: Capacity analysis of wireless mesh networks with omni or directional antennas. In: 28th IEEE international conference on computer communications. IEEE INFOCOM. IEEE Communications Magazine, **47**(1), 130–138 (2009)
18. Yi, S., Pei, Y., Kalyanaraman, S.: On the capacity improvement of ad hoc wireless networks using directional antennas. In: ACM MobiHoc 2003, June 1–3, 2003, Annapolis, Maryland, USA (2003)
19. Das, S.M., Pucha, H., Koutsonikolas, D., Hu, Y.C., Peroulis, D.: DMesh: incorporating practical directional antennas in multichannel wireless mesh networks. IEEE Sel. Areas Commun. archive **24**(11), 2028–2039 (2006)
20. Winters, J.H.: Smart antenna techniques and their application to wireless adhoc networks. IEEE Wireless Commun. 77–83 (2006)
21. Ruttik, K., Koufos, K., Jäntti, R.: Spectrum sensing with multiple antennas. In: Proceedings of the 2009 IEEE Systems, Man, and Cybernetics, pp. 2281–2286, October 2009
22. Taherpour, A., Nasiri-Kenari, M., Gazor, S.: Multiple antenna spectrum sensing in cognitive radios. IEEE Trans. Wireless Commun. **9**(2), 814–823 (2010)
23. Pandharipande, A., Linnartz, J.P.: Performance analysis of primary user detection in a multiple antenna cognitive radio. IEEE Signal Process. Soc. (2007)
24. Kuppusamy, V., Mahapatra, R.: Primary user detection in OFDM based MIMO cognitive radio. Parallel Sensing (2009)
25. Neihart, N.M., Roy, S., Allstot, D.J.: Parallel, multi-resolution sensing technique for multiple antennas cognitive radios. IEEE. ISCAS 2007, 2530–2533, (2007)
26. Shen, L., Wang, H., Zhang, W., Zhao, Z.: Multiple antennas assisted blind spectrum sensing in cognitive radiochannels. IEEE Commun. Lett. **9**(2), 814–823 (2010)

27. López-Valcarce, R., Vazquez-Vilar, G., Sala, J.: Multiantenna spectrum sensing for cognitive radio: overcoming noise uncertainty. In: 2010 IAPR Workshop on Cognitive Information Processing, CIP2010. IEEE (2010)

28. Du, K.L., Mow, W.H.: Affordable cyclostationarity-based spectrum sensing for cognitive radio with smart antennas. IEEE Trans. Veh. Technol. **59**, 1877–1886 (2010)

29. Kim, S., Lee, J., Wang, H., Hong, D.: Sensing performance of energy detector with correlated multiple antennas. IEEE Signal Processing Letters. **16**(8), 671 (2009)

30. Zeng, Y., Liang, Y.C.: Maximum-minimum eigenvalue detection for cognitive radio. IEEE Trans. Commun. **58**(1), 84–88 (2007)

31. Font-Segura, J., Wang, X.: GLRT-based spectrum sensing for cognitive radio with prior information. IEEE Trans. (2010)

The Design and the Use of Knowledge Management System as a Boundary Object

Dejen Alemu[1]([⊠]), Murray E. Jennex[2], and Temtem Assefa[1]

[1] Information Systems, Addis Ababa University, Addis Ababa, Ethiopia
dejenfasil@gmail.com, temtim@yahoo.com
[2] Management of Information Systems, San Diego State University,
San Diego, USA
mjennex@mail.sdsu.edu

Abstract. Agricultural knowledge management system (KMS) involves various members coming from different social groups who possess their own knowledge which need to be combined in the system development. However, the current development of the technology ignored the indigenous knowledge of the local communities. The multi-methodological approach to KMS research in action research perspective was employed to understand the design and use of KMS for knowledge integration. Primary qualitative data were acquired through semi-structured interviews and observations. The research shall have theoretical contribution in addressing the incorporation of variety of knowledge in agriculture and practical implication to provide management understanding in developing strategies for the potential of a shared KMS as a boundary object for knowledge integration to support marginalized smallholder farmers.

Keywords: Agriculture · Knowledge · System development · Farmers

1 Introduction

Today, literature is awash with the potential of ICTs as enablers of socio-economic development [1]. ICTs are, therefore, increasingly recognized by the governments of developing countries and being implemented to backing-up different economic sectors, especially to increase agricultural productivity as a strategic priority [2]. Technological advancements have been applied for the betterment of poor farmers and developed tools that are potentially capable of supporting agricultural sector [3]. However, their use and relevance are still alien to the local rural communities [3]. Agricultural knowledge management systems (KMS) are, therefore, unsuccessful to provide the full promised potential of ICTs in developing countries [1, 3].

Agricultural KMS development is a complex team activity involving participants coming from different CoPs, each of them contributing specific knowledge that needs to be incorporated in the IT system. In agricultural KMS, there are participants from different communities of practice (CoPs), who possess indigenous knowledge and scientific knowledge, for example, local farmers and scientific communities, respectively [1–3]. However, little has been realized for the integration of IK with the scientific knowledge in KMS development that can involve relevant participants from

© ICST Institute for Computer Sciences, Social Informatics and Telecommunications Engineering 2018
F. Mekuria et al. (Eds.): ICT4DA 2017, LNICST 244, pp. 193–202, 2018.
https://doi.org/10.1007/978-3-319-95153-9_18

different CoPs. This research is interested in identifying boundary objects which links users from different CoPs. Boundary objects are any objects such as artefacts, documents, terms, concepts, and other forms of reification around which communities of practice can organize their interconnections [4]. Besides, research in KMS development must also address the design tasks faced by practitioners. Accordingly, the research is also interested in understanding the design of technological artifact as a boundary object and investigating the use of it.

2 Literature Review and Theoretical Framework

Davenport and Prusak [5] [p. 5] defined knowledge as a fluid mix of framed experience, values, contextual information, and expert insight that provides a framework for evaluating and incorporating new experiences and information. Despite the fact that knowledge is a key organizational asset, it is a resource difficult to access that is challenging to share, imitate, buy, sell, store, or evaluate [6]. This is due to organization's knowledge is mainly embedded in the minds of its members, working routines and processes, organizational rules, practices, and norms [6, 7]. Jennex [6] stated that in order to make knowledge repository useful, it must capture and store the context in which the knowledge generated such as when it occurred; who is knowledgeable about it; who provided it; and social conditions. It is crucial to understand knowledge with its context in order to facilitate the capturing of knowledge from individuals in agricultural KMS development and making it available for reuse.

Knowledge management (KM) is one that has come to be used to refer to explicit strategies and practices applied to make knowledge as a resource for the organization. Jennex [8] defined KM as the practice of selectively applying knowledge from previous experiences of decision making to current and future decision making activities with the express purpose of improving the organization's effectiveness. KM processes are viewed as cyclic process that encompasses processes and practices concerned with the creation, storing, sharing and applying of knowledge and experience rather than as a linear process. As existing knowledge and experience is applied, it also leads to new knowledge creation, thus the process follows a circular flow and a nonstop process that continuously updates itself.

Organizational knowledge creation and transfers takes place when all four modes are organizationally managed to form a continual cycle: combination, internalization, socialization and externalization [9] (see also Fig. 1).

- Internalization (explicit-to-tacit): this refers to the conversion of explicit knowledge into new tacit knowledge within an individual by learning and experience.
- Externalization (tacit-to-explicit): it refers to conversion of tacit knowledge into new explicit knowledge through narratives and analogies to convey an individual's conceptualization to others.
- Socialization (tacit-to-tacit): this mode refers to the conversion of tacit knowledge to new or other form of tacit knowledge by social interaction, face-to-face interaction, dialogue, and shared experience among members of the organization.

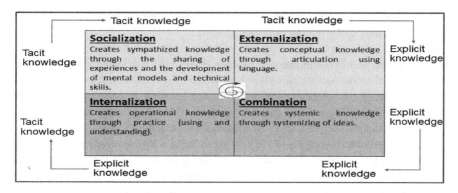

Fig. 1. Nonaka's [9] four modes of knowledge creation and transfer.

- Combination (explicit-to-explicit): the combination mode is the process of recombining discrete pieces of explicit knowledge into a new form [7]. It refers to the creation of new or other form of explicit knowledge from the existing explicit knowledge through manipulation such as merging, categorizing, sorting, reclassifying, modeling, and synthesizing [9].

Previous researches such as Jennex [7] and Jennex and Olfman [10] have suggested that the KM activities need to be supported through KMS in order to foster the organization effectiveness. A KMS, a class of information systems, is a managerial, technical, social, and organizational system structured to support the implementation of KM within an organization, thereby enables organization to manage knowledge effectively and efficiently [12]. A KMS can be seen as an activity system that involves people making use of objects such as tools and technologies to create artifacts and products that represent knowledge in order to achieve a shared goal [7] [p. 167]. It is not, therefore, the technology that distinct KMS from the other type of information systems; however, it is the highly involvement of human activity in their operation and designed to put organizational participants in contact with recognized experts in a variety of topic areas [13].

Web 2.0 tools are today widely used to develop an online KMS in order to understand users' interaction for knowledge sharing and integration. Web 2.0 refers to a set of Web-based technologies such as wiki, blogs, content aggregators, social networking sites, podcasting, and other emerging forms of participatory applications and social media [14, 15]. Web 2.0 tools are characterized by being user-centered, enhance social network formation, promote communication, interaction, and collaboration, and harness collective intelligence [15]; thereby help to systematize the processes of knowledge sharing, creation, and integration. For example, social networking tool can be used for connecting people and locate each other with similar interest; Wiki for collaborative, mediated, content production and organization; blogs enable user to subscribe to a blog and post comments in an interactive format; and real time collaboration tools to provide real time voice communication for interaction and knowledge sharing. These tools are important for KM processes including explicit knowledge publishing and the tacit knowledge extraction, dissemination, integration, and utilization across various CoPs having common interest.

In order to understand the integration of knowledge in agriculture, the theory of situated learning within community of practice (CoP) [16] is selected since it helps in creating a social infrastructure and view knowledge as socially constructed rather than view of knowledge as objective entities. Situated learning is conceptualized as the social context of learning in CoPs and defined as an informal aggregation of individuals engaged in common enterprise and distinguished by the manner in which its members interact and share interpretations [4, 16]. In agricultural KMS development, IK having the tacit format possessed by the local communities needs to be captured and integrated in the system. The theory of situated learning within CoP [16] provides the concept of boundary objects important for understanding knowledge integration across CoPs.

Different communities through time develop their own practices, routines, documents, rituals, artifacts, symbols, tools, conventions, websites, stories and histories [4]. They are any objects that are relevant to the practices of multiple communities, but they may be used and viewed differently by each of CoPs [17, 18], and support collaboration, interaction, and knowledge sharing across CoPs [1]. Boundary objects mediate and coordinate productive breakdowns in collaboration across different social perspectives, distributed organizational workgroups and geographical boundaries [1, 4]. Previous researches are resulted in the identification of wide range of boundary objects in different context, for example, diagrams, system documentations, user training materials, standards, policies, technical extraction, physical prototypes, report printouts [17]. In the context of knowledge sharing and integration in KMS development that involves local rural communities, little have been worked on the identification and roles of boundary objects. In previous researches such as the work of Puri [1], maps (e.g., paper maps and scale models) are served as boundary objects as visualization tools to draw out community expertise and local knowledge, thereby contribute to the integration of IK with scientific knowledge.

Local rural communities and agricultural domain experts possess different knowledge types and individuals in each social groups use boundary objects for their interaction. Additionally, members from different social groups also use shared boundary objects for their interactions. However, the development of agricultural KMS for knowledge sharing in developing countries did not involve the objects possessed by local communities [1, 3]. As a result, the KMS does not allow local communities to use knowledge in the systems and contribute and share their knowledge through it. Information system professionals who develop and support the agricultural KMSs are, therefore, to learn the work practices and objects of each user community. Thus, in the development of agricultural KMS, system developers should involve objects possessed by relevant CoPs in particular local communities in turn the shared KMS as a boundary object enables all relevant participants coming from different CoPs to interact and collaborate for their common practice. As such, this research seeks to investigate the boundary objects possessed by different relevant social groups and integrate in the development of the shared agricultural so as to understand the use of a shared KMS as a boundary object.

3 Methodology

This research followed applied systems development action research approach. Accordingly, the multi-methodological approach to IS research in action research perspective which consists of four strategies including theory building, experimentation, observation, and system development was employed [19]. As stated by Burstein and Gregor [19], theory building refers development of new ideas and concepts, which guides the design of experiments, and conduct systematic observations. The KMS development in agriculture is considered to provide a theoretically relevant organizational setting for this investigation due to the presence of multiple project participants from different communities with differing expertise.

Primary data were collected by employing mainly in-depth semi-structured interviews. Participant observations were also carried out to understand the nature of the working relationships among the various local communities in agricultural practices. Of the total 23 informants, 5, 3, 8 and 7 were selected from domain experts, technologists, extension agents, and farmers, respectively. Data were immediately transcribed using respondents' own words as fast as possible. Through the iterative process of data collection and analysis, the initial concepts were expanded and revised. An agricultural KMS is further developed and applied in order to understand the use of KMS.

4 Result

The research has identified three different social groups in the agricultural KMS development: agricultural researchers, extension agents, and local farmers. Agricultural researchers possess scientific knowledge arises from their educational background, findings of researches and their everyday institutional practices. Local farmers are important source of indigenous knowledge and also use the scientific knowledge and technology from research. However, the KMS development process relies on data extracted from scientific experts and data generated on the basis of recognized scientific principles, draw upon spatial inputs derived mainly from the interpretation of remotely sensed satellite data. This research understood the potential of IK in order to bring the full potential of the KMS in agriculture and the development needs to involve both indigenous and scientific knowledge. In Ethiopian agricultural extension system, there are extension agents who are transferring knowledge and technology from research to local farmers.

Informants from all subjects reported a wide range of boundary objects for knowledge sharing process among others, EthioSIS (Ethiopian Soil Information Systems), oral mapping, audio visual, guidelines, procedure, system documentation, report printout, publication, newsletter, bulletin, user training manuals, websites, and ICT Kiosks. These all support the extension agents as boundary objects while they provide knowledge and technology transfer from research to local farmers. Local farmers employ observation, traditional music and ceremonies, symbols, farming materials, storytelling, oral expressions, and oral mapping for indigenous knowledge sharing which serve as boundary object. However, such boundary objects for sharing IK are not considered in the development of agricultural KMS. Consequently, the development efforts do not fully enable farmers to participate and collaborate in the use of such systems. A shared technological artifact such as a KMS as a boundary object needs to be created through participating all relevant social groups and their need of knowledge and information to establish common ground for different participants and enables to cross the knowledge boundary among participants [4].

4.1 Designing of a KMS

The KMS needs to support the different participants including extension agent as a knowledge broker, local rural communities, and agricultural researchers. To this effect, critical components of the agricultural KMS for knowledge sharing and integration and relevant issues are identified. Following the terminologies presented by Saade et al. [20] and Jung et al. [21], three basic subsystems of KMS for effective knowledge process specifically for knowledge sharing and integration were identified: the people, resources, and technological subsystems.

In building this research, the human subsystem includes the local farmers, agricultural researchers, and extension agents, who are the core of the KMS and it needs to be designed based on the capability of those agents. Table 1 indicated the human agents and their roles in the development of agricultural KMS. In order to share and integrate knowledge, active participation and collaboration among these social groups are highly critical in the KMS development process. There are also extension agents mediating knowledge exchange between the knowledge contributors and the users of the knowledge. Hence, development of the technological artifact as a boundary object is required for sharing and integration of knowledge by paying attention to those people.

Table 1. The roles of relevant social groups in KMS development

Social groups	Roles
Agricultural researchers	Scientific knowledge systems creation, recreation, and presentation Use IK from local farmers for further research Interact with extension agents Evaluate the ongoing implementation of new knowledge and technology
Local farmers	Indigenous knowledge creation, recreation and presentation Use scientific knowledge and technology from research Interact with extension agents and researchers
Extension agents as knowledge brokers	Extension agents exchange knowledge and technology between farmers and researchers, and coordinate the interaction and collaboration among users from different social groups

Resource subsystem consists of knowledge resources from the local and scientific communities, rules including guidelines and procedures for social interaction in system development. There are two different categories of domain-specific knowledge relevant in agricultural KMS development: farmers' indigenous knowledge and scientific knowledge from research. The scientific knowledge includes scientifically processed or analyzed data, which were collected from researchers through field survey, interviews, and observations and from documents such as publications, reports, newsletter, bulletins on soil fertility management and conservation. In the existing agricultural KMS, only the explicit scientific knowledge and procedures are considered and managed statically. However, the indigenous knowledge from local communities which is tacit and embedded in the minds of human being and practice is ignored. Few explicit indigenous knowledge are collected form documented on lesson learned, best practices, and storytelling. However, indigenous knowledge is mostly tacit and collected through ongoing interaction with local farmers in the development and the use of KMS. Explicit knowledge from researchers and local farmers is primarily stored in the knowledge repository of a KMS.

The KMS consists of technological artifact and processes used by users from different social groups to support KM activities [10]. The implementation subsystem entails the use of concepts derived from theory of social learning systems such as the roles and practices of relevant social groups having common interest for knowledge sharing and integration. To this effect, the implementation subsystem is primarily concerned with the identification and development of applications for supporting KM activities in particular knowledge sharing and integration. When investigating the concepts for knowledge sharing and integration, it was discovered that such processes are built on previous knowledge systems. For this purpose, the shared boundary object (i.e., KMS) can support human communication, interaction, collaboration, and negotiation for knowledge sharing and integration from the existing knowledge repositories and maps. The existing explicit scientific and indigenous knowledge are represented in knowledge repositories.

Primarily, users start KM activities through accessing the existing explicit knowledge from different members and knowledge repositories and perform their tasks. Through such processes users can learn new knowledge, expand their existing knowledge and experience. This internalization process converts explicit knowledge to tacit knowledge. Additionally, knowledge users content communication can occur either via acquiring knowledge directly from the knowledge repositories and maps or by constructing meaning from interaction, dialog, and reflection. This socialization process enable users to sharing experiences by observation, imitation, and practice in order to create new tacit knowledge (i.e., tacit-to-tacit). Socialization promotes a mutual understanding by the sharing of mental models [7] which is important precondition for sharing tacit knowledge. The tacit knowledge from different members in particular from local communities with indigenous knowledge highly tacit can be transcribed. Consequently, tacit knowledge from different members can be converted into explicit knowledge. Finally, pieces of knowledge from members coming from different social groups can be shared and combined. For this purpose, through employing the people, the resource and rules, and technological components, a KMS prototype is developed using Web 2.0 tools.

4.2   The Use of the KMS for Knowledge Sharing and Integration

We provided access to 23 informants of this research to the online KMS following its development from January 2017 to March 2017, who were voluntary to participate in the research as respondent and informed in advance. Other users were also joining from different social groups. Finally, participants are observed while using the system and further interviewed for understanding the significance of the shared KMS as a boundary object.

The participants from the rural communities and agricultural researchers access the existing knowledge, enriching dialogue/forum to enhance interaction, contribute their knowledge and create new knowledge. Knowledge contents presented in different languages (i.e., farmers' local language) and presentation of content in different forms (i.e., textual, image, audio, and video) enables farmers and others to easily access information and be able them to interact. Farmers share their own knowledge (i.e., indigenous knowledge) using oral mapping, storytelling, and observation. Hence, audio blogging and podcasting, instant message, and visualization tools employed in the KMS help farmers to access knowledge from others and share their own through posting audio.

During the use time of the online KMS, it has been observed the communication and participation of participants from local communities and research groups who are geographically disparate. Their communication and interaction employed several forms such as text-based (chat), voice and video communication through instant messaging, audio and video conferencing, and podcasting. As such, the attractiveness of these Web 2.0 tools lies in the direct contact between participants whereby highly decrease the feeling of distance among them. Moreover, audio and video communication and mapping in the KMS foster the externalization of indigenous tacit knowledge from local farmers through visualization. The shared KMS is highly important not only to reach too many users geographically disparate and enhances the interaction between researchers, extension agents and farmers but also provide distributed environment to disseminate knowledge two-way instantly. The use of the KMS can also eliminate the existing hierarchical structure of the country extension, which promotes one-way knowledge and technology dissemination from research to local farmers.

The online KMS enable users to connect with others informally in their CoPs and with other users from different CoPs. The social network tools in a shared KMS also enable them to identify the knowledgeable and interact on one-to-one, one-to-many, and many-to-many among users from different CoPs independent of the existing hierarchical structure of the extension systems. Such networking is important for exposing users to different knowledge. Consequently, users from different groups highly communicate, interact and collaborate for their common interest, whereby, knowledge sharing and integration are enhanced.

5   Conclusion and Recommendation

In order to integrate knowledge, it is critical to identify the relevant social groups who are capable of influencing the KMS development, information needs and the knowledge they possess. This research identified relevant social groups in agricultural IS development: local farmers who possess IK, researchers who practices scientific knowledge and extension agents who exchange knowledge. However, result of this research and extant literatures such as Puri [1] and UNDP [2] indicated that knowledge in agriculture have been applied in an isolated and fragmented manner.

Despite the fact that several boundary objects are identified in the agricultural KMS development process for knowledge sharing and integration; boundary objects employed by local farmers for IK sharing, preservation, and integration are not considered in the current KMS development process. In response, a shared KMS for knowledge systems sharing and integration is designed in this research to meet the challenges raised by diverse groups of participants. Thus, a shared boundary objects should be flexible to be used by different participants to promote communication, interaction, and collaboration among relevant participants for sharing and integration knowledge and support them to build shared understanding. The research demonstrated the use of a shared KMS by a large number of users coming from diverse CoPs in a distributed environment. Therefore, KMS using Web 2.0 tools can be implemented for various areas of agriculture with low cost for knowledge sharing and integration. Freely available social Medias with some modification such as Facebook, Twitter, Linked, and Wikipedia can also be used for knowledge sharing and integration in agriculture. Relevant agricultural organizations or policy makers need to understand the roles of Web 2.0 tools for their knowledge management activities.

The research can contributes to the extension of the theory of situated learning in CoP [16] for knowledge integration in KMS development. It also advances the literature on the roles of a shared KMS as a boundary object for knowledge sharing and integration. Practically, the research can provide management understanding in developing strategies for the potential of a shared KMS as a boundary object for the integration and sharing of knowledge ultimately to support marginalized smallholder farmers.

References

1. Puri, S.K.: Integrating scientific with indigenous knowledge: constructing knowledge alliances for land management in India. MIS Q. **31**(2), 355–379 (2007)
2. UNDP: "Promoting ICT based agricultural knowledge management to increase production and productivity of smallholder farmers in Ethiopia," UNDP Ethiopia's Development Brief Series (2012)
3. Masinde, M.: Survivability to sustainability of biodiversity: what do ICTs and indigenous knowledge have to do with it? (2013). http://dx.doi.org/10.1145/2517899.2517900. Accessed 13 Oct 2014
4. Wenger, E.: Communities of Practice: Learning, Meaning and Identity. Cambridge University Press, Cambridge (1998)

5. Davenport, T.H., Prusak, L.: Working Knowledge. Harvard Business School Press, Boston (1998)
6. Jennex, M.E.: A proposed method for assessing knowledge loss risk with departing personnel. VINE J. Inf. Knowl. Manag. Syst. **44**(2), 185–209 (2014)
7. Dalkir, K.: Knowledge Management in Theory and Practice. Elsevier Butterworth-Heinemann, Burlington (2005)
8. Jennex, M.E.: What is knowledge management? Int. J. Knowl. Manag. **1**(4), i–iV (2005)
9. Nonaka, I.: A dynamic theory of organizational knowledge creation. Organ. Sci. **5**(1), 14–37 (1994)
10. Jennex, M.E., Olfman, L.: Development recommendations for knowledge management/organizational memory systems. In: Sein, M.K., et al. (eds.) Contemporary Trends in Systems Development, pp. 209–222. Springer, Boston (2001). https://doi.org/10.1007/978-1-4615-1341-4_18
11. Jennex, M.E., Smolnik, S., Croasdell, D.: The search for knowledge management success. In: Hawaii International Conference on Systems Sciences (2012)
12. Arisha, A., Ragab, M.A.F.: Knowledge management and measurement: a critical review. J. Knowl. Manag. **17**(6), 873–901 (2013)
13. King, W.R.: Knowledge management and organizational learning. Ann. Inf. Syst. **4**, 3–13 (2009)
14. Jennex, M.E.: Knowledge management in support of education. J. Adm. Dev. **1**(2), 15–28 (2007)
15. Wang, W., Xiong, R., Sun, J.: Design of a web 2.0-based knowledge management platform. In: Wang, W., Li, Y., Duan, Z., Yan, L., Li, H., Yang, X. (eds.) Integration and Innovation Orient to E-Society, vol. 252, pp. 237–245. Springer, Boston (2007). https://doi.org/10.1007/978-0-387-75494-9_29
16. Lave, J., Wenger, E.: Situated Learning: Legitimate Peripheral Participation. Cambridge University Press, Cambridge (1991)
17. Rosenkranz, C., Vranesic, H., Holten, R.: Boundary interactions and motors of change in requirements elicitation: a dynamic perspective on knowledge sharing. J. Assoc. Inf. Syst. **15**(6), 306–345 (2014)
18. Brown, J.S., Duguid, P.: Organizing knowledge. Calif. Manag. Rev. **40**(3), 90–111 (1998)
19. Burstein, F., Gregor, S.: The systems development or engineering approach to research in information systems: an action research perspective. In: Proceedings of 10th Australasian Conference on Information Systems, Wellington NZ 1–3 December 1999, School of Communications and Information Management Victoria University of Wellington, Wellington, New Zealand, pp. 122–134 (1999)
20. Saade, R., Nebebe, F., Mak, T.: Knowledge management systems development: theory and practice. Interdiscip. J. Inf. Knowl. Manag. **6**, 35–72 (2011)
21. Jung, J., Choi, I., Song, M.: An integration architecture for knowledge management systems and business process management systems. Comput. Ind. **58**, 21–34 (2007)

Autonomous Flyer Delivery Robot

Tesfaye Wakessa Gussu$^{(\boxtimes)}$ and Chyi-Yeu Lin

Department of Mechanical Engineering,
National Taiwan University of Science and Technology,
No. 43, Sec. 4, Keelung Road, Da'an District, Taipei City 106, Taiwan (R.O.C.)
tesfayewakessa@gmail.com, jerrylin@mail.ntust.edu.tw

Abstract. In this study, we developed a socially interactive service robot with an innovative autonomous flyer distribution function. This robot is equipped with innovative flyer storage and delivery system and could store numerous A5 to A7 flyers sizes and tissue packs at a time. Each flyer passes through an internal channel to reach the palm of the robot, which is configured at a commonly reachable height for the majority of people. Every time a flyer or tissue pack is taken from the palm of the robot, the next flyer autonomously arrives at the robot's palm every 8 s. The developed robot was designed to have autonomous cassette and battery swapping mechanisms and could work exclusively within a localized working zone. Furthermore, it is equipped with strategies for localizing and avoiding obstacles. Thus, the robot was observed to perform flyer delivery without human intervention. The developed robot was displayed in various exhibitions held in Taiwan. The robot was seen to perform the expected task of flyer delivery which proves the robots full commercial value and a huge potential of becoming a product in the intelligent service robot market.

Keywords: Social robot · Autonomous robot · Flyer delivery
Swappable battery and cassette · Localized environment

1 Introduction

These days, various types of indoor and outdoor service robots were developed to fully or partially replace the work of humans and to provide various services. Such human-robot interactions may occur once or multiple times and may have single or multiple users, depending on the sociability and intelligence of the robots. A socially interactive courier robot for hospitals [1] was developed to provide service all day long, every day per week. A social robot [2] that allows the user to exercise twice longer in home thereby cutting down their calorie consumption was developed and thus allowed the user to maintain more intimacy with the robot. However, most people including young and elderly are still seen to be more hostile to such robots [3]. This could be due to the fact that humanoid robots servicing in a home environment require a balance between local autonomy and user intervention [4]. The mobile guest companion robot presented in [5] can interact with the residents in various ways such as teleconferencing, verbal query and behaving with integral privacy policy. Services robots are being designed replace people in areas involving hazardous and heavy-duty industry line, remote areas that are rather difficult-to-access, assist, and provide service on busy roads and in

F. Mekuria et al. (Eds.): ICT4DA 2017, LNICST 244, pp. 203–208, 2018.
https://doi.org/10.1007/978-3-319-95153-9_19

overcrowded areas. However, social robots serving the purpose of flyer delivery is rarely seen in any kind of environmental settings and we believe that no to less attempt is made to develop such kind of robots resembling human in its appearance and performance flyer delivery intelligently. Thus, this introduces a family of socially interactive service robot with autonomous flyer delivering capability through interaction with the recipient when in operation. To equip this robot with the intended functionality of delivering either flyer or pack of tissues wrapped with flyer, the state-of-art-of-the-art development of this robot is achieved by breaking it down into various modules. The design was modularized because of the intricate nature of the mechanism that ensured the smooth operation of flyer delivery. Moreover, flexibility during mechanism development and the rapid deployment of the customized robotic system design were achieved with ease. Furthermore, Since this robotic system consists of different modules that are functionally independent of each other, modularization allows ease of control of each module. The designed robot comprises a supporting rigid frame, flyer feeding mechanism, and flyer picking and forwarding mechanism. A removable cassette with partitioning is developed to enable autonomous cassette swapping. A conveying mechanism is used to transport the flyer and the tissue- packs from the end of the robot's shoulder to its palm. A display unit with a built-in visually interactive images and audio system is integrated into the head of this robot to enable a coordinated and smooth interaction with the recipient autonomously. Finally, a mobile robotic platform is developed to move the robot within its working area.

2   Design Approach to the Developing of Flyer Delivery Robot

The design approach to the development of socially interactive robots can span from human-centered approach [6–8] to affective-centered approach [5] and related approaches. In this paper, a modular design approach is implemented to the design of the flyer delivery robot shown in Fig. 1(a), moreover, new design metrics is set with respect to the performance, delivery capacity and ergonomics to achieve an efficient delivery mechanism. Thus, the mechanical design of the robot was divided into two main parts: the mobile platform module that provided mobility and the upper body module that provided autonomous flyer delivery.

2.1   Performance Specifications of Flyer Delivery Robot

The robot should be able to contain and deliver flyers or packs of tissues wrapped with flyers and to operate autonomously with minimal human intervention.

It should also incorporate an autonomous flyer cassette and battery swapping mechanism.

2.2   Flyer Delivery Capacity Specifications

The robot has a holding capacity of 3000 flyers of A5 to A7 sizes or 600 packs of tissues with 6 mm thicknesses. The average delivery time should not exceed 10 s per flyer or tissue packs.

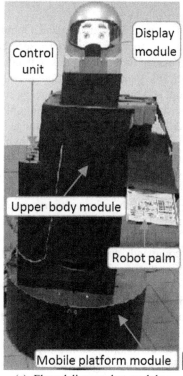

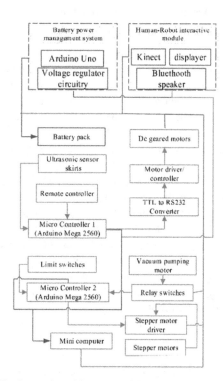

(a) Flyer delivery robot modules.   (b) Control architecture of flyer delivery task

Fig. 1. Flyer deliver robot module and control architecture

2.3 Overall Dimensions of Flyer Delivery Robot

The flyer delivery robot should human-likeness in appearance as it is going to operate among people. Thus, the overall dimensions of the flyer delivery robot were adopted from the anthropometric data and design for ergonomics [9]. These dimensions are summarized in the Table 1. When developing this robot, the minimum height of the robotic palm is designed to provide access to all group of people including kids and disabled persons on wheelchairs. Special consideration is also made to include tall people by setting the robotic height to a minimum value of 0.9 m for ease of comfortable reach when crouching.

Table 1. Overall dimensions of flyer delivery robot

Description	Dimension in meters
Robot maximum height	1.38
Shoulder maximum height	1.09
Robot minimum width	0.551
Robot maximum height	0.612
Maximum height the robotic palm	0.99

2.4   Design of Upper Body Module

The flyer delivery robot shown in Fig. 1(a) consists of upper body module and a mobile platform module. The upper body module comprises a supporting structure for securely positioning the internal mechanisms, a swappable cassette for holding piles of flyers or tissue packs, and a feeding unit having one movable platform. This module also consists of flyer and tissue pack picking, forwarding, and transmission channel as sub-modules. The Tray and the movable platform has a slot for inserting a portioning plate whose usage is dependent on the size of the flyer to be delivered. The feeding, the picking, forwarding and transmission sub-modules are driven by a two-phase hybrid stepper motors. The end-to-end motion of the stepper motors is controlled by the state of the limit switches that are configured at the extreme end of the respective stepper motors. The flyer delivering process is achieved through the coordinated motion of these motors, the limit switches, the reflectance sensor, and the mini-vacuum pumping motor. In This module, the mini vacuum pump is turned on and off during picking and releasing, respectively by using a relay switch. The state of the reflectance sensor configured at the extreme end of the robot palm commands the autonomous feeding, picking, forwarding, and transmission of the top most flyer or tissue pack every time a flyer is taken from the palm. The upper body module has another sub-module integrated in the robot head. This sub-module has a built-in audio and display graphics to facilitate smooth interaction between the robot and receiving people. In general, the flyer delivery process began with the loading of the cassette containing flyers or tissue packs. The system was set to a homing position before feeding took place. At this stage, the feeding distance should be the same as the thickness of the flyer; otherwise, the feeding distance should be adjusted according to Eq. 1

$$feed = n * \alpha \tag{1}$$

where n is the number of steps per revolution for the feeding stepper motor, and α is a constant for adjusting the feed. For example, every time the state of the signal received from the reflectance sensor changes from high to low or it shows a change from the set threshold, the value of α must be 7.5 for the feeding motor running with 200 steps per revolution. As a result, the upward advance of the movable platform is limited to the thickness of the flyer chosen for delivery.

2.5   Design of Mobile Robotic Platform Module

The developed flyer delivery robot only delivers the flyers and tissue packs, interact with people through the display module but also has a capability of avoiding obstacles self-localization within the set working environment. In order to develop this mobile platform, a tri-omnidirectional wheel configuration with circular profile proposed and solved with the help of an optimization tool in MATLAB. Thus, the mobile robotic platform is developed using the optimal design values. This robotic platform obstacle both static and dynamic obstacles using a geometry based obstacle avoidance technique presented in [10].

3   Control Architecture of Flyer Delivery Robot

Socially interactive robots could be controlled in various ways, such as a distributed sensor network system that covers an area of a block in a town with many houses, buildings, and roads. This approach is used to manage robot services by monitoring events that occur in the town with the help of an RFID tag is used for tracking moving people within the constructed 3D geometrical models of large-scale environments [11]. However, a combination of inexpensive microcontrollers and sensors was used in this work. The details of the robot control architecture is shown in Fig. 1(b). Due to independent autonomous operation of the upper body and mobile platform module, the two modules are controlled and allowed to operate separately using two Arduino mega 2560 microcontroller boards. A third microcontroller board, Arduino Uno is used as a master controller and to monitor the battery voltage levels. Finally, a graphical user interface was used to manage the three microcontrollers, the Kinect sensor, and the Bluetooth speaker placed within the upper body module of the flyer delivery robot.

4   Conclusion

A flyer delivery robot comprising the following is designed: a mobile platform module for autonomous movement; an upper body module placed on top of the this platform comprising picking, feeding, forwarding, and transmission sub-modules; a swappable cassette and battery pack module for stacking flyers and tissue pack, respectively; a display and audio sub-module for interacting with people; a Kinect camera for detecting an approaching person; and a control system that mainly uses an Arduino microcontroller. The prototype of this robot is developed at a full-scale and displayed in two exhibitions in Taipei (2016). The robot was seen capturing the attention of most visitors. Following visitors interest, reactions, interaction, and their feedback's, it can be concluded that the affective state and affective quality of the developed robot is positive and acceptable during the interaction.

Acknowledgements. This work was financially supported by the Ministry of Science and Technology of Taiwan (R.O.C) under grant number 103-2221-E-011-104-MY2 at National Taiwan University of Science and Technology, Mechanical Engineering Department.

References

1. Evans, J.M.: Helpmate: an autonomous mobile robot courier for hospitals. In: Proceedings of the IEEE/RSJ/GI International Conference on Intelligent Robots and Systems'. Advanced Robotic Systems and the Real World', IROS 1994, vol. 3, pp. 1695–1700. IEEE (1994)
2. Kidd, C.D., Breazeal, C.: Robots at home: understanding long-term human-robot interaction. In: IEEE/RSJ International Conference on Intelligent Robots and Systems, IROS 2008, pp. 3230–3235. IEEE (2008)
3. Hudson, J., Orviska, M., Hunady, J.: People's attitudes to robots in caring for the elderly. Int. J. Soc. Robot. **9**(2), 1–12 (2016)

4. Kawamura, K., Wilkes, D.M., Pack, T., Bishay, M., Barile, J.: Humanoids: future robots for home and factory. In: International Symposium on Humanoid Robots, pp. 53–62 (1996)
5. Ziegler, A., Jones, A., Vu, C., Cross, M., Sinclair, K., Campbell, T.L.: Companion robot for personal interaction. US Patent 7,957,837 (2011)
6. Vaz, C.J., Wade, E.: Design of a low-cost social robot for children with complex communication needs. J. Med. Devices **10**(3), 030943 (2016)
7. Agah, A., Cabibihan, J.J., Howard, A., Salichs, M.A., He, H.: Social Robotics. Springer, Cham (2016). https://doi.org/10.1007/978-3-319-47437-3
8. Sung, J.Y.: Towards the human-centered design of everyday robots. Ph.D. thesis, Georgia Institute of Technology (2011)
9. Pheasant, S., Haslegrave, C.M.: Bodyspace: Anthropometry Ergonomics and the Design of Work. CRC Press, Boca Raton (2016)
10. Gussu, T.W., Lin, C.-Y.: Geometry based approach to obstacle avoidance of triomnidirectional wheeled mobile robotic platform. J. Sens. **2017**, 10 p. (2017). https://doi.org/10.1155/2017/2849537. Article ID 2849537
11. Kurazume, R., Iwashita, Y., Murakami, K., Hasegawa, T.: Introduction to the robot town project and 3-D co-operative geometrical modeling using multiple robots. In: Christensen, H., Khatib, O. (eds.) Robotics Research, vol. 100, pp. 505–523. Springer, Cham (2017). https://doi.org/10.1007/978-3-319-29363-9_29

Minimal Dependency Translation: A Framework for Computer-Assisted Translation for Under-Resourced Languages

Michael Gasser[✉]

Indiana University, Bloomington, IN, USA
gasser@indiana.edu
http://homes.soic.indiana.edu/gasser/

Abstract. This paper introduces Minimal Dependency Translation (MDT), an ongoing project to develop a rule-based framework for the creation of rudimentary bilingual lexicon-grammars for machine translation and computer-assisted translation into and out of under-resourced languages as well as initial steps towards an implementation of MDT for English-to-Amharic translation. The basic units in MDT, called **groups**, are headed multi-item sequences. In addition to wordforms, groups may contain lexemes, syntactic-semantic categories, and grammatical features. Each group is associated with one or more translations, each of which is a group in a target language. During translation, constraint satisfaction is used to select a set of source-language groups for the input sentence and to sequence the words in the associated target-language groups.

1 Introduction

For the majority of the world's languages we lack adequate resources to make use of the machine learning techniques that have become the standard for modern computational linguistics. For machine translation (MT) and computer-assisted translation (CAT), the lack is even more serious because what is required for machine learning is sentence-aligned translations, which are even less common than monolingual corpora. However, linguistic descriptions and sizable communities of native speakers do exist for many under-resourced languages, including Asian languages such as Telugu and Burmese, African languages such as Amharic and Hausa, and indigenous American languages such as Quechua and Guarani. There is thus a need for frameworks that facilitate the rapid creation of computational grammars and lexica by people and their automatic extension through the limited corpora that are available.

The lack of computational linguistic resources for a language usually correlates with a lack of written material in the language, an even more serious disadvantage for the community of speakers. The gap in available material is easily seen on Wikipedia, where the Amharic edition currently has 13,767 articles

© ICST Institute for Computer Sciences, Social Informatics and Telecommunications Engineering 2018
F. Mekuria et al. (Eds.): ICT4DA 2017, LNICST 244, pp. 209–218, 2018.
https://doi.org/10.1007/978-3-319-95153-9_20

and the Hausa edition 1,504 articles. Compare these numbers with the editions for more privileged languages with comparable numbers of speakers: 1,909,454 articles for Dutch and 1,237,519 for Polish [14]. One way to alleviate this gap between the more privileged and less privileged languages is to accelerate the translation of documents into the under-resourced languages.

For this reason, this project focuses on MT, and especially CAT, into languages like Amharic. The long-term goal is a system that allows users with little or no linguistic experience to write bilingual lexicon-grammars for low-resource languages that can also be updated on the basis of corpora, when these are available, and that can be easily integrated into a CAT system, where they are also updated on the basis of feedback from users.

This paper describes Minimal Dependency Translation (MDT), a lexical-grammatical framework for MT and CAT. The core of MDT is a lexicon of phrasal units called groups. A group's entry specifies translations to groups in one or more other languages. Our focus to date has been on the language pairs Spanish-Guarani and English-Amharic. Examples and implementation details discussed in this paper are from the English-Amharic system, called MIT'MIT'A.

2   Lexica and Grammars

2.1   Phrasal Lexica

The idea of treating phrases rather than individual words as the basic units of a language goes back at least to the proposal of a Phrasal Lexicon by Becker [3]. In recent years, the idea has gained currency within the related frameworks of Construction Grammar [13] and Frame Semantics [6] as well as in phrase-based statistical machine translation (PBSMT). Arguments in favor of phrasal units are often framed in terms of the ubiquity of idiomaticity, that is, departure from strict compositionality. Seen another way, phrasal units address the ubiquity of lexical ambiguity. If a verb's interpretation depends on its object or subject, then it may make more sense to treat the combination of the verb and particular objects or subjects as units in their own right.

Arguments based on idiomaticity and ambiguity are semantic, but they extend naturally to translation. If the meaning of a source-language phrase fails to be the strict combination of the meanings of the words in the phrase, then it is unlikely that the translation of the phrase will be the combination of the translations of the source-language words. Adding lexical context to an ambiguous word may permit an MT system to select the appropriate translation.

2.2   A Simple Phrasal Lexicon

The basic lexical entries of MDT are multi-word units called **groups**. Each group represents a catena [11]. Catenae go beyond constituents, including all combinations of elements that are continuous in the vertical dimension within a dependency tree. For example, in the sentence *I gave her a piece of my mind*, {*I,gave*} and {*gave,her,piece*} are catenae but not constituents of the sentence.

A catena has a head, and each MDT group must also have a head, which indexes the group within the lexicon. The other elements in the group are dependents of the head, but the group has no further structure; it is thus a *minimal dependency structure*. A group's entry also specifies translations to groups in one or more other languages. For each translation, the group's entry gives an **alignment**, representing inter-group correspondences between elements, as in the phrase tables of PBSMT. Entry 1 shows a simple group entry of this sort. The English group <one way or the other> with head way[1] has as its Amharic translation the group <በዚህም ሆነ በዚያ> (*bɛzzihɨm honɛ bɛzziya*) which has its own entry in the Amharic lexicon. In the alignment, three of the words in the English group are associated with positions in the Amharic group; the others (indicated with "0") correspond to no word in the Amharic group.

Entry 1 Group entry for *one way or the other* and its Amharic translation

<one [way] or the other>

→amh በዚህም ሆነ በዚያ
    align:[0,1,2,0,3]

2.3 The Lexicon-Grammar Tradeoff

A rudimentary lexicon with entries of this sort is simple in two senses: given an appropriate interface, a user with no formal knowledge of linguistics can add entries in a straightforward manner, and the resulting entries are easily understood. Such a lexicon permits the translation of sentences that are combinations of the wordforms in the group entries, as long as group order is preserved across the languages and there are no constraints between groups that would affect the form of the target-language words. However, such a lexicon permits no *generalization* to combinations of wordforms that are not explicit in the lexicon. It would require a group entry for every reasonably possible combination of wordforms.

At the other extreme from this simple lexicon is a full-blown grammar that is driven by the traditional linguistic concern with parsimony: every possible generalization must be "captured". Although such a grammar has the advantage of compactness and of reflecting general principles of linguistic structure, it is difficult to write, to debug, and to understand, requiring significant knowledge of linguistics.

In the MDT project, the goal is a range of possibilities along the continuum from purely lexical (and phrasal) to syntactic/grammatical, with the emphasis on ease of entry creation and interpretation.

2.4 Lexemes

We can achieve significant generalization over simple groups consisting of wordforms by permitting lexemes in groups. As an example, consider the English

---

[1] In the figures, heads are enclosed in brackets.

group <lose_v hope>, where lose_v is the verb lexeme *lose*. In order to make such a group usable, the system requires knowledge of verb morphology, either in the form of a morphological analyzer or a list of wordforms associated with each lexeme in the lexicon. For example, the system needs to be able to recognize that *loses* is the third person singular present tense form of the lexeme *lose_v*. MDT assumes such a resource for the source language and in addition a part-of-speech tagger to reduce the syntactic and morphological ambiguity that can result when words are analyzed in isolation.

Because a source-language lexeme will normally be translated as a lexeme rather than a wordform, the system also requires knowledge of target-language morphology, specifically either a morphological generator or a list of wordform associated with each combination of lexeme and grammatical features. For example, the system needs to know that for the Amharic verb ጠፋ (*t'ɛffa*)[2], one translation of *lose*, the forms corresponding to *loses* are ይጠፋል (*yit'ɛfal*) and ትጠፋለች (*tit'ɛfalɛčč*), for masculine and feminine respectively. Entry 2 shows the entry for the expression *lose hope* and its Amharic translation ተስፋ ቆረጠ (*tɛsfak'orrɛt'ɛ*), literally 'cut hope'.

Entry 2 Group entry for *lose hope* and its Amharic translation

```
<[lose_v] hope>

    →amh ተስፋ ቆረጠ
        align:[2,1] ; agr:[(([2,1],(tam:tam,sb:sb))]
```

Because this entry accommodates multiple sequences of English wordforms, we need to map these onto appropriate target-language sequences. This is accomplished through pairs of agreement features for the lexeme, constraining the corresponding target language form to agree with the source form on those features. In the example, the head lose_v and its translation in the Amharic group agree on the tense-aspect-modality (tam) and subject (sb) features. For example, if this group is selected in the translation of the sentence *John loses hope*, the head of the corresponding Amharic group will be constrained to be third person singular present tense: ጆን ተስፋ ይቆርጣል (*ǰon tɛsfa yik'ort'al*)[3] For more about where the features of source-language words come from, see the section on morphosyntactic transformations below.

2.5 Lexical/Grammatical Categories

Another straightforward way to generalize across groups is to introduce syntactic or semantic categories. Consider the English expression *make fun of somebody*.

---

[2] For simplification, Amharic verb lexemes are given in their usual citation form, the third person singular masculine perfect form. In fact they are represented internally in terms of their abstract roots, the sequence of consonants that characterize words in Semitic languages.

[3] In fact the system would also generate the (incorrect) feminine of the verb in this case since the group does not include the subject itself: ትቆርጣለች.

We can generalize across specific word sequences such as *made fun of her* and *made fun of the mayor* by replacing the specific wordforms in position 4 in the group with a category that includes the wordforms that can fill that position. This requires a dictionary of category labels for wordforms. Entry 3 shows how this appears in the lexicon. Category names are preceded by $.

Entry 3 Group entry for *make fun of somebody* and its Amharic translation

<[make_v] fun of $sbd>

   → amh $sbd[+acc] አሾፈ.
      align:[2,0,0,1] ; agr:[([2,1],(tns:tns,sb:sb)),([4,1],(num:num))]

Because group positions that are filled by categories do not specify a surface form, during translation they must be merged with other groups that match the category and do specify a form. For example, in the translation of the sequence *made fun of the mayor*, position 4 in the group <make_v fun of $sbd> may be filled by the head of the group <the mayor>. This **node merging** process is illustrated in Fig. 1.

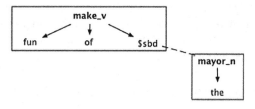

Fig. 1. Merging of two groups in *make fun of the mayor*

Finally, the Amharic group that is the translation of *make fun of $sbd* includes the constraint that whatever word fills the role of *$sbd* in the Amharic sentence must be accusative since it is the direct object of the verb አሾፈ.

2.6 Morphosyntactic Transformations

For languages pairs, such as English and Amharic, that differ greatly in their syntax and morphology, a further elaboration of the framework permits many generalizations that save on the number of groups required. Amharic verb morphology is extremely complex, including tense-aspect-modality, subject and sometimes object agreement, as well as morphemes indicating whether the verb is negative and the main verb of a relative clause. In English almost all of these features are indicated syntactically rather than morphologically. Consider the sentence *they do not know her* and its Amharic translation አያውቋትም (*ayawk^w'atim*). With a different subject, different object, or an affirmative rather than a negative verb, the single Amharic verb translating this sentence would differ. Clearly without including the subject, the object, or the word *not* in groups, there is no way the

Amharic morphology can end up correct. However, doing this entails a significant combinatorial explosion: for each English verb there would need to be hundreds of groups to cover all the different combinations of subject, object, polarity, and tense-aspect-modality.

We can deal with some aspects of this problem by incorporating a pre-processing phase that modifies the English input to make it more like Amharic. Following morphological analysis of the input sentence, it is matched against a set of morphosyntactic transformation rules, each of which may delete words and/or modify the features of words. One of these is shown in Entry 4. This rule matches sequences in input sentences consisting of the words *they do not* followed by a verb. It modifies the features of the verb to make its subject third person plural, its aspect imperfective (corresponding roughly to English present and future), and its polarity negative, and it deletes the first three words of the sequence.

Entry 4 Morphosyntactic transformation rule for *they do not $v*

```
they do not $v[sb=3p,tam=impf,+neg] ; del 1, 2, 3
```

Getting all of this morphology right is a challenge, and the MDT approach only handles some of the cases. Since the morphosyntactic transformation phase does not actually involve a syntactic parse of the input sentence, gaps present a problem. For example, adverbs can intervene between *not* and the main verb in English, in which case a rule such as that in Entry 4 would not apply.

3   Constraint Satisfaction and Translation

The steps in MDT translation are illustrated in Fig. 2 for the input sentence *she made fun of the mayor.*

Following tokenization of the input sentence, the wordforms in the sentence are tagged for part-of-speech and analyzed morphologically (2). Next, the sequence of analyzed words is matched against the morphosyntactic transformation rules (3). In the example sentence two rules match, one for *she* followed by a past tense verb, one for *the* followed by a noun. The first rule assigns perfective aspect to the verb and deletes *she*. The second assigns definiteness to the noun and deletes *the* (definiteness is expressed by a suffix in Amharic). Next the words or lexemes resulting from this first pass are used to look up candidate groups in the groups dictionary (4).

To complete sentence analysis, the system assigns a set of groups to the input sentence. A successful group assignment associates as many words in the sentence as possible with a group, and no word to more than one group, unless that word represents a node merging (see below). Longer groups over sequences of shorter groups. Node merging takes place during this phase; in the example, the $sbd node in the instantiation of the group <make_v fun of $sbd> is merged with an instantiation of the group <mayor_n> (5).

Group selection is implemented in the form of constraint satisfaction, making use of insights from the Extensive Dependency Grammar framework (XDG) [5].

(1) She made fun of the mayor.

(2) she make_v[tns=pst] fun_n of the mayor_n

(3) make_v[tns=pst,tam=prf,sb=3psf] fun_n of mayor_n[+def]

(4) <make_v fun of $sbd><mayor_n>

(5) <make_v[tns=pst,tam=prf,sb=3psf] fun of <mayor_n[+def]>>

(6) <<ከንቲባ_n[+def,+acc]> አሾፈ_v[tam=prf,sb=3psf]>

(7) ከንቲባውን አሾፈች

Fig. 2. Steps in the translation of *she made fun of the mayor*

Although considerable source-sentence ambiguity is eliminated because groups incorporate context, ambiguity is still possible, particularly for figurative expressions that also have a literal interpretation. In this case, the constraint satisfaction process undertakes a search through the space of possible group assignments, creating an analysis for each successful assignment.

During the transfer phase, a source-language group assignment is converted to an assignment of the corresponding target-language groups (6). In this process some target-language items are assigned grammatical features on the basis of cross-language agreement constraints from the source group's entry. In the example sentence, the Amharic verb gets its tam and sb feature values from the English verb, and the noun gets its def feature value from the English noun. A source-language group may have more than one translation; unless specified otherwise, the transfer phase returns all of these.

During the realization phase, surface forms are generated for each target-language group assignment, based on the lexemes and grammatical features that resulted from the transfer phase (7).

4   Related Work

Our goals are similar to those of the Apertium [7] project. As with Apertium, we are developing open-source, rule-based systems for MT, and we work within the framework of relatively shallow, chunking grammars. We differ mainly in our willingness to sacrifice linguistic coverage to achieve our goals of flexibility, robustness, and transparency. We accommodate a range of lexical-grammatical possibilities, from the completely lexical on the one extreme to phrasal units consisting of a single lexeme and one or more syntactic/semantic categories on the other, and we are not so concerned that MDT grammars will accept many ungrammatical source-language sentences or even output ungrammatical (along with grammatical) translations. Because MDT focuses on the translation of phrases and outputs usually outputs multiple translations rather than complete sentences, it is more appropriate for CAT than for full-scale MT.

In terms of long-term goals, MDT also resembles the Expedition project [10], which makes use of knowledge acquisition techniques and naive monolingual informants to develop MT systems that translate low-resource languages into English. Our project differs first, in assuming bilingual informants and second, in aiming to develop systems that are unrestricted with respect to target language. In fact we are more interested in MT systems with low-resource languages as target languages because of the lack of documents in such languages.

Although MDT is not intended as a linguistic theory, it is worth mentioning which theories it has the most in common with. Like Construction Grammar [13] and Frame Semantics [6], it treats linguistic knowledge as essentially phrasal. Like synchronous context-free grammar (SCFG) [4], it associates multiword units in two languages, aligning the elements of the units and representing word order within each. MDT differs from SCFG in having nothing like rewrite rules or non-terminals. MDT belongs to the family of dependency grammar (DG) theories because the heads of its phrasal units are words or lexemes rather than non-terminals. However, it remains an extremely primitive form of DG, permitting only flat structures with unlabeled arcs and no relations between groups other than through the merge operation described in Sect. 2.5. This means that complex grammatical phenomena such as long-distance dependencies and word-order variability can only be captured through specific groups.

5   English-Amharic Implementation

We are in the process of creating an English–Amharic implementation of MDT, called MIT'MIT'A (ሚጥምጢጥ). In doing so, we have relied on the tokenizer and POS tagger from spaCy [12], the Amharic-English dictionary of Amsalu Aklilu [2], the Amharic morphological generator within the HornMorpho system for morphological processing [8], the extensive grammatical descriptions of Amharic, and the author's own knowledge of the grammars of English and Amharic. Although far from finalized, the implementation already contains approximately 7000 groups and 500 morphosyntactic transformation rules. The MDT framework offers a range of possibilities with respect to how many grammatical generalizations are captured through the use of morphosyntactic transformations and category nodes in groups, and MIT'MIT'A falls on the heavily grammatical end of the spectrum. Thus there are transformation rules accommodating combinations of pronoun subjects with all English tenses and modal verbs in both affirmative and negative forms. The result is that the system often, though by no means always, gets Amharic morphology right.

Evaluation of an MDT implementation should be of two types: for accuracy of the translations and for usability of the system with CAT. Since MIT'MIT'A is still under development, we have not undertaken a systematic evaluation of either of these sorts. However, we have begun to informally compare the system's accuracy with that of existing statistical MT systems.

There are several commercial English–Amharic machine translation systems, including Google Translate [9] and Abyssinica Translator [1], developed by Ethio-Cloud. We can highlight the strengths of MIT'MIT'A by examining the grammaticality of the output of Google Translate fpr the grammatical patterns that MIT'MIT'A is designed to capture. MIT'MIT'A knows how to translate all patterns consisting of a pronoun subject followed by a negative or affirmative verb in any of eight possible English tenses/aspects and combinations of modal and main verbs, as well as combinations of transitive verbs with personal pronoun objects. Given the roughly 2,700 English verbs that the system has Amharic translations for, the result is hundreds of thousands of translatable patterns such as *she is about to break it*. Randomly selecting from the possible verb patterns, pronouns, and six common verbs, we get an idea of how well Google Translate performs on such combinations. Of the 54 resulting sentences, Google Translate outputs only one grammatically correct verb. MIT'MIT'A, on the other hand, makes only one minor mistake on three sentences, treating *him* in *write him* as a direct rather than an indirect object. MIT'MIT'A also has the advantage of returning multiple translations when there is ambiguity, for example, translating English *you* in three ways (feminine singular, masculine singular, plural). Needless to say, this is not really a fair comparison since it is based on examples that MIT'MIT'A is designed to handle, but it does give an idea of what sorts of advantages this rule-based system can have over a statistical system for a morphologically complex language in the context of limited training data.

6   Status of Project, Ongoing and Future Work

MDT code, including implementations for Spanish–Guarani and English–Amharic, is available at https://github.com/hltdi/mainumby and https://github.com/hltdi/mitmita under the GPL license.

In order to develop more complete lexicon-grammars for English–Amharic and Spanish–Guarani, we are working on methods for automatically extracting groups from the limited bilingual corpora that are available. We are also implementing an interface for the use of MDT implementations for CAT; working versions for Spanish-Guarani and English-Amharic can be found at https://plogs.soic.indiana.edu/mainumby/ and https://plogs.soic.indiana.edu/mitmita/. Here it will be important to evaluate to what extent translators find their task simplified through the use of the system. Finally, since the interface records the user's translations whether or not they make use of the suggestions from MDT, there is the opportunity to update the system's lexicon-grammar on the basis of those translations.

7   Conclusions

Relatively sophisticated computational grammars, parsers, and/or generators exist for perhaps a dozen languages, and usable MT systems exist for at most dozens of pairs of languages. This leaves the great majority of languages and the communities who speak them even more disadvantaged than they were before the digital revolution. What is called for are methods that can be quickly and easily deployed to begin to record the grammars and lexica of these languages and to use these tools for the benefit of the linguistic communities. The MDT project is designed with these needs in mind. Though far from achieving our ultimate goals, we have developed a simple, flexible, and robust framework for bilingual lexicon-grammars and MT/CAT that we hope will be a starting point for a large number of under-resourced languages.

References

1. Abyssinica Translator. http://translator.abyssinica.com/
2. Aklilu, A.: Amharic-English Dictionary. Addis Ababa, Kuraz (1979)
3. Becker, J.: The phrasal lexicon. In: Schank, R., Nash-Webber, B. (eds.) Theoretical Issues in Natural Language Processing, pp. 38–41. Association for Computational Linguistics (1975)
4. Chiang, D.: Hierarchical phrase-based translation. Comput. Linguist. **33**, 201–228 (2007)
5. Debusmann, R.: Extensible dependency grammar: a modular grammar formalism based on multigraph description. Ph.D. thesis, Universität des Saarlandes (2007)
6. Fillmore, C.J., Baker, C.F.: Frame semantics for text understanding. In: Proceedings of WordNet and Other Lexical Resources Workshop, NAACL (2001)
7. Forcada, M.L., Ginestí-Rosell, M., Nordfalk, J., O'Regan, J., Ortiz-Rojas, S., Pérez-Ortiz, J.A., Sánchez-Martínez, F., Ramírez-Sánchez, G., Tyers, F.M.: Apertium: a free/open-source platform for rule-based machine translation. Mach. Transl. **25**, 127–144 (2011)
8. Gasser, M.: HornMorpho: a system for morphological processing of Amharic, Oromo, and Tigrinya. In: Proceedings of Conference on Human Language Technology for Development, Alexandria, Egypt (2011)
9. Google Translate: English-Amharic. https://translate.google.com/#en/am/
10. McShane, M., Nirenburg, S., Cowie, J., Zacharski, R.: Embedding knowledge elicitation and MT systems within a single architecture. Mach. Transl. **17**, 271–305 (2002)
11. Osborne, T., Putnam, M., Gross, T.: Catenae: introducing a novel unit of syntactic analysis. Syntax **15**, 354–396 (2012)
12. Honnibal, M.: spaCy: industrial-strength natural language processing in python (2016). https://spacy.io/
13. Steels, L. (ed.): Design Patterns in Fluid Construction Grammar. John Benjamins, Amsterdam (2011)
14. Wikipedia (English): List of Wikipedias (2017). https://en.wikipedia.org/w/index.php?title=List_of_Wikipedias&oldid=796394102. Accessed 29 Aug 2017

Massive MIMO for 5G Cellular Networks: Potential Benefits and Challenges

Bekele Mulu Zerihun$^{(\boxtimes)}$ and Yihenew Wondie

School of Electrical and Computer Engineering, AAiT, AAU,
Addis Ababa, Ethiopia
{bekele.mulu,yihenew.wondie}@aait.edu.et

Abstract. The concept of deploying multiple antenna arrays in the base station (i.e. massive MIMO) among other technologies, such as millimeter wave communication and network densification, that it is one of the key enabling methods in the design and development of future cellular networks. Massive MIMO is a disruptive technology; it is considered as a cornerstone in the design of future cellular networks. In this paper, we investigate the benefits of massive MIMO in terms of capacity and energy efficiency. Performance evaluation of massive MIMO is also presented with respect to spectral efficiency and energy efficiency. Moreover, the major challenges for practical deployment of massive MIMO are discussed in details.

Keywords: Massive MIMO · 5G · Cellular network · Capacity
Network efficiency

1 Introduction

In recent years, cellular network operators are facing challenges to satisfy the exponential traffic growth due to the popularity of smart devices. This exponential data traffic growth and continuous emergence of various services and applications triggered the investigation of the fifth generation (5G) for future cellular systems [1].

To address the future high traffic demands, 5G networks is required to be designed to improve the network performance in terms of capacity, energy efficiency, latency, network security and robustness at large [1, 13]. However, the dramatic network performance improvement targeted by 5G could not be achieved by a mere evolution of the legacy network architecture. Therefore, the future cellular network architecture is required to incorporate different new radio access technologies. Thus, 5G is not only envisioned as an evolution of LTE, but it should also consider new potential technologies that were not included in the previous networks. There are many new applications that should be served in 5G, such as machine type communications (MTC), Internet of things (IoT), tactile Internet, connected vehicles etc. [1, 3].

These services and 5G requirements set by 5G-PPP were defined in different test cases, each of them aiming at representing one possible deployment and utilization of 5G. According to different research results, the standardization of 5G will be composed of two radio access technologies: an evolution of LTE, and new radio systems. The

© ICST Institute for Computer Sciences, Social Informatics and Telecommunications Engineering 2018
F. Mekuria et al. (Eds.): ICT4DA 2017, LNICST 244, pp. 219–227, 2018.
https://doi.org/10.1007/978-3-319-95153-9_21

main concept of the new radio system is to use higher frequency bands. Utilization of unlicensed band is also expected in 5G, as used in LTE-Unlicensed.

Software-defined networking (SDN), network function virtualization (NFV), and network slicing and spectrum sharing can be used to improve the network efficiency and minimize the cost of network operators, and in turn for users. To that end, the future 5G cellular network should exploit the potential gains from different emerging technologies including massive antenna arrays (i.e., massive MIMO technologies), deployment of ultra-dense small cells, and utilization of millimeter wave frequency bands.

The rest of this paper is organized as follows: In Sect. 2, we describe the details of five key emerging technologies towards the development of the future 5G cellular network. Comprehensive discussions on basics of massive MIMO, its benefits, associated research challenges, and performance evaluations are then presented in Sect. 3. Finally, a concluding remark is drawn in Sect. 4.

2   Emerging Technologies Towards 5G Cellular Networks

To satisfy the ambitious goals set by 5G-PPP, it is required to evaluate the potential technologies to investigate and produce solutions, architectures, and standards for 5G. As explained in the introductory part, 5G will be composed of different emerging technologies which will bring a revolutionary change in cellular principles. İn this section, we describe five disruptive technologies which lead to both architectural and component design changes, as depicted in Fig. 1.

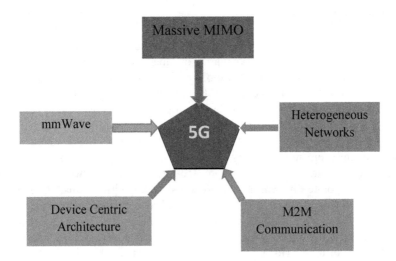

Fig. 1. Five new technologies for the design of future 5G cellular networks.

Device Centric Architecture. In previous network design, the network structure is based on cells in the radio access network. However, in future 5G cellular network design, a device-centric architecture is required. Device centric architecture changes the traditional view, where users and network providers are two different entities. İn device centric architecture, nodes might serve as a relay between a user equipment and BS. For example, with connected vehicles, both vehicle to vehicle and vehicle to infrastructure communications will be important, either to serve users in the vehicle or for new services such as collision avoidance for unmanned cars. Device centric architectural network design will compensate multiple transmission by resource aggregation [2].

Millimeter Wave (mmWave). The frequency spectra in the microwave range currently in use for cellular communication is almost saturated. Therefore, most of the studies consider the millimeter waves as the best candidate to achieve a bandwidth in gigabit range. Millimeter waves refer to the frequency bands in the 3–300 GHz range. Theoretical and experimental studies have been carried out to determine which band is the most suitable within this range. The exponential growing traffic demand in mobile communications and bandwidth limit in RF range has recently drawn increased attention to use spectrum in the millimeter wave bands. Using millimeter wave will increase network capacity in 5G more than 100 times compared to current 4G cellular network [3].

Heterogeneous Networks (HetNets). HetNets are composed of a macro layer, with traditional BSs and small cells using different cell size or coverage within the same network installed in strategic locations. HetNets can be seen as a concept designed for LTE. However, HetNets were used only to improve the network performance locally, whereas ultra-dense network is seen as a cornerstone of future deployments. Ultra-dense networks can be considered as one of the most promising technique to meet the new requirements. While this paradigm is seen as a cornerstone of 5G, densified networks were already present in the existing cellular networks. İn ultra-dense networks, small cells can be deployed within macro-coverage to serve small areas with hotspots. Solutions like carrier aggregation or dual connectivity can be used to boost system performance [4, 5].

Machine-to-Machine (M2M) Communication. Including M2M communication in the design of 5G will change the network architecture and help to satisfy the high data rate requirements using; (i) large number of devices to be connected and operated without human intervention, (ii) guaranteed minimum data rate in all conditions, (iii) data could be transferred in a very short transmission time interval. In M2M, nodes can serve as a relay, or two equipment might communicate together without using the serving base station.

Massive MIMO. Massive MIMO is considered as a promising technology to improve the network performance in the next generation of cellular systems. The gains promised by massive MIMO are augured to overcome the capacity crunch in today's mobile networks and to pave the way for the ambitious goals set for 5G. The details of massive MIMO is presented in Sect. 3.

3 Massive MIMO

3.1 Basics of MIMO Technology

In conventional point-to-point MIMO, user equipment, and BSs are equipped with more than one transmitter and receiver. MIMO is used for spatial multiplexing to improve the data rate where messages transmitted at the same time. However, MIMO technology was fundamentally designed to serve a single user at a time. Massive MIMO is a large-scale MIMO, with hundreds of antenna elements in single BS. A large number of users can be served simultaneously [6].

Massive MIMO is one of the promising technology in the design and development of the future 5G cellular network. It is expected to increase the network capacity by 10 times and energy efficiency by 1000 times compared with the conventional MIMO. Massive MIMO offers numerous advantages. It can be built with inexpensive, low-power transceivers make it robust, secure and use spectrum efficiently. However, high mobility is a challenge in massive MIMO since channel estimation and spatial beamforming required a lot of signaling. A typical massive MIMO network is depicted in Fig. 2. In recent years, Massive MIMO attracts the attention of many researchers due to its promising capability of improving spectral efficiency, energy efficiency, and robustness of the system [6, 7].

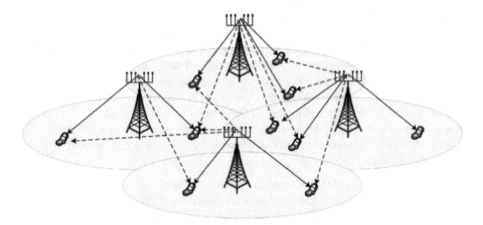

Fig. 2. Illustration of massive MIMO systems.

3.2 Benefits of Massive MIMO for 5G HetNet

As explained in the introductory section, the future 5G cellular network requires new technologies to provide extra high throughput for many users simultaneously. Among these new technologies, massive MIMO takes the lion's share. Using massive MIMO, we can achieve a huge energy efficiency and spectral efficiency when the array and multiplexing gains are large. These gains are obtained under favorable propagation conditions and using optimal signal processing technique at the BS [8]. Therefore, one of the important benefits from massive MIMO is to improve the network throughput by serving many users in the same frequency band and time frame, which is a very critical requirement in 5G.

Another major benefit from massive MIMO is improved energy efficiency and reduced cost. Since it can be built with inexpensive low-power components, circuit complexity and cost will be highly reduced. İn addition, energy consumption will be reduced using beamforming techniques, where each transmitter emits only some portion of its transmit power directed to the location of active users. This, in turn, minimizes the operational cost of the network and reduce carbon emissions [7]. Moreover, massive MIMO is very useful in interference management. Since BSs are equipped with very large antenna elements compared to the number of user equipment in a given cell region, transmitted signals can be easily shaped to null interference [9].

Massive MIMO improves not only the network performance and energy efficiency, but also it increases the system robustness. İntentional jamming and cyber security threat is a serious issue in wireless systems. Since massive MIMO offers an excess degree of freedom, it could be used as the best tool to cancel signals from intentional jammers [10].

Generally, deploying multiple antenna elements in a BS will highly improve the overall network performance and energy efficiency. Especially, a 1000 times energy efficiency requirement set by 5G can be easily achieved by implementing massive MIMO in the new architectural design of future cellular networks.

3.3   Performance Analysis of Massive MIMO

Since the number of antenna elements is very large, the channel vectors between the BS and user equipment are orthogonal. Considering the data transmission in favorable propagation conditions, the performance of massive MIMO can be evaluated using simple linear signal processing techniques, such as MRC, ZF, and MMSE in the receiver section. A comparison among these receivers in realistic test-case is presented in [11]. İn the following, we evaluate the performance of massive MIMO using simple linear processing techniques and analyze some numerical results in terms of sum rate, spectral efficiency, and energy efficiency.

Figure 3 shows that the performance of massive MIMO using different linear processing techniques in terms of the achievable sum rate. Where K is a multiplexing gain and P_u is the uplink power. As clearly observed from Fig. 3, we can give the following analysis. The achievable sum rate increases exponentially as the number of antenna elements increased in the BS. On the other hand, as the number of BS antennas increased, the spectral efficiency with linear receivers is almost the same with Shannon sum capacity achieved by optimal receivers.

The other basic parameter to evaluate the performance of massive MIMO is energy efficiency. Fundamentally, the significant improvement of energy efficiency in massive MIMO can be obtained by extremely sharpening the radiated energy from the transmitter to focus into small regions where active user equipment located. By using a

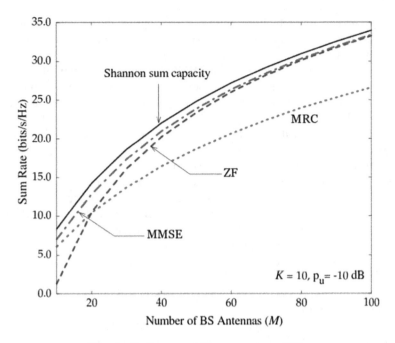

Fig. 3. Performance of linear receivers [10].

beamforming technique the transmitted signals emitted by all antenna elements at the BS can be constructively added and directed into the location of intended user equipments.

Strictly speaking, the energy efficiency and spectral efficiency are two trade-off parameters. Since spectral efficiency is directly proportional to the transmit power, to improve the spectral efficiency of the system the signal power is required to be increased. On the other hand, as the signal power increased, the power consumption in the system will increase and in turn reduce the energy efficiency. However, by using moderately large antenna arrays we can jointly improve spectral efficiency and energy efficiency in orders of magnitude compared with a single antenna system.

Figure 4 shows the trade-offs between the spectral efficiency and energy efficiency with 100 antennas at the BS using different linear processing techniques. In Fig. 4 it is clearly observed that ZF processing performs strictly better than MRC processing in a wider range. However, in the lower region of spectral efficiency, we can achieve a better energy efficiency using MRC processing.

Generally, using appropriate signal processing technique we can jointly achieve a better energy efficiency and spectral efficiency by deploying a moderately large number of antenna arrays at the BS.

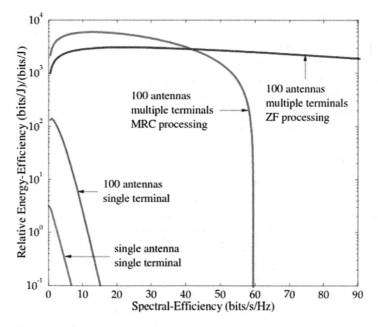

Fig. 4. Trade-offs between energy efficiency and spectral efficiency [10].

3.4   Research Challenges

Despite the fact that massive MIMO has numerous advantages to meet the ambitious requirements of 5G, a number of issues and challenges are required to be investigated. There are many open research directions and various challenges to be addressed before its practical deployment. In the following, some of the key challenges related to the practical implementation of massive MIMO and the potential solution approaches are discussed.

Pilot Contaminaton. Pilot contamination is one of the fundamental limitations which significantly reduces the performance of massive MIMO. Pilot contamination is the effect of interference from other cells during the pilot training sequences. In multi-cell systems, we cannot assign orthogonal pilot sequences for each user in all cells. One of the best methods to minimize the pilot contamination effect is to use high frequency-reuse factors. But, this will degrade the spectral efficiency of the system [12]. An appropriate design of frequency-reuse factor during the pilot sequence and power control to reduce pilot contamination effect is an important research direction.

Radio Resource Management. The future 5G cellular network is required to fully exploit all available resources at a maximum level. Current approaches to resource management and scheduling algorithms will not be the best solution for future networks. To properly coordinate and utilize all available resources, a new radio resource management technique is required. Some advanced technologies, such as cloud based radio access networks are proposed to centrally cooperate all network elements. Centralized cloud based radio access network is the best method to efficiently centralize resources and brings flexible options for radio resource management. İn cloud based radio access network architecture design, adaptive and intelligent technologies, such as NFV and SDN can be included. However, the current mobile networks are designed based on the 3GPP standards, both network architecture and radio access are an evolution from it. Therefore, the future network architecture is expected to support both central and distributed radio access control system. This will create a trade-off between centralized radio resource management as in cloud based network architecture and decentralization as in the current networks' resource management system. Further research is required to address this trade-off and to design optimal resource management technique.

Beamforming and CSI Acquisition. The acquisition of CSI is very important in massive MIMO. In massive MIMO, the BS needs a perfect CSI to detect the signals transmitted from the users. Each user is assigned an orthogonal pilot sequence and sends this pilot sequence to the BS. Beamforming and CSI are the two very important tools in the design of future 5G cellular network which highly affect the network efficiency. Acquisition of CSI is an energy consuming technique and equipments are very expensive. CSI acquisition vary depending on the channel estimation techniques and system duplexing mode [13]. In this regard, many problems are not yet addressed. How to optimally assign a pilot sequence for new users? Which pilot sequences should be used? These are some of the problems related to CSI acquisition. Therefore, the design of low-cost CSI acquisition system and optimal assignment of pilot sequences is a good research direction.

Hardware Impairements. Massive MIMO will be built with inexpensive low-power components. Ultra-linear high power equipment used in the previous system will be replaced by this inexpensive low-power equipment. However, the design of future cellular network is required to be backward compatible and seamlessly support the legacy network. Therefore, there will be a potential challenge to practically implement and integrate massive MIMO with the physical layer of the current technology. Designing a new efficient system to smoothly combine these technologies will be a good research area.

4   Conclusion

In this paper, the benefits of massive MIMO as a promising technology for the design of future 5G networks is highlighted. The technology offers huge advantages in terms of network efficiency, robustness, and reliability. As the performance evaluation result shows by deploying a large number of antenna arrays in the BS, spectral and energy efficiency can be improved in a significant level. However, to fully exploit the numerous advantages of massive MIMO, further research is required to address some challenges such as pilot contamination, hardware impairments, radio resource management, beamforming, and channel state information acquisition.

References

1. Chen, Y., Zhang, S., Xu, S., Li, G.Y.: Fundamental trade-offs on green wireless networks. IEEE Commun. Mag. **49**, 30–37 (2011)
2. Rusek, F., Persson, D., Lau, B.K., Larsson, E.G., Marzetta, T.L., Edfors, O., Tufvesson, F.: Scaling up MIMO: opportunities and challenges with very large arrays. IEEE Sig. Process. Mag. **30**, 40–60 (2013)
3. Ma, Z., Zhang, Q., Ding, G.: Key techniques for 5G wireless communications: network architecture, physical layer, and MAC layer perspectives. Sci. China. Inf. Sci. **58**, 1–20 (2015)
4. Feng, D., Jiang, C., Lim, G., Cimini, L.J., Feng, G., Li, G.Y.: A survey of energy-efficient wireless communications. IEEE Commun. Surv. Tutor. **15**, 167–178 (2013)
5. Lopez-Perez, D., Guvenc, I., Roche, G.D.L., Kountouris, M., Quek, T.Q.S., Zhang, J.: Enhanced intercell interference coordination challenges in heterogeneous networks. IEEE Trans. Wirel. Commun. **18**, 22–30 (2011)
6. Zhang, D., Liu, Y., Ding, Z., Zhou, Z., Nallanathan, A., Sato, T.: Performance analysis of non-regenerative massive-MIMO-NOMA relay systems for 5G. IEEE Trans. Commun. **65** (11), 4777–4790 (2017)
7. Marzetta, T.L.: Noncooperative cellular wireless with unlimited numbers of base station antennas. IEEE Trans. Wirel. Commun. **9**, 3590–3600 (2010)
8. Ali, S., Chen, Z., Yin, F.: Pilot decontamination in TDD multicell massive MIMO systems with infinite number of BS antennas. Can. J. Electr. Comput. Eng. **40**(3), 171–180 (2017)
9. Larsson, E.G.: Very large MIMO systems: opportunities and challenges (2012)
10. Ngo, H.Q., Larsson, E.G., Marzetta, T.L.: Energy and spectral efficiency of very large multiuser MIMO systems. IEEE Trans. Commun. **61**, 1436–1449 (2013)
11. Nguyen, S., Ghrayeb, A.: Compressive sensing-based channel estimation for massive multiuser MIMO systems. In: Proceedings of the 2003 IEEE Wireless Communication and Networking Conference, Shanghai, China (WCNC), pp. 2890–2895 (2013)
12. Knievel, C., Noemm, M., Hoeher, P.A.: Low-complexity receiver for large-MIMO space-time coded systems. In: Proceedings of the IEEE Vehicle Technology Conference (VTC), San Francisco, USA (2011)
13. Liand, L., Wei, Y.: Massive device connectivity with massive MIMO. In: IEEE International Symposium on Information Theory (ISIT) (2017)

Mathematical Modeling and Dynamic Simulation of Gantry Robot Using Bond Graph

Tadele Belay Tuli[✉]

Department of Electromechanical Engineering, Addis Ababa Science and Technology University, Addis Ababa, Ethiopia
tademech2008@gmail.com

Abstract. This paper presents an initial mathematical modeling and dynamic simulation of gantry robot for the application of printing circuit on board. The classical modeling methods such as Newton-Euler, Kirchoff's law and Lagrangian fails to unify both electrical and mechanical system models. Here, bond graph approach with robust trajectory planning which uses a blend of quadratic equations on triangular velocity profile is modeled in order to virtually simulate it. In this paper, the algebric mathematical models are developed using maple software. For the sake of simulation, the model is tested on matlab by integrating robot models which are developed by using Solidwork.

Keywords: Robot · Bond graph · Dynamic simulation
Trajectory planning

1 Introduction

Robots are electromechanical devices that can perform different tasks that are difficult, dangerous, repetitive or dull for human beings [4]. They are programmable devices that follow a set of instructions to perform certain tasks. Now a day's robotics is so advanced that we have different kinds of robots, but all have something in common. First, all have mechanical structure to achieve a desired task. Second, all have a power supply and electrical units to control it. Third, robots have a programming aspect to help them decide how to interact with the environment [1,5,7].

A gantry robot consists of a manipulator mounted onto an overhead system that allows movement across a horizontal plane. Servo motors are used to deliver power to each axis by using a rack and pinion mechanism. They are usually large systems that are suitable for applications such as pick and place, cutting, welding and others.

Gantry robot systems provide the advantage of large work areas and better positioning accuracy which enables the robot to place a part correctly. They are easier to program with respect to motion, because they use with an X, Y, Z

© ICST Institute for Computer Sciences, Social Informatics and Telecommunications Engineering 2018
F. Mekuria et al. (Eds.): ICT4DA 2017, LNICST 244, pp. 228–237, 2018.
https://doi.org/10.1007/978-3-319-95153-9_22

coordinate system. Another advantage is that they are less limited by floor space constraints [8]. Though they seem cheap compared to other robots like SCARA or articulated robots; they are not affordable to be implemented in emerging small scale industries that are flourishing in developing countries like Ethiopia. So, mathematical modeling and dynamic simulation of gantry robot using bond graph contributes a step toward the design and manufacture of gantry robot.

2   Kinematic Model of Gantry Robot

Kinematic modeling of gantry robot refers the study of link motions without considering the causing forces. The study takes place by assigning frames on links and joints. **Denavit-Hartenberg** (DH) convention simplifies the matters of frame assignment and creates a common language to fix frames in certain convection. In this paper modern DH-parameter convection is used.

2.1   Link Description

A link is a mechanical structure that connects two joint axes in space. Joint axes are vector that show direction of motion of link i with respect to $i-1$. The perpendicular distance between axes of $i-1$ and i is called link length a_{i-1} to joint axis i about a_{i-1} in right hand rule sense.

2.2   Intermediate Links in the Chain

Other parameters are defined based on common axes of consecutive links are link off set and joint angle. Link off set d_i is a parameter that describes the distance between two links (link lengths) along a joint axis. The off set on link i is d_i. Joint angle θ_i is the angle from link $i-1$ to i in right hand rule sense about these common axes.

2.3   Conventions on Modern DH - Parameter

Always assign Z_i-axis along axes of motion of joint i. While frame i is located at the intersection of a_i and joint i axis or Z_i-Axis. The axis of x_i points along a_i in the direction from joint i to joint $i+1$. The remaining axis will be completed using right hand rule [3].

The Homogeneous transformation matrix for modern DH-Matrix for link i is given by Eq. 1.

$$
{}^{i-1}_{i}T = \begin{bmatrix} c\theta_i & -s\theta_i & 0 & a_{i-1} \\ s\theta_i c\alpha_{i-1} & c\theta_i c\alpha_{i-1} & -s\alpha_{i-1} & -s\alpha_{i-1}d_i \\ s\theta_i s\alpha_{i-1} & c\theta_i s\alpha_{i-1} & c\alpha_{i-1} & c\alpha_{i-1}d_i \\ 0 & 0 & 0 & 1 \end{bmatrix} \tag{1}
$$

Where $c\theta_i$ and $s\theta_i$ are the short hands for $cos\theta_i$ and $sin\theta_i$ respectively.

Table 1. DH-parameters of Gantry robot

i	α_{i-1}	a_{i-1}	d_i	θ_i
1	0	0	q_1	0
2	90	0	q_2	90
3	90	d	q_3	0

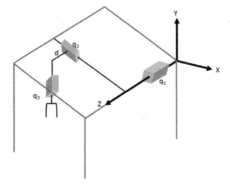

Fig. 1. Assignment of DH-reference frames

The DH parameters for this robot is shown on the Table 1.

Substituting the DH-parameters given on Table 1 in Eq. 1, we obtain reference frames for each links Fig. 1 as they are presented following.

Accordingly, link 1 is defined as,

$$
{}^0_1T = \begin{bmatrix} 1 & 0 & 0 & 0 \\ 0 & 1 & 0 & 0 \\ 0 & 0 & 1 & q_1 \\ 0 & 0 & 0 & 1 \end{bmatrix}
\tag{2}
$$

Reference frame for link 2 is given as;

$$
{}^1_2T = \begin{bmatrix} 0 & -1 & 0 & 0 \\ 0 & 0 & -1 & -q_2 \\ 1 & 0 & 0 & 0 \\ 0 & 0 & 0 & 1 \end{bmatrix}
\tag{3}
$$

Reference frame for link 3 is given by

$$
{}^2_3T = \begin{bmatrix} 1 & 0 & 0 & d \\ 0 & 0 & -1 & -q_3 \\ 0 & 1 & 0 & 0 \\ 0 & 0 & 0 & 1 \end{bmatrix}
\tag{4}
$$

The Transformation of end effector frame to the base frame (reference frame) is the matrix product of each transformation matrices, Hence

$$
{}^0_iT = {}^0_1T \times {}^1_2T \times {}^2_3T \ ... \ {}^{i-1}_iT
\tag{5}
$$

where i is the number of links.

Hence, the description of end effector of gantry robot position relative to base frame is,

$$
{}_3^0 T = \begin{bmatrix} 0 & 0 & 1 & q_3 \\ 0 & -1 & 0 & -q_2 \\ 1 & 0 & 0 & d+q_1 \\ 0 & 0 & 0 & 1 \end{bmatrix} \tag{6}
$$

Since no joints are revolute all rotational variables are set to zero. Therefore velocity of end effector relative to base frame is;

$$
V_3^0 = \dot{q}_3 i - \dot{q}_2 j + \dot{q}_1 k \tag{7}
$$

Acceleration of links is calculated as the same as velocity but effect of gravity is introduced by assuming the base is accelerating up ward at $g = 9.8\,\mathrm{m/s^2}$. Finally a_3 with respect to base is given as;

$$
a_3^0 = (\ddot{q}_3 i - g)i - \ddot{q}_2 j + \ddot{q}_1 k \tag{8}
$$

3   System Modeling Using Bond Graph Method

Classical system modeling uses Newton's equations of motion to model mechanical systems and the Kirchoff's law is applicable for modeling the electrical systems behavior. If we consider hydraulic system, it is common to consider electric circuit analogy [6].

However, Bond graph method utilizes conservation of energy principle with a logical approach for studying a dynamic systems. It is a logical way to deal with multidisciplinary problems. They are used to map flow of power from one part of a system to another. It consists of subsystems linked together by lines representing power bonds.

3.1   Dynamic Model Formulation

Once we have defined the basic components of a system, the following is the modeling approach of dynamic model of gantry robot.

Bond graph of each motion axes are shown below.

Link 3

Link three has two effort sources; one for applied force and one for gravitational force (Fig. 2).

Note: p and q are state variables.

Here, we will attempt to derive the governing equations using questions and answers.

Question: What does the elements give to the system?

Bond 1

$$
e_1 = F_3 \tag{9}
$$

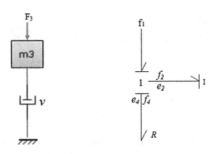

Fig. 2. Bond graph for Link 3

Bond 2
$$e_2 = G \tag{10}$$

Bond 3
$$f_1 = \frac{p_3}{m_3} \tag{11}$$

Bond 4
$$e_4 = v_3 f_4 \tag{12}$$

Question: What does the system give to storage elements?
It gives e_3 to bond 3.
Where
$$e_3 = \dot{p}_3 = e_1 + e_2 - e_4 \tag{13}$$

Because we said that,

$$e = \dot{p} \tag{14}$$
$$f = \dot{q} \tag{15}$$

And
$$\begin{aligned}
e_3 &= m_3 \ddot{q}_3 \\
e_1 &= F_3 \\
e_2 &= G \\
e_4 &= v_3 \dot{q}
\end{aligned} \tag{16}$$

From the substitution of the values of e_1, e_2, e_3 and e_4 into Eq. 13, we arrive at;
$$m_3 \ddot{q}_3 = F_3 + G - v_3 \dot{q} \tag{17}$$

However, since
$$G = m_3 g \tag{18}$$

Finally, the governing system equation of link 3 is;

$$F_3 = m_3 \ddot{q}_3 + v_3 \dot{q}_3 - m_3 g \tag{19}$$

Note: (F_3) represents force applied on the system.

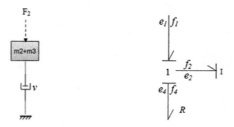

Fig. 3. Link 2

Link 2

Link two has one effort sources as it is given on Fig. 3.
Question: What does the elements give to the system?

$$\begin{aligned} e_1 &= F_2 \\ f_2 &= \frac{p_2}{m_2+m_3} \\ e_3 &= v_2\, f_3 \end{aligned} \qquad (20)$$

Note: F_2 represents force applied on the system.
Question: What does the system give to storage elements?

$$e_2 = e_1 - e_3 \qquad (21)$$

$$e_2 = \dot{p}_2 = e_1 - e_3 \qquad (22)$$

Further simplifying, we obtain the governing equation as;

$$F_2 = (m_2 + m_3)\, \ddot{q}_2 + v_2\, \dot{q}_2 \qquad (23)$$

Link 1

Link two has one effort sources.
Question: What does the elements give to the system?

$$e_1 = F_1 \qquad (24)$$

$$f_1 = \frac{p_1}{(m_3 + m_2 + m_1)} \qquad (25)$$

$$e_3 = v_1\, f_3 \qquad (26)$$

Note: F_1 represents force applied on the system.
Question: What does the system give to storage elements?

$$e_2 = \dot{p}_1 = e_1 - e_3 \qquad (27)$$

Finally by simplifying further, we will arrive at the final governing equation which is given by Eq. 28.

$$F_1 = (m_1 + m_2 + m_3)\, \ddot{q}_1 + v_1\, \dot{q}_1 \qquad (28)$$

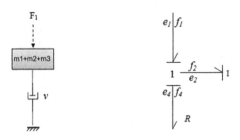

Fig. 4. Link 1

The dynamic system equation which unifies all the motion of the links of the gantry robot can be given in state space equation form as it is shown in equation,

$$F = \begin{bmatrix} m_1 + m_2 + m_3 & 0 & 0 \\ 0 & m_2 + m_3 & 0 \\ 0 & 0 & m_3 \end{bmatrix} \begin{bmatrix} \ddot{q}_1 \\ \ddot{q}_2 \\ \ddot{q}_3 + g \end{bmatrix} + \begin{bmatrix} \dot{q}_1 \\ \dot{q}_2 \\ \dot{q}_3 \end{bmatrix} \tag{29}$$

where

$$v = \begin{bmatrix} v_1 & 0 & 0 \\ 0 & v_2 & 0 \\ 0 & 0 & v_3 \end{bmatrix} \tag{30}$$

And

$$F = \begin{bmatrix} F_1 \\ F_2 \\ F_3 \end{bmatrix} \tag{31}$$

4   Direct Dynamics

Direct dynamics involves determining joint accelerations, velocity as well as position of end effector resulted by an applied force of link actuator.

$$\ddot{q} = M^{-1} [F - G(q) - F(\dot{q})] \tag{32}$$

M is the mass matrix which its inverse is given by Eq. 33.

$$M^{-1} = \begin{bmatrix} \frac{1}{m_1 + m_2 + m_3} & 0 & 0 \\ 0 & \frac{1}{m_2 + m_3} & 0 \\ 0 & 0 & \frac{1}{m_3} \end{bmatrix} \tag{33}$$

The gravitational force $G(q)$ and it is represented with Eq. 34.

$$G(q) = m_3 \begin{bmatrix} 0 \\ 0 \\ -g \end{bmatrix} \tag{34}$$

The non conservative forces which is due to frictional forces is given as $F(q)$ by Eq. 35.

$$F(q) = \begin{bmatrix} v_1 & 0 & 0 \\ 0 & v_2 & 0 \\ 0 & 0 & v_3 \end{bmatrix} \begin{bmatrix} \dot{q}_1 \\ \dot{q}_2 \\ \dot{q}_3 \end{bmatrix} \qquad (35)$$

5   Trajectory Planning

In order to simulate the dynamic system model of the robot, it is necessary to plan a trajectory for the motion of the robot links. As a result, a quadratic blend of triangular velocity with a known time of maximum velocity is computed by considering three control points of the quadratic function [2].

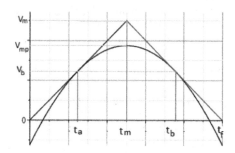

Fig. 5. Planning a triangular velocity profile with a quadratic blend

In order to study the motion profile, we approach by classifying the velocity motion in three regions. These are linearly accelerating, quadratic blending and linearly decreasing.

Case I: Linearly accelerating velocity profile

For all t, $t \in [t_0, t_a]$ the linear velocity for this case is forward one, which is given by;

$$v_a = a * t \qquad (36)$$

where a is the constant linear acceleration absorbed by the links, t is the instantaneous time and v is the linear instantaneous velocity.

Case II: Quadratic blending velocity profile

For all t, $t \in [t_a, t_b]$ the linear velocity is not forward. Instead, we derive by using control points shown on Fig. 5 which are (t_a, v_b), (t_m, v_{mp}), and (t_b, v_b). And solving the quadratic equations, we obtain;

$$v_{ab} = \frac{-(t - t_m)(t - t_a - t_b + t_m)v_b + v_{mp}(t - t_b)(t - t_a)}{(t_b - t_m)(t_a - t_m)} \qquad (37)$$

Considering v_b as the velocity where the linear motion starts to be in the state of quadratic motion, and v_{mp} is the rescaled maximum velocity of the motion.

From Fig. 5, we can understand that v_m is computed as;

$$v_m = a * t_m \tag{38}$$

And we can solve v_b and v_{mp} as

$$v_{mp} = \frac{v_m + v_b}{2} v_b = a * ta \tag{39}$$

Finally, we can simplify Eq. 37 as;

$$v_{ab} = -a \left(\frac{(-t - tb + 2 * tm) * ta + t * (t - tb)}{2 * tb - 2 * tm} \right) \tag{40}$$

Case III: Linearly decelerating velocity profile
For all t, $t \in [t_b, t_f]$, there is the linearly decelerating motion profile;

$$v_{bf} = v_b + a * (t - t_b) \tag{41}$$

However, v_b is computed by equating $t = t_b$ in Eq. 40. And finally come with;

$$v_{bf} = -(-ta + t - tb) * a \tag{42}$$

6   Simulation and Discussion

By considering motion characteristics of motor 1, we observe that the applied linear force to the motor from the stepper motor is linear (Fig. 7) for the quadratic portion of the velocity profile and remains constant where the velocity is in linear motion behavior. Accordingly, power required by the motor exhibits non linear property for the quadratic portion of the velocity profile (Fig. 6).

Now, by programming the mathematical models on matlab, we can simulate the robot in order to study the behavior of the dynamics. In this paper, matlab and solidworks software's are used as it is shown on Figs. 8 and 9

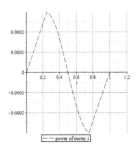

Fig. 6. Power required by Motor 1

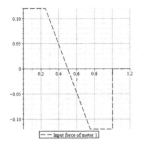

Fig. 7. Input force to Motor 1

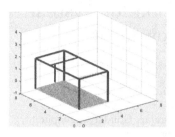 

Fig. 8. Simulation of the robot on matlab.

Fig. 9. The simulation of gantry robot using CAD tools

7   Conclusion

In this paper, mathematical modeling of gantry robot for the application of printing on circuit board, is performed using bond graph modeling method. In order to simulate the dynamics of the robot model, I integrated matlab software with solidwork. Here, solidwork replicates the physical model of the robot where matlab controls the trajectory plan of the robot. The trajectory of the robot is planned by using a blend of quadratic function with a triangular velocity profile which is suitable for small interval of time in between subsequent points.

References

1. Sciavicco, L., Villani, L.: Robotics: Modelling, Planning and Control. Springer, Heidelberg (2009). https://doi.org/10.1007/978-1-84628-642-1
2. Corke, P.: Robotics, Vision and Control Fundamental Algorithms in MATLAB, vol. 73. Springer, Heidelberg (2011). https://doi.org/10.1007/978-3-319-54413-7
3. Craig, J.J.: Introduction to Robotics: Mechanics and Control. Pearson/Prentice Hall, Upper Saddle River (2005)
4. Williams, B.: An Introduction to Robotics. http://www.ohio.edu/people/williar/html/PDF/IntroRob.pdf
5. Dietz, T., et al.: Programming system for efficient use of industrial robots for deburring in SME environments. In: Proceedings of 2012 7th German Conference on Robotics ROBOTIK. VDE (2012)
6. Das, S.: Mechatronic Modeling and Simulation Using Bond Graphs. CRC Press, Boca Raton (2009)
7. Cubero, S.: Industrial Robotics: Theory, Modelling and Control. Pro Literatur Verlag, Augsburg (2006)
8. www.robots.com/faq/show/what-are-gantry-robots

Web Usage Characterization for System Performance Improvement

Alehegn Kindie[1(✉)], Adane Mamuye[1], and Biniyam Tilahun[2]

[1] Faculty of Informatics, University of Gondar, Gondar, Ethiopia
alehegn12@gmail.com
[2] Department of Health Informatics, University of Gondar, Gondar, Ethiopia
http://www.uog.edu.et

Abstract. Web usage mining discovers patterns of user behaviors from web log files. In this study web usage mining is employed to identify business-critical and non-business critical web traffics in University of Gondar. Apriori and FP tree algorithms are applied to extract the web browsing behavior in terms of frequently accessed sites along with their web traffics. Our research findings can be used as an input for bandwidth management and system performance improvement.

Keywords: Web usage characterization · Web usage mining
Pattern discovery

1 Introduction

World Wide Web is a global village and rich source of information [1]. Million of users engage with different web services and their browsing behavior evolve as rapidly as the business landscape underlying it. This evolution, however, is difficult to observe because of the users behavior. As a result, accurate picture of how users engage with the web is lacked [11]. Web usage mining, hence, aims to discover interesting and frequent user access patterns and trends from web [5, 7]. The identified usage patterns are used for web usage characterization, bandwidth management, system performance improvement and web personalization [2–4].

Several approaches have been forwarded to extract knowledge from the Web. There are three broad categories of web mining: web content mining, web structure mining and web usage mining [2–4]. The web log files are major source of data for web usage mining. The users find relevant information easily and want to download the web resources with least amount of time [2, 7]. System administrators want to create new knowledge from the usage pattern and want to improve the performance of the system. It is not possible to manage users access and improve the system performance without knowing their behavior. Web usage mining provides the key to understand interest of users and web traffic behavior which can in turn be used for network transmission and load balancing policy development [12]. For any organization, one can categorize web users

© ICST Institute for Computer Sciences, Social Informatics and Telecommunications Engineering 2018
F. Mekuria et al. (Eds.): ICT4DA 2017, LNICST 244, pp. 238–245, 2018.
https://doi.org/10.1007/978-3-319-95153-9_23

as business-critical web user and non-business-critical web user or bandwidth abuser. For network and system performance improvement, adding more bandwidth can be one of the solution. However, since there are bandwidth abusers, adding bandwidth could not be a solution. Allocating required bandwidth to the business-critical network traffic and reducing non-business related network traffic (unwanted traffic) are the primary solutions for network and system performance improvement. This can be done using load balancing and task priority techniques [12]. Therefore, with the right policies in place, there is a possibility to improve the system performance.

In this paper, we investigated the web usage behavior of University of Gondar (UoG) community. The remainder of the paper is organized as follows. Section 2 illustrates the methodology followed in our study. Section 3 discusses the results achieved. While conclusions is given in Sect. 4.

2   Methodology

2.1   Data Collection

A total of 90,058,655 unprocessed web log data was collected from UoG proxy server.

2.2   Web Usage Mining Process

Our web usage mining process is divided into three major activities, namely data preprocessing, pattern discovery and pattern analysis, as presented in Fig. 1.

Data Preprocessing: The unprocessed web log data is cleaned using Glogg and Data Preparator. Then the data is clustered into students and staffs based on their VLANs. A total of 170,821 clean web log was used for experimentation purpose.

Pattern Discovery: Statistical analysis and association rule mining techniques are used for pattern discovery. Statistical Analysis is employed to identify access frequence [8]. Association rule mining algorithms, namely Apriori and Frequent Pattern (FP) tree, are used to extract interesting patterns. Though there are a number of techniques, as noted by Han and Kamber [10], the most widely used algorithms for association rule discovery are Apriori and FP tree. Since Apriori algorithm repeatedly scans all web log data, it takes long running time. While FP tree algorithm is faster than Apriori algorithm it scans the web log data only twice. On the other hand, FP tree algorithm takes only binary value. Even if the attribute VLAN has more than two binary values; it is not considered in FP tree algorithm experiment. As a result, the Apriori algorithm discovers an interesting pattern from each VLAN.

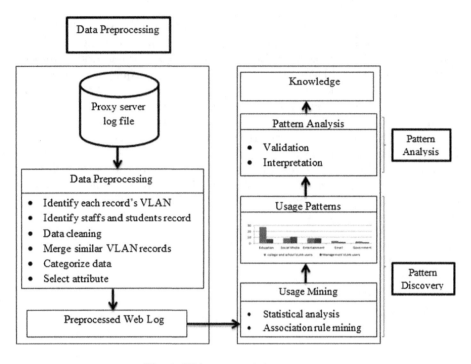

Fig. 1. Web usage mining process.

3   Result and Discussion

Six experiments are conducted. The first two experiments are statistical analysis and the remaining four are association rule mining.

3.1   Statistical Analysis

Experiment I: On Staffs Web Log Dataset: In this case a total of 60,019 data is used. As represented in Fig. 2, the x-axis represents web users VLAN and the y-axis represents the access frequency. Accordingly, two results are observed. Firstly, in some of the VLANs educational sites and in some others social media and entertainment sites accessed more frequently. In VLANs 80, 81 and 110, for instance, educational tutorials are accessed more frequently in the first priority. YouTube and Facebook are accessed next to educational tutorial sites. This is because VLANs 80, 81 and 110 are assigned to academic staffs. On the other hand, in the remaining VLANs (assigned for administrative staffs), Facebook is accessed more frequently in the first priority. The implication is that the interest of academic staffs is mostly accessing educational sites. While administrative staffs mostly accessed social media and entertainment sites. Secondly, the web traffic is analyzed based on number of query and download types. In the same VLANs, the web traffics is high since so many queries are submitted. As the

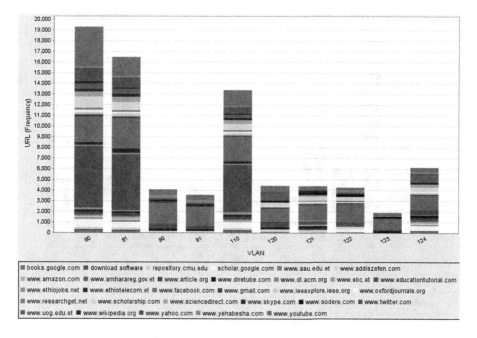

Fig. 2. Top frequently accessed sits and web traffic in the staffs VLANs.

number of query increases in the given bandwidth, the response time of the server decreases. Additionally, as the file content increase, such as video and audio and more people are accessing them, it consumes more bandwidth. This results more web traffic. Thus, for allocating bandwidths, knowing web traffic, access priorities and organizations mission are quite important.

Experiment II: On Students Web Log Dataset: In this experiment, a total of 110,802 data is used. As it has been shown in Fig. 3, in different VLANs educational, social media and entertainment sites were accessed. In VLANs 10, 11, 12, 13, 50, 73 and 74 Facebook is accessed more frequently, followed by educational tutorials and YouTube. As pointed out by domain experts, the previously specified VLANs are school (class room) computer laboratories. In VLANs 20, 21, 30, 41 and 42 educational tutorials sites are accessed more frequently. Entertainment and email sites are accessed next to educational sites. VLANs 20, 21, 30, 41 and 42 are library computer laboratories. Since Facebook is prohibited in library, students Facebook access frequency is null. However, in school computer laboratories, Facebook is accessed more frequently in the first priority. In some of the VLANs the web traffic is high, particularly in school (class room) computer laboratories than in the library computer laboratories.

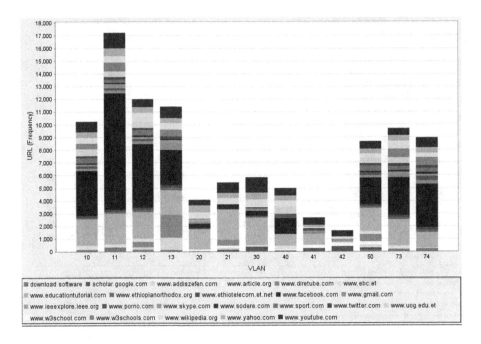

Fig. 3. Top frequently accessed sits and web traffic in the students' VLANs.

3.2   Browsing Behavior Characterization

In the previous experiments, we have shown that the web access behavior of staffs and students are different. This result is also supported by the statistical analysis as presented in Figs. 4 and 5. Accordingly, mostly the web browsing behavior of staffs is focus on educational sites in the first priority and then social media, entertainment and email sites, as depicted in Fig. 4. While students are interested in accessing social media in the first priority and then educational, entertainment and email sites, as depicted in Fig. 5.

There is also high web traffic in some school VLANs. This is due to high number of educational queries are submitted by the users in the first place. In administrative (management) VLANs social media and entertainment queries are submitted in the first and second place. In students VLANs, more web traffic is observed in schools and low web traffic is observed in library. The cause of more web traffic in schools are due to socila media, educational and entertainment queries, in first, second and third place, respectively. On the contrary, students accessed educational sites in library in the first place. Therefore, the web usage at UoG can be characterized as educational, social media, entertainment, email and government sites. The web traffic anaysis is made based on submitted query and file content type. Considering institutional mission, there are business critical activites and non-business activities. Obviously, in higher education, teaching and research activities can be considered as business critical activities. For higher educations social media and entertainment web traffics

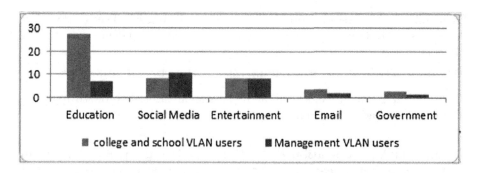

Fig. 4. Staffs' behavior characterization.

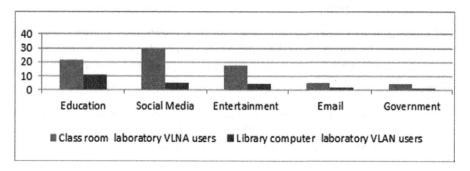

Fig. 5. Students' behavior characterization.

can be categorized under non-business related traffic. Therefore, allocating the required bandwidth to the business-critical traffic like is the primary solution for network performance improvement. Our findings can be used as an input for system performance and bandwidth management. As a result, this can be done using load balancing techniques.

3.3 Association Rule Discovery

We used objective (support and confidence) and subjective (domain experts) evaluations to determine interestingness of the rules [9].

Experiment III: Association Rule Discovery Using Apriori Algorithm on Staffs Web Logs: The value of min support and confidence was 0.01 and 0.9, respectively.

VLAN=81 URL24=accessed 4320 ==> URL35=accessed 4320   <conf.(1)> lift :(5.56) lev:(0.06) [3543] conv:(3543.58)

If URL24 accessed in VLAN 81 (academic staff), then URL35 had 100% probability to be accessed. This shows educational sites are accessed in VLAN 81,as presented in Experiment I.

Experiment IV: Association Rule Discovery Using FP Tree Algorithm on Staffs Web Logs: The value of min-support and confidence was 0.1 and 0.9, respectively.

[URL16=accessed, URL4=accessed]: 14382 ==> [URL1=accessed]: 14382   <conf:(1)> lift:(1.99) lev:(0.14) conv:(7167.78)

This rule states that if yahoo mail and educational tutorials browsed together, then Facebook had 100% probability to be accessed with them.

Experiment V: Association Rule Discovery Using Apriori Algorithm on Students Web Logs: The value of min-support and confidence was 0.01 and 0.9, respectively.

VLAN=11 URL8=accessed 3831 ==> URL1=accessed 3831   <conf:(1)> lift:(3) lev:(0.02) [2553] conv:(2553.72)

As of this rule, if URL8 accessed in VLAN 11, then Facebook had 100% probability to be access in the same VLAN. This shows entertainment and social media sites are accessed in VLAN 11 by the students, as presented, in Experiment II.

VLAN=30 URL4=accessed 1656 ==> URL20=accessed 1656   <conf:(1)> lift:(3) lev:(0.01) [1103] conv:(1103.88)

This rule shows that if educational tutorials accessed in VLAN 30, then URL20 had 100% probability to be access in this VLAN. Educational sites are accessed in library by the students, as presented in Experiment II.

Experiment VI: Association Rule Discovery Using FP Tree Algorithm on Students Web Logs: The value of min-support and confidence was 0.1 and 0.9, respectively.

[URL4=accessed, URL8=accessed]: 22635 ==> [URL1=accessed]: 22635   <conf:(1)> lift:(3) lev:(0.14) conv:(15088.37)

This rule states that if students browse educational tutorials and YouTube together, then they also accessed Facebook with 100% probability. To sum up, association rule discovered, social media and entertainment sites accessed more frequently in the students and administrative VLANs. On the contrary, educational and email sites accessed more frequently in academic staff VLANs.

4   Conclusion

The aim of this study was to understand web browsing behavior of UoG community. Statistical analysis and association rule mining algorithms are employed. The experimental results show that academic staffs focused on accessing educational sites and administrative staffs focused on social media and entertainment sites. On the other hand, it is also observed that students web browsing behavior in school and library are different. The identified usage patterns can be used for bandwidth management and system performance improvement.

References

1. Vellingiri, J., Pandian, S.C.: Survey on web usage mining. Glob. J. Comput. Sci. Technol. **11**(4) (2011)
2. Munilatha, R., Venkataramana, K.: A study on issues and techniques of web mining. Int. J. Comput. Sci. Mob. Comput. Mon. J. Comput. Sci. Inf. Technol. **3**(5) (2014)
3. Madhak, N.N., Kodina, T.M., Jayesh N. Varnagar, R.C.R.: Web usage mining using association rule mining on clustered data for pattern discovery. Int. J. Data Min. Tech. Appl. **2**(1) (2013)
4. Vijiyarani, S., Suganya, E.: Research issues in web mining. Int. J. Comput.-Aided Tech. (IJCAx) **2**(3), 55–64 (2015)
5. Santhosh Kumar, B., Rukmani, K.V.: Implementation of web usage mining using apriori and FP growth algorithms. J. Adv. Netw. Appl. **1**(6), 400–404 (2010)
6. Oskouei, R.J.: Identifying students behaviors related to internet usage patterns. IEEE Computer Science and Engineering Department Motilal Nehru National Institute Of Technology Allahabad (2010)
7. Amutha, K., Devapriya, M.: Web mining: a survey paper. Int. J. Comput. Trends Technol. (IJCTT) **4**(9), 3038–3042 (2013)
8. Uma Maheswari, B., Sumathi, P.: A comparative study of rule mining based web usage mining algorithms. Int. J. Sci. Res. (IJSR) **4**(11), 2540–2543 (2015)
9. Parvatikar, S., Joshi, B.: Analysis of user behavior through web usage mining. Int. J. Comput. Appl. (09750–8887) 27–31 (2014)
10. Han, J., Kamber, M.: Data Mining: Concepts and Techniques. 2nd edn, pp. 243–246. Elsevier, Amsterdam (2006)
11. Kumar, R., Tomkins, A.: A characterization of online browsing behavior. In: International World Wide Web Conference Committee (IW3C2), 26–30 April 2010
12. Srivastava, J., Cooley, R.: Web usage mining: discovery and applications of usage patterns from web data. SIGKDD Explor. **1**(2), 12 (2000)

Critical Success Factors and Key Performance Indicators for e-Government Projects-Towards Untethered Public Services: The Case of Ethiopia

Dessalegn Mequanint Yehuala[✉]

Department of Computer Science, Addis Ababa University,
Addis Ababa, Ethiopia
dessalegn.mequanint@aau.edu.et

Abstract. The road to digital transformation of the governance system of developing countries has been a steep uphill climb- in addition to massive investment in ICT infrastructure and applications e-Government projects often require changes in legislation, major policy decisions and restructuring of the public sectors. In this paper, pertinent issues that stand in the way of digital government ascent of Ethiopia have been investigated. To give the issues addressed a context, an e-Service that enabled consumers to pay utilities bill for water, telephone and electricity in one-stop service center has been analysed with respect to metrics developed as well as on the basis of consumers rating of the service. The main findings from consumers response of the service ratings are that, e-Government projects success cannot be judged solely by monetary return of investments which could be obtained among other things by cutting down the work force required to run the service and improvements achieved compared to how the service was delivered in manual settings before it went electronics. In fact as evidenced by the findings, monetary return of investments might not be achieved. However, other metrics such as time to process transactions, service responsiveness, availability of government services or the ability to conduct transactions anytime and anywhere, and costs associated to getting the service weighs more significance.

Keywords: e-Government · e-Services · e-Government success factors
Performance indicators of e-Government · Untethered e-Services

1 Introduction

During the last decade, Information and Communication Technologies (ICTs) have emerged as critical tools for development processes worldwide. Their application has transcended almost all sectors including healthcare, education, agriculture and governance, to name just a few. With respect to the latter, the use of ICTs in governance processes has taken root in some countries. Governments in developed countries; central, regional and municipal; as well as political parties and campaigners are using the Internet as well as other ICT tools to interact with citizens. The concept of

F. Mekuria et al. (Eds.): ICT4DA 2017, LNICST 244, pp. 246–258, 2018.
https://doi.org/10.1007/978-3-319-95153-9_24

e-Governance is emerging as part of the governance vocabulary. Despite these developments, in much of the emerging economies, there is yet to be an effective environment to maximize the benefits from ICTs. There is therefore fear that the digital divide might deepen into other forms of divides.

World governments have recognized the immense potential of ICT tools and they have been progressively acting towards integrating them in the governance processes to achieve cost savings and greater operational efficiencies, among other purposes. The government of Ethiopia is one of those who invested significant sum of money in ICT for national development and public sector governance reforms- notably the development of the WoredaNet infrastructure[1]. However due to a plethora of factors e-Government services in the country are not just only limited in number but restricted in their pervasiveness as well. In this paper, the challenges that the government along with other actors, public and private sectors, academia and development partners need to address towards embarking on a harmonized e-Government ecosystem have been discussed; and accordingly a strategic considerations that need to be taken have been recommended.

The rest of the paper is organized as follows. Section 2 sets out the study objectives; Sect. 3 introduces the research methodology used; Sect. 4 discusses summary of the study findings; Sect. 5 discusses elements of untethered e-Government ecosystem. Section 6 finally presents recommendations or the way forward.

1.1 e-Service Description

Before 2013 bill settlement service for water, telephone and electric power consumptions were delivered separately in separate service centers established at the lowest local administrative unit of the city administration of Addis Ababa. Since 2013 Kifiya launched a software system named "Lehulu" to offer bill settlement service for the three utilities in a unified manner at more than 34 newly established e-Service centers. The newly established e-Service centers have been furnished with the necessary facilities with a significant amount of investment and it operates in a public private partnership model. The cost attached to establishing the e-Service centers and running them has been more expensive than what it was before. Hence transforming the service into electronics makes no financial sense, and the monetary return of investments might not be achieved. However, the electronic transformation of the service has brought fundamental and significant changes that might not be quantifiable in monetary terms.

1.2 The Research Questions

Though not to the required level, in Ethiopia, the widespread use of ICT tools in the various public and private sectors is gathering pace. The governance sector is one of those benefiting to a degree from the ongoing electronic transformations taking place in the country. Despite these ongoing developments, challenges that stand in the way of e-Government remain unaddressed. With those challenges remain unaddressed it would

---

[1] http://unpan1.un.org/intradoc/groups/public/documents/un-dpadm/unpan034887.pdf.

be impossible to see the true effects of ICT in transforming government services. This paper through the e-Service named "Lehulu" show cases the challenges that lie ahead in untethered e-Government diffusion for providing improved public services.

The paper investigates the following interdependent issues:

– What are the key challenges of untethered e-Government in developing countries?
– How can the gaps towards untethered e-Government ecosystem be bridged?
– What are the factors that stand in the way of e-Government in its truest sense in developing countries?
– What are the Critical Success Factors and Key Performance Indicators for e-Government Projects?
– What strategic considerations are needed to mitigate the factors?

In order to be able answer the above set of research questions, primary data via questionnaire as well as secondary data from the e-Government implementation strategy [2] have been collected, and from the collected data actionable recommendations toward mitigating the challenges have been generated.

1.3   Methodology

A random sampling technique was used to collect questionnaire data at the e-Service centers by trained enumerators about service users' quality of experience of the unified utility billing system and the response rate was 100%. The distribution of respondents by sex was that 55% of respondents are male while the rest 45% are women. Since the respondents are selected randomly among the population or service users equal distribution of gender was not attained. It can be said that this small imbalance has not affected the outcome of the research.

2   Summary of the Findings

For services that involve payment, in Ethiopia, virtually there is no truly online service as services offered by the various organizations or institutions demand the physical presence of service users at service centers to at least effect payment. In this study, users quality of experience on the government service that went electronic very recently named "Lehulu- Kifiya", a unified utilities billing system available for residents of the capital, Addis Ababa has been analysed. The table below, Table 1, summarises service users response to questions asked in the scoring scale of 1–5 (using Likert scale), from strongly disagree(1) to strongly agree(5).

2.1   Respondents View on Service Delivery Improvements Compared to What It was Before

The average mean score of respondents' rating of service improvements in settling utility bills since the e-Service system named in Amharic "Lehulu- Kifiya" has become operational was 3.8, which in the scoring scale of 1–5 is nearly high indicating that there has been significant service improvements as a result of the utility billing services

Table 1. Users ratings of the e-Service "Lehulu-Kifiya"

	N	Average mean
Service delivery since the e-Service system get operational is better	100	3.84
With the e-Service system on average I get the service within 30 min time	100	2.74
With the e-Service system queuing up time for the service is small	100	2.85
After the current e-Service system got operational getting the service has become easier	100	3.85
After the current e-Service system got operational there has been significant waiting times reduction	100	3.00
After the current e-Service system got operational there has been times I was told to come another day as the service was not available due to connection related problems	100	2.35
I have no complaint(s) on the current service delivery process	100	2.97
The current e-Service system is prone to errors and it has caused me inconvenience as a result	100	1.97
The most important limitation of the service is its inaccessibility at places other than the service centers	100	2.76
Level of satisfaction with the e-Service system	100	3.59

going into electronic. Utility billings in the past have been handled by separate offices for that service users had to go to separate offices to settle bills for their monthly electric power, water and telephone consumptions, however through the current unified utility billing system consumers can settle their bill at same time at one service center for all utilities consumed, which is a lot more easier than what it was before. However this should not mask the reality that further improvements are needed in the service delivery process particularly consumers inconvenience such as the demand on physical presence at service centers to effect payments for consumed utilities needs to be eliminated- the achilles heel that needs immediate addressing to drive the creation of truly online government as well as other forms of services in Ethiopia is the lack of secured online payment systems.

2.2 Respondents Getting the Service in Less Than 30 min

The average mean score of respondents' rating on getting the service in less than 30 min time once they arrive at a service center was 2.7, which in the scoring scale of 1–5 is slightly above average. By any standard 30 min of service time is big for services that went online even for offline electronic, thus there is an indication that service rates at service centers lags significantly behind service consumers arrival rate and queue as a result builds up.

2.3 Respondents Queuing Up Time for the Service

The average mean score of respondents' who think the queuing time for service is small was 2.8, which in the scoring scale of 1–5 is slightly above average. Respondents' compare the current service waiting time in light of what it was before the system going electronic, and their rating only has to be seen in that respect. However, it is common to find significant number of service users queuing up for the service at any time during working hours in any of the service centers.

2.4 Respondents' Perception of How Getting the Service is Easier

The average mean score of respondents' who think getting the service in the electronic unified billing system is much easier was 3.9, which in the scoring scale of 1–5 is nearly high. Respondents' compare the current service delivery improvement in light of what it was before the system going electronic, and their rating only has to be seen in that respect. However, it would be important to take account of service users experiencing several inconveniences such as traveling to nearby service center which could be a few kilo meters away and queuing up for the service - when taken together service users spend significant amount of time to get the service which could have been avoidable had the system truly been an online one.

2.5 Respondents' Perception of Waiting Time for the Service

The average mean score of respondents' who think there has been service waiting time reduction in the electronic unified billing system was 3.0, which in the scoring scale of 1–5 is above average. Respondents' compare the current service delivery process in light of what it was before the system going electronic, and their rating only has to be seen in that respect. However, service waiting time in the electronic unified billing system is still significantly high.

2.6 e-Service Availability

The average mean score of respondents' rating on service availability since the electronic unified billing system has been operational was 2.7, which in the scoring scale of 1–5 is slightly above average. Service availability of the unified billing system, as is the case in other e-Services, is not guaranteed in that the operation experience a glitch at times which could be mainly related to network connectivity that can last from a few hours to a day. This adds another burden on service users, as they have to travel to the service center for a second or more number of times to settle their bills.

2.7 Complaints on the e-Service

The average mean score of respondents' rating on their level of satisfaction on the service since the electronic unified billing system has been operational was 2.9, which in the scoring scale of 1–5 is above average. This needs to be put into perspective that despite the significant amount of time service consumers are required to spend for travelling to a service center, queuing up as well as service time, a considerable part of the respondents are satisfied with the e-Service. However it should be noted that most service users have little or no idea of the degree to which the service could have been improved; certainly with the support of online payment system the service's accessibility and convenience for service users could have been significantly improved.

2.8   Degree of Unreliability of the e-Service

The average mean score of respondents' rating on the degree of error proneness of the e-Service was 1.9, which in the scoring scale of 1–5 is significantly below average. However, chances are still there for service consumers to experience inconvenience as in the current setting there is a possibility to commit errors that can happen in the form of misreading of consumed utilities.

2.9   The Most Important Limitation of the e-Service

The average mean score of respondents' who think the service inaccessibility other than places at service centers is its main limitation was 2.8, which in the scoring scale of 1–5 is slightly above average. The inconveniences like service consumers traveling a few kilo meters to get to a nearby service center, and the considerable amount of time spent on getting the service as well as queuing up have significantly dwarfed the e-Service impact.

2.10   Overall Respondents Rating of the e-Service

The average mean score of respondents' who rate the e-Service as satisfactory was 3.6, which in the scoring scale of 1–5 is significantly above average. However things need to be put into perspective that most respondents are satisfied with the e-Service for one obvious reason that they compare it with how the service was delivered before- when they used to go to three separate offices to settle for water, electric power and telephone bills separately. Otherwise the e-Service potential remains unexploited particularly the new system lack of online payment support is costing service consumers their time as well as money dearly.

2.11   Distance Service Users Travel and Queue Time

In the following tables the percentage distribution of distances respondents travel to get a service center and percentage distribution of time respondents queue up for the service are presented (Table 2).

As it can be seen from the table above, an astounding 67% of respondents travel more than 1 km to service centers (Table 3).

As it can be seen from the table above, an astounding 64% of respondents queue up longer than 30 min for getting the service.

Table 2. Percentage distribution on distance respondents travel to get the service.

	N	%
Less than 1 km	33	33.0
1 km–2 km	24	24.0
2 km–3 km	18	18.0
3 km>	25	25.0
Total	100	100

Table 3. Percentage distribution of time respondents queue up for the service.

	N	%
Less than 15 min	12	12
15–30 min	24	24
30–45 min	22	22
45–60 min	19	19
Longer than 1 h	23	23
Total	100	100

3   Metrics and Key Performance Indicators

As there is no unanimous agreement among scholars on whether e-Government services without online accessibility are truly e-Government service or not, in this paper e-Government services online inaccessibility is treated as a deficiency and making e-Government services tethered. The primary data collected via questionnaire has been used to derive the key performance indicators. The following metrics and Key Performance Indicators (KPIs) have been developed to measure the effectiveness and efficiency of public sector services which are transformed to e-Government services and systems but with a lack of digital money or online payment system integration:

- Round trip distance to effect payments for settling utilities bill without digital money or online payment system integration;
- Time to travel and effect payments for utilities bill without digital money or online payment system integration;
- Service and queue waiting time;
- Time to respond to queries from service consumers;
- Time for service consumers to obtain information/guidelines;
- Service availability;
- Timely settlement of bills;
- and Costs of getting the service.

Particular cases have been observed and measured and the results of the observation have been analysed in the section below, Sect. 3.1.

3.1   Analysis of the Findings with Respect to KPIs

a. Distance Traveled to Effect Payments for Utilities Bill

In this paper the round trip travel service consumers make to effect payments for utility bill is considered as one of the metrics in order to equate the inconvenience that service consumers have to bear which for e-Government systems with digital or online payment system integrated is non-existent.

As evidenced by the study, the cost of round trip distance is a concern for e-Services that lack the integration of online payment system and the findings describe how far service consumers need to travel to get to a nearby service center.

- About 67% of service consumers travel more than 1 km on average to get to a nearby service center to effect payment and a total of 2 km on average for their round trip. Users physical presence is a must because of a lack of online payment system integration with the e-Service.

b. Time to Travel to Effect Payments for Utility Bill

Because of the same reason as above the round trip time metric which is about the time it takes for service consumers to reach to a nearby service center is significant.

- As it stands on average about 63% of service consumers spend on average 15 to 20 min of time to reach to a nearby service center.

c. Service and Queue Waiting Time

The amount of time that service consumers spend on average for queuing up as well as service delivery is 20 to 30 min. Service delivery as well as queue time are not uniformly distributed throughout the month and at the beginning of the month service and queue waiting time could even get longer than 30 min.

d. Time to Respond to Queries from Service Consumers

Service consumers submit queries when they have one in the traditional way, and follow up to their queries require physical presence and which is demanding and at times unbearable.

e. Time for Service Consumers to Obtain Information/Guidelines

Information or guidelines pertinent to the e-Service are disseminated via the traditional means such as printed broachers and flying papers which could have been made accessible more easily and cost effectively with online presence.

f. Service Availability

Service availability is a great concern for service consumers as it not uncommon to go to a service center and being told the e-Service is not available due to power outages and to come back on another time or day. This adds to the inconveniences that service consumers have to bear- mainly caused by a lack of digital money or online payment systems integration to the e-Service.

g. Timely Settlement of Bills

Due to inconveniences associated with the current e-Service system it is also not uncommon for service consumers to effect payments past settlement due dates. This could have been easily avoided with the integration of digital money or online payment systems with the e-Service.

h. Costs of Getting the e-Service

Costs associated to getting the service are generally categorised into two- those quantifiable in monetary terms and those non-quantifiable ones. Time spent for travelling to service center, money spent for travelling, queuing and service delivery time constitute the costs that can be quantified in monetary terms, and generally in conveniences caused by a lack of digital money or online payment systems integration to the e-Service such as the inconvenience of travelling to a service center, inconveniences caused by power outages or service unavailability or extended waiting constitute the non-quantifiable cost of getting the service.

e-Government implementation frameworks proposed in the literature lack dynamism, and they have been too often slipping off the pace with the technology dynamics [2, 3, 5]. Thus, most of them have quickly outlived their usefulness. Due to emerging trends and continuous advancements in the technology sphere e-Government implementation frameworks need to embody characteristics such as adaptability as well as extensibility to elongate their usefulness thereby bringing in the desired outcomes such the realization of good governance constructs. In this paper, a conceptual framework for untethered e-Government ecosystem is proposed to address the major issues that surround adaptability and extensibility of e-Government implementation frameworks. The classification of issues into tethered and untethered in e-Government implementations is the distinguishing feature of this paper. It points out the key elements to bridge the gap from tethered to the untethered e-Government functional model.

4   A Conceptual Framework for Tethered and Untethered e-Government

In this paper, a conceptual framework for tethered and untethered e-Government with the metrics and key performance indicators (KPIs) defined above as the main distinguishing features have been proposed. The conceptual framework highlights the constraints that need addressing and it also informs the strategic considerations that particularly governments in developing countries need to pursue for transforming traditional public services into digital as well as online (Fig. 1).

e-Government services in the tethered setting are characterised by intermittent connectivity with low level of public or private access to Internet or ICT, mode of payments systems heavily conventional or at best semi-electronic, services requiring physical presence, low level of digital literacy rate (service consumers familiarity with the Internet and ICT tools is low), slow response to queries, unguaranteed service availability with services offered predominantly offline and the cost of getting the service for consumers is high. E-Government services in the untethered setting to the contrary possesses the necessary ingredients to provide impeccable services to citizens-pervasive Internet which enables service users to conduct transaction at the comfort of

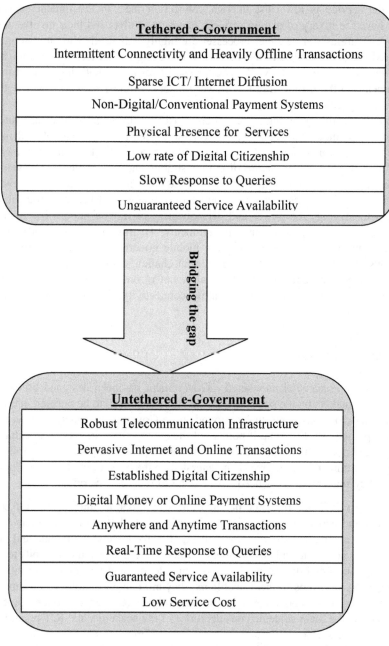

Fig. 1. Bridging the gap to untethered e-Government ecosystem.

being anywhere and anytime, services require no physical presence, citizens are capable of using the Internet and ICT tools to interact with the government, real-time responses for queries, with high services availability and reliability, and the cost of getting the service is low (just Internet connection fee). In the untethered setting citizens have the luxury of getting services in several outlets and their involvement in decision making as well as other processes are highly enhanced. The ultimate goal in untethered e-Government is to use current or emerging digital technologies for better public services to citizens as well as better use of resources with less impact on the environment via the use of ultra-low power sensors, wireless networks, and web and mobile-based applications [6, 7].

The unified utilities billing system (Lehulu-Kifiya) investigated as a case study in this paper falls under this category. In the tethered setting e-Services offered mostly involve the physical presence of service users at least to effect payments. Given the diverse as well as complex nature of the constraints and governments in developing countries operating with restricted or limited resources or fiscal wherewithal, addressing them in the shorter term might look unviable and hence a strategic consideration to leverage the power and pervasiveness of mobile phones has to be the priority aim of developing country governments. To this end, there needs to be a strategic focus on the expedition of more mobile government (m-Gov) services and indigenous innovations or solutions for current challenges- for instance transforming existing payments systems to support digital money or online transaction like m-pesa[2], localizing e-Service systems and mitigating connectivity slowness and unreliability related problems.

5   Recommendations

In this paper, a conceptual untethered e-Government has been designed primarily to inform policy makers on the strategic considerations that need to be pursued in order to mitigate issues or constraints that surround the e-Government sphere of developing countries, particularly Ethiopia. It points out the strategic considerations in enhancing existing e-Services with respect to the KPIs developed. Accordingly, the following actionable recommendations have been generated on the basis of the KPIs developed to inform policy makers on what needs to be done to unleash e-Services.

- **Scaling up ICT or Internet penetration** - in order to unlock the full social, political and economic benefits of the Internet as well ICT towards improving e-Services outcome, besides the government, all stakeholders, the private and public sectors, the academia and development partners should contribute their bits towards bridging the digital divide gap in rapidly broadening and deepening capacity;
- **Indigenous solutions to local problems** - beyond being technology consumer and adopters, crafting innovative solutions to mitigate tethered e-Services problems needs to be the main strategic considerations of the academia and ICT practitioners in the private sector;
- **Telecommunication regulatory reforms** - rigidity in telecom regulatory frameworks are to blame for some of constraints that stand in the way of untethered e-Services and reforms in telecom regulatory are critical.

---

[2] https://www.mpesa.in/portal/.

- **Following the opportunities insight** - planning ahead to maximize the benefits of the ongoing telecom infrastructure expansion project is critical [4]. The 3G plus and 4G mobile networks infrastructure deployment can be used to great effect in terms of bridging the digital divide gap within the society at both urban and rural areas. However, endowing infrastructure access to citizens amounts to addressing only one facets of the digital divide problem which can impact e-Services delivery because of service users lack of access to ICT or inability to use ICT tools effectively. More is required to use the infrastructure to its full potential for better government services provision as well as citizens full participation. To this effect, developing localised mobile-based applications for mobile-based government services needs a strategic consideration.
- **Digital Citizenship** - Ethiopia is known for the lowest rate of digital literacy. The low rate of digital literacy is one of the most difficult hurdles the country needs to cross in order to dispense the benefits of e-Services to a wider segment of the society. Thus, conducting digital literacy campaigns sooner rather than later in broadening and deepening capacity needs a strategic consideration.

6 Conclusion

Globally, efforts to transform government services in to digital or electronic are gathering pace; however electronic transformation of government services in developing countries are yet to exhibit the true effects of the Internet and ICT tools potential in the realisation of good governance constructs- effectiveness, efficiency, responsiveness, participation in decision making, accountability and transparency are not taking roots. Besides service consumers convenience to get government services at the comfort of anytime and anywhere have become elusive as existing e-Government systems lack pervasiveness as well as support for digital money or online payment systems. In this study, in order to capture the look and feel of e-Government landscape of developing countries (with Ethiopia as a case study), one popular and widely used e-Service, the unified billing system named "Lehulu" was chosen. The e-Service is designed to help consumers pay their utility bills for electric, water and telephone in a nearby service center in a unified manner. With the current setting service consumers physical presence to effect payments for utilities bills is a must. About 67% of respondents travel more than 1 km to get to a nearby service center and 64% of respondents claim they spend more than 30 min for queuing up as well as service time. These inconveniences consumers experience once in every month could have been easily avoided with the creation of an enabling environment for the use of digital money or online payment systems.

The transformation of the fragmented utility bill payment services into electronic as well as being served under one-stop centers has brought significant benefits to utility consumers. The cost attached to establishing the e-Service centers and running them has been more expensive than what it was before. There is significant cost attached to recruiting computer literate skilled man power and furnishing the e-Service centers with computers and related devices. Hence transforming the service into electronics makes no financial sense, and the monetary return of investments might not be achieved.

References

1. Beardsley, S., von Morgenstern, I.B., Enriquez, L., Verbeke, W.: Towards a new regulatory compact. The Global Information Technology Report 2003–2004: Towards An Equitable Information Society, pp. 71–86. Oxford University Press, New York (2004)
2. Clement, D.: The Ethiopian National Electronic Government Implementation Strategy and the ICT4D-2010 E-Government Action Plan, May 2006
3. Roslind, K.: Malaysian e-Government implementation framework, May 2006 http://www.shebacss.com/docs/ecompo001–10.pdf
4. Ongoing and Completed Telecom Services Initiatives in Ethiopia - Translated from Documents available in Amharic Language
5. van den Berg, L., van der Meer, A., van Winden, W., Woets, P.: e-Governance in European and South African Cities: The Cases of Barcelona, Cape Town, Eindhoven, Johannesburg, Manchester, Tampere, The Hague, and Venice. Ashgate Publishing, Ltd., Farnham (2006)
6. Maria, N., Constantina, C.: Agricultural e-government services: an implementation framework and case study. Comput. Electron. Agric. **70**(2), 337–347 (2010)
7. Ruthbea, Y.C.: Smart Cities and the Internet of Everything: The Foundation for Delivering Next-Generation Citizen Services, October 2013. https://www.cisco.com/web/strategy/docs/scc/ioe_citizen_svcs_white_paper_idc_2013.pdf
8. Michael, B., Kay, A., Giannotti, F., Alexei, P., Armando, B., Monica, W., Georgios, O., Yuval, P.: Smart Cities of the Future, October 5. ISSN 1467-1298. https://www.bartlett.ucl.ac.uk/casa/pdf/paper188

Intelligent License Plate Recognition

Yaecob Girmay Gezahegn[1]([⊠]), Misgina Tsighe Hagos[2],
Dereje H. Mariam W. Gebreal[1], Zeferu Teklay Gebreslassie[2],
G. agziabher Ngusse G. Tekle[3], and Yakob Kiros T. Haimanot[3]

[1] Addis Ababa University, Addis Ababa, Ethiopia
yaecob.girmay@gmail.com, dereje.hailemariam@aait.edu.et
[2] Ethiopian Biotechnology Institute, Addis Ababa, Ethiopia
misgina.tsighe@ebti.gov.et, teklayg2002@gmail.com
[3] Mekelle University, Mekelle, Ethiopia
gezubashay@gmail.com, yakobkiros81@gmail.com

Abstract. Road traffic accident is the leading cause of deaths and injuries in the world according to the World Health Organization (WHO). Every year many deaths and injuries are reported and most of them are in developing countries; the problem has great impact in Africa. Intelligent License Plate Recognition and reporting (ILPR) plays an important role in minimizing traffic accidents by implementing traffic monitoring and management systems. Since the number of vehicles are increasing, breaking traffic rules, entering restricted areas are becoming a trend. So, to control these actions, a system which can recognize vehicles by their License Plate (LP) is crucial. In this paper, we have developed ILPR system, which aims at reducing traffic accidents by processing an input image of a vehicle and reporting on its legality status. The ILPR starts with preprocessing and then extracts the LP using edge detection and vertical projection algorithms. To identify the License Plate Number (LPN), characters found on the LP are extracted and recognized by Artificial Neural Networks (ANN), which we trained with sample characters. If the recognized LPN is found to be a suspect after cross checking it with a pre-stored database, it will be sent to a person in charge via Short Message Service (SMS). In the recognition part, different papers use template matching, but is sensitive to noise. In order to mitigate the noise problem, our system uses ANN. We have also added SMS module. The system is implemented using MATLAB and Java.

Keywords: Filtering · Edge detection · Segmentation · Recognition
Artificial neural networks · Vertical projection · Template matching

1 Introduction

According to the WHO, road traffic accident is the leading cause of death worldwide. Since 2007, more than 1.25 million people die and 50 million injuries occur every year by traffic accidents. Most of these deaths are in low and middle-income countries. The loss is approximately 3% of their GDP's. Developing countries account more than 85% of the injuries. The problem is severe in Africa, specifically Sub-Saharan; they have only 4% of the global vehicles but account 10% of the global death. On the other hand,

© ICST Institute for Computer Sciences, Social Informatics and Telecommunications Engineering 2018
F. Mekuria et al. (Eds.): ICT4DA 2017, LNICST 244, pp. 259–268, 2018.
https://doi.org/10.1007/978-3-319-95153-9_25

60% of global vehicles are in the developed countries with only 14% of deaths. As can be seen in Fig. 1, the traffic accidents affect the economically active workforce group (15–50 age), in low and middle income countries [1].

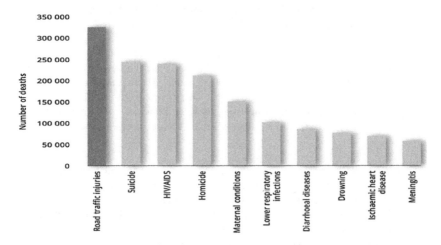

Fig. 1. Top ten causes of death among people aged 15 to 29 years in 2012 (Source WHO)

According to the report of Ethiopian Ministry of Transport, 1700 lives are lost and 7000 injuries occur each year. These are from the formal report of the police. However, there are many deaths and injuries which are not reported. Although the number of vehicles is very small in number, Ethiopia is one of the leading countries in traffic accident rate [2].

There are many reasons for the causes of traffic accidents, but the root causes are failing to observe the priority of pedestrians, passing the speed limit, human poor road network, absence of knowledge on road traffic safety, mixed traffic flow system, poor legislation and failure of enforcement, poor conditions of vehicles, lack of emergency medical services, poor road design, lack of automation or system computerization and monitoring [3–5]. World Bank warns that unless effective safety measures are taken, global road fatalities will increase by more than 65% between the years 2000 and 2020 [6]. The World Bank emphasized that traffic safety is the responsibility of governments, industries, business, non-governmental organizations and international agencies, with participation of people from all walks of life and disciplines [7].

Some of the problems associated with driving beyond speed limit, annual mechanical checkup verification, hit and run may be addressed by using ILPR systems.

In Ethiopia, Ministry of Transport carries out annual mechanical inspection of vehicles to ensure the technical competence of vehicles and their functionality. And if a vehicle has passed this test, a small sticker, which is valid for one year, will be posted to the vehicles windshield. A traffic police, on the road, undergoes a manual task of identifying vehicles that have not passed the annual mechanical inspection by stopping and checking whether it has the right sticker posted or not. However, there is no way to get information about any vehicle on the road using its LPN without stopping it. ILPR system will help computerize this manual task. Application of ILPR system is wide, for example in access control giving access only to vehicles of authorized personnel.

2   Previous Works

In traffic control, vehicles can be directed to different lanes for a better congestion control in busy urban communications during rush hours [8]. It is also used in tracking, automatic toll collection [9], automatic monitoring of traffic rules & maintaining law enforcement on public roads, surveillance, security, parking lots [10], monitoring vehicles passing through restricted areas [11], to mention few. The main parts of LPN recognition system are image acquisition, LP extraction, character segmentation, and character recognition [12]. In [13] cascade combination of adaptive boosting and Haar-like features are used to extract LP. The advantage of using Haar-like features is that irrespective of illumination variation, color, size, and position the LP can be detected. In [14], fast Vertical Edge Detection Algorithm (VEDA) was proposed, VEDA showed that it is faster than Sobel operator. Combination of edge detectors and mathematical morphology is used in [15] but, at the cost of computational time. Hence, [16] uses block-base algorithm for detection. Wavelet transform-based algorithm is also used in [17] for localization. Neural network based color extraction and template matching recognition of characters can be found in [18]. Genetic algorithm segmentation is used in [19] to extract the plate region. In [20] Gabor filter is applied for character recognition. As can be seen, it is possible to use many different features to find the location of the LPs, such as, shape, color, orientation and frequency. Edge detection is often used to help locate LPs. Systems detect vertical edges to find two parallel edges on each side of the LP, or to find characters [21]. Machine learning algorithms such as neural networks can be used to increase accuracy and computational speed [22]. Fuzzy algorithms like fuzzy C-means can also be used for plate detection [23]. Template matching based character recognition has been used in [27]. ANN have been adopted for increasing the speed of computation in [28] and Support Vector Machine (SVMs) [29] can be applied for classification.

While studying the literatures, we came across two papers which are studied in Ethiopia for the license plate recognition [25, 26]. Both of them are more or less similar. In the recognition part they both used template matching. But, ours differs, as will be discussed in detail under the "Proposed System", the ILPR system uses ANN based character recognition and SMS reporting system. The recognized LPN is stored in a database for law enforcement, traffic control and facility management purpose. In this paper, we have used a still digital camera to acquire images of vehicles.

3   Proposed System

The proposed system basically consists of image acquisition, preprocessing and information retrieval (ILPR) components. Among current LP systems, the simplest example is that of European LPs. It contains black numerical and English characters on white background. The United States LP is complex because it contains figures, state names, different fonts and colors. Chinese or Japanese LP are similar to that of Europe. However, they contain many texts and complicated fonts [24]. In our system, the Ethiopian alphabets and numbers are more or less similar to the European LPs.

Figure 2, shows the process flow of our ILPR system.

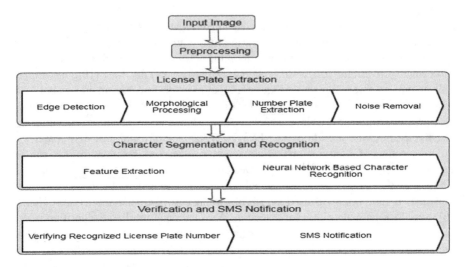

Fig. 2. Flowchart of ILPR

3.1 Capturing an Image and Preprocessing

Preprocessing is carried out on the image to improve its quality by removing noise. The following steps were followed for this phase.

Step1: get picture of a vehicle with a still digital camera from the road
Step2: Convert RGB to gray scale, as depicted in Fig. 3
Step3: Then filter the image using Gaussian filter.

Fig. 3. RGB image (left) and gray image (right)

3.2   License Plate Area Detection (Localization)

The second phase is plate localization. It is assumed that the LP is a rectangular area with increased occurrence of horizontal and vertical edges. The high density of horizontal and vertical edges on a small area is in many instances caused by an LP. This process can sometimes detect a wrong area that does not correspond to an LP. Because of this, we often detect several candidates for the plate, and then we choose the best one by a further heuristic analysis. Detection of an LP area consists of a series of operations. Modified snapshot is then projected into axes x and y. These projections are used to determine an area of an LP.

3.3   Image Segmentation

3.3.1   Edge Detection

This phase detects the presence of an edge within an image [30]. Edge detection simplifies processing speed, data and computational time [31]. Generally, an edge is characterized by an abrupt frequency or amplitude change in an image [32]. There are many different types of edge detection techniques. Here Sobel operator is used due to its high computational speed, accuracy and simplicity, see Table 1 and Fig. 4.

Table 1. Edge detection methods and their rate of success [33]

Total image	Method	Prewitt	Log	Canny	Sobel	Robert	Zero cross
100	Success rate	83%	60%	85%	93%	88.22%	70%

G_x detects vertical edges and the G_y detects horizontal edges.

Fig. 4. Detected edges

3.3.2   Detecting and Cropping License Plate Area

We followed the following steps to detect, select and crop the LP area.

Step 1: Image Filling
   Fill holes, an area in the image surrounded by rounding lines, so that LP area can be identified to be isolated from the image. Output of this step is shown in Fig. 5 (Left).

Step 2: Scan and count each pixel in the following manner, where size of the LP area is supposed to be between x and y:
   If number of 'white pixels' < x;

```
            pixels become 'black'
        Else; no change
        If number of 'white pixels' > y;
            pixels become 'black'
        Else; no change
```
Step 3: Use Step 2 in both horizontal and vertical direction, changing x and y correspondingly.
Step 4: Check number of possible areas.
```
        If number of areas > 1,
            go to step 5
        Else; go to step 6
```
Step 5: Select true candidate for the LP.
This function first calculates on aspect ratio; it then selects the candidate area with the most edges per area as the true LP. An example of the output of this stage is shown in Fig. 5 (Center).
Step 6: Logically AND with binary image obtained at "Edge Detection"
Step 7: Crop the LP
This step determines position of the true candidate LP and uses that position to crop the LP from the original binary image. An example of the output of this stage can be seen in Fig. 5 (Right).

Fig. 5. LP detection and cropping. Image with LP candidates (left), Image with a true candidate (center), Image of a cropped LP (right)

3.3.3   License Plate Normalization

The brightness and contrast characteristics of segmented characters vary due to different light conditions while the camera captures the image. The LP can sometimes be partially shadowed or non-uniformly illuminated. Because of this, it is necessary to normalize the LP. Histogram normalization, global, adaptive thresh-holding etc., can be used to enhance the brightness and contrast of an image. We used adaptive thresh-holding, since it computes threshold value for each pixel separately using its local neighborhood which increases the intensity and resolution of the LP.

3.4   Character Extraction

All the remaining steps depend on segmentation. If segmentation fails, a character can be improperly divided into two pieces, or two characters can be improperly merged. We can either use a horizontal projection of an LP for the segmentation or one of the more sophisticated methods, such as segmentation using the neural networks. If we assume only one-row plate, the segmentation is a process of finding horizontal boundaries between characters.

3.4.1   Segmentation of LP Using a Horizontal Projection

By detecting spaces in horizontal projection, the plate image can be segmented. After the adaptive thresh-holding, a horizontal projection of the LP is computed. This projection is used to determine horizontal boundaries between segmented characters.

3.5   LP Segmentation

Character segmentation is done using the following main steps:

Step 1: Connected components extraction.

Step 2: Bounding-boxes detection.

    Aspect ratio and percentage area of the connected components are first computed. If the aspect ratio 'r' of the bounding box of a connected component is in an open interval, i.e.,]rMin, rMax[, and the percentage area pA,]pAreaMin, pAreaMax[, then the character is segmented and its bounding box coordinates are stored in a vector R. Otherwise, the candidate is discarded. Note that, this process is run to every bounding box of connected components in the binary image obtained from "Detecting and Cropping License Plate Area."

Step 3: Characters detection:

    The horizontal distance of each pair of nearest characters detected in the previous step is used as criterion in order to find new candidate characters.

Table 2.   Extracted/Isolated characters

Vehicle Code/ LP Identifier	Region Codes	LP Digits
🔲	🔲 🔲	🔲 🔲 🔲 🔲 🔲

Now, it is preferable to divide extracted LP into individual images, each containing one isolated character. Static bounds, vertical projection, and connected component are used for isolating. Here, connected component technique is applied. Bounding box is used to extract individual characters from the license.

3.6   Recognition of Characters Using ANN

Using the segmented images collected, as depicted in Table 2, as inputs we created and trained 3 feed forward neural networks which have two hidden layers each, for LP digits classification (digits 0 to 9), for LP region codes classification (AA, AM, OR, TG, ET) and for the LP identifier classification (digits 1 to 5). In all of the 3 artificial neural networks, we have used a gradient descent with momentum and adaptive learning rate back-propagation algorithm and log-sigmoid transfer function (Fig. 6).

Fig. 6.   An example of a segmented neural network input character

Figure 7 is an example showing input, output and hidden layer nodes for the first neural network using the input image shown in Fig. 8. We have resized the images of the characters to 7 × 5 pixels (height = 7 and width = 5), so as to have 35 input pixels to the neural network architecture.

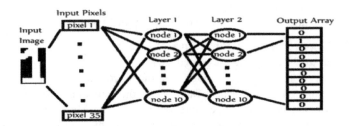

Fig. 7. Feed forward back-propagation neural network for identifying digits 0 to 9.

3.7   Notification

From the above steps we have acquired the LP identifier, region code and LP digits, which make up the LPN together. If an LPN was not found to be on the list of vehicles that have passed the annual mechanical inspection or if it was previously stored in a black list of LPs, a traffic police or a person in charge will be notified of the LPN. To facilitate this action, an android device has to be connected to a Personal Computer (PC), on which the MATLAB LPN recognition program is running, in USB debugging mode. The PC and the android device communicate through Android Debug Bridge (ADB) utility. Java program (which runs on the PC) is written to send an SMS of suspected LPNs, which it has accepted from the MATLAB program, using ADB through the connected android mobile device. SMS is used to send the LPN of the illegal car to the person in charge. Because of its reliability SMS based notification is chosen, it can even work in a very remote area where other access networks are hard to get.

4   Conclusion

It can be inefficient to manually keep track of vehicles on a busy road or parking lot. In order to overcome this problem, the ILPR is very helpful. Given an input image of a vehicle the ILPR should identify its LPN using ANN, undergo a comparison with previously stored database and send an SMS to a nearby traffic police if the detected LPN is found to be of a suspect vehicle. There may be commercial solutions available to automatic LP recognition which use different algorithms in other places, but the main purpose of our work is to develop a solution that also helps traffic police or any other concerned body identify a suspect vehicle automatically with a cheap or no price in order to minimize the death or injury which is reported every year.

References

1. World Health Organization (WHO): Global Status Report on Road Safety (2015)
2. Ethiopian Roads Authority: How Safe are Ethiopian Roads, April 2013
3. Tulu, G.S., et al.: Characteristics of police-reported road traffic crashes in Ethiopia over a six year period. In: Proceedings of the 2013 Australasian Road Safety Research, Policing & Education Conference, August 2013
4. Persson, A.: Road traffic accidents in Ethiopia: magnitude, causes and possible interventions. Adv. Transp. Stud. **15**, 5–16 (2008)
5. Mekasha, F.: Road traffic accident: causes and control mechanisms. Master's thesis, Addis Ababa University, Addis Ababa City, June 2015
6. Kopits, E.: Traffic Fatalities and Economic Growth. Policy Research Working Paper Number 3035, World Bank, Washington, DC (2003)
7. Bliss, T., et al.: Implementing the recommendations of the world report on road traffic injury prevention. World Bank Global Road Safety (2009)
8. Cowell, J.R.: Syntactic pattern recognizer for vehicle identification numbers. Image Vis. Comput. **13**(1), 13–19 (1995)
9. Lotufo, R.A., et al.: Automatic number plate recognition. Inst. Elect. Eng. Colloquium on Image Analysis for Transport Applications, pp. 61–66 (1990)
10. Bartolome, L.S., et al.: Vehicle parking inventory system utilizing image recognition through artificial neural networks, pp. 1–5, IEEE, May 2012
11. Draghici, S.: A neural network based artificial vision system for license plate recognition. Int. J. Neural Systems **8**, 113–126 (1997)
12. Lotufo, R.A., et al.: Automatic license plate recognition a state-of-the-art review. Iccc Trans. Circ. Syst. Video Technol. **23**, 311–325 (2013)
13. Zhang, H., et al.: Learning-based license plate detection using global and local features. Int. Conf. Pattern Recognit. **2**, 1102–1105 (2006)
14. Al-Ghaili, A.M., et al.: A new character segmentation is successful when the character Vertical edge detection algorithm and its application. In: Proceedings of International Conference on Computer Engineering Systems, pp. 204–209 (2008)
15. Zheng, D., et al.: An efficient method of license plate location. Pattern Recogn. Lett. **26**(15), 2431–2438 (2005)
16. Lee, H.J., et al.: Extraction and recognition of license plates of motorcycles and vehicles on highways. In: Proceedings of ICPR, pp. 356–359 (2004)
17. Hsieh, C.T., et al.: Multiple license plate detection for complex background. Int. Conf. AINA **2**, 389–392 (2005)
18. Lee, E.R., et al.: Automatic recognition of a car license plate using color image processing. In: Proceedings of International Conference on Image Processing (1994)
19. Kim, S.K., et al.: A Recognition of vehicle license plate using a genetic algorithm based segmentation. In: Proceedings of 3rd IEEE International Conference, pp. 661–664 (1996)
20. Tavsanoglu, V., Saatci, E.: Feature extraction for character recognition using Gabor-type filters implemented by cellular neural networks. In: Proceedings of the 6th IEEE International Workshop, pp. 63–68, Piscataway, NJ, USA. IEEE (2000)
21. Ahmed, M.J., et al.: License plate recognition system. In: ICECS, Proceedings of the 2003 10th IEEE International Conference, vol. 2, pp. 898–901, December 2003
22. Kim, K.K., et al.: Learning-based approach for license plate recognition. In: Proceedings of the IEEE Signal Processing Society Workshop, vol 2, pp. 614–623 (2000)
23. Comelli, P., Ferragina, P., Granieri, M.N., Stabile, F., et al.: Optical recognition of motor vehicle license plates. IEEE Trans. Veh. Tech. **44**, 790–799 (1995)

24. Zhu, S.: An end-to-end license plate localization and recognition system. Master thesis. Rochester Institute of Technology, New York, March 2015
25. Ahmed, H.Z.: Design and implementation of car plate recognition system for ethiopian car plates. Master's thesis, Addis Ababa, November 2011
26. Nigussie, S., Assabie, Y.: Automatic recognition of ethiopian license plates. In: IEEE AFRICON, Addis Ababa, Ethiopia (2015)
27. Pan, R., et al.: An efficient method for skew correction of license plate. In: Second International Workshop, vol. 2, pp. 90–93, March 2010
28. Park, S.H., et al.: Locating car license plates using neural networks. Electron. Lett. **35**, 1475–1477 (1999)
29. Arth, C., et al.: Real-time license plate recognition on an embedded DSP-platform. In: Computer Vision Pattern Recognition, pp. 1–8, June 2007
30. Frei, W., et al.: Fast boundary detection: a generalization and new algorithm. IEEE Trans. Comput. **C-26**, 988–998 (1977)
31. Canny, J.: A computational approach to edge detection. IEEE Trans. Pattern Anal. Mach. Intell. **8**(6), 679–698 (1986)
32. Pratt, W.K.: Digital Image Processing, pp. 491–556. Wiley, Hoboken (1991)
33. Azad, R., et al.: Real-time and efficient method for accuracy enhancement of edge based license plate recognition system. In: International Conf. on computer, Information Technology and Digital Media (2013)

Comparison of Moving Object Segmentation Techniques

Yaecob Girmay Gezahegn[1(✉)], Abrham Kahsay Gebreselasie[2],
Dereje H. Mariam W. Gebreal[1], and Maarig Aregawi Hagos[3]

[1] Addis Ababa University, Addis Ababa, Ethiopia
yaecob.girmay@gmail.com,
dereje.hailemariam@aait.edu.et
[2] Addis Ababa Science and Technology University, Addis Ababa, Ethiopia
kgabrham@gmail.com
[3] Mekelle University, Mekelle, Ethiopia
maarig2000@gmail.com

Abstract. Moving object segmentation is the extraction of meaningful features from series of images. In this paper, different types of moving object segmentation techniques such as Principal Component Analysis (PCA), K-Means clustering (KM), Genetic Algorithm (GA) and Genetic Algorithm Initialized K-means clustering (GAIK) have been compared. From our analysis we have observed that PCA reduces dimension or size of data for further processing, which in return reduces the computational time. However, the segmentation quality sometimes becomes unacceptable. On the other hand, due to random initialization of its centroids, KM clustering sometimes converges to local minimum which results in bad segmentation. Another algorithm which has been considered in this study is GA, which searches all the feature space and results in a global optimum clustering. Although the segmentation quality is good, it is computationally expensive. To mitigate these problems, KM and GA are merged to form GAIK, where GA helps to initialize the centroids of the clustering. From our study, it has been found out that GAIK is superior to GA in both the quality of segmentation and computational time. Therefore, in general, the analyses of the four algorithms shows that GAIK is optimal for segmenting a moving object.

Keywords: Clustering · Segmentation · PCA · KM · GA · GAIK

1 Introduction

Segmentation is the process of extracting meaningful features from an image or series of images (frames) in time domain. It is widely used in object detection, surveillance, tracking, content based image retrieval, medical imaging such as locating tumors, machine vision, locating objects in satellite imagery, pattern recognition etc.

There are several types of image segmentation techniques, some of which are thresholding, Edge-based, Region-based, Hybrid and Clustering. Thresholding delineates peaks, valleys, and shapes in its corresponding intensity histogram to segment an image, whereas edge-based segmentation is a set of linked pixels lying on the boundary

© ICST Institute for Computer Sciences, Social Informatics and Telecommunications Engineering 2018
F. Mekuria et al. (Eds.): ICT4DA 2017, LNICST 244, pp. 269–279, 2018.
https://doi.org/10.1007/978-3-319-95153-9_26

between different regions, where there are intense discontinuities such as gray change, color distinctness, variation in texture and other similar features. Moreover, edge-based segmentation uses abrupt changes in intensity, color, and texture for segmenting an object [1]. By detecting the discontinuities, a moving object can be segmented. There are two types of Edge-based segmentations - Gray-histogram method and Gradient-based method [2].

Region-based segmentation divides an image into sections that are alike on some predefined criteria. Pixels within the same region need to have similar values of intensity, color or texture [3]. Hybrid techniques may use both region based and edge detection technique. The other segmentation technique is clustering. It is the process of grouping data into clusters in a certain metric, where objects within each cluster have high similarity, but are dissimilar to the objects in other clusters [4]. Each of these groups is called a cluster [5, 6]. Most of the time, the similarity is measured with distance, namely two or more objects belong to the same cluster if they are close enough according to a given distance limit. Patterns within a cluster are more similar to each other than patterns fit into different clusters [7].

Another method of segmentation is the fuzzy set theory. This method can be used in clustering and it allows fuzzy or soft boundaries to exist between different clusters. The main drawback of this algorithm is that it is difficult to confirm the attribute of fuzzy members [8]. There is also neural network based segmentation, in which every pixel is mapped to every neuron when the algorithm is applied to image processing. To segment a moving object using neural network, series of images are mapped into a neural network architecture. By using dynamic equations to optimize every neuron's energy image edges are extracted [9].

Table 1 summarizes some of the techniques that are used in image segmentation. This paper makes further comparison on PCA, KM, GA and GAIK using python libraries Numpy and OpenCV.

Table 1. Types of segmentation techniques [10].

Main categories	Techniques		Interpretation
Edge-based segmentation	Gray-histogram technique		Partition an image through detecting edge among different regions
	Gradient-based method	Differential coefficient techniques	
		Laplacian of a Gaussian (LoG)	
		Canny technique	
Region-based segmentation	Thresholding	Otsu	Extract the objects from the background by setting reasonable gray threshold for image pixels
		Optimal thresholding	

(continued)

Table 1. (*continued*)

Main categories	Techniques		Interpretation
		Thresholding image	
	Region operating	Region growing	Partition an image into regions that are similar according to a given criteria, such as gray character, color character or texture character
		Region splitting and merging	
		Image matching	
Segmentation based on Clustering, Hybrid and other methods	Fuzzy clustering segmentation		Introduce fuzzy set theory into image segmentation
	PCA Based		Segmentation based on PCA
	KM Clustering Segmentation		Segmentation based on KM clustering
	Neural networks based segmentation		It is a learning algorithm imitating the working pattern of neural networks
	GA based segmentation		Utilizes GA for segmentation
	GAIK Based segmentation		Uses hybrid of GA and KM clustering

The rest of the paper is organized as follows. PCA based moving object segmentation is discussed in Sect. 2. Section 3 expresses how KM can be used in image segmentation. Section 4 presents GA and its application in image processing. The hybrid of GA and KM is discussed in Sect. 5. Section 6 discusses the result & analysis, and Sect. 7 provides the conclusion of the study.

2 PCA

PCA focuses on finding orthogonal projections of dataset that contain the highest variance possible in order to 'find hidden linear correlations' between variables of the dataset. Most of the time, features are correlated. So, PCA de-correlates data for feature extraction and reducing the size. Many features rely on each other or on an unknown variable. A single feature can embed/hide a lot of information with in it. Removing such a feature can remove sensitive information. Hence, before eliminating features or reducing the size, the data is transformed into feature space for the purpose of avoiding dependency among variables, i.e. the feature space becomes de-correlated. So, the data is projected onto the largest eigenvectors of its covariance matrix in the feature space which encodes the most information; covariance matrix uses a sequence of rotation and scaling operations on data, where the rotation matrix is the eigenvectors of this covariance matrix.

In information theory, the valuable information or largest entropy is found in the feature with the highest variance. The data is defined by the largest eigenvectors or principal components, whereas the smallest eigenvectors are neglected as noise [11].

PCA reduces linear M-dimensional subspace of the original N-dimensional data, where $M \leq N$. Furthermore, if the unknown, uncorrelated components are Gaussian distributed, then PCA actually acts as an independent component analysis since uncorrelated Gaussian variables are statistically independent. However, if the underlying components are not normally distributed, PCA merely generates decorrelated variables which are not necessarily statistically independent. Principal components' are obtained by the Eigen Decomposition of the covariance matrix of the data. The size is then reduced by projecting the data onto the largest eigenvectors. The covariance matrix in the x-direction is given as

$$\sigma_x^2 = \frac{1}{M} \sum_{i=1}^{M} (x_i - \mu)^T (x_i - \mu) \tag{1}$$

$$\sigma_x^2 = \frac{1}{M} \sum_{j=1}^{M} (x_i - \mu)^2$$
$$= E[(x - E(x))(x - E(x))]$$
$$= \sigma(x, x)$$

Where $x_i - \mu$ the zero is mean and x_i is the input data.

The variance $\sigma(x, x)$ shows spread of the data in the x-direction and the variance $\sigma(y, y)$ depicts the spread in the y-direction. However, there is no correlation between x and y. When one variable is dependent on the other one, we use covariance matrix.

$$\sigma(x, y) = E[(x - E(x))(y - E(y))] \tag{2}$$

For two dimensional data, the covariance matrix can be stated as

$$\begin{bmatrix} \sigma(x, x) & \sigma(x, y) \\ \sigma(y, x) & \sigma(y, y) \end{bmatrix} \tag{3}$$

Similarly, we can generalize the covariance matrix for an $N \times N$ dimensional data.

Following the covariance matrix, the singular value decomposition (SVD) can be calculated as

$$\sigma_x^2 = O\Lambda O^T, \tag{4}$$

Where O is the eigenvector matrix and Λ is the diagonal matrix. The Eigen-decomposition extracts transformation matrices; the eigenvectors depict the direction and the eigenvalues represent the magnitude [11].

Steps Used in PCA
Step 1: Center the Data (frames)
    The data is centered in order to get zero average.
Step 2: Normalize the Data
    Divide each feature by its standard deviation.
Step 3: Calculate the Eigen Decomposition
    It is calculated using Singular Value Decomposition
    (SVD).
Step 4: Project the Data
    Data is projected onto the largest eigenvectors.

3   KM Algorithm

There are different methods for clustering data [5]. K-means clustering is widely used due to its good computational performance [12]. It optimizes the distance criterion, mostly Euclidian distance, either by minimizing the within cluster spread or by maximizing the distance among clusters. Clustering may be performed based on other criteria's like graph theoretical approach and hierarchical approach. Survey and comparative analysis of different clustering methods are presented in [13] and suggests that there is no general strategy which works equally in every domain. The Algorithm (Pseudo-code) for KM Clustering is presented in [14] as follows.

Step 1: Choose K initial cluster centers $z_1, z_2, \cdots, z_k$ randomly from the n points $\{x_1, x_2, \cdots, x_n\}$.
Step 2: Assign point x_i, $i = 1, 2,..., n$ to cluster $C_j = j \in \{1, 2. \cdots K\}$ iff

$$\left\| x_i - z_j \right\| < \left\| x_i - z_p \right\|, p = 1, 2, \ldots, K, \text{ and } j \neq p. \tag{5}$$

Step 3: Compute new cluster centers $z_1^*, z_2^*, \cdots, z_k^*$ as follows

$$z_i^* = \frac{1}{n_i} \sum_{x_j \in C_i} x_j, \, i = 1, 2, \ldots, K, \tag{6}$$

Where n_i is the number of elements belonging to cluster C_j.
Step 4: If $z_i^* = z_i$, $i = 1, 2, ..., K$ then terminate.

Otherwise, continue from step 2.
    KM may sometimes converge to a local minimum which is undesired process. This depends on the random initialization of the centroids. Simply put, different runs of KM on the same input data might produce different results.

4   GA Algorithm

Evolutionary algorithms such as simulated annealing, evolution strategies, evolutionary programming, ant colony, genetic algorithms and swarming (honey bee) are stochastic optimization algorithms based on the theory of survival of the fittest for an optimum solution to a given problem, [15]. By using evolutionary or genetic operators such as selection, recombination, crossover, mutation, migration, locality and neighborhood at each generation and iterating those leads to a natural adaptation, strong population which adapts to its environment in genetics sense [16].

Many researchers have proposed genetic algorithms for clustering data [13]. The basic idea is to simulate the evolution process of nature and evolve solutions from one generation to the next. In contrast to KM, which might converge to a local optimum, genetic algorithm is insensitive to the initialization process and always converges to the global optimum. However, these algorithms are usually computationally expensive. In all iterations of the GA, the individuals in the populations whose fitness score was in the top half were chosen to directly join the next generation population without mutation. In all the tests, the probability of mutation considered was 0.001, and the population size was 20.

Goldberg's Pseudo-code of GA

```
      Begin
Step 1: t = 0
Step 2: Initialize population P(t)
Step 3: Compute fitness P(t)
Step 4: t=t+1
Step 5: If termination criterion achieved go to step 10
Step 6: Elect P(t) from P(t-1)
Step 7: Crossover P(t)
Step 8: Mutate P(t)
Step 9: Go to step 3
Step 10: Output best and stop

      End
```

Genetic algorithms enhance the searching capability of cluster centers for the purpose of optimization in the feature space. Chromosomes encode the centroids. GA-clustering is superior to KM for it always converges globally [14]. Genetic Algorithm encodes its parameters as chromosomes. Initially, a random population is created from the data at hand, which represents different points in the search space. An objective and fitness function is associated with each string that represents the degree of goodness of the string. Based on the principle of survival of the fittest, a few of the strings are selected and each is assigned a number of copies that go into the mating pool. Operators like crossover and mutation yield a new generation of strings.

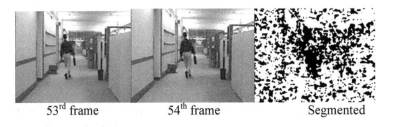

53rd frame   54th frame   Segmented

Fig. 1. Segmentation using PCA

The process of selection, crossover and mutation continues for a fixed number of generations or till a termination condition is satisfied as can be seen in Fig. 1.

5   GAIK Algorithm

It is a combination of KM and GA. It takes the best quality of each algorithm and combines them. KM is simple and computationally faster. It works for large number of variables, and GA is insensitive to the initialization process and its output converges optimally because it searches all the feature space of the input data. So, GAIK applies genetic algorithm as an initialization method for the KM clustering technique to enhance the segmentation of a moving object [17].

Input:

```
      Mutation Probability, Pm;

      Population size, N;

      Maximum Number of Generation, MAX_GEN;

Output: Solution string, s*;

{Initialize the population, P;

   Geno = MAX_GEN;

   s* = P1;  (Pi is the ith string in P)

   while (geno > 0)

   {Calculate Fitness values of strings in P;

    P* = Selection (P);

    for i = 1 to N, Pi = Mutation (P*);

    for i = 1 to N, k-means (Pi);

       s  =  string  in  P  such  that  the  corresponding
       weight matrix Ws has the minimum SE measure;

    if (S(Ws*) > S(Ws)), s* = s;

    geno = geno-1;

   }

   Output s*;

}
```

In all the tests, the probability of mutation considered was 0.001, and the population size was 20.

6   Result and Analysis

The different test frames that have been simulated are Hall frames [18] in an Intel corei3, 4 GB RAM with CPU 1.9 GHZ. Python libraries OpenCV and Numpy were used to implement all the algorithms. As can be seen in the results, PCA and KM need less computational time. However, they are not accurate; Figs. 1 and 2 are good examples. On the other hand, GA and GAIK are accurate. GAIK is preferable to GA because it is fast and has good quality output. Figures 3 and 4 and Tables 2, 3 and 4 clearly show all the differences among PCA, KA, GA and GAIK. There is a trade-off between accuracy and computational time. Furthermore, there is an additional requirement for KM, GA and GAIK, the background frame is needed as a reference. But, in some situations we may not have the background image in advance. So, optical flow, PCA or similar method of moving object segmentation seems preferable at the cost of computational time (for optical flow) and accuracy (for PCA). In this paper, we have used only two consecutive frames and a background (background, Hall 53rd & 54th [18]). But, the whole video test frames are tested for completeness, for instance all the 249 Hall frames are tested. Furthermore, there was no iteration in PCA. However, in KM we have used different iterations from 1 to 100 to get good segmentation result. GA and GAIK were iterated only twice by varying the population generation from 1 to 100. The different simulated results and their computational performances are shown from tables and figures. The metrics that are used for measuring the quality of the segmentations are objective (computational time) and subjective (accuracy, i.e. visual) methods. In other words, the results shown in the table are measured using objective method. The reason is that we have used the same standard, 'computational time' for all the algorithms, see the tables. But, the figures show subjective way of evaluation, by looking into the segmented images we can comment whether the quality is good or bad. For example, in Fig. 1, the segmented object is hard to identify, this is one simple instance of bad segmentation using PCA. We may sometimes get acceptable segmented quality using PCA if the data size is relatively small. KM clustering for moving object segmentation is demonstrated in Fig. 2. As can be observed, the segmentation is not really good. Figure 3 is segmented by using GA. It is better than PCA and KM, but still it has some noises around the segmented object which is undesired. GAIK based

Background image   53rd frame   54th frame   Segmented Object

Fig. 2. Segmentation using KM (5 iterations)

segmented object is shown in Fig. 4, and it can be observed that it is accurate, neat and computationally acceptable when it is compared with the other three methods.

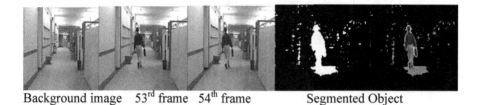

Background image   53rd frame   54th frame   Segmented Object

Fig. 3. Segmentation based on GA (5 generations)

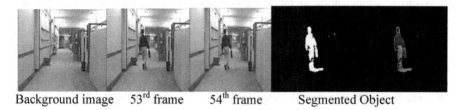

Background image   53rd frame   54th frame   Segmented Object

Fig. 4. Segmentation based on GAIK (5 generations)

Table 2. Computational time and accuracy for a 'Hall' test frame for 1 generation.

	Accuracy (visual)	Computational t(sec)	Comment
PCA	Less accurate	0.0326185483252	Not applicable
KM	Less accurate	0.213585236708	1 iteration
GA	Accurate	1.25684074966	1 generation
GKA	Accurate	0.998757	1 generation

Table 3. Computational time and accuracy for a 'Hall' test frame for 5 generations.

	Accuracy (visual)	Computational t(sec)	Comment
PCA	Less accurate	0.0326185483252	Not applicable
KM	Less accurate	0.215545061382	5 iterations
GA	Accurate	4.05593981372	5 generations
GKA	Accurate	4.01345731871	5 generations

Table 4. Computational time and accuracy for a 'Hall' test frame for 50 generations.

	Accuracy (visual)	Computational t(sec)	Comment
PCA	Less accurate	0.0326185483252	Not applicable
KM	Not always accurate	0.216087956580	50 iterations
GA	Accurate	38.038828081	50 generations
GKA	More accurate	37.51	50 generations

7 Conclusion

In this research, comparison of four image segmentation algorithms (PCA, KM, Genetic Algorithm (GA), and GAIK) has been made using different test frames of a Hall. The objective of the research was to distinguish which algorithm is optimal in both accuracy and computational cost. The metrics that are used for measuring the quality of the segmentation methods are objective (for computational time) and subjective (for accuracy, i.e. visual). From the results, it has been observed that PCA and KM need less computational time at the expense of segmentation accuracy. On the other hand, GA and GAIK are accurate but not computationally as fast as PCA or KM. Furthermore, it has been observed that GAIK is faster and has better segmented image output than GA. Therefore, GAIK based segmentation has been found to be accurate and computationally acceptable (optimal) when compared with the other three methods.

References

1. Otsu, N: Discriminant and least square threshold selection. In: Proceedings of the 4th International Joint Conference on Pattern Recognition, pp. 592–596 (1978)
2. Wang, et al.: Threshold segmentation for hand vein image. In: Control Theory and Application, pp. 19–22. Publishing House of Electronics Industry, Beijing (2005)
3. Shi, J., Malik, J.: Normalized cuts and image segmentation. IEEE Trans. Mach. Intell. **22**, 888–905 (2000)
4. Han, J., Kamber, M.: Data Mining: Concepts and Techniques. Morgan Kaufmann Publishers, Burlington (2001)
5. Pena, J., Lozano, J., Larranaga, P.: An empirical comparison of four initialization methods for the K-means algorithm. Pattern Recogn. Lett. **20**(10), 1027–1040 (1999)
6. Kaufman, L., Rousseeuw, P.: Finding Groups in Data: An Introduction To Cluster Analysis. Wiley, Hoboken (1990)
7. Jeyakumari, D., Somasundareswari, D.: Analysis on genetic current trends in color image segmentation. Int. J. Mod. Sci. Eng. Technol. (IJMSET) **1**(5), 1–12 (2014)
8. Gao, X.: Fuzzy Cluster Analysis and Application, pp. 124–130. Xidian University Press, Xi'an (2004)
9. Wang, Q.: One image segmentation technique based on wavelet analysis in the context of texture. In: Data Collection and Processing, vol. 13, p. 1216 (1998)
10. Kang, W.X., et al.: The comparative research on image segmentation algorithms. In: IEEE, First International Workshop on Education Technology and Computer Science, pp. 703–707 (2009)

11. www.visiondummy.com/2014/05/feature-extraction-using-pca/index.html
12. Dubes, R.C., Jain, A.K.: Clustering techniques: the user's dilemma. Pattern Recogn. **8**(4), 247–260 (1976)
13. Maulik, U., Bandyopadhyay, S.: Genetic algorithm based clustering technique. Pattern Recogn. **33**(9), 1455–1465 (2000)
14. Fogel, D.B.: An introduction to simulated evolutionary optimization. IEEE Trans. Neural Netw. **5**(1), 3–14 (1994)
15. http://www.geatbx.com/docu/algindex-01.html#TopOfPage
16. Lu, Y., Lu, S., Fotouhi, F., Deng, Y., Brown, S.: FGKA: a fast genetic k-means clustering algorithm. In: ACM Symposium on Applied Computing (2004)
17. Krishna, K., Murty, M.N.: Genetic k-means algorithm. IEEE Trans. Syst. Man Cybern. Part B Cybern. **29**(3), 433–439 (1999)
18. https://media.xiph.org/video/derf/y4m/hall_objects_qcif.y4m

ICT4DA Workshops

Towards Group Fuzzy Analytical Hierarchy Process

George W. Musumba[1(✉)] and Ruth D. Wario[2]

[1] Department of Computer Science, Dedan Kimathi University of Technology,
P.O. BOX 657, Nyeri 10100, Kenya
george.musumba@dkut.ac.ke
[2] Department of Computer Science and Informatics, University of Free State,
Private Bag X13, Kestell, Bloemfontein 9866, South Africa
wariord@ufs.ac.za

Abstract. Group decision making takes place in almost all domains. In building construction domain, a team of contractors with disparate specializations collaborate. Little research has been done to propose group decision making technique for this domain. As such, specific teams' competitiveness enhancements are minimal as it takes more time for individual evaluators to choose the right partners. Qualitative and quantitative methods were used. Themes and categorizations were based on deductive approach. Subsequently, Group Fuzzy Analytical Hierarchy Process (GFAHP), Multi-Criteria Decision Making (MCDM) algorithm, was designed and applied. It uses all evaluation criteria unlike Fuzzy AHP (FAHP) which excludes some criteria that are assigned zero weights. GFAHP reduces the number of pairwise comparisons required when a large number of attributes are to be compared. Validation of the technique carried out by five case studies, show that GFAHP is approximately 98.7% accurate in the selection of partners.

Keywords: Multi criteria decision making
Group Fuzzy Analytical Hierarchy Process
Partners evaluation and selection problem

1 Introduction

In almost all economic sectors globally, supply chains are composed of a complex sequence of processing stages, ranging from raw materials supplies, parts manufacturing, components and end-products assembling, to the delivery of end products [1]. In supply chain management (SCM), supplier selection decision is considered as one of the key issues faced by project managers to remain competitive. Supplier evaluation, selection and management can be applied to a variety of suppliers throughout a product's life cycle from initial raw material acquisition to end-of-life service providers. Thus, the breadth and diversity of suppliers make the process even more cumbersome [2]. In construction industry, apart from supply of physical materials, services are also supplied. In this case, the services supplied are key to the projects' completion.

© ICST Institute for Computer Sciences, Social Informatics and Telecommunications Engineering 2018
F. Mekuria et al. (Eds.): ICT4DA 2017, LNICST 244, pp. 283–307, 2018.
https://doi.org/10.1007/978-3-319-95153-9_27

In the construction industry, a project is normally implemented by a team of professionals and an alliance of companies [3]. Alliance of companies is formed by consultants who evaluate contractors (or service suppliers) for specific project tasks. A client hires an architect/consultant who makes designs for the project and engages other consultants to carry out the various tasks. For example, in a building construction project, the main consultant who is normally the architect, contracts civil/structural, electrical, mechanical, plumbing, interior design and land-scaping engineers. They work as a team to accomplish the tasks. The main consultant selects the best engineer/engineering firm among many firms who might have similar or near similar required attributes for the project. These companies coordinate among each other.

Evaluation and selection of a candidate among many alternative contestants, like is done for building construction projects, is a multi-criteria decision-making (MCDM) process [4]. MCDM process has been widely used in various fields such as location selection, information project selection, material selection, management decisions, strategy selection, and problems relating to decision-making [5]. This study defines a multiple criteria decision making problem for construction projects as "Partner Evaluation and Selection Problem (PESP)" so that each prospective partner (service supplier) can be evaluated against each defined criterion. A multi criteria decision making technique is designed that can be applied to derive each partner's weight and determine the best partner that is eventually selected for each project task.

Partner Evaluation and Selection Problem (PESP) can be represented mathematically as:

$$\gamma(t) = f(Z(h), S(p), P(m), T) \tag{1}$$

where:

$\gamma(t)$: partner evaluation and selection problem.
$Z(h)$: a set of tasks of the project,

$$Z(h) = \{z_1, z_2, \ldots z_m\}, m \geq 1.$$

$S(p)$: a set of selection criteria for assigning tasks to partner companies,

$$S(p) = \{s_1, s_2, \ldots s_n\}, n \geq 1.$$

$P(m)$: a set of prospective partner companies that satisfies the selection criteria, s_p and project tasks, z_h.

$$P(m) = \{p_1, p_2, \ldots p_m\}, m \geq 1.$$

T = expected completion time.

The PESP for the project is formulated as follows:

"Which partner companies $p_m(m > 1)$ are capable of performing the task $z_h(h > 1)$ according to the selection criteria $s_p(p > 1)$ for expected completion time T?" This requires the determination of the number of companies that are qualified to carry out tasks.

The same problem for a single task is formulated as follows:

"Which partner company p_m is capable of performing the task z_h according to the selection criteria s_p for expected completion time T?" This requires the determination of a company that is qualified to carry out a task.

In general, the PESP is a multi-criteria and multi-objective decision making problem [6]. With its need to trade-off multiple criteria exhibiting vagueness and imprecision, partner selection is a highly important multi-criteria decision making (MCDM) problem [8]. The classical MCDM methods that consider deterministic or random processes cannot effectively address decision problems incorporating imprecise and linguistic information. Fuzzy set theory is one of the effective tools to deal with uncertainty and vagueness.

The rest of the paper is organized as follows: The following section presents a brief literature review on supplier selection. In Sect. 3, methodology is presented. In Sects. 4 and 5, partner evaluation and selection factors, and Fuzzy Analytical Hierarchy Process approach are discussed respectively. Section 6 presents the proposed Group Fuzzy Analytical Hierarchy Process (GFAHP) and provides its stepwise representation. In Sect. 7, application of GFAHP is shown. Finally, concluding observations and directions for future research are given in the last section.

2 Literature Review

The partner selection process can be considered as a Multi-Criteria Decision-Making (MCDM) process, characterized by a substantial degree of uncertainty and subjectivity due to limited information about potential partners. Construction project partners are like suppliers to organizations [7]. In this regard, this review is based on suppliers in supply chain management which is applicable to construction domain. Supplier evaluation is a management decision-making process that addresses how organizations select strategic suppliers to enhance their competitive advantage [8].

According to the vast literature on supplier selection, the following properties need to be considered while resolving the supplier selection problem [9]. First, the supplier selection process requires considering multiple conflicting criteria. Second, several decision-makers are oftentimes involved in the decision process. Third, decision-making is often influenced by uncertainty in practice. Studies have shown that the classical MCDM methods which often consider deterministic or random processes have not been able to effectively address decision problems that incorporate imprecise and linguistic information [8].

Earlier studies on supplier selection focused on identifying the criteria used to select suppliers. Dickson [10] conducted one of the earliest works on supplier selection and identified 23 supplier attributes that managers consider when choosing a supplier. Among these criteria, quality, on time delivery, and performance history were noted as the most significant ones. Another study conducted by Lehmann and O'Shaughnessy [11] found that the key criteria generally claimed to affect supplier selection decisions were price, reputation of supplier, reliability, and delivery. Weber et al. [12] classified the articles published between 1966 and 1990 according to the considered criteria.

Based on 74 papers, they concluded that supplier selection is a multi-criteria problem, and price, delivery, quality, and production facility and location are the most frequently employed criteria.

In light of the multi-criteria nature of partner selection problem, it would appear that the application of multi-criteria decision making (MCDM) techniques to the problem is a fruitful area of research. Such techniques would allow project initiators to systematically examine the trade-offs among various criteria when selecting specific suppliers. As firms become involved in strategic partnerships with their suppliers, a new set of supplier selection criteria, termed as soft criteria, need to be considered in supplier selection decisions. These criteria are subjective factors that are difficult to quantify. Fuzzy set theory appears as an effective tool to deal with uncertainty inherent in supplier selection process. This section will briefly review the research works on supplier selection that employ fuzzy MCDM techniques.

Several authors have used fuzzy MCDM techniques such as fuzzy analytic hier-archy process (F-AHP), fuzzy analytic network process (F-ANP), fuzzy technique for order preference by similarity to ideal solution (F-TOPSIS), fuzzy multi-criteria opti-mization and compromise solution (F-VIKOR), fuzzy preference-ranking-organization-method-for-enrichment-of-evaluation (F-PROMETHEE), fuzzy suitability index, 2-tuple fuzzy linguistic representation model, and grey approach. Bevilacqua and Petroni [13] proposed a methodology for supplier selection based on the use of fuzzy suitability index. Bottani and Rizzi [14] addressed the problem of supplier selection in an e-procurement environment. Fuzzy AHP was employed to determine the most viable supplier. Chen et al. [9] developed a methodology for solving supplier selection problems in fuzzy environment. This was based on TOPSIS. Chan and Kumar [15] identified the decision criteria including risk factors for the development of an efficient system for global supplier selection. Fuzzy extended AHP based methodology was used in the selection procedure.

Chan et al. [16] employed a fuzzy modified AHP approach to select the best global supplier. Wang [17] used 2-tuple fuzzy linguistic representation model to determine the overall supplier performance with dynamic supply behaviors. Chen and Wang [18] provided an integrated VIKOR framework under fuzzy environment for determining the most appropriate supplier and compromise solution from a number of potential suppliers in information system/information technology outsourcing project. Kavita and Kumar [19] extended TOPSIS for interval-valued intuitionistic fuzzy data. Wang [20] developed a model based on 2-tuple fuzzy linguistic representation model to evaluate the supplier performance.

Vinodh et al. [21] utilized fuzzy ANP for supplier selection process and presented a case study in an electronics switches manufacturing company. In their study, Baskaran et al. [22] evaluated the Indian textile and clothing industry suppliers employing grey approach. The sustainability criteria were considered in the evaluation process. Chu and Varma [23] suggested a hierarchical MCDM model under fuzzy environment to evaluate and select suppliers. Govindan et al. [24] employed fuzzy TOPSIS for supplier selection considering environmental, social, and economic aspects of supplier selection problem. Roshandel et al. [25] used fuzzy hierarchical TOPSIS for evaluating suppliers in detergent production industry. Application of fuzzy TOPSIS and fuzzy AHP to supplier selection problem is seen in [26] where the results obtained are compared.

Integrated MCDM techniques based approaches have also been developed to select the most appropriate supplier [8]. Haq and Kannan [27] proposed an integrated supplier selection and multi-echelon distribution inventory model utilizing fuzzy AHP and genetic algorithm (GA). Sevkli et al. [28] developed a supplier selection approach that integrates AHP and fuzzy linear programming. Yang et al. [29] introduced a fuzzy MCDM method for supplier selection problem. First, they used interpretive structural modeling to obtain the relationships among the sub-criteria. Then, they applied fuzzy AHP to compute the relative weights for each criterion. Finally, they employed fuzzy integral to obtain the fuzzy synthetic performance and determined the rank order of alternative suppliers.

Tseng et al. [30] presented a hierarchical supplier evaluation framework combining ANP and Choquet integral. Razmi et al. [31] proposed a hybrid model based on ANP to evaluate and select supplier under fuzzy environment. The proposed approach was enhanced with a non-linear programming model to elicit weights of comparisons from comparison matrices in the ANP structure. Ordoobadi [32] combined Taguchi loss function and AHP to develop a decision making model for the selection of the appropriate supplier. Ravindran et al. [33] introduced two-phase multi-criteria supplier selection models incorporating supplier risk. In phase 1, initial set of supplier alternatives was reduced to a smaller set employing AHP. In phase 2, order quantities are allocated among the suppliers using a multi-objective optimization model [34].

Chen and Yang [35] combined constrained fuzzy AHP and fuzzy TOPSIS for supplier selection. Liao and Kao [36] proposed an integrated fuzzy TOPSIS and multi-choice goal programming model to solve multi-sourcing supplier selection problems. Pitchipoo et al. [37] proposed a structured decision model for evaluating suppliers by integrating fuzzy AHP and grey relational analysis. Rodriguez et al. [38] proposed a combination of AHP and TOPSIS in fuzzy environment for the selection of customized equipment suppliers.

Shidpour et al. [39] integrated fuzzy AHP, TOPSIS and multi-objective linear programming to determine the most appropriate configuration product design, assembly process, and supplier of components in the new product development process. Singh [40] combined TOPSIS and mixed linear integer programming for supplier selection and order allocation problem. Hashemian et al. [41] integrated fuzzy AHP and fuzzy PROMETHEE for supplier evaluation. Fuzzy AHP was used to determine the weight of the criteria and fuzzy PROMETHEE was employed for obtaining the final ranking of suppliers.

Although previously reported studies developed approaches for supplier (and for this study partner) selection process, further studies are necessary to integrate imprecise information concerning the partner assessment criteria, and dependencies between partner assessment criteria into the analysis. This study concentrates on the partner assessment criteria, even as dependencies between partner assessment criteria is left for future work. A sound decision aid for partner selection should also aim to rectify the problem of loss of time when computing with linguistic variables for a large set of selection criteria. In this paper, a fuzzy multi-criteria group decision making approach based on fusion of fuzzy information is developed. The weights of partner selection criteria and the final ranking of partners are obtained benefiting from FAHP methodology using geometric mean prioritization technique. The proposed approach uses the AHP method in partners' weights prioritization of linguistic information. The subjective information provided by decision-makers is unified into a specific linguistic labels. The collective performance values that are also fuzzy sets are obtained by geometric mean operator. Then, the collective preference values are defuzzified.

These techniques are applicable in supplier selection and there is no available research that investigated their applicability in the construction projects' partner evaluation and selection. However, although most of these techniques may be used to rank all the available partners for construction projects, they are still unable to take into account the requirements of the construction projects as a whole that may require that partners' attributes are varied to take into account partner or project changes. Given a pool of partner companies, these methods rank the partners according to their satisfaction of the evaluation and selection criteria without considering the tendencies of the decision makers to be imprecise when making judgements about partner abilities to perform a task. To account for this impreciseness, there is need for incorporating techniques that can address the imprecise judgements from evaluators. Covella and Olsina [42] as cited by Nyongesa et al. [6] suggested the use of fuzzy logic to deal with impreciseness (subjectivity) of the evaluators.

Many research studies have analyzed and solved multi-criteria decision making problems using multi-level analysis of alternatives. Analytical Hierarchy Process (AHP) [43] is a MCDM algorithm that uses pairwise comparisons of alternatives to derive weights of importance from a multi-level hierarchical structure of objectives, criteria, sub-criteria and alternatives depending on the problem. In cases where the comparisons are not perfectly consistent, AHP provides an uncomplicated method for improving the consistency of the comparisons, by using the eigenvalue method and consistency checking method [44].

The hierarchical structure fits well with the structure of partner evaluation and selection problem. Cheng et al. [45] identified the shortcomings of AHP as follows: (i) it is used in nearly crisp (exact) decision applications, (ii) does not take into account any uncertainty associated when mapping human judgement to a number scale, (iii) the subjective assessment of decision makers, and change of scale have great influence on the AHP outcome. Furthermore, Wang and Chin [46] found out that the increase in the number of characteristics geometrically increases the number of pairwise comparisons by $O(n^2/_2)$ which can lead to inconsistency or failure of the algorithm. Furthermore, AHP cannot solve non-linear models [45].

Another weakness of AHP identified by Mikhailov [47] is that it cannot be used when judgements are considered to be uncertain. In practice, human evaluation can sometimes be vague [6]. The factors that contribute to ambiguity/fuzzy/uncertainty of judgements are: (i) lack of sufficient information about the problem domain, (ii) incomplete information, (iii) lack of methods for data validation, (iv) changing nature of the problem, (v) lack of appropriate scale. Mikhailov [47] argues that the best way to solve uncertain judgement is to express it in terms of fuzzy sets or fuzzy numbers [47].

In an attempt to address the shortcomings of AHP, Mikhailov [47] introduced fuzzy logic in AHP. Fuzzy logic [48] deals with a continuum of variables and best addresses uncertainty and vagueness in input variables, in order to make rational decisions under such conditions. Fuzzy logic is derived from fuzzy set theory that has proven advantages within fuzzy, imprecise and uncertain decision situations and is an abstraction of human reasoning in its use of approximate information and uncertainty to generate decisions [49]. It implements grouping of data with boundaries that are not sharply defined. Fuzzy logic is considered the best method compared to deterministic approaches, algorithmic approaches, probabilistic approaches and machine learning [50] for problems that users are not certain of the value of parameters to use.

Fuzzy AHP [47] being an extension of conventional AHP, comprises the steps of conventional AHP, with fuzzy logic, namely: (i) structuring the problem into hierarchy; (ii) computing the pairwise comparison matrix to obtain the weight or priority vector and (iii) computing the global prioritization weight. Structuring of the problem into hierarchy involves decomposing the problem into objectives, sub-objectives and alternative solutions. AHP analyses how the alternative solutions satisfy the sub-objectives and how sub-objectives influence objectives of the problem. This is done by computing priority weights (PW) for alternatives in all levels of the hierarchy.

Wang et al. [51] describes FAHP challenges as follows; (a) Once a criteria is assigned a zero weight, it will not be considered in the decision making process, (b) This method may lose some useful information in the form of judgment ratios in the fuzzy comparison matrices as some of the criteria are assigned zero weight, (c) Weights calculated through this method may not represent the true relative importance of that criterion, and (d) This method might select the worst decision alternative as the best one and thus leads to wrong decision making. To handle weaknesses of FAHP, this study proposes Group FAHP (GFAHP). GFAHP can handle group fuzzy values of evaluation and is effective, that is it uses all evaluation criteria even if some are assigned zero values. It is also more accurate than FAHP.

3 Methodology

Steps followed in this study were as follows: Step 1: Literature review on decision making models and their application to the partner evaluation and selection problem to help identify MCDM technique that could be used for evaluation and selection of construction projects partners. Step 2: Design and Implementation of a MCDM technique for partner evaluation and selection problem. Step 3: Data collection from case study construction projects through interviews and evaluation tool (in the appendix). Focus group interviews and evaluation tools were used to collect data from participants. Step 4: Data analysis from case studies' data. The analysis of qualitative data was done by finding patterns in the collected data, as suggested by Seidel [52]. In analyzing the data and identifying patterns, themes and subcategories were developed. Sub categories were arrived at by analyzing the data further. Additionally, triangulation (interview questions and evaluation tools) was used to increase the reliability of research findings. Step 5: Categorization and themes based on deductive approach:- Selective coding for choosing partners' selection criteria; open coding for identifying selection sub-criteria; axial coding for making connections/relationships among sub criteria and between sub-criteria and criteria.

Representatives of construction companies based in Nairobi were invited for a focus group interview. These companies were selected by purposive sampling [53] from the National Construction Authority (NCA) database. NCA is the body mandated to regulate construction industry in Kenya. The purposive sampling procedure was used because of the difficulty in getting these participants. Results of the interview were used to design an evaluation tool. The applicability and validity of the evaluation tool for the collection of quantitative data was evaluated and discussed with experienced quantitative data analysis experts.

Data was collected between September 2016 and December 2016. Ten construction companies with ongoing construction projects within and in the environs Nairobi city were identified from the NCA database. Each organization was given twenty evaluation tools (the appendix). A total of 83 responses (response rate of 41.5%) were collected. Taking into consideration the length and complexity of the evaluation tool, this response rates compares well above other surveys such as Bailey et al. [54], and Culley et al. [55] that obtained 31%, and 23.6% response rate respectively. To corroborate results of the study, five case studies were conducted. Each case had ten construction companies selected from various sub counties in Nairobi County. However, some sub-counties did not have construction firms based in them. These respondents were given profiles of five companies, P1 to P5 as suggested by Musumba and Wario [56]. They used the companies' profiles information to evaluate each company according to how they satisfied a selection criterion for a particular task in the construction project [6]. Respondents of evaluation tool were required to indicate the level of importance of one selection criterion over another in implementing the task, the level of importance of a sub-criterion over another in satisfying a criterion and how preferable a company (partner) was over another in satisfying a sub-criterion.

The data from focus group interview was largely qualitative while data from evaluation tools were largely quantitative. Techniques to analyze both qualitative and quantitative data were employed. Analyzed data was used to evaluate and select partners. Merriam [57] and Creswell [58] recommend simultaneous data collection and analysis for generating categories. As data were being categorized, the responses were compared within categories and between categories (constant comparative analysis) [59]. Constant comparative analysis occurs as the data are compared and categories and their properties emerge or are integrated together. Data from focus group interviews was categorized into evaluation and selection criteria and sub-criteria.

4   Evaluation and Selection Criteria

To determine partner evaluation and selection criteria, data from focus group (experts) interviews were categorized. Categories include: Technical capability (TC), development speed (DS), cost of development (CD), Information Technology (IT), financial security (FS), business strength (BS), strategic position (SP), collaboration record (CR), cultural compatibility (CC) and management ability (MA). Specific categories were then put in general categories. Technical skills comprised TC, DS, CD and IT while FS, BS, SP and CR, CC, MB were categorized as Business Skills and Management Skills respectively. Constant comparative analysis aided in identifying patterns and categories.

At the lowest level, TC comprised the following factors: capacity, customer services, value-adding capabilities, skills, experience, complementation in core capabilities; DS comprised delivery time, development speed, task completion probability; CD comprised price/cost, task price; IT comprised design capabilities, communication techniques while FS comprised financial position, credit worthiness, risk, uncertainty, caution price; BS comprised commitment to quality, partner flexibility, reputation, communication mechanism, market position, size of company, reliability, partner resources, security; SP comprised partner performance, location, strategic goals; CR comprised previous collaboration experience, ability to work as a team, relationship between staff; CC comprised matching of corporate cultures, trust, confidentiality. Finally, MA comprised management style and openness.

The following section explains the sub criteria considered. Technical capabilities, requires that partners should have relevant types of skills and experience for the task. Development speed, assesses the capability of a partner to complete tasks within project timelines. Financial security, is important because it reveals the financial strength of the partner. The partner deposits some amount of money before project commencement. Collaborative record, determines the ability of the partner to work in a team. This is done by examining the successful projects the partner has been part of. Business strength, examines the necessary equipment and qualified staff of the partner. Cost of development, determines the ability of the partner to implement a task within the project budget. Corporate cultural compatibility, examines staff management style in the previous projects and corporate culture of the partner. In determining the strategic position, examination of the partnerships with other firms like financiers during previous projects is done. Management ability, indicates how the partner relates with staff and handles staff issues. Use of Information Technology, determines the partner's ability to use software for designs, finance and staff related issue management.

These categorizations of evaluation and selection factors can be represented in a hierarchical structure. The hierarchy proposed by Nyongesa et al. [6], shown in Fig. 1 represents a decision problem for a specific task. This hierarchy is composed of four levels: objective (the problem), criteria, sub-criteria and partners (alternatives). The overall objective of the problem is the task of partner evaluation and selection, the criteria for evaluating and selecting partners are technical, management and business, sub-criteria for each criterion are defined and the partners to be considered. The process was simplified into finding the best partner for a structural engineering works of a building. This could be replicated to find best partners for other tasks like electrical, mechanical and plumbing, interior design and landscaping works.

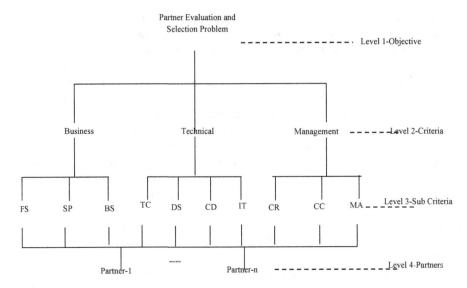

Fig. 1. A task specific decision problem representation [4]

5 Fuzzy Analytical Hierarchy Process Approach

Fuzzy theory has proven advantages for dealing with imprecise and uncertain decision situations and models human reasoning in its use of approximate information [48]. Fuzzy set theory implements grouping of data with boundaries that are not distinctly defined. In conventional AHP, the pairwise comparison is established using a nine-point scale which indicates the human preferences between alternatives [45]. The discrete scale of AHP has the advantage of ease of use but, it cannot handle the uncertainty associated with the mapping of evaluators' preferences to a number [60]. The evaluators' judgements are normally vague and difficult to represent in terms of exact numbers but could best be given as interval judgements than fixed value judgements. Different types of fuzzy numbers (triangular or trapezoidal) are used to decide the priority of one decision variable over other [61, 62]. A triangular fuzzy number (TFN), Ñ is given by $a \leq b \leq c$ where b, a, and c are the most likely, the lower bounds and upper bounds decision values, respectively [61, 62]. The triangular fuzzy numbers (TFNs), Ñ are linear piece-wise membership functions, $\mu_n(x)$ of the form;

$$\mu_n(x) = \begin{cases} (x-a)/(b-a), & a \leq x \leq b \\ (c-x)/(c-b), & b \leq x \leq c \\ 0, & \text{Otherwise} \end{cases}$$
$$\text{where } \infty < a \leq b \leq x \leq c < \infty$$

When Saaty's nine scale values are converted into fuzzy numbers and the values used in AHP, the resulting algorithm is Fuzzy AHP (FAHP). First, obtain preference values/level of importance of alternatives. This is done by choosing the linguistic attributes e.g. the statement "Indicate how important each of the following criterion is when your company is selecting partners for structural engineering works in a building construction project" needs an evaluator to choose one answer from (extremely important, very important, important, weakly important and not at all important) to answer.

Secondly, the chosen linguistic attributes are converted into numerical crisp values [6]. In the partner evaluation tool (in the appendix), alphabetical symbols (A, B, C, D, E) with matching nominal scales (extremely important, very important, important, weakly important and not at all important) are provided. These are converted to Saaty scale [43]. Thirdly, once the linguistic opinions are converted to numerical values, the crisp values are converted to fuzzy scale using Table 1.

Table 1. Conversion of nominal or crisp to fuzzy scale

Alphabetical symbol	A	B	C	D	E
Nominal scale	Extremely important	Very important	Important	Weakly important	Not at all important
Crisp number	1	3	5	7	9
Fuzzy membership function	(1, 1, 3)	(1, 3, 5)	(3, 5, 7)	(5, 7, 9)	(7, 9, 9)

Notes: According to Akadiri et al. [76] as cited by Nyongesa et al. [6], in crisp AHP, a scale of one to nine is used to decide the priority of one decision variable over another whereas in fuzzy AHP fuzzy numbers or linguistic variables are used.

The linguistic symbols obtained from individual evaluators can be converted directly to TFNs [6]. TFN values are divided in three parts. That is lower bound, middle and upper bound triangular fuzzy values. In the fourth step, compute the pairwise comparisons matrices of the values of alternatives. This step gives the fuzzy pairwise comparison matrix in form of triangular fuzzy number (l, m, u). The pairwise comparison judgement matrix gives the preference of one alternative over the other (A_j), and is given by

$$A_{ij} = \frac{Ai}{Aj} \, for \, i, j = 1, 2, 3, \ldots n. \tag{4}$$

In the fifth step, apply the fuzzy extent analysis to the pairwise comparison matrix. The basic procedures for fuzzy extent are adopted from Zhu et al. [39] thus, Let $X = \{x_1, x_2, x_3 \ldots x_n\}$ be an object set (for this study object set is either the objective, criteria, or sub-criteria) and $G = \{g_1, g_2, g_3, \ldots g_n\}$ be a goal defined for each level in the hierarchical structure. Thus, G can change depending on the level of the hierarchy.

M extent analysis on each object is taken

$$\acute{M}_{gi}^1, \acute{M}_{gi}^2, \acute{M}_{gi}^3, \ldots \ldots \acute{M}_{gi}^m, \quad i = 1, 2, 3, \ldots \ldots, n$$

where $\acute{M}_{gi}^j (j = 1, 2, 3, \ldots, m)$ are triangular fuzzy numbers (TFNs).

6 Proposed Group Fuzzy AHP

This section outlines the Group Fuzzy AHP which is a multi-criteria decision making algorithm that builds on Fuzzy AHP. The proposed decision making approach uses the geometric mean operator to aggregate decision makers' preferences. This algorithm has both features for AHP and FAHP. First, obtain evaluation comparison judgements of different alternatives in crisp values, as it is done in AHP. Then crisp values are fuzzified using triangular fuzzy number as it is done in FAHP. The arithmetic average of the fuzzified evaluators' opinions is found and a fuzzy pairwise comparison matrix is formed. From literature, this is based on Group Decision Making Algorithm [63]. The steps of the GFAHP are illustrated in Fig. 2.

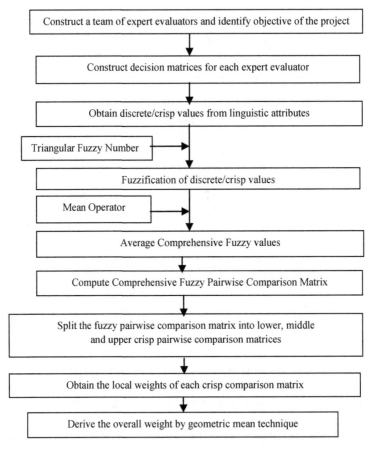

Fig. 2. Group Fuzzy AHP for PESP

Detailed stepwise representation of the proposed Group Fuzzy AHP algorithm is given below.

Step 1. Put in place a team of expert evaluators $E(e = 1, 2, \ldots E)$ and identify the requirements (objective) of the project in order to meet the client's needs and the criteria (CRs) and sub criteria (SCRs) relevant to partner assessment

Step 2. Construct the decision matrices for each decision-maker that denote the fuzzy assessment to determine the relative importance of CRs, SCRs, and the overall evaluation scores of each considered partner.

Step 3. Obtain preference values/level of importance of alternatives (appendix) as done in FAHP.

Step 4. The chosen linguistic attributes are converted into numerical crisp values using Table 1 as done in FAHP.

Step 5. Once the linguistic opinions are converted to numerical values, computation of the arithmetic mean of the numerical values is done and the average of crisp values, are converted to fuzzy using Table 1. The linguistic symbols obtained from evaluators can also be converted directly to TFNs and their arithmetic mean computed. The use of weight mean operator helps to get the collective opinion of all participants. This is done to all lower bound, middle and upper bound triangular fuzzy values. The outcomes of this step are comprehensive fuzzy opinions.

Step 6. Compute the pairwise comparisons matrices of the values of alternatives. This step gives the fuzzy pairwise comparison matrix in form of triangular fuzzy number (l, m, u). The pairwise comparison judgement matrix gives the preference of one alternative (A_i) over the other (A_j), and is given by $A_{ij} = Ai/Aj$ for $i, j = 1, 2, 3, \ldots n$.

Step 7. The fuzzy comparison matrix is split into three parts. The lower bound values are used to form lower pairwise comparison matrix (PCM), middle values are used to form middle PCM while upper bound values form upper PCM. These PCMs have crisp values, therefore, AHP approach is used to derive priority vectors after confirming the evaluators' consistency using Saaty and Kearns [64]'s method. Priority vector of lower PCM, middle and upper PCM are combined using geometric mean.

Step 8. Computing global weights. This is the step whereby the relative importance of each element within the level (local weights) is merged/multiplied with the relative importance of each element in the parent level. This gives the global weights for each alternative.

6.1   Time Complexity of GFAHP

Time complexity refers to time in which the algorithm runs. It is determined by finding the upper bound on the execution time [65]. In AHP, the computational time is affected by the size of a matrix with bigger matrices requiring more time [69]. Considering a prioritization of n elements stated as $T_1, T_2, \ldots, T_n$, the intensity of preference element T_i over element T_j which represent a judgment is indicated as a_{ij} for $i, j = 1, 2, \ldots, n$ [66]. If element T_i is preferred to T_j, then $a_{ij} > 1$ or otherwise $a_{ij} < 1$ and $a_{ij} = 1$ (for all $i, j = 1, 2, \ldots, n$) when the two elements is of the same importance. Hence, the reciprocal property $a_{ji} = 1/a_{ij}$ by assumption will always hold, with $a_{ij} = 1$ (for all $i = 1, 2, \ldots, n$) [67, 68]. Finally, a positive reciprocal matrix of pairwise comparison with the property $A = a_{ij}$ is constructed by having a dimension of $n \times n$ [69].

Consider an AHP reciprocal matrix A with weights,

$$A = \begin{array}{c} \\ T_1 \\ T_2 \\ \ldots \\ T_n \end{array} \begin{array}{cccc} T_1 & T_2 & \ldots\ldots & T_n \\ \begin{pmatrix} a_{11} & a_{12} & \ldots\ldots & a_{1n} \\ a_{21} & a_{22} & \ldots\ldots & a_{2n} \\ \ldots & \ldots & \ldots\ldots & \ldots \\ a_{n1} & a_{n2} & \ldots\ldots & a_{nn} \end{pmatrix} \end{array}, \quad \text{Weights} = \begin{pmatrix} W_1 \\ W_2 \\ \ldots \\ W_n \end{pmatrix}$$

where n is the number of elements and T are the objects while W is the derived weights from the reciprocal matrix. For the elements of the main diagonal in matrix A which are $a_{ii}, \ldots, a_{nn}$, the elements will always be equal to 1. Due to the reciprocal nature of AHP matrix, judgments are only required to the upper diagonal of the matrix and only need n $(n - 1)/2$ of the judgments to generate a matrix for prioritization while the symmetrical elements are communally reciprocal [67]. This means that the elements below the diagonal elements are satisfying the equation which is $a_{ji} = 1/a_{ij}$.

If there are n selection criteria and m candidates, the evaluators would have to make $n(n - 1)/2 + n(m(m - 1)/2)$ pairwise comparisons, a substantial number even for a small n and m (<8). Chang [65] found FAHP (for n criteria) has the time complexity of $n(n + 6)$ and AHP has a time complexity equal to $\frac{n(n-1)}{2}$. The number of comparisons in GFAHP is thrice that of AHP. This is due to the fact that once linguistic evaluations are converted to fuzzy values, three matrices are formed. One matrix is formed using lower bound elements, another one formed using middle elements and the other matrix is formed using the upper bound elements. Pairwise comparisons for each matrix are computed using AHP approach. One matrix of n criteria will take $p = \frac{n(n-1)}{2}$ comparisons. For the three matrices, the number of comparisons is thrice p comparisons, $3 \times \frac{n(n-1)}{2} = \frac{3n(n-1)}{2}$. Therefore, using these illustrations, GFAHP has a time complexity of $\frac{3n(n-1)}{2}$.

7   Application of the Proposed Group Fuzzy AHP

Data collected from evaluators was converted from crisp values to fuzzy/continuous values. It was done for all levels of the hierarchy. The arithmetic mean values for business (CR_1), technical (CR_2) and management (CR_3) criteria by evaluators were (9, 7, 7) respectively. These crisp values were fuzzified using TFNs to get (7, 9, 9) for CR_1, (5, 7, 9) for CR_2 and (5, 7, 9) for CR_3. A fuzzy pairwise comparison matrix was formed as shown in Table 2.

Table 2. Fuzzy pairwise comparison matrix for partner selection criteria

Criteria	CR_1	CR_2	CR_3
CR_1	1, 1, 3	7/5, 9/7, 9/9	7/5, 9/7, 9/9
CR_2		1, 1, 3	1, 1, 3
CR_3			1, 1, 3

Then the fuzzy pairwise comparison matrix is divided into three matrices consisting of lower, middle and upper bound elements as shown in Tables 3, 4 and 5.

Table 3. Lower bound PCM for selection criteria

Criteria	CR_1	CR_2	CR_3
CR_1	1.00	1.40	1.40
CR_2	0.714	1.00	1.00
CR_3	0.714	1.00	1.00

Table 4. Middle PCM for selection criteria

Criteria	CR_1	CR_2	CR_3
CR_1	1.00	1.29	1.29
CR_2	0.778	1.00	1.00
CR_3	0.778	1.00	1.00

Table 5. Upper bound PCM for selection criteria

Criteria	CR_1	CR_2	CR_3
CR_1	3.00	1.00	1.00
CR_2	1.00	3.00	3.00
CR_3	1.00	0.33	3.00

After that the local weight of each pairwise comparison matrix is done like in the conventional AHP. Table 6 shows the local weights for the lower and upper bound elements.

Table 6. Local and global weights for selection criteria

Criteria	Lower local weight	Middle local weight	Upper local weight	Overall weight (Geometric mean)
CR_1	0.412	0.386	0.325	0.372
CR_2	0.294	0.324	0.401	0.337
CR_3	0.294	0.361	0.228	0.289

After obtaining the results for the local weights of the lower and upper elements then the final step is to combine three respective local weights (for the lower, middle and upper element) in order to get the overall weights for alternatives. The same procedure was applied to all levels of hierarchy. It should be noted business criterion sub-criteria were denoted as $SCR_{1,1}$ to $SCR_{1,3}$ for FS, Sp and BS respectively.

Likewise, technical criterion sub-criteria were denoted as $SCR_{2,1}$ to $SCR_{2,4}$ for TC, DS, CD and IT respectively. Finally, management criterion sub-criteria were denoted as $SCR_{3,1}$ to $SCR_{3,3}$ for CR, CC and MA respectively. Table 7 shows the overall outcome of the GFAHP.

Table 7. Results of evaluations using GFAHP

Criteria	CR_1			CR_2				CR_3			
CR LW	0.372			0.337				0.289			
SCR	$SCR_{1,1}$	$SCR_{1,2}$	$SCR_{1,3}$	$SCR_{2,1}$	$SCR_{2,2}$	$SCR_{2,3}$	$SCR_{2,4}$	$SCR_{3,1}$	$SCR_{3,2}$	$SCR_{3,3}$	
SCR LW	0.417	0.302	0.253	0.312	0.211	0.126	0.351	0.449	0.298	0.254	
GW	0.155	0.112	0.094	0.105	0.071	0.042	0.118	0.13	0.086	0.073	
											Priority weights
P1	0.203	0.263	0.215	0.128	0.109	0.21	0.103	0.267	0.12	0.06	0.218
P2	0.137	0.157	0.113	0.22	0.245	0.12	0.237	0.313	0.09	0.24	0.242
P3	0.213	0.101	0.313	0.147	0.105	0.348	0.237	0.201	0.046	0.255	0.222
P4	0.112	0.101	0.154	0.274	0.122	0.211	0.194	0.022	0.289	0.179	0.157
P5	0.155	0.188	0.085	0.121	0.259	0.021	0.139	0.067	0.345	0.006	0.152
										Total	0.991
										Error	0.009

Note: CR LW denotes criteria local weight
SCR denotes sub criteria
SCR LW denotes sub criteria local weight
GW denotes global weight

To calculate the priority weight (PW) of partners, the global weights for each sub-criterion in each criterion is multiplied by the local weights of each partner according to a sub-criterion. After this, the sum of the products (partner local weights multiplied by sub-criterion global weights) of each partner is computed. This is illustrated in the following section.

$$\begin{bmatrix} 0.203 & \cdots & 0.155 \\ \vdots & \ddots & \vdots \\ 0.060 & \cdots & 0.006 \end{bmatrix} \times \begin{Vmatrix} 0.155 \\ \vdots \\ 0.006 \end{Vmatrix} = \begin{Vmatrix} 0.218 \\ \vdots \\ 0.152 \end{Vmatrix}$$

The global weight (GW) for $SCR_{1,3}$ (BS) is derived by multiplying local weight of business criterion by local weight of $SCR_{1,3}$, which is $0.372 \times 0.253 = 0.094$, GW for $SCR_{2,3}$ (DS) is $0.337 \times 0.211 = 0.071$. Likewise the GW for $SCR_{3,1}$ (CR) is $0.289 \times 0.449 = 0.130$. Finally PW for partners is derived by finding the sum of products of global weights of each sub criterion and the local weight of the partner in the sub criterion. For instance PW for partner 1 is $0.155 \times 0.203 + 0.112 \times 0.263 + 0.094 \times 0.215 + 0.105$ $0.128 + 0.071 \times 0.109 + 0.042 \times 0.210 + 0.118 \times 0.103 + 0.130 \times 0.267 + 0.086$ $0.120 + 0.073 \times 0.060 = 0.218$. PWs for partners 2, 3 to 5 are derived in the same way. If all was perfect the sum of the weights for partners should be 1. From Table 7 the sum is

0.991 with an error of 0.009. The PWs of Partners 1 through 5 was 0.218, 0.242, 0.222, 0.157 and 0.152 respectively. Partner 2 has the highest weight value and is consequently selected.

Ideally, in any algorithm that ranks alternatives, the sum of the PWs of alternatives should be 1. If this is not the case, then the algorithm has not performed optimally therefore resulting in errors. The higher the error the worse the algorithm's performance. Since the consistency ratio correlate to the judgemental errors in pairwise comparisons [70, 50], it can be concluded that these mean errors correspond to the consistency ratio [19]. GFAHP algorithm ranked all the partners in the following order, P2, P1, P3, P4 and P5 with P2 with the highest weight and P5 having the lowest weight. GFAHP has an error of 0.009. In order to verify the results of the algorithm, sources of data was varied from additional five cases of evaluators and projects. However, evaluation tool and company profiles were not varied. Table 8 shows the results of the five cases.

Table 8. Results of all cases

	P1	P2	P3	P4	P5	Total	Error
Case 1	0.251	0.232	0.206	0.145	0.154	0.988	0.012
Case 2	0.253	0.223	0.206	0.145	0.154	0.981	0.019
Case 3	0.251	0.232	0.206	0.154	0.143	0.986	0.014
Case 4	0.253	0.234	0.202	0.152	0.149	0.990	0.010
Case 5	0.251	0.252	0.206	0.134	0.145	0.988	0.012
Mean						0.987	0.013

According to the results of the analysis for cases 1 and 2, partners P1 is determined as the most suitable supplier, which is followed by P2, P3, P5 and P4 in that order. For cases 3 and 4, partners P1, P2, P3, P4 and P5 had priority weights in that order with P1 with the highest and P5 with the least. For case 5, P2, P1, P3, P4 and P5 had priority weights in that order with P2 with the highest and P5 with the least. The arithmetic mean total and error of the algorithm are 0.987 and 0.013 respectively. P1 averagely had the best types of skills and relevant experience; was best placed to complete the project task within reasonable time; had more financial strength than the rest; had shown better previous team collaborations; had better necessary equipment; better staff management capability among others. In the converse P5 had the reverse competencies to P1. Prior to this analysis, the cases had been working with P1, P2 and P3 using their own evaluation and selection system. The results obtained from the proposed decision making approach are similar to the findings from real life selection of partners in then cases, which demonstrates the robustness of the methodology and promotes its use as a decision aid for further partner evaluation and selection situations faced by project initiators.

Over the past decade, several researchers have used various fuzzy MCDM techniques for supplier selection process. While fuzzy MCDM techniques enable consideration of imprecision and vagueness inherent in partner evaluation, they also incorporate several shortcomings. Defuzzification has been commonly employed in a number of fuzzy MCDM methods. Freeling [71] revealed that by reducing the whole analysis to a single number, much of the information which has been intentionally kept throughout calculations is lost. Thus, defuzzification might essentially contradict with the key objective of minimizing the loss of information throughout the analysis [8].

Moreover, obtaining pairwise comparisons in AHP and ANP may become quite complex especially when the number of attributes and/or alternatives increases. Apart from this, Saaty and Tran [72] claimed that uncertainty in the AHP was successfully remedied by using intermediate values in the 1–9 scale combined with the verbal scale and that seemed to work better to obtain accurate results than using fuzzy AHP. The lack of a precise justification for the values chosen for concordance and discordance thresholds in fuzzy ELECTRE as well as the absence of a clear methodology for the weight assignment in fuzzy PROMETHEE may pose limitations for their use in partner selection. To the best of researchers' knowledge, an earlier study, which is apt to account for the impreciseness of human judgments in the partners evaluation and selection when information available about partners is either inadequate or uncertain in a decision setting with multiple information sources, does not exist in the partner evaluation and selection literature. In here, the partner selection and evaluation methodology which has made use of fuzzy logic is designed and employed. However, this methodology has neither considered the inner dependencies among partner attributes nor enabled the use of different semantic types by decision-makers.

8 Discussions

Considering the inherent challenges in the construction sector, project initiators have to select the right partners to work with in order to remain competitive. To reach this aim, firms must device better ways to get the right partners to improve on their overall performance. Selecting the right partners significantly reduces the project management cost and improves corporate competitiveness. Partner evaluation and selection problem, which requires the consideration of multiple selection criteria incorporating vagueness and imprecision with the involvement of a group of experts, is an important multi-criteria group decision making problem. The classical MCDM methods that consider deterministic or random processes cannot effectively address partner evaluation and selection problems since fuzziness and imprecision coexist in real-world. In this study, a fuzzy multi-criteria group decision making algorithm is presented to rectify the problems encountered when using classical decision making methods in partner evaluation and selection.

Using GFAHP, it has been shown how preference and consensus can be attained if a group decision-making process is used in the partner evaluation and selection problem. It resembles the traditional AHP method, which uses preferences and consensus generated from crisp values to evaluate and select partners. The level of accuracy of the prioritization outcome when GFAHP was 98.7%. It can be stated that GFAHP can be incorporated in the design and development of new techniques for the partner evaluation and selection. GFAHP have those advantages of conventional AHP [73], which are: It is flexible, integrates deductive approaches, acknowledge interdependence of alternatives (selection criteria and sub-criteria), has hierarchical structure, measure intangibles, track logical consistency, give an overall estimation, consider relative weights and improves judgements. It also has advantages for FAHP which are: It is applied in evaluation and selection when imprecise values are used.

PESP is solvable if pragmatic scientific approaches were employed with appropriate mathematical models. This paper proposed an GFAHP algorithmic paradigm for evaluating and selecting right partners for building construction projects. The algorithm was used to demonstrate the choice of the most preferred partner based on business, technical and management skills among five potential partners. The consistency of the selected partner was tested using some mathematical tools. It was observed that the selected partner falls within the acceptable limit of the error margin. Precisely, we can say that the requirement of consistency is the most critical issue in the practical application of GFAHP. The use of the balanced scale improves consistency, but it would be most helpful to have well defined, theoretically founded cut-off limits, independent from scales and priority derivation methods. GFAHP employed FAHP process. PCM were divided into three, lower, middle and upper because Triangular Fuzzy Numbers were used. This could be applied to Trapezoidal Fuzzy Numbers where the PCM would be divided into four.

The procedure used in this paper considers the GFAHP as a fuzzy multi-criteria group decision tool and constructs three matrices to compute the weights of partner selection criteria and the ratings of partners. It utilizes the geometric mean of TFN, which enables decision-makers to tackle the problems of multi-criteria decision making impreciseness. The proposed methodology possesses two merits compared to some other MCDM techniques presented in the literature for partner selection. First, the developed method is a group decision making process which enables the group to identify and better appreciate the differences and similarities of their judgments. Second, the proposed approach is apt to incorporate imprecise data into the analysis using fuzzy set theory.

Finally, This study examines multi-criteria decision-making (MCDM) "under uncertainties", in particular the linguistic uncertainties and proposes the incorporation of fuzzy logic in AHP algorithm thus addressing issues of partner evaluation and selection while information available about partners is subjective. This study sought to evaluate and select partners for tasks in the construction projects. Research has shown the importance of using multiple evaluators in the evaluation and selection of partners. This is important for the project sustainability in terms of the evaluators being able to work as a team.

9   Further Work

Future research will focus on implementation of the decision technique presented in here for real-world group decision making problems in diverse disciplines. That research should be carried out to determine the applicability of this technique to other industries and other research fields. The limitations of GFAHP should probably be addressed in future research. Examples of limitations are: (i) checking if GFAHP preserve the consistency of the evaluator's judgement; and (ii) whether GFAHP ignore the dependence between the elements at the same level of the hierarchy, as is the case with AHP. A study should be done to determine how the incorporation of the Analytical Network Process (ANP) in this algorithm can address its weaknesses.

Moreover, as pointed out in several recent works [74, 75], supplier segmentation which in this study means, partner segmentation has an important role in supply chain management. Partner segmentation that succeeds partner evaluation and selection is the process of classifying the partners on the basis of their similarities. This classification or segmentation enables to choose the most suitable strategies for handling different segments of selected partners. Therefore, further development of the proposed method for partner segmentation may also be considered as a direction for future research.

Appendix: Partner Evaluation Tool

Collaboration of Construction Projects

Indicate your choice with a tick (✓) on the label provided. For the purpose of this study the term "collaboration" is defined as participation in a project between organizations that operate under a different management.

Section A-Partners Evaluation and Selection Criteria

1. Indicate how important each of the following criterion is when your company is selecting partners for a task in a building construction project. Use the symbols "A to E" with A being "Extremely important" and E being "Not at all important". Choose the symbol which best indicates your choice

Criterion	Extremely important	Very important	Important	Weakly important	Not at all important
Business Skills	A	B	C	D	E
Technical Skills	A	B	C	D	E
Management Skills	A	B	C	D	E

2. Considering Business Skills Criterion; indicate how important each of the following sub-criteria is when your company is selecting partners for a task in a building construction project. Use the symbols "A to E" with A being "Extremely important" and E being "Not at all important". Choose the symbol which best indicates your choice

Sub-Criteria	Extremely important	Very important	Important	Weakly important	Not at all important
Business Strength (BS)	A	B	C	D	E
Financial Security (FS)	A	B	C	D	E
Strategic Position (SP)	A	B	C	D	E

3. Considering Technical Skills Criterion; indicate how important each of the following sub-criteria is when your company is selecting partners for a task in a building construction project. Use the symbols "A to E" with A being "Extremely important" and E being "Not at all important". Choose the symbol which best indicates your choice

Sub-Criteria	Extremely important	Very important	Important	Weakly important	Not at all important
Technical Capabilities (TC)	A	B	C	D	E
Development Speed (DS)	A	B	C	D	E
Cost of Development (CD)	A	B	C	D	E
Information Technology (IT)	A	B	C	D	E

4. Considering Management Skills Criterion; indicate how important each of the following sub-criteria is when your company is selecting partners for a task in a building construction project. Use the symbols "A to E" with A being "Extremely important" and E being "Not at all important". Choose the symbol which best indicates your choice

Sub-Criteria	Extremely important	Very important	Important	Weakly important	Not at all important
Collaboration Record (CR)	A	B	C	D	E
Cultural Compatibility (CC)	A	B	C	D	E
Management Ability (MA)	A	B	C	D	E

Section B-Partner Selection

Use the company profiles of companies P1, P2, ..., P5 provided at the end of this questionnaire. Indicate how preferable is each company against each other according to partner selection sub-criterion to perform a task in a building construction project. Use the symbols "A to E" with A being "Extremely preferable" and E being "Not at all preferable". Choose the symbol which best indicates your choice

Sub-Criteria	Extremely preferable	Strongly preferable	Preferable	Weakly preferable	Not at all preferable
	P1 P2 P3 P4 P5	P1 P2 P3 P4 P5	P1 P2 P3 P4 P5	P1 P2 P3 P4 P5	P1 P2 P3 P4 P5
Technical capabilities (Have relevant types of skills)	A A A A A	B B B B B	C C C C C	D D D D D	E E E E E
Development speed (Can complete tasks within project timelines)	A A A A A	B B B B B	C C C C C	D D D D D	E E E E E
Financial security (Amount of money deposited before project commencement)	A A A A A	B B B B B	C C C C C	D D D D D	E E E E E

Collaborative record (Have been part of large projects)	A A A A A	B B B B B	C C C C C	D D D D D	E E E E E
Business strength (Have necessary equipment and qualified staff)	A A A A A	B B B B B	C C C C C	D D D D D	E E E E E
Cost of development (The projected task cost within the project budget)	A A A A A	B B B B B	C C C C C	D D D D D	E E E E E
Corporate cultural compatibility (Staff management style in the previous projects)	A A A A A	B B B B B	C C C C C	D D D D D	E E E E E
Strategic position (Partnership with other firms like financiers)	A A A A A	B B B B B	C C C C C	D D D D D	E E E E E
Management ability (Handles staff issues amicably)	A A A A A	B B B B B	C C C C C	D D D D D	E E E E E
Use of Information Technology (Use software for designs, finance and staff issues management)	A A A A A	B B B B B	C C C C C	D D D D D	E E E E E

References

1. Wu, D., Olson, D.L.: Supply chain risk, simulation, and vendor selection. Int. J. Prod. Econ. **114**, 646–655 (2008)
2. Bai, C., Sarkis, J.: Integrating sustainability into supplier selection with grey system and rough set methodologies. Int. J. Prod. Econ. **124**, 252–264 (2010)
3. Talukhaba, A.A.: An investigation into factors causing construction project delays in Kenya. Case study of high rise building projects in Nairobi. Doctoral dissertation, University of Nairobi (1999)
4. Chen, Y., Lien, H., Tzeng, G., Yang, L.: Fuzzy MCDM approach for selecting the best environment-watershed plan. Appl. Soft Comput. **11**, 265–275 (2009)
5. Chiou, H.K., Tzeng, G.H., Cheng, D.C.: Evaluating sustainable fishing development strategies using fuzzy MCDM approach. Omega **33**(3), 223–234 (2005)
6. Nyongesa, H.O., Musumba, G.W., Chileshe, N.: Partner selection and performance evaluation framework for a construction- related virtual enterprise: a multi-agent systems approach. Archit. Eng. Des. Manag. **13**, 1–21 (2017)
7. Musumba, G., Kanyi, P., Nyongesa, H., Wario, R.: Techniques for evaluation and selection of partners for construction projects. In: Pan African Conference on Science, Computing and Telecommunication (PACT) (2017)
8. Karsak, E.E., Dursun, M.: An integrated fuzzy MCDM approach for supplier evaluation and selection. Comput. Ind. Eng. **82**, 82–93 (2015)
9. Chen, C.T., Lin, C.T., Huang, S.F.: A fuzzy approach for supplier evaluation and selection in supply chain management. Int. J. Prod. Econ. **102**, 289–301 (2006)
10. Dickson, G.: An analysis of vendor selection systems and decisions. J. Purch. **2**, 5–17 (1966)
11. Lehmann, D.R., O'Shaughnessy, J.: Difference in attribute importance for different industrial products. J. Mark. **38**(2), 36–42 (1974)
12. Weber, C.A., Current, J.R., Benton, W.C.: Vendor selection criteria and methods. Eur. J. Oper. Res. **50**, 2–18 (1991)
13. Bevilacqua, M., Petroni, A.: From traditional purchasing to supplier management: a fuzzy logic-based approach to supplier selection. Int. J. Logist. Res. Appl. **5**(3), 235–255 (2002)

14. Bottani, E., Rizzi, A.: A fuzzy multi-attribute framework for supplier selection in an e-procurement environment. Int. J. Logist. Res. Appl. **8**(3), 249–266 (2005)
15. Chan, F.T.S., Kumar, N.: Global supplier development considering risk factors using fuzzy extended AHP-based approach. Omega **35**, 417–431 (2007)
16. Chan, F.T.S., Kumar, N., Tiwari, M.K., Lau, H.C.W., Choy, K.L.: Global supplier selection: a fuzzy-AHP approach. Int. J. Prod. Res. **46**(14), 3825–3857 (2008)
17. Wang, S.Y.: Applying 2-tuple multi-granularity linguistic variables to determine the supply performance in dynamic environment based on product-oriented strategy2-tuple. IEEE Trans. Fuzzy Syst. **16**(1), 29–39 (2008)
18. Chen, L.Y., Wang, T.C.: Optimizing partners' choice in IS/IT outsourcing projects: the strategic decision of fuzzy VIKOR. Int. J. Prod. Econ. **120**, 233–242 (2009)
19. Kavita, Yadav, S.P., Kumar, S.: A multi-criteria interval-valued intuitionistic fuzzy group decision making for supplier selection with TOPSIS method. In: Sakai, H., Chakraborty, M. K., Hassanien, A.E., Ślęzak, D., Zhu, W. (eds.) Rough Sets, Fuzzy Sets, Data Mining and Granular Computing. LNCS, vol. 5908, pp. 303–312. Springer, Heidelberg (2009). https://doi.org/10.1007/978-3-642-10646-0_37
20. Wang, W.P.: A fuzzy linguistic computing approach to supplier evaluation. Appl. Math. Model. **34**, 3130–3141 (2010)
21. Vinodh, S., Ramiya, R.A., Gautham, S.G.: Application of fuzzy analytic network process for supplier selection in a manufacturing organization. Expert Syst. Appl. **38**, 272–280 (2011)
22. Baskaran, V., Nachiappan, S., Rahman, S.: Indian textile suppliers' sustainability evaluation using the grey approach. Int. J. Prod. Econ. **135**, 647–658 (2012)
23. Chu, T.C., Varma, R.: Evaluating suppliers via a multiple levels multiple criteria decision making method under fuzzy environment. Comput. Ind. Eng. **62**, 653–660 (2012)
24. Govindan, K., Khodaverdi, R., Jafarian, A.: A fuzzy multi criteria approach for measuring sustainability performance of a supplier based on triple bottom line approach. J. Clean. Prod. **47**, 345–354 (2013)
25. Roshandel, J., Miri-Nargesi, S.S., Hatami-Shirkouhi, L.: Evaluating and selecting the supplier in detergent production industry using hierarchical fuzzy TOPSIS. Appl. Math. Model. **37**, 10170–10181 (2013)
26. Junior, F.R.L., Osiro, L., Carpinetti, L.C.R.: A comparison between Fuzzy AHP and Fuzzy TOPSIS methods to supplier selection. Appl. Soft Comput. **21**, 194–209 (2014)
27. Haq, A.N., Kannan, G.: Design of an integrated supplier selection and multi-echelon distribution inventory model in a built- to-order supply chain environment. Int. J. Prod. Res. **44**(10), 1963–1985 (2006)
28. Sevkli, M., Koh, S.C.L., Zaim, S., Demirbag, M., Tatoglu, E.: Hybrid analytical hierarchy process model for supplier selection. Ind. Manag. Data Syst. **108**(1), 122–142 (2008)
29. Yang, J.L., Chiu, H.N., Tzeng, G.H., Yeh, R.H.: Vendor selection by integrated fuzzy MCDM techniques with independent and interdependent relationships. Inf. Sci. **178**, 4166–4183 (2008)
30. Tseng, M.L., Chiang, J.H., Lan, L.W.: Selection of optimal supplier in supply chain management strategy with analytic network process and choquet integral. Comput. Ind. Eng. **57**, 330–340 (2009)
31. Razmi, J., Rafiei, H., Hashemi, M.: Designing a decision support system to evaluate and select suppliers using fuzzy analytic network process. Comput. Ind. Eng. **57**, 1282–1290 (2009)
32. Ordoobadi, S.M.: Application of AHP and Taguchi loss functions in supply chain. Ind. Manag. Data Syst. **110**(8), 1251–1269 (2010)
33. Ravindran, A.R., Bilsel, R.U., Wadhwa, V., Yang, T.: Risk adjusted multi-criteria supplier selection models with applications. Int. J. Prod. Res. **48**(2), 405–424 (2010)

34. Guo, L.L., Fang, Z.M.: Modeling study of lot-sizing in virtual enterprise based on multi-objective. In: 2011 IEEE 18th International Conference on Industrial Engineering and Engineering Management (IE&EM), pp. 933–937 (2011)
35. Chen, Z., Yang, W.: An MAGDM based on constrained FAHP and FTOPSIS and its application to supplier selection. Math. Comput. Model. **54**, 2802–2815 (2011)
36. Liao, C.N., Kao, H.P.: An integrated fuzzy TOPSIS and MCGP approach to supplier selection in supply chain management. Expert Syst. Appl. **38**, 10803–10811 (2011)
37. Pitchipoo, P., Venkumar, P., Rajakarunakaran, S.: Fuzzy hybrid decision model for supplier evaluation and selection. Int. J. Prod. Res. **51**(13), 3903–3919 (2013)
38. Rodríguez, A., Ortega, F., Concepción, R.: A method for the selection of customized equipment suppliers. Expert Syst. Appl. **40**, 1170–1176 (2013)
39. Shidpour, H., Shahrokhi, M., Bernard, A.: A multi-objective programming approach, integrated into the TOPSIS method, in order to optimize product design; in three-dimensional concurrent engineering. Comput. Ind. Eng. **64**, 875–885 (2013)
40. Singh, A.: Supplier evaluation and demand allocation among suppliers in a supply chain. J. Purch. Supply Manag. **20**, 167–176 (2014)
41. Hashemian, S.M., Behzadian, M., Samizadeh, R., Ignatius, J.: A fuzzy hybrid group decision support system approach for the supplier evaluation process. Int. J. Adv. Manuf. Technol. **73** (5–8), 1105–1117 (2014)
42. Covella, G.J., Olsina, L.A.: Assessing quality in use in a consistent way. In: Proceedings of the 6th international Conference on Web Engineering, pp. 1–8, Palo Alto, California, USA. ACM Press, New York (2006)
43. Saaty, T.L.: The Analytic Hierarchy Process: Planning, Priority Setting, Resource Allocation. McGraw-Hill International, New York (1980)
44. Saaty, T.L.: Decision making with the analytic hierarchy process. Int. J. Serv. Sci. **1**(1), 83–98 (2008)
45. Cheng, C.H., Yang, K.L., Hwang, C.L.: Evaluating attack helicopters by AHP based on linguistic variables weight. Eur. J. Oper. Res. **116**(2), 423–435 (1999)
46. Wang, Y.M., Chin, K.S.: A linear goal programming priority method for fuzzy analytic hierarchy process and its applications in new product screening. Int. J. Approx. Reason. **49** (2), 451–465 (2008)
47. Mikhailov, L.: Deriving priorities from fuzzy pairwise comparison judgments. Fuzzy Sets Syst. **134**(3), 365–385 (2003)
48. Yager, R.R., Zadeh, L.A. (eds.): An Introduction to Fuzzy Logic Applications in Intelligent Systems, vol. 165. Springer, Berlin (2012). https://doi.org/10.1007/978-1-4615-3640-6
49. Zadeh, L.A.: Fuzzy sets. Inf. Control **8**(3), 338–353 (1965)
50. Ahmed, F., Kiliç, K.: Modification to fuzzy extent analysis method and its performance analysis. In: Proceedings of the 6th IESM Conference, Seville, Spain (2015)
51. Wang, Y.M., Elhag, T.M.S., Hua, Z.S.: A modified fuzzy logarithmic least squares method for fuzzy analytic hierarchy process. Fuzzy Sets Syst. **157**, 3055–3071 (2006)
52. Seidel, J.V.: Qualitative data analysis (1998). www.qualisresearch.com. Accessed May 2016
53. Van Vuuren, D., Maree, A.: Survey methods in market and media research. In: Research in practice: Applied methods for the social sciences, pp. 269–286 (1999)
54. Bailey, W.J., Masson, R., Raeside, R.: Choosing successful technology development partners: a best-practice model. Int. J. Technol. Manag. **15**(1–2), 124–138 (1998)
55. Culley, S.J., Boston, O.P., McMahon, C.A.: Suppliers in new product development: their information and integration. J. Eng. Des. **10**(1), 59–75 (1999)
56. Musumba, G.W., Wario, R.D.: Partner performance evaluation problem for construction projects. J. Appl. Sci. Eng. Technol. Dev. **2**(1), 1–29 (2017)
57. Merriam, S.B.: Case Study Research in Education. Jossey-Bass, San Francisco (1988)

58. Creswell, J.W.: Research Design: Qualitative and Quantitative Approaches. Sage, Thousand Oaks (1994)
59. Glaser, B.G., Strauss, A.L.: The Discovery of Grounded Theory: Strategies for Qualitative Research. Aldine, Chicago (1967)
60. Kwong, C.K., Bai, H.: A fuzzy AHP approach to the determination of importance weights of customer requirements in quality function deployment. J. Intell. Manuf. **13**(5), 367–377 (2002)
61. Buckley, J.J.: Fuzzy hierarchical analysis. Fuzzy Sets Syst. **17**(3), 233–247 (1985)
62. Dubois, D., Kerre, E., Mesiar, R., Prade, H.: Fuzzy interval analysis. In: Dubois, D., Prade, H. (eds.) Fundamentals of Fuzzy Sets. FSHS, vol. 7, pp. 483–581. Springer, Boston (2000). https://doi.org/10.1007/978-1-4615-4429-6_11
63. Tang, H., Zhang, J.: Study on fuzzy AHP group decision-making method based on set-valued statistics. In: FSKD, vol. 3, pp. 689–693 (2007)
64. Saaty, T.L., Kearns, K.P.: Analytical Planning: The Organization of System, vol. 7. Elsevier, Amsterdam (2014)
65. Chang, D.Y.: Applications of the extent analysis method on fuzzy AHP. Eur. J. Oper. Res. **95**(3), 649–655 (1996)
66. Indrani, B.: On the use of information in analytic hierarchy process. Eur. J. Oper. Res. **141**, 200–206 (2002)
67. Srdjevic, B.: Combining different prioritization methods in the analytic hierarchy process synthesis. Comput. Oper. Res. **32**(7), 1897–1919 (2005)
68. Mikhailov, L., Singh, M.G.: Comparison analysis of method for deriving priorities in the analytic hierarchy process. In: IEEE SMC 1999 Conference Proceedings of System, Man, and Cybernetics, vol. 1, pp. 1037–1042 (1999)
69. Golany, B., Kress, M.: A multi-criteria evaluation of methods for obtaining weights from ratio-scale matrices. Eur. J. Oper. Res. **69**(2), 210–220 (1993)
70. Karlsson, J., Wohlin, C., Regnell, B.: An evaluation of methods for prioritizing software requirements. Inf. Softw. Technol. **39**(14–25), 939–947 (1998)
71. Freeling, A.N.S.: Fuzzy sets and decision analysis. IEEE Trans. Syst. Man Cybern. **10**, 341–354 (1980)
72. Saaty, T.L., Tran, L.T.: On the invalidity of fuzzifying numerical judgments in the analytic hierarchy process. Math. Comput. Model. **46**, 962–975 (2007)
73. Sanga, C., Venter, I.M.: Is a multi-criteria evaluation tool reserved for experts? Electron. J. Inf. Syst. Eval. (EJISE) **12**(2), 165–176 (2009)
74. Rezaei, J., Ortt, R.: A multi-variable approach to supplier segmentation. Int. J. Prod. Res. **50**(16), 4593–4611 (2012)
75. Rezaei, J., Ortt, R.: Multi-criteria supplier segmentation using a fuzzy preference relations based AHP. Eur. J. Oper. Res. **225**, 75–84 (2013)
76. Akadiri, P.O., Olomolaiye, P.O., Chinyio, E.A.: Multi-criteria evaluation model for the selection of sustainable materials for building projects. Autom. Constr. **30**, 113–125 (2013)

Overview of Spectrum Sharing Models: A Path Towards 5G Spectrum Toolboxes

Gcina Dludla$^{(\boxtimes)}$, Luzango Mfupe, and Fisseha Mekuria

CSIR Meraka Institute, Pretoria 0001, South Africa
{gdludla, lmfupe, fmekuria}@csir.co.za

Abstract. In this paper three spectrum sharing models are studied and their relative merits are outlined to allow dynamic spectrum sharing in all bands of interest. The main criterion is to improve the availability of underutilized spectrum for secondary wireless broadband networks. The three database-assisted spectrum sharing models studied in this paper are the Licensed Shared Access (LSA), Spectrum Access System (SAS) and Television White Space (TVWS). This paper proposes a unified spectrum sharing database-assisted model as solution for improving the broadband connectivity of underserved communities and improving spectrum availability for high bandwidth services in the fifth generation (5G) networks.

Keywords: DSM · Spectrum sharing · LSA · SAS · TVWS
Spectrum database · Interference · 5G spectrum · Broadband

1 Introduction

Radio frequency (RF) spectrum is the superhighway for the wireless communications systems and associated information and communication technology (ICT) services that are exponentially expanding. Spectrum regulators around the world are increasingly becoming aware of the importance to efficiently managing their national RF spectrum resources. They are beginning to adopt flexible spectrum management frameworks that enables opportunistic sharing of spectrum [1]. This trend plays an important role in addressing the demand for broadband connectivity in underserved areas and also in preparation for the gigabits wireless services in the upcoming fifth generation (5G) ICT eco-systems [2–4]. Dynamic spectrum management (DSM) is regarded as a process of regulating the use of RF spectrum to promote efficient utilisation of spectrum resources. The term RF spectrum typically refers to the full frequency range from 3 kHz to 300 GHz that may be used for wireless communication. Increasing demand for services such as mobile telephones and many others has required changes in the philosophy of spectrum management. Demand for wireless broadband has soared due to technological innovation, such as third generation (3G) and fourth generation (4G) mobile services, and the rapid expansion of wireless internet services.

Dynamic spectrum sharing approaches enables third-party users to share spectrum bands licensed to incumbent users while adhering to the interference limitations of the incumbents (i.e., such sharing approaches could be on the secondary or tertiary basis). Database-assisted DSM frameworks such as the Licensed Shared Access (LSA),

© ICST Institute for Computer Sciences, Social Informatics and Telecommunications Engineering 2018
F. Mekuria et al. (Eds.): ICT4DA 2017, LNICST 244, pp. 308–319, 2018.
https://doi.org/10.1007/978-3-319-95153-9_28

Authorised Shared Access (ASA) and Television white spaces (TVWS) allow spectrum that has been licensed for use by the International mobile telecommunications (IMT), Citizen broadband radio services (CBRS) and TV broadcasting to be shared with unlicensed users. This is said to increase the use of the radio spectrum by allowing shared access when and where the primary licensee is not using its selected frequencies [5–7]. The major drawback of the aforementioned database-assisted spectrum sharing approaches is that they are all band specific (i.e., each model is applicable in a given band of interest). This drawback could be a costly hindrance in the 5G network ecosystem in which heterogeneous wireless access networks are expected, possibly each network operating in different spectrum bands. This paper investigates and compares the LSA, SAS and TVWS frameworks. The key contribution of this paper is a proposed unified spectrum sharing database assisted model that will enable seamless spectrum sharing in many bands of interest for the 5G networks.

1.1 Spectrum Underutilisation

The motivation for research and development in spectrum sharing models comes from the fact that spectrum is grossly underutilized in both time and space domains, by all licensed network services and in all bands of interest. Studies by national regulatory authority such as the Independent Communications Authority of South Africa (ICASA), the Federal Communications Commission (FCC) of USA, and the Office of communications (Ofcom) of UK clearly had shown this [3, 6, 8]. A typical example is shown in Fig. 1 (below). The figure shows the study done using the Council for Scientific and Industrial Research (CSIR) geolocation spectrum database (GLSD), near the city of Polokwane, northern South Africa [9]. The system could identify 30 TVWS channels (This is approximately to 240 MHz of unused bandwidth). The TVWS channels could be shared by broadband network service operators to provide broadband ICT services.

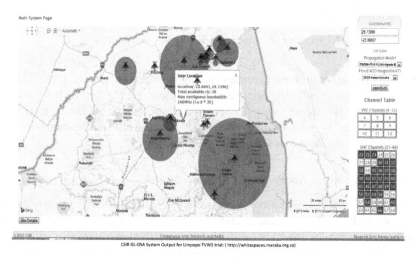

CSIR GL-DSA System Output for Limpopo TVWS trial: (http://whitespaces.meraka.org.za)

Fig. 1. GLSD based spectrum underutilisation study in the UHF band.

Regulators all over the globe are now scrambling to enable new models of spectrum sharing, using modern technologies such as GLSD, spectrum sensing, advanced spectrum sharing algorithms, cloud computing and artificial intelligence.

2 Spectrum Sharing Models Overview

Spectrum sharing models such as the LSA, SAS and TVWS enable regulators to manage spectrum sharing between existing licensed and unlicensed secondary networks. The spectrum sharing models aim to facilitate the introduction of radio communication systems operated by a limited number of licensees under an individual licensing regime in a frequency band already assigned or expected to be assigned to one or more incumbent users [10, 11].

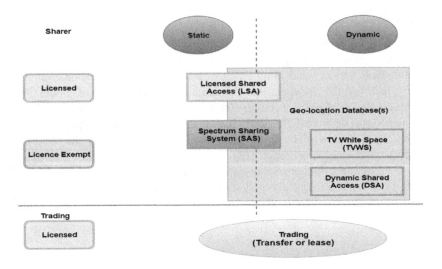

Fig. 2. Spectrum sharing mechanisms and spectrum trading [4].

Figure 2 illustrates different spectrum sharing mechanisms namely; LSA, SAS, and TVWS in the context of DSA. Important observations are twofold (i) the close connections between spectrum sharing in licensed and unlicensed (license exempt) modes (ii) spectrum trading which opens the gates of business and commercialisation opportunities for database-enabled white space networks.

2.1 Licensed Shared Access (LSA) Sharing Model

LSA model enables harmonization of spectrum sharing between the incumbents (primary users) and the LSA licensees (secondary users) of the band [7]. The LSA licensee are authorised to use the spectrum (or part of the spectrum) in accordance with sharing rules included in their rights of use of spectrum, thereby allowing all the authorized users, including incumbents, to provide a certain Quality of Service (QoS) [7, 10, 12].

The LSA spectrum sharing approach is intended to ensure immediate access to the spectrum to commercial operators, without binding their investments to the times of the traditional process of refarming. The generic LSA concept encompasses sharing between any types of radio systems, most activities in standardization and regulation are concentrating on the application of LSA to the IMT bands [7]. This could enable mobile communication systems to access the bands available on a shared basis that are currently not available for them on an exclusive basis.

The 2.3–2.4 GHz band is under study as the first use case for LSA. In the regulatory domain, European Conference of Postal and Telecommunications (CEPT) has considered harmonised implementation measures and introduced cross border coordination procedures for this band [11, 12].

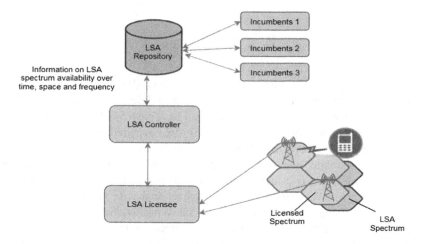

Fig. 3. LSA architecture.

Figure 3 demonstrate the LSA model architecture as defined by the European Telecommunications Standards Institute (ESTI) [13]. The spectrum is managed through a centralized database; LSA Repository. The incumbents are required to provide their spectrum usage information to the database over time and space. Based on the provided information by the incumbents, the LSA licensee will be given a permission to use or vacate the band through LSA controller.

2.2 Spectrum Access System (SAS) Sharing Model

SAS is a model used for enabling sharing of the CBRS in the 3.5 GHz, currently this model has attracted interest in USA [5, 7]. SAS supports spectrum sharing with three levels of hierarchy in spectrum usage.

Figure 4 illustrates the architecture of SAS. The incumbent Access are given the highest level of usage rights including exclusive spectrum access and guaranteed protection from harmful interference when and where they deploy their networks [5, 7]. Secondary licensees occupy the middle level and are generally expected to be a

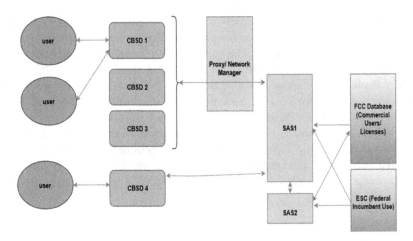

Fig. 4. SAS architecture.

commercial service provider i.e. a cellular service provider. The secondary licensee would have short-term priority operating rights, that is, Priority Access License (PAL), for a specified geographic area [7]. PAL is issued for a predefined term and bandwidth, such as, one minute or even one year for a 10 MHz unpaired channel with possibly varying spectral location. PAL could also guarantee the secondary licensee interference protection from the third level of the hierarchy often referred to as opportunistic use.

Third level of access is called the General Authorized Access (GAA) and is light licensed similarly to a Wi-Fi with the critical distinction that the GAA device or system must be capable of effectively interacting with the controlling SAS [5, 14]. GAA users are allowed to opportunistically access a specific spectrum band in a geographical area or time period when it is otherwise unoccupied by both the incumbent and the PAL licensee. The amount of spectrum reserved for PAL and GAA and the PAL license durations will strongly influence their demand.

The main functions of SAS include determining and assigning available frequencies at a given geographic location; registration, authentication and identification of user information and location as well as protection of the incumbent from harmful interference; through enforcing an Interference Limits Policy based approach to insure that harm claims threshold limits are not exceeded in exclusion or coordination zones. The SAS model is a general framework that could be applied to any bands and between any networks.

2.3 Television White Spaces (TVWS) Sharing Model

TVWS spectrum is found in VHF and UHF bands. TVWS are frequencies made available for unlicensed use at location where the spectrum is not being used by licensed services, such as Television broadcasting.

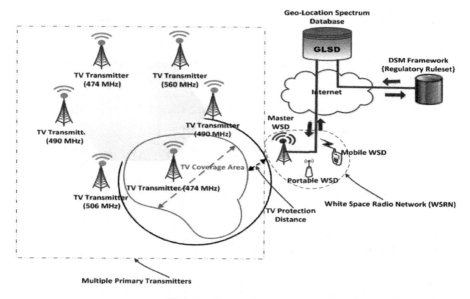

Fig. 5. TVWS architecture.

Figure 5 illustrates the TVWS sharing model. TVWS has become a focal point for research and development effort for the last couple of years [4, 6, 8, 9] due to its long range communication capabilities, good propagation and excellent in-building penetration. TVWS are enabled through GLSD; through GLSD harmful interference to the incumbents of the band is reduced.

3   Comparison of LSA, SAS and TVWS Models

All regulatory spectrum sharing models described in Sect. 2 present the state of the art sharing models. These models present the incumbent system on the highest level as shown in Fig. 6. LSA is a two tier model whereas SAS is a three tier model and TVWS is a two tier model [15]. The protection of the incumbent spectrum users' rights is the starting point for both models [4]. Additional users are introduced on times and geographical areas where the incumbent user is not using the spectrum.

LSA is foreseen to be based on the voluntariness and the incumbent can define on which bands, geographical areas and times to allow additional usage via licensing. While SAS is based on the assumption that the incumbent has an exclusive right to actual use but all spectrum resources unused by the incumbent user would be subject to additional usage. The second level on both spectrum sharing models introduce additional users on a controlled manner based on individual licensing [7, 10]. The major difference between the two models is that the SAS introduces a third level of usage rights. This additional level of the SAS introduces opportunistic access for light licensed users. Table 1 below represent the differences between the LSA, SAS and TVWS.

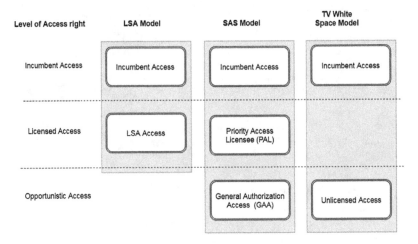

Fig. 6. LSA, SAS and TVWS at different levels of access rights.

Table 1. Comparison of LSA, SAS and TVWS spectrum sharing models [10]

Criteria	Licensed Shared Access (LSA)	Spectrum Access System (SAS)	TV White Space (TVWS)
Efficient spectrum utilisation	Enhanced utilisation through shared access spectrum	Enhanced utilisation through shared access spectrum, further efficiency obtained via GAA	Enhanced utilisation through unlicensed shared spectrum
Protection from the interference	Spatial separation obtained via LSA license and protection zones enforced by LSA database and management system	Spatial separation obtained via SAS license and protection zones enforced by SAS database. Number and character of GAA devices create interference concerns	Protection enforced by the geolocation database
Minimum impact to the technology of the system	The incumbent reports changes in licensing terms, LSA licensee needs means to respond to possible changes	Reporting all spectrum usage in SAS, direct interactions between systems pose changes to systems	Incumbents reports changes in the system, that's allow the secondary users to vacate or continue using the spectrum in the selected band
Reliable access and usage conditions	License, spectrum sharing framework, voluntariness	PAL license, access not guaranteed GAA	Access is not guaranteed for secondary users (unlicensed users)

(continued)

Table 1. (*continued*)

Criteria	Licensed Shared Access (LSA)	Spectrum Access System (SAS)	TV White Space (TVWS)
Implementation and enforcement by regulatory authorities	Based on licensing procedure	PAL, device standardization for opportunistic access, enforcement for GAA more challenging	Enforcement for unlicensed users is challenging
Fairness and pro-competition	Based on licensing procedure, negotiations between the incumbent and LSA licensee challenging	Based on licensing procedure, but GAA option provides a "pro-competition edge" to SAS	There is no negotiations between incumbents and unlicensed users
Legal certainty	License provides legal certainty, database security	Legal certainty is provided for PAL level licensees, GAA licenses are only provided with opportunistic access to the spectrum. Both are provided with, database security	Secondary users are only provided with opportunistic access to the spectrum
Foster innovation	Makes spectrum available, flexible regulatory framework allows access to new systems and new innovative	Makes spectrum available, flexible regulatory framework allows access to new systems and new innovative services, GAA allows for broad set of innovators	TVWS allows for broad set of functions for innovative use of spectrum
Quality of Service (QoS)	QoS is guaranteed through licensing	QoS for PAL users is guaranteed while as for GAA is not guaranteed	Secondary users QoS for TVWS operation is not guaranteed
Market Acceptance	There is market acceptance and support from manufactures	There is market acceptance and support from manufactures	Market acceptance is low and remains below the original expectations

4   Discussion

Table 1 compares the LSA, SAS and TVWS spectrum sharing models. LSA, SAS and TVWS models enhance spectrum utilisation through shared access, they allow spectrum to be shared while giving the priority to the incumbents of the chosen bands. This is essential since there is a demand for new spectrum for the growing radiocommunication services [10]. The incumbents of the bands are protected from interference through database the unlicensed users of SAS (GAA) and TVWS pose a slightly concern to assure an interference free environment. The unlicensed users of SAS and TVWS are not guaranteed to get the QoS, they are required to vacate the band whenever the licensed users' needs to use the spectrum in the selected bands.

5 Recommendations

The proposed 5G standard and its services ecosystem require the availability of sufficient spectrum allocation to provide high bandwidth (gigabit wireless) services and massive machine-2-machine (M2M) communications [16]. 5G standards identified a number of frequency bands as shown in Table 2.

Table 2. Identified frequency bands for the 5G ecosystem.

Band range	Spectrum and application types		
	Typical spectrum types	5G App1	5G App2
54 kHz – 1 GHz	Widespread coverage range, 700, 800, 900 MHz	Rural/unlicensed	Urban, WLAN (IoT)
1 GHz– 6 GHz	Mixed range and capacity, 1800 MHz, 3.3–3.8 GHz	Urban/rural/unlicensed	IoT/ITS
>6 GHz	Gigabits wireless broadband (6– 28 GHz)	UWB, wireless fiber	Wireless VOD

LSA, SAS and TVWS models enables dynamic spectrum sharing to increase the spectrum utilisation and also to meet the ever-increasing demand of the new spectrum in the rapidly growing radiocommunication services. However, LSA, SAS and TVWS are currently defined for usage only in specific frequency bands of interest.

Since LSA, SAS and TVWS are all database-assisted models; we propose that a unified spectrum sharing database containing the local regulatory rules for wireless networks co-existence, geo-location information and dynamic licensing mechanism as a solution for future wireless network deployments.

Artificial Intelligence (AI) techniques coupled with cloud-based distributed ledger (blockchain) architectures are being considered to solve the computational resources challenges associated with big-data. The proposed unified approach will enable seamless dynamic spectrum access in the bands of interest by heterogeneous networks in the 5G ecosystem. This will provide the required quality of service for each application. Figure 7 depicts a high-level proposed architecture of the unified database-assisted spectrum sharing framework.

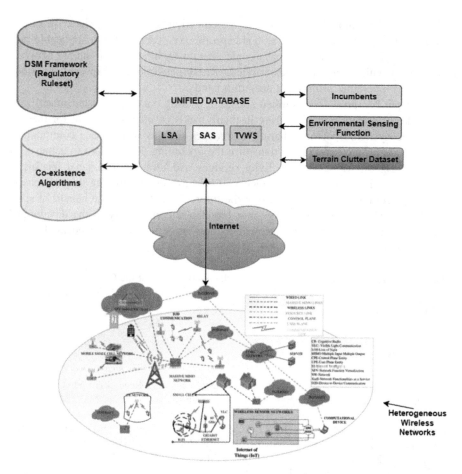

Fig. 7. Proposed high-level architecture of a unified database-assisted spectrum sharing framework for the 5G ecosystem.

6 Conclusion

The commercial access and use of spectrum is generally authorised in two ways (i) either through individual licenses or; (ii) in accordance with license exempt (unlicensed or 'commons') rules. Database-assisted dynamic spectrum management models investigated in this paper namely; LSA, SAS and TVWS brings the benefit of enabling dynamic allocation and sharing of spectrum in the bands of interest. LSA and SAS guarantee the QoS for the users of the band through licensing part of the spectrum for other services whereas the TVWS doesn't guaranteed the QoS. SAS and TVWS allows more dynamic spectrum sharing model which is likely to promote competition and foster innovation. In LSA there is no requirement for sensing mechanism for supporting the system for the identification of the incumbents as compared to the SAS where it is a mandatory requirement, while in TVWS it is optional.

However, the major drawback of the aforementioned database-assisted spectrum sharing approaches is that they are all band specific (i.e., each model is applicable in a given band of interest). This drawback could be a costly hindrance in the 5G network ecosystem in which heterogeneous wireless access networks are expected, possibly each network operating in different spectrum bands.

This paper has proposed a unified spectrum sharing database-assisted model that will enable dynamic spectrum sharing in many bands of interest relevant for the 5G networks ecosystem. Spectrum sharing approaches such as white space communications technologies are expected to transform the upcoming 5G standard to achieve its promise of gigabit wireless connectivity services. Additionally, the paper has highlighted the importance of research which will lead towards promoting the unlicensed sharing of spectrum as a new use case in the future 5G networks. The benefit of such research is to allow provision of low-cost broadband connectivity in the developing countries particularly in the rural areas. This new drive has been termed as the "4th Pillar of 5G" [17].

Acknowledgement. The authors would like to thank colleagues at the CSIR Meraka Institute and The CSIR R&D units for funding this work, under the auspices of the CSIR Thematic R&D funding.

References

1. Sohul, M.M., Yao, M., Ma, X., Imana, E.Y., Marojevic, V., Reed, J.H.: Next generation public safety networks: a spectrum sharing approach. IEEE Commun. Mag. **54**(3), 30–36 (2016)
2. Irnich, T., Kronander, J., Selén, Y., Li, G.: Spectrum sharing scenarios and resulting technical requirements for 5G systems. In: IEEE International Symposium on Personal, Indoor and Mobile Radio Communications, PIMRC, pp. 127–132 (2013)
3. ITU: Final Acts WRC-15 World Radio Conference (2016)
4. Carlson, J., et al.: Studies on the use of television white spaces in South Africa : recommendations and learnings from the Cape Town television white spaces trial (2013)
5. Palola, M., Höyhtyä, M., Aho, P., Mustonen, M., Kippola, T., Heikkilä, M.: Field trial of the 3.5 GHz citizens broadband radio service governed by a spectrum access system (SAS) (2017)
6. Ofcom: TV white spaces : approach to coexistence, September 2013
7. Mueck, M.D., Srikanteswara, S., Badic, B.: Spectrum sharing: licensed shared access (LSA) and spectrum access system (SAS) (2015)
8. T. M. Opinion and T. O. F. Contents: Third Memorandum Order and Opinion, vol. 1, no. 12–36, pp. 3692–3726 (2012)
9. Mfupe, L., Mekuria, F., Mzyece, M.: Geo-location white space spectrum databases: models and design of South Africa's first dynamic spectrum access coexistence manager. KSII Trans. Internet Inf. Syst. **8**(11), 1–6 (2014)
10. Mustonen, M., Matinmikko, M., Roberson, D., Yrjölä, S.: Evaluation of recent spectrum sharing models from the regulatory point of view. In: 1st International Conference on 5G for Ubiquitous Connectivity, pp. 11–16 (2014)

11. Ponomarenko-Timofeev, A., Pyattaev, A., Andreev, S., Koucheryavy, Y., Mueck, M., Karls, I.: Highly dynamic spectrum management within licensed shared access regulatory framework. IEEE Commun. Mag. **54**(3), 100–109 (2016)

12. Frascolla, V., et al.: Dynamic licensed shared access - a new architecture and spectrum allocation techniques. In: IEEE Vehicular Technology Conference, pp. 1–5 (2017)

13. Technical Specification: Reconfigurable Radio Systems (RRS); for operation of Licensed Shared Access (LSA), vol. 1, pp. 1–28 (2015)

14. Sohul, M.M., Yao, M., Yang, T., Reed, J.H.: Spectrum access system for the citizen broadband radio service. IEEE Commun. Mag. **53**(7), 18–25 (2015)

15. IEEE Computer Society: IEEE Standard for Information technology - Local and metropolitan area networks - Specific requirements Part 11: Wireless LAN Medium Access Control (MAC) and Physical Layer (PHY) Specifications Amendment 5: Television White Spaces (TVWS) Operation, vol. 2013 (2013)

16. Ofcom: M2M application characteristics and their implications for spectrum final report. AEGIS Spectr. Eng., no. May, p. 78 (2014)

17. Mekuria, F.: 5G and the Next Billion Mobile Users a view from Africa. IEEE COMSOC CTN, December 2015. http://www.comsoc.org/ctn/5g-and-next-billion-mobile-users-view-africa

Towards Affordable Broadband Communication: A Quantitative Assessment of TV White Space in Tanzania

Jabhera Matogoro$^{(\boxtimes)}$, Nerey H. Mvungi, Anatory Justinian, Abhay Karandikar, and Jaspreet Singh

College of Informatics and Virtual Education, The University of Dodoma, P.O Box 490, Dodoma, Tanzania
jaberamatogoro@udom.ac.tz, nhmvungi@udsm.ac.tz, anatory@engineer.com, karandi@ee.iitb.ac.in, jaspreet.singh@iitb.ac.in

Abstract. A quantitative assessment of TV White Space in Tanzania was conducted to assess the level of spectrum utilization as well as a key milestone towards the use of white space for affordable broadband communication. Two approaches have been used; pollution and protection viewpoints and experimental spectrum measurements based on energy detection principle. The study focused on 470–694 MHz UHF spectrum band which is used for digital terrestrial television in Tanzania. It was found that, more than 120 MHz is available as white space in various locations in Tanzania when pollution and protection view point was used and about 184 MHz are available as white space in Dodoma urban using experimental spectrum measurements and almost 100% of the available frequencies are not used in Dodoma rural. Both approaches revealed that there is low spectrum utilization and therefore presents a best case towards development of dynamic spectrum access technologies in Tanzania.

Keywords: White space · Spectrum analyzer · Energy detection principle
Dynamic spectrum access

1 Introduction

Tanzania has experienced an exponential increase in the number of voice telephone and Internet users in the last few years. According to Tanzania Communications Regulatory Authority (TCRA) statistics, the number of voice telephone subscribers has increased from 6.3 million users in March, 2007 to 39.9 million users in March, 2017 [1, 2]. Furthermore, the estimated number of Internet users has increased from 5.3 to 19.9 million users in 2011 to 2016 respectively [2]. From 2016 Internet users statistics above, the distribution of Internet users according to technology type is 90.7%, 6.1% and 3.2% for mobile wireless, fixed wireless and fixed wired respectively. The increase of both voice telephone and Internet users in Tanzania has resulted to more demand of spectrum resources to meet the current and future needs.

There is growing recognition across the globe that dynamic spectrum access, especially on the Television White Spaces (TVWS) has significant potential to address

© ICST Institute for Computer Sciences, Social Informatics and Telecommunications Engineering 2018
F. Mekuria et al. (Eds.): ICT4DA 2017, LNICST 244, pp. 320–330, 2018.
https://doi.org/10.1007/978-3-319-95153-9_29

challenges associated with the raising importance of radio spectrum and can optimize spectrum utilization. In this paper, an investigation was conducted to quantify the availability of TVWS in 470–694 MHz Ultra High Frequency (UHF) spectrum band in Tanzania. The overarching objectives of this paper is three-fold; firstly, is to guide a range of stakeholders so as to increase the use of the currently underutilized TV UHF spectrum band; secondly, to attract more Research and Development (R&D) invest-ments on dynamic spectrum access using TVWS and thirdly, necessitate the discussion to establish a sound technical and legal framework to embrace the dynamic spectrum access paradigm towards affordable broadband communication in Tanzania.

2 Related Work

An estimation of TV White Space has been regarded as a critical step for the efficient and effective spectrum management scheme. TVWS estimation informs various stakeholders including regulators, researchers, industrial, scientific and medical com-munities on the current spectrum usage and possible values that can be harvested from using the licensed but under-utilized TV UHF radio spectrum band. The spectrum scarcity experienced by many regulatory authorities can be seen as an artificial problem due to lack of effective technical solutions that make use of the available spectrum band at all times and in all locations. In order to understand how UHF spectrum band is utilized in various locations around the globe, many studies have been carried out and revealed that there is low spectrum utilization especially in TV UHF spectrum band −55.5% to 55.8% in United States [3], 66.58% in Spain [4], 43.06% for urban and only 11.42% for rural in Romania [5], 7.14% in Philippines [6], 13.46% at University of Hull in United Kingdom [7], 56% in Europe [8], 32% in a study conducted in Italy, Spain and Romania [9], 20% in South Africa [10] and approximately 150 MHz and 112 MHz is available as white space in United Kingdom [11] and India [12] respec-tively. In the literature, it is clearly shown that spectrum utilization differ from one country to another and this is due to the fact that every country is an autonomous regarding local frequency allocation and is also bound by local regulatory bodies [13]. It is therefore important for country specific studies to be conducted to be able to understand local spectrum utilization in various countries around the globe. This is also important when working for technical and legal framework aimed to favor the use of TVWS for broadband communication in a specific self-governing country. It has also observed that spectrum utilization is high in urban area as compared to rural area [5, 14] and hence making rural area the best case to efficiently utilized the unused spectrum band to bridge the digital divide.

3 Methodology

In order to answer the question on "how much white space is there in Tanzania", this paper uses two methods. Firstly, a computational tool based on Mat lab simulation to generate a color-coded map of the United Republic of Tanzania showing how many MHz of white-space is available as shown in Figs. 3 and 4. The tool used the pollution and protection viewpoint that was introduced by [15] to establish the pollution and protection regions and Hata empirical formula [16] was used for propagation loss calculation of the TV UHF transmitters. Among other reasons of choosing this propagation model is due to the fact that it was derived from extensive measurement of data over various situations of irregular terrain and environmental clutter to some extent meeting local environment. Secondly, an experimental spectrum measurement was conducted in Dodoma Region using inexpensive handheld spectrum analyzer [17] to find out how TV UHF spectrum band is utilized in rural and urban areas in Dodoma Region. The measurement was based on energy detection principle where a threshold value was used to determine whether a certain frequency is occupied or not. Furthermore, a Monitoring Software R&S ARGUS [18] was used to validate results obtained from pollution and protection view points as well as that from inexpensive handheld spectrum analyzer. In the literature, two approaches are the commonly used to estimate the white space in a location; pollution and protection viewpoints base on TV transmitters' databases [12, 19, 20] and energy detection principle [10, 14, 21, 22].

3.1   Study Location

This study was designed to estimate TV White Space in Tanzania Mainland. According to 2012 census [23], Tanzania Mainland has a population of 43.6 Million to which 21.2 million are males and 22.4 are female. In addition, Dodoma Region was selected for a measurement campaign in order to assess spectrum utilization in both rural and urban areas. Dodoma Region has a population of 2.08 million in its seven districts councils [23] and is the capital city of Tanzania. The rationale of choosing Dodoma Region for an experimental spectrum measurement is due to the fact that, it is among the fast growing regions of Tanzania presenting high demand for affordable broadband services. Furthermore, the College of Informatics and Virtual Education of the University of Dodoma which is the host institution of this study received an authorization letter from TCRA to conduct a research on dynamic spectrum access using TVWS in Dodoma Region.

3.2   Pollution and Protection Viewpoints

In the literature, the pollution and protection viewpoints approach have been used to estimate white space in United States [20] and India [12]. In pollution viewpoint perspective, the primary user is considered to raise the noise floor at secondary user location and therefore each television tower should have a pollution radius around it in which the secondary user is not allowed to transmit. Whereas, in protection viewpoint, a secondary user is permitted to transmit in a location with the condition that, it is should not cause any harmful interference to the primary receivers in its vicinity [12, 15]. In order to quantify the availability of white space using pollution and protection viewpoints, the researcher of this study received transmitters' information from TCRA. This information included position of the tower (latitude and longitude), transmission power of the TV transmitters, frequency of operation and height of the antenna for all Digital Terrestrial Television (DTT) transmitters in Tanzania. The study used a matlab tool to process the given data in order to quantify the amount of TVWS in Tanzania.

Currently, there are no TV white space regulations in Tanzania. The regulations of FCC (US) are borrowed for the estimation of TV white space in Tanzania. Microphones are ignored in the computation due to lack of available information.

3.3   Measurement Locations and Equipments

A spectrum measurements campaign was conducted in Dodoma Municipal Council, Kondoa, Bahi and Chamwino District Councils to establish spectrum utilization in these locations. Selected locations in Dodoma Municipal Council are categorized as urban area whereas those from Kondoa, Bahi and Chamwino District Councils are rural areas in nature. Figure 1 shows locations considered for measurement campaign in Dodoma Region.

Equipments used for the experimental spectrum measurement consists: RF Explorer WSUB1G Spectrum Analyzer, Toshiba Laptop with Ubuntu Operating System (OS) and Inverter connected to a car battery to power the devices and Nagoya NA-773 wideband telescopic antenna with SMA male connector. RF Explorer spectrum analyzer has the following specifications: Frequency band (240–960 MHz), Frequency span (112 kHz–100 MHz), amplitude resolution (0.5 dBm), dynamic range (−115 dBm to 0 dBm), absolute max input power (+5 dBm) and average noise level (−110 dBm).

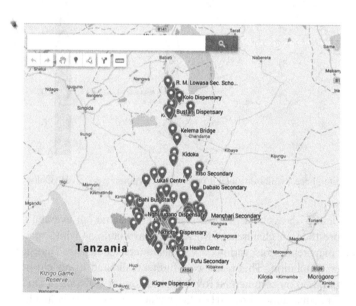

Fig. 1. Locations considered for measurement campaign (Source: Google maps)

For a successful static spectrum measurement, Rfestatic application was installed in Ubuntu OS. To start data acquisitions, a bash script was launched to collect power levels of UHF channels for DTT which ranges from channel 21 to 48 (470–694 MHz). The collected data files were further analyzed to decide if a channel is occupied or not. A threshold value of −85 dBm and 80% of the samples below this threshold value were used to consider a channel is occupied. In each location, duration of 15 min was configured to collect reading of power levels of TV UHF transmitters in a given location. In addition, spectrum utilization results generated from inexpensive RF Explorer WSUB1G model was further validated using commercial R&S Argus Monitor software, which is the standard software for spectrum monitoring and evaluation in accordance with ITU recommendations [18].

4   Results and Major Observations

In this study, two approaches have been used to estimate white space in Tanzania. The pollution and protection viewpoint was used to generate a color-coded map of Tanzania Mainland showing the amount of spectrum available as white space in MHz as shown in Figs. 2 and 3. This estimate is based on the transmitters' information obtained from TCRA.[1]

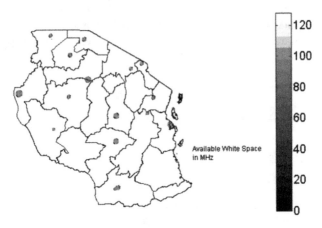

Fig. 2. TV white space availability using pollution viewpoint $\gamma = 15$ dB (Color figure online)

Figures 2 and 3 shows that in most places of Tanzania, an average of more than 120 MHz (more than 15 channels of 8 MHz) are available as white space. The color cycles in the map represents various TV transmitters located in Tanzania generated from computer simulation. This result was further validated using physical measurement campaign based on commercial R&S Argus Monitor software in Dodoma Region and it was found that about 184 MHz (23 channels of 8 MHz) is available as white space in urban area. In Dodoma Region, the digital terrestrial television transmitters are located in Imagi Hills with −6.213 and 35.753 coordinates of latitude and longitude respectively.

---

[1] While TV transmitters' information is publicly available in other countries including US, it is not so in Tanzania. This information is only available upon request to Tanzania Communications Regulatory Authority.

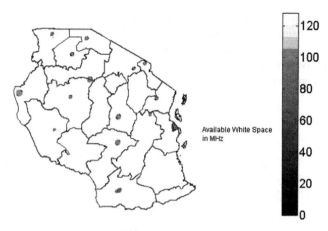

Fig. 3. TV white space availability using protection viewpoint Δ = 1 dB (Color figure online)

The results of the data collected in Nyerere Sqaure (−6.178, 35.748) a location in Dodoma Municipal Council was analyzed using a threshold value of −85, it was found that about 23 channels (82.1%) are free and only 5 channels are occupied (17.9%). Figure 4 shows a heat map graph with Received Signal Strength Indicator (RSSI) in dBm was generated using inexpensive handheld spectrum analyzer at Nyerere Sqaure in Dodoma Region. The color legend represents various power levels, whereby a threshold value of −85 dBm was used to decide if a channel is occupied or not. A result generated in Fig. 4 was validated using commercial R&S Argus Monitor software and found only 40 MHz (5 channels) are available as occupied channels shown in Fig. 5.

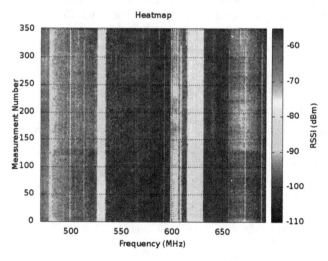

Fig. 4. Spectrum utilization graph for data collected at Nyerere Square (−6.178, 35.748), Dodoma Municipal Council using handheld spectrum analyzer. (Color figure online)

In order to validate results obtained from both computer simulation and measurement campaign using inexpensive handheld spectrum analyzer, commercial R&S Argus Monitor software was used to validate spectrum utilization results in Tanzania, specifically in Nyerere Sqaure as shown in Fig. 5. It was found that only 5 channels were found occupied and 23 channels are available as free channels in this location.

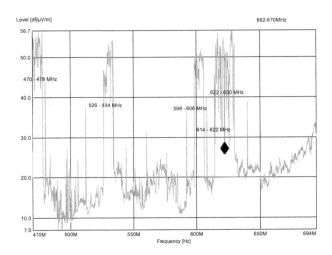

Fig. 5. Spectrum utilization graph for data collected at Nyerere Square, Dodoma Municipal Council from R&S Argus Monitoring Software.

Table 1 shows the results of free and occupied channels in Dodoma Municipal Councils. It is clearly shown that in most of locations, 23 channels out of 28 channels (82.1%) of the spectrum are unused in Dodoma Municipal Council. This is an indication that there is a high possibility of using the identified unused UHF spectrum for other services such as broadband communication without affecting broadcasting services.

Table 1. Free and occupied channels in various locations in Dodoma Municipal Council.

Location name	Coordinates (Lat & Long)	Free channels	Occupied channel
Kikuyu Secondary	−6.201, 35.729	23	5
The University of Dodoma	−6.216, 35.789	23	5
Miyuji Secondary	−6.132, 35.740	27	1
Nyerere Square	−6.178, 35.748	23	5
College of Business Education	−6.177, 35.758	25	3

The study further revealed that almost all 28 channels (100%) of TV UHF spectrum is unused in Kondoa District Council as shown in Table 2. Kondoa District Council is located about 140 km from Dodoma Municipal Council where all digital terrestrial transmitters are located.

Table 2. Free and occupied channels in various locations in Kondoa District Council.

Location name	Coordinates (Lat & Long)	Free channels	Occupied channel
Masange Secondary	−4.606, 35.804	28	0
Busi Health Centre	−4.850, 36.051	28	0
ULA Secondary School	−4.900, 35.765	28	0
Kondoa Girls High School	−4.888, 35.769	28	0
Bustani Teacher's College	−4.898, 35.789	28	0
Pahi Centre	−4.716, 35.917	28	0

Figure 6 heat map graph for spectrum utilization at Ibihwa Dispensary in Bahi District Councils and Table 3 shows the number of free and occupied channels in various locations in Chamwino District Council. The blue color indicates that all channels have power level below −85 dBm. Similarly, the study revealed that almost all 28 channels (100%) of TV UHF spectrum band are unused in these locations. Bahi and Chamwino District Councils are located about 60 km and 40 km from Dodoma Municipal Council respectively.

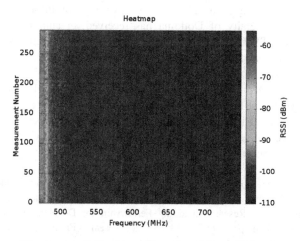

Fig. 6. Spectrum utilization graph for data collected at Ibihwa Dispensary (−6.005, 35.432), Bahi District Council using handheld spectrum analyzer. (Color figure online)

Table 3. Free and occupied channels in various locations in Chamwino District Council.

Location name	Coordinates (Lat & Long)	Free channels	Occupied channel
Dabalo Secondary	−4.606, 35.804	28	0
Itiso Secondary	−4.850, 36.051	28	0
Chilonwa Secondary	−4.900, 35.765	28	0
Fufu Secondary	−4.888, 35.769	28	0
Makwawa Secondary	−4.898, 35.789	28	0
Mvumi Mission Secondary	−4.716, 35.917	28	0

5   Conclusion and Recommendation

In this paper, a quantitative assessment of TV White Space in Tanzania was conducted. In Tanzania, digital terrestrial television is allocated to use spectrum band in the range of 470–694 MHz with about 28 channels of 8 MHz. When the pollution and protection view point approach was used, it was found that more than 120 MHz of TV UHF spectrum band is available as free channel in most of locations in Tanzania. In addition, the study found that almost 82.1% of TV UHF spectrum is unused in most of urban areas of Dodoma Region when energy detection principle was used. Experimental measurements that were conducted in Kondoa, Bahi and Chamwino District Councils also revealed that 100% of TV UHF spectrum band is not used in most of these locations. This study is an important milestone towards development of dynamic spectrum access technologies in Tanzania. The College of Informatics and Virtual Education of the University of Dodoma has received an authorization letter from TCRA to transmit in TV UHF spectrum band for dynamic spectrum access researches. In future, a test bed network will be deployed in Dodoma Region to make use of the identified white space for wireless broadband communication. The test bed network will also be a critical step to help various stakeholders in the development of legal and technical framework that favors the use of dynamic spectrum access in Tanzania. For efficient spectrum utilization in Tanzania, a geo-location database is currently under development at the University of Dodoma, the results of this work will further be published for public access.

Acknowledgments. Mr. Jabhera Matogoro, a first author of this study would like to extend his thanks to NAM S&T Centre of New Delhi and Indian Institute of Technology Bombay, India for the award of Six Months Research Training Fellowship for Developing Country Scientists (RTF-DCS) where he participated in TV White Space Research Project in India. This work was also supported by various stakeholders in different capacity, including; The University of Dodoma, Higher Education Students' Loans Board, International Centre for Theoretical Physics, Internet Society, Council for Scientific and Industrial Research and Tanzania Communications Regulatory Authority.

References

1. TCRA: Telecommunication Statistics as at March 2007 (2007). https://www.tcra.go.tz/index.php/2007/March-2007. Accessed 29 June 2017
2. TCRA: Quarterly Communications Statistics Report: January–March 2017 Quarter. Dar es Salaam (2017)
3. McHenry, M.A., Tenhula, P.A., McCloskey, D., Roberson, D.A., Hood, C.S.: Chicago spectrum occupancy measurements & analysis and a long-term studies proposal. In: TAPAS' 2006, Proceedings of the First International Workshop on Technology and Policy for Accessing Spectrum, Article No. 1 (2006)
4. López-Benítez, M., Umbert, A., Casadevall, F.: Evaluation of spectrum occupancy in Spain for cognitive radio applications. In: VTC Spring 2009 - IEEE 69th Vehicular Technology Conference, Barcelona, pp. 1–5 (2009)
5. Martian, A.: Evaluation of spectrum occupancy in urban and rural environments of Romania. Rev. Roum. des Sci. Tech. - Ser. Electrotech. Energ. **59**(1), 87–96 (2014)
6. Pintor, A.L.C., To, M.R.S., Salenga, J.S., Geslani, G.M., Agpawa, D.P., Cabatuan, M.K.: Spectrum survey of VHF and UHF bands in the Philippines. In: TENCON 2012, IEEE Region 10 Conference, Cebu, pp. 1–6 (2012)
7. Mehdawi, M., Riley, N., Paulson, K., Fanan, A., Ammar, M.: Spectrum occupancy survey in HULL-UK for cognitive radio applications: measurement & analysis. Int. J. Sci. Technol. Res. **2**(4), 231–236 (2013)
8. Van de Beek, J., Riihijarvi, J., Achtzehn, A., Mahonen, P.: TV white space in Europe. IEEE Trans. Mob. Comput. **11**(2), 178–188 (2012)
9. Fadda, M., Popescu, V., Murroni, M., Angueira, P., Morgade, J.: On the feasibility of unlicensed communications in the TV white space: field measurements in the UHF band. Int. J. Digit. Multimed. Broadcast. **2015** (2015)
10. Barnes, S.D., Jansen Van Vuuren, P.A., Maharaj, B.T.: Spectrum occupancy investigation: measurements in South Africa. Meas. J. Int. Meas. Confed. **46**(9), 3098–3112 (2013)
11. Nekovee, M.: Quantifying the availability of TV white spaces for cognitive radio operation in the UK. In: 2009 IEEE International Conference on Communications Workshops, Dresden, pp. 1–5 (2009)
12. Naik, G., Singhal, S., Kumar, A., Karandikar, A.: Quantitative assessment of TV white space in India. In: 2014 Twentieth National Conference on Communications (NCC), pp. 1–6 (2014)
13. Brown, T.X., Pietrosemoli, E., Zennaro, M., Bagula, A., Mauwa, H., Nleya, S.M.: A survey of TV white space measurements. In: International Conference on E-Infrastructure and E-Services for Developing Countries, pp. 164–172 (2014)
14. Kumar, P., Rakheja, N., Sarswat, A., Varshney, H., Bhatia, P., Goli, S.R., Ribeiro, V.J., Sharma, M.: White space detection and spectrum characterization in urban and rural India. In: 2013 IEEE 14th International Symposium on "A World Wireless, Mobile and Multimedia Networks" (WoWMoM), Madrid, pp. 1–6 (2013)
15. Mishra, S.M.: Maximizing Available Spectrum for Cognitive Radios. University of California at Berkeley, Berkeley (2010)
16. Hata, M.: Empirical formula for propagation loss in land mobile radio services. IEEE Trans. Veh. Technol. **29**(3), 317–325 (1980)
17. RF Explorer: RF Explorer User Manual. http://j3.rf-explorer.com/download/docs/RFExplorerSpectrumAnalyzerUserManual.pdf. Accessed 27 June 2017
18. Rohde-Schwarz: Monitoring Software R&S ARGUS. http://www.rohde-schwarz-ad.com/docs/specmon/TI_ARGUS.pdf. Accessed 17 May 2017

19. Makris, D., Gardikis, G., Kourtis, A.: Quantifying TV white space capacity: a geolocation-based approach. IEEE Commun. Mag. **50**(9), 145–152 (2012)
20. Harrison, K., Mishra, S.M., Sahai, A.: How much white-space capacity is there? In: 2010 IEEE Symposium on New Frontiers in Dynamic Spectrum Access Network (DySPAN), Singapore, pp. 1–10 (2010)
21. Zennaro, M., Pietrosemoli, E., Mlatho, J., Thodi, M., Mikeka, C.: An assessment study on white spaces in Malawi using affordable tools. In: 2013 IEEE Global Humanitarian Technology Conference (GHTC), San Jose, CA, pp. 265–269 (2013)
22. Dinh, C.H., Van Tien, P.: Assessment of TV white space in Vietnam. In: 2014 International Conference on Advanced Technologies for Communications (ATC 2014), Hanoi, pp. 637–640 (2014)
23. United Repubic of Tanzania (URT): 2012 Population and Housing Census Population Distribution by Administrative Areas. National Bureau of Statistics, Dar es Salaam (2013)

An Evaluation of the Performance
of the University of Limpopo TVWS Trial
Network

Bongani Fenzile Mkhabela[(✉)] and Mthulisi Velempini

Department of Computer Science, University of Limpopo,
Polokwane, Mankweng 2735, South Africa
fanzile.bongani@gmail.com, mvelempini@gmail.com

Abstract. A comparative study of the performance of the TV White space (TVWS) network and WiFi is presented. The Software Defined Radios and Cognitive Network Technology have presented many opportunities and possibilities, which advances the wireless technology. This paper investigates the effectiveness of the TVWS technology in comparison with the legacy broadband WiFi technology. The TVWS technology utilizes the spectrum holes in the broadcasting frequency bands. The vacant frequencies can be used opportunistically by the TVWS technology in providing broadband solutions to rural areas among other areas. It is therefore imperative to investigate the effectiveness of this technology and its performance in relation to existing technologies. The comparative study of TVWS and WiFi is therefore presented. For this study, performance-monitoring techniques were employed to analyze the basic performance metrics such as throughput and latency of the TVWS and WiFi technologies. To evaluate the performance of the technologies, two-performance analysis tools were used, Internet performance open group (Iperf) and Java Performance/Scalability Testing Framework (jperf) tool. Speedtest was also used as an additional tool. The performance data were gathered and analyzed. The results show that the performance of the TVWS of the University of Limpopo trial network still requires significant improvement for it to at least match the performance of the legacy technologies such as WiFi.

Keywords: Cognitive Networks · Software Defined Radios · TVWS

1 Background

The lack of broadband technologies in rural areas is widening the digital divide. The current technologies can not be deployed in rural areas due to a number of reasons. For example, it is not cost effective for telecommunication operators to deploy broadband technologies in rural areas given the terrain, barriers, density, sparsely populated communities with no disposable incomes. There is therefore a need for cost effective technology, which can be deployed in rural communities. Wireless technologies have emerged as promising rural technologies and are attracting significant research attention [1]. The TV White Spaces (TVWS) technology is one such technology, which is

© ICST Institute for Computer Sciences, Social Informatics and Telecommunications Engineering 2018
F. Mekuria et al. (Eds.): ICT4DA 2017, LNICST 244, pp. 331–344, 2018.
https://doi.org/10.1007/978-3-319-95153-9_30

envisioned as a potential rural technology [2]. However, there is a need to investigate its performance in remote rural communities.

The TVWS technology is considered a rural technology largely because of its good signal penetration and efficiency. It also offers better coverage however, at the cost of low information content. Lastly, the technology does not require any new spectrum and it addresses the spectrum scarcity challenge through the utilization of the licensed TV channels opportunistically, for broadband communications. The University of Limpopo (UL) in collaboration with Microsoft, Multisource and Council for Scientific and Industrial Research (CSIR) implemented a trial TVWS network which connects five (5) rural schools. The UL trail project is the second such a trail project in South Africa after the Cape Town project [3]. The Cape Town project was implemented in an urban area while the UL one was deployed in a rural setting.

The term TVWS refers to "part of the spectrum, available for a radio-communication application (service, system) at a given time in a given geographical area on a noninterfering/non-protected basis with regard to primary and other services" [4]. The TV broadcast bands, between 450 and 700 MHz can be utilized for broadband communication [5]. The vacant or unused portions of the radio spectrum can be used as an alternative for wireless broadband communication and access in both rural communities and urban centres [5].

In [6] white space spectrum is defined as "frequencies that are not being used by existing licensees at all times or at all locations". The TVWS technology utilizes the unused or unassigned frequency opportunistically for wireless broadband communications. It is envisioned that the TVWS technology will address the underutilization of the licensed spectrum and the overcrowding of unlicensed spectrum against the backdrop of ever-increasing number of wireless devices requiring wireless spectrum bands for communications. The advert of the TVWS technology and the deployment of the trail projects in South Africa will benefit the growing economy if they succeed [3].

2 Related Work

TVWS is yet to be implemented as an operational network however, a number of trial networks have been deployed. The performance analysis of the technology still requires further investigation. There are many wireless technologies that exist namely 2G, 3G, IEEE 802.11 and 4G however; our research is a comparative study of the performance the UL trial TVWS network and WiFi. The study focuses on the performance of these two technologies in terms of bandwidth, jitter, and latency. This study is significant in the light of the observation in [7], which concluded that the availability rural broadband technologies are hardly compared to urban technologies. The success of teaching and learning depends largely on the access to the broadband technology and these broadband technologies are not deployed in rural areas. The TVWS technology however, addresses this digital divide for the benefit of the rural communities.

Malawi - Performance Assessment of TV White Spaces Technology

There are a number of performance analyses on TV White Spaces technology that have been conducted. The study in [8] conducted a preliminary performance assessment of TVWS technology in Malawi after a successful deployment of the technology. In addition to the monitoring and analysing the performance of the network, they also evaluated the performance the network through simulations. However, for the scope of this paper, we focus on the monitoring and performance of the technology.

The results [8] of the performance were based on the students accessing contents or material availed through the electronic system of the university library. Students also use the services of the network to interact with the university faculty. The evaluation of the performance was to ascertain the usability of the technology. The evaluation was also designed to inform the industry regarding the capability of the technology including its effective coverage and bandwidth. However, the evaluation did not present results, which relate to the experiences of the end users in terms of downloading and uploading rates. In this case, a learner may want to download study material and lecturers may want to upload notes and reading material. Our study takes into consideration the end user experiences.

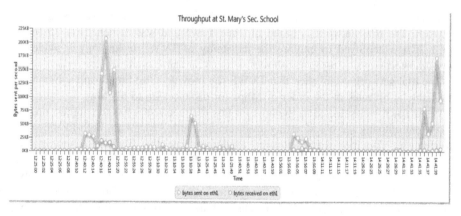

Fig. 1. Achieved end to end throughput at St. Mary's School [8]

The results of the preliminary measurements of throughput and latency were generated. The results are presented in Fig. 1.

The measurement were done for a period of two hours and the maximum throughput achieved was 2 Mb/s. The results show that the technology offers reasonable connection speeds; however, large buffers and higher connection speeds are required for large files and multimedia files. A 2 Mbps connection may be sufficient for voice and may be a challenge in rural areas due to fading, attenuation, shadowing effects and distance. The average latency of the network was also generated and the results are presented in Fig. 2.

Latency, the delay between an input being processed and corresponding output has a negative impact on time bounded data such as voice and video data.

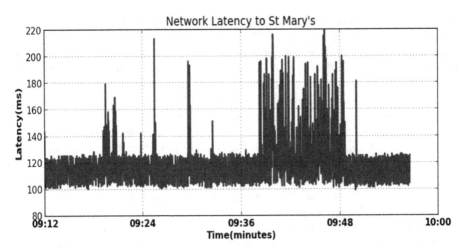

Fig. 2. Latency at St. Mary's School [8]

Cape Town Trial

The study in [3] made a contribution in TVWS in South Africa by deploying a trail network. The trial network is based in Cape Town and was launched on 25 March 2013. It was deployed to explore the capability of TVWS technology in widening network access.

The trial network established that TVWS can provide a fast broadband solution that is reliable at bit rates in the order of Mbps for distances up to 6.5 km.

Cape Town was selected as the host for this trial because it has the highest number of players utilizing the broadcasting spectrum in South Africa with high likelihood of interference. The trial was conducted to demonstrate that TVWS technology can deliver low-cost broadband services without interfering with the TV reception.

The trail network has multiple base stations located at Stellenbosch University's Faculty of Medicine and Health Sciences in Tygerberg, Cape Town. The network provides connectivity to ten schools located within a radius of ten kilometers. The links to each school have a capacity of 2.5 Mbps. The schools are equipped with Carlos Wireless RuralConnect TVWS radios with a backup ADSL line.

The results show an uplink peak of 4 Mbps while the downlink peak speed was 12 Mbps. The results show the great potential of the technology. However, the latency results show that the technology still requires improvement. High latency is largely caused by the Software Defined Radio. This study presents similar performance results of the UL trail network which provides connectivity to five rural schools [9, 10]. However, in contrast with the Cape Town trail network, the UL trial network's evaluation is based on data gathered over longer durations.

The Extension of LTE Operation Mode over TV White Spaces

The work in [3] extended LTE to TVWS. The motivation of their work was the digital switch over which releases Ultra High Frequency to be used for TVWS technology. Network simulations were employed to evaluate the scheme. The simulation framework modeled an urban scenario. The results of the simulation are presented in Figs. 3 and 4. The results compare the performance of the LTE with TVWS.

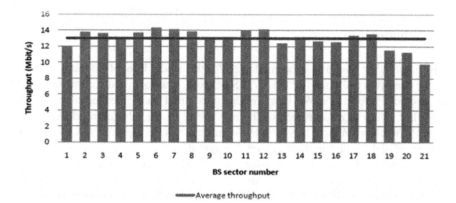

Fig. 3. Legacy carrier

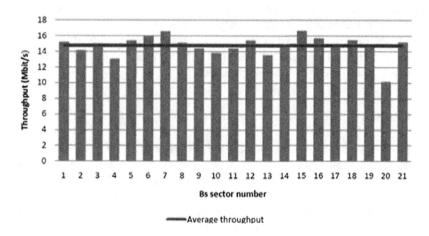

Fig. 4. TVWS carrier

The results show that the TVWS outperformed the LTE in terms of coverage and achievable throughput. The TVWS offered a wider coverage than the LTE technology. The TVWS also achieved higher throughput in all the sectors. The adoption of TVWS is motivated by its characteristics, and its good coverage.

A number of TVWS trail projects have been implemented elsewhere. For example in Cambridge [11], Kenya [12], and EI, Dorado County [13]. The implementation of cognitive radios has gained popularity since 1999 when Mitola [14] proposed it. As a result, specifications of TVWS has been recommended in [15] and [16]. In [17], a number of spectrum access algorithms were reviewed and the technology is presented as a candidate of the next generation networks. Lastly, studies [5, 18–24] either present the TVWS as a possible rural technology or as a promising alternative technology to existing technologies.

3 Methodology

Active monitoring method has been adopted for this study. It involved the collected of data between two end points in the TVWS network. The tool used for the monitoring was Internet Performance Working Group tools (Iperf) which collected bandwidth, delay jitter, and loss measurements. The monitoring was conducted on different days during the week when there was high traffic in the network. The data was collected for a minimum of 12 h during the week on different days.

The throughput was measured using Iperf. Iperf was configured using command lines. The tool was used to test the point to point bandwidth. Three computers were configured and were placed at different locations and measured the performance of the network between endpoints. The experiment was designed to monitor TVWS network at three sites, specially three schools, namely Mamabudusha, Doasha and Mapeloana.

A clock was used to measure the file transmission speed. TCP and UDP traffic was generated to measure the performance of the network. The network was evaluated using the jitter, bandwidth, and the latency metrics.

Jperf was used to collect WiFi data. Two computers were configured as a server and the other as a client. The speedtest was used as well to test the upload and download rate, as well as the latency of the WiFi network.

4 Results

The goal of this research was to compare the performance of TVWS with the existing technologies such as WiFi. The data was collected using three different network analysis tools namely, Iperf, Java Performance/Scalability Testing Framework (Jperf), and speedtest. Figure 5 presents the bandwidth results of the WiFi network.

Figure 5 represents the end user's experience on WiFi network. The measurement results between the 170 and 200 s are presented. The results show that from 170 s the bandwidth was less than 0.5 Mbps. It remained under 0.5 Mbps until it peaked momentarily to 6 Mbps after 195 s before dropping to 2.5 Mbps. At the time of the measurements, there were few active users, which accounted for low bandwidth. The results also show that when active users reduce, the bandwidth for a given user increases. The users received more bandwidth after 195 s largely because some users had to close their sessions in preparation for the next class. Around this time of the measurement, students move from one lecture to the next. Students tend to have short sessions during these breaks to access emails, messages, the learning management systems, and other applications. Figure 6 presents more bandwidth results. The results were gathered approximately six seconds after the results in Fig. 5.

Figure 6 shows that users were consuming less than 0.7 Mbps on the Wi-Fi network. It only reached the highest pick of 0.7 mbps. The bandwidth usage later dropped

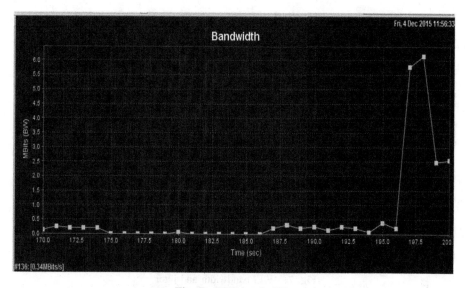

Fig. 5. WiFi bandwidth

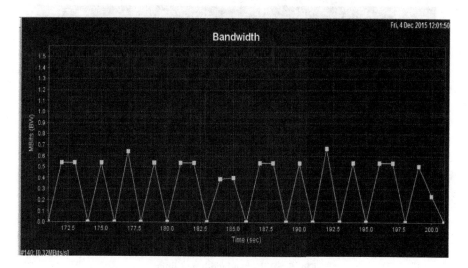

Fig. 6. More WiFi bandwidth

to as low as 0.2 mbps. This shows bandwidth increased when active users closed their sessions and thereafter it began degrading as new users began accessing the Internet after the lectures. The jitter results are presented in Fig. 7 together with the bandwidth results.

Figure 7 represents both bandwidth and jitter. According to the results, there was no observed delay and jitter in the performance of the network. The TVWS technology requires more improvement in delay and jitter. The technology cannot guarantee the

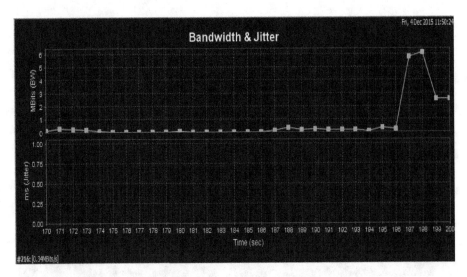

Fig. 7. WiFi bandwidth and jitter

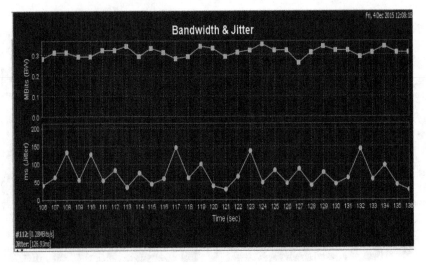

Fig. 8. WiFi bandwidth and jitter

QoS requirements due to jitter and delay. Figure 8 presents more jitter and bandwidth results.

Figure 8 shows both jitter and bandwidth. The jitter reached the highest pick of 150 ms which shows a lot of delays of packet transition on the Wi-Fi network. The network was degraded by many active users. Figure 9 presents more bandwidth and jitter results.

The jitter results show that when the number of active users reduces, jitter improves. The jitter results reached a maximum of 100 ms, which delays packets on

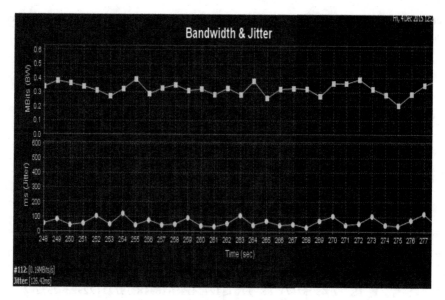

Fig. 9. WiFi bandwidth and jitter

the network while the bandwidth was ranging between 0.2 Mbps and 0.4 Mbps. The jitter was less than 100 ms while bandwidth increased marginally.

In Fig. 10, we present the TVWS results and compare them to the results of the WiFi technology. The WiFi had more active users compared to the TVWS network.

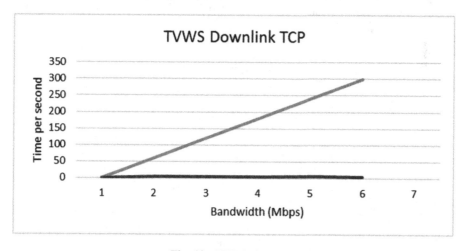

Fig. 10. TVWS downlink

The TVWS downlink results depicted in Fig. 10 show a steady increase in bandwidth from 1 Mbps to 6 Mbps. The measurement results for a five minutes duration were extracted and reported on. During this period, the achievable throughput increased steadily. Figure 11 depicts the latency results for an uplink.

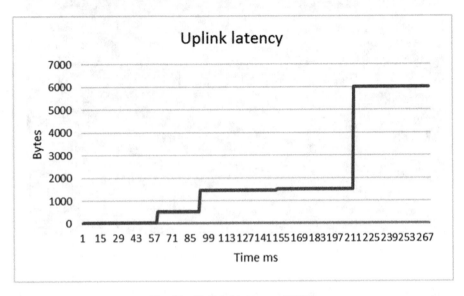

Fig. 11. Uplink latency on TVWS

The latency results show that in TVWS technology an increase in traffic increases latency. They also show that the TVWS in its current performance level cannot meet the QoS of time bounded data. The TVWS UDP jitter results are presented in Fig. 12.

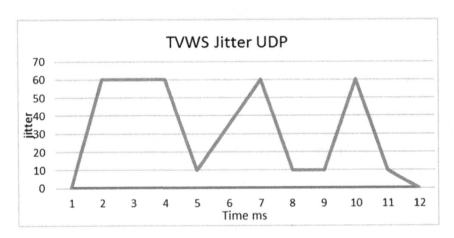

Fig. 12. TVWS jitter

The TVWS technology outperformed the WiFi in terms of jitter results. The number of active users can be the cause of this good performance. There were many active users in the WiFi network as compared to the TVWS network. The TVWS jitter results are significantly lower than the Wi-Fi jitter results. The Wi-Fi jitter was over 100 ms whereas the TVWS jitter is less than 70 ms. The TVWS delay results are also reasonable and can be tolerated by the client. The jitter results, in general, they vary in the network, fluctuating between 10 ms and 60 ms. The performance of the TVWS network was also monitored for a longer duration in Fig. 13.

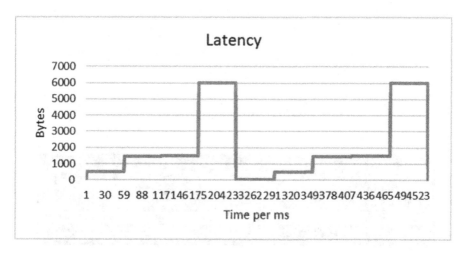

Fig. 13. TVWS latency results

The latency results were generated which depicts that technology is not performing well with regards to latency. Figure 14 presents additional results of the TVWS network in which the uplink speed was measured.

These tests show that 120 bytes were transferred in 116 s. The curve increased as the bytes transferred rate increased. Figure 15 presents the speedtest results of the WiFi network.

The speedtest used to gather performance results shows that the network was able to reach 4.99 Mbps of download speed and 8.52 Mbps upload speed. The WiFi offers higher uploading and downloading speeds compared to the TVWS technology. The speed results show that the TVWS seemed to be performing well due to the fact that it had fewer active users.

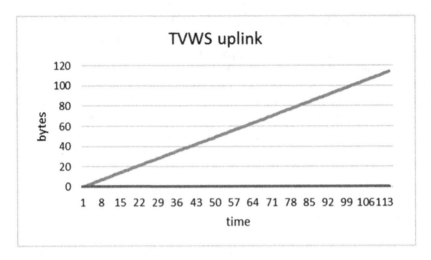

Fig. 14. TVWS uplink speed

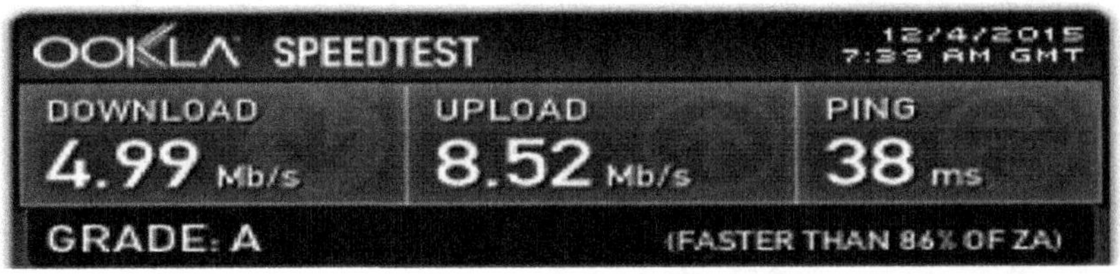

Fig. 15. Speedtest results on Wi-Fi network

5   Conclusion

The results of this study in relation to the literature provide insights to the future research directions in TVWS. In general, the characteristics of TVWS that makes it attractive to broadband access. Attributes such as its capabilities to cover long distances, and to penetrate walls and hard substances clearly show that TVWS is a promising technology. However, the performance of the technology still requires indepth investigation. Most of the studies do not perform through performance analysis of the technology.

This study contributes to the need for further investigation by presenting practical results based on a trial network. It also presented comparative results of the TVWS and WiFi networks.

The research findings of this study are consistent with the findings of several performance related studies in the evaluation of TVWS technology. This study extended the existing evaluations by presenting comparative results of TVWS and WiFi technologies in a rural setup. An efficient broadband technology customized for rural areas is sought after. This study and the related work show that TVWS can be successfully deployed in the rural areas. Though in our study, TVWS outperformed the

WiFi network there is need for further investigation of the technology in more scalable, robust, large, and heavily loaded TVWS networks offering many multi hop links in a mesh like topology.

References

1. Murty, M.S., Veeraiah, A., Rao, S.: Performance evaluation of Wi-Fi comparison with WiMAX networks. Int. J. Distrib. Parallel Syst. (IJDPS) 3(1), 321–329 (2012)
2. Haque, A., Amola, Y., Singh, N.K.: Performance of WiMAX over WIFI with reliable QoS over wireless communication network over wireless communication network. World Appl. Program. 1(5), 322–329 (2011)
3. Silva, C.F., Alves, H., Gomes, A.: Extension of LTE Operation Mode Over TV White Spaces 2011. www.ictcogeu.eu/pdf/.../Y2/FUNEMS_2011_COGEU_paper_n2.pdf
4. Apia, Samoa - April 2013. Cristian Gomez Spectrum Regulation and Policy Officer Radio Communication Bureau (BR), ITU. http://www.itu.int/ITU-D/asp/CMS/.../ITU-APT-S3_Cristian_Gomez.pdf. Accessed 23 Feb 2015
5. Kerk, S.G.: TV White Space for Super Wi-Fi and Beyond 2012. http://icto.dost.gov.ph/wp-content/uploads/2014/05/tvws-white-paper_power-automation_rev1.pdf
6. Ofcom: TV White Spaces: A Consultation on White Space Device Requirements (2012). https://www.ofcom.org.uk/__data/assets/pdf_file/0022/40477/condoc.pdf
7. Beede, D., Neville, A.: Broadband Availability Beyond the Rural/Urban Divide, Washington (2013)
8. Mikeka, C., Mlatho, J.S., Thodi, M., Pinifolo, J., Kondwani, D., Momba, L., Zennaro, M., Arcia-Moret, A., Fonda, C., Pietrosemoli, E.: Preliminary Performance Assessment of TV White Spaces Technology for Broadband Communication in Malawi (2014). http://wireless.ictp.it/Papers/TVWS_hum.pdf
9. Masonta, M.T., Kola, L.M., Lyskol, A.A., Pieterse, L., Velempini, M.: Network performance analysis of the Limpopo TV White Space trial network. In: IEEE AFRICON 2015, Addis Ababa, Ethopia, 14–17 September 2015
10. Ramoroka, T.: Wireless internet connection for teaching and learning in rural schools of Africa: the University of Limpopo TV White Space trial project. Mediter. J. Soc. Sci. 5(15), 382 (2014)
11. Cambridge TV White Space Consortium-Microsoft Research: Cambridge TV White Space Trial Findings. http://research.microsoft.com/en.../cambridge-tv-white-spaces-trial-findings.pdf. Accessed 23 Mar 2015
12. Rural Broadband Trial Laikipia County Kenya (2014). http://dynamicspectrumalliance.org/assets/TVWS_Report_for_Kenya_final_final_24_Aug.pdf
13. Garnett, K.: Deployment of TVWS Technology in El, Dorado County California. https://www.whitespacealliance.org/documents/Cal-Net%20TVWS%20Deployment%20Review%20140222a.pdf
14. Mitola, J.: Cognitive radio: making software radios more personal. IEEE Pers. Commun. 6 (6), 13–18 (1999)
15. International Telecommunications Union, Report ITU-R M.2370-0 1, "IMT Traffic Estimates for the Years 2020 to 2030", REPORT ITU-R M.2370-0 (2015)

16. Electronic Communication Committee (ECC): Technical and operational requirements for the possible operation of cognitive radio systems in the white spaces of the frequency band 470–790. In: European Conference of Postal and Telecommunications Administrations (CEPT), Technical report: ECC Report 159, January 2011. http://www.ietf.org/mailarchive/web/paws/current/pdf6LNQT4Lb6S.pdf

17. Akyildiz, I.F., et al.: NeXt generation/dynamic spectrum access/cognitive radio wireless networks: a survey. Comput. Netw. **50**, 2127–2159 (2006)

18. Brewer, J.: TV White Space Technology for Rural Telecommunication (2012). https://internetnz.nz/.../2012/telco2_whitespace_study_community_exam

19. TV White Space: Ready for Prime Use? (2014). http://www.unh.edu/broadband/sites/www.unh.edu.broadband/files/media/kb-reports/bcoe_tvws_2014_report.pdf

20. Waddell, M., Thilakawardana, S., Harrold, T., Kesby, P., Cherry, S.: Performance of an Experimental TV White space Base Station For Mobile and Fixed Broadband Applications (2012). www.bbc.co.uk/rd/publications/whitepaper253

21. Mohapatra, S.K., Choudhury, R.R., Das, P.: The Future Directions In Evolving Wi-Fi (2014). www.airccse.org/journal/ijngn/papers/6314ijngn02.pdf. Accessed 26 Apr 2014

22. Lopez-Benitez, M., Moessner, K.: LTE Uplink Extension in TV White Spaces (2013). http://www.compeng.ulster.ac.uk/iu-atc/publications/LTE%20Uplink%20Extension%20in%20TV%20White%20Spaces.pdf

23. Ricci, F.: An Introduction to Wireless Technologies Part 1 (2010/2011). www.inf.unibz.it/~ricci/MS/slides-2010.../9-WirelessTechnologies-P1.pd, Accessed 26 Aug 2015

24. Lo, E.C.-C.: An Investigation of the Impact of Signal Strength on Wi-Fi Link Throughput through Propagation Measurement (2007). http://aut.researchgateway.ac.nz/bitstream/handle/10292/698/LoE.pdf?. Accessed 26 Aug 2015

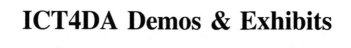

ICT4DA Demos & Exhibits

Review on Cognitive Radio Technology for Machine to Machine Communication

Negasa B. Teshale$^{(\boxtimes)}$ and Habib M. Hussien

School of Electrical and Computer Engineering, Addis Ababa Institute of Technology,
Addis Ababa, Ethiopia
negasabasha4@gmail.com, habibmohammed2001@gmail.com

Abstract. Recently, due to the rapid and fast ever growth number of connected devices/machines starting from our house hold appliances to the large industrial machines connected through wired/wireless communication network is becoming greater or larger. Hence, the electromagnetic undesirable state and interference become very critical issue as the spectrum resources we have is limited. However, a cognitive radio technology which automatically detects available channel spectrum, then accordingly changes its transmission or reception parameters to allow more occurring or operating at the same time in wireless communications in a given spectrum band at one location is a promising method for the challenges machine to machine communication facing this days. In this paper work, some detail survey of machine to machine communication and cognitive radio technology is introduced. Moreover, the challenges and advantages we get from combining cognitive radio and Machine to machine will be discussed.

Keywords: Cognitive radio · M2MS communication
Spectrum detection and sharing

1 Background

1.1 Introduction

The fast and continuous growth of the amount of data to be transferred/received through wireless communication networks is one of the main motivations to seek for the application of new communication systems all over the world. Nowadays, people are allowed to conveniently exchange voice, audio, video, emails and images with anyone, any-time and any-place with any terminals, machines or devices. In addition to the conventional human communications, new aspects and use of machine-to-machine (M2M) communications are drawing overwhelming attention in both the academia and the industry [1].

The M2M wireless communication has recently included to where devices can connect and communicate over wireless channels with less or without human intervention. The data are produced, processed, and exchanged through a fully automatic fashion. Very few human intervening and control is substituted by

© ICST Institute for Computer Sciences, Social Informatics and Telecommunications Engineering 2018
F. Mekuria et al. (Eds.): ICT4DA 2017, LNICST 244, pp. 347–355, 2018.
https://doi.org/10.1007/978-3-319-95153-9_31

Table 1. Number of connected devices [2]

World population	6.3 billion	6.8 billion	7.2 billion	7.6 billion
Connected devices	500 million	12.3 billion	25 billion	50 billion
Connected devices/person	0.08	1.84	3.47	6.58
Year	2003	2010	2013	2020

self-configuration, self-management, self-organization, and self-healing processes from smart services, such as smart city, grid, home, meter, etc. M2M communications reduce prices and allow a large degree of efficiency that affect individual as well as industrial uses [1,2].

Any devices can be connected with M2M system networks and be larger in number the world population as depicted in Table 1 below. The joined devices in the system involves entities like: power and gas meters that report usage data, wearable monitors that tell a doctor when a patient needs to come in for a check-up, traffic monitors, and cars that describe their place and condition to authorities in the event of an accident, any other sensors, cameras, computers, pumps, heating modules etc.

As indicated in the table above there are a number of issues that M2M Communication by having billions of devices connected/inter connected, our world is facing some problems like the main reason of spectrum congestion due to the scarcity of the limited spectral resources, power consumption and electromagnetic pollution problems. Furthermore, wireless coverage to rare density around countryside areas (M2M facing blockage in remote areas), due self-existence or co-existence interference problem and large number of different machines as well as diverse services, which causing diversity in network protocols and data formats(machines heterogeneity) is experienced [2].

To tackle these problem by looking at the spectral tuning to deal with the ceaseless increment of connected machines, currently some researchers proposing a new communication paradigm cognitive radio technology for machines to raise the scalability, flexibility, efficiency and reliability of M2M communications. Cognitive radio technology enabled machines are able to sense and utilize idle frequency bands in their environments. This technology utilizes the existing in possibility that wireless system has when they are context attentive and capable of readjustment based on their environment conditions and their own attributes.

Usually, two systems coexist in same frequency ranges which are named as the primary user and the secondary user in M2M system. The primary user has the sole right to use the assigned frequency spectrum. The secondary user is the opportunistic access unused spectrum from licensed frequency spectrum, e.g., TV broadcast systems. By adding a new cognition dimension, cognitive radio for M2M is intelligent and easily adjustable and much more capable than normal M2M communication. For example, using cognitive in M2M communication can extract unused radio spectrum resources such that the notorious spectrum congestion problems in conventional M2M can be highly maintained [1].

1.2   Objective

1.2.1   General Objective

The main propose of this paper work is to explore application of using cognitive radio technology in machine to machine communication.

1.2.2   Specific Objective

The specific objective of this paper is:

- To make a detail survey on machine to machine communication.
- To discuss some main challenges of M2M communication system.
- To explain the practical applications of cognitive radio in detail.
- To discuss fundamental characteristics of cognitive radio technology.
- To analyze the difference between conventional and cognitive radio M2M wireless communication system.

2   Machine to Machine (M2M) Communication

2.1   Introduction

Machine communication system depict mechanisms, algorithms and technologies that enable networked devices, whether it is wireless or wired, and services to exchange information or control data seamlessly, with only very limited human interaction. It is about enabling direct communications among electronic devices, and it can use both wireless and fixed network communication [3].

2.2   General Architecture of M2M Communication

The characteristics of M2M communications are completely different from those of traditional system networks. M2M networks are framed of very large amount of nodes, since the main target of participating in communication is a device or object. Because most devices/objects are battery operated, energy efficiency is the greatest significant issue, as for the machines senses itself or its physical surrounding condition, the aggregation per connected things becomes very small. However, data are generated from a large number of objects, and because the data generation period, amount, and format are all different, a large quantity of data is generated. While M2M communication can occur with very limited human intervene, functional constancy and sustainability are also required.

In 2009, the ETSI were established the M2M technical committee with the purpose to develop an end-to-end architecture for M2M communications. According to ETSI, an M2M system is composed of the five key elements with its functions are mentioned in [4,5]. In the M2M domain, a potentially large number of nodes and M2M gateway (GW) are integrated to enable automated and diverse services. Each embedded node as flexible and smart device should be equipped with various functions, such as data acquisition, data preprocessing, data storage, distinctive address, wireless transceiver, power supply, etc. [7].

In the network domain, a high quantities of heterogeneous Points of Attachment (PoA) potentially coexist. Here, convergence of heterogeneous networks (e.g., xDSL, LTE, WiMax, WiFi, etc.) in an optimal way supply cost effective and reliable channels for sensing signal information packet transmission from M2M to the application layer.

Finally, in the application area, various real time services for remote management monitoring are provided and can be classified into several categories, such as traffic, logistic, business, home, etc. Back-end server is the key component for the whole M2M communication system. It makes the integration point for all gathered data from M2M device area [5].

2.3   Challenges of M2M Communication

Currently M2M communication has an active application in different areas such as surveillance, intelligent transportation, emergency alert, ehealth, security, smart grid, home automation and smart metering. Hence, a capably large number of machines are deployed with the purpose of gathering information and transmitting it over a network to processing units. LTE cellular networks try to present a strong contender for M2M communications due to its native IP connectivity and its scalability to support a massive number of devices in wide areas [8].

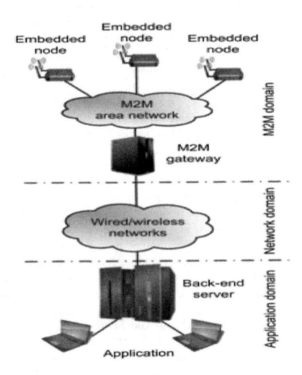

Fig. 1. General M2M communication architecture [6]

The major challenges for M2M communication networks include the following:

1. Group-based of M2M: The ultimate propose of grouping a number of M2M machines is to make easier the traffic pollution on the air interface by reducing communication loads between an M2M device and 3GPP E-UTRA and EPC. Additionally, an other very curial main requirements in wireless M2M network system is to lower energy dissipation [9].

2. Heterogeneity: The technological potential requirements to integrate many types of devices, especially,in terms a of their technologies and services are the main highly expected achievements from M2M communications in current and future networks to be successful. At the device domain, this includes a lot of various features in terms of packet/data exchange capabilities (e.g., data rates, latency, and reliability, flexibility in handling different technologies, availability of energy, computational and storage power, etc. [8]).

3. Scalability: One of the main consideration when we deal with M2M communications is scalability. Of-course, the produced information as well as the network traffic will rise as the number of devices raises from time to time, which may contribute to the scalability issues. Lets consider, for instance, the case of several devices trying to simultaneously perform network authentication. Since the existing mobile technologies have not been designed to hold up such a massive number of machines, this would probably will be the main consequence of traffic network system pollutant [10].

Therefore, the design of scalable authentication mechanisms is very important particularly in the case of real-time scenarios. On an other point of view, some scenarios (e.g. home automation, city automation,) going to include numerous M2M machines that ensure their data exchange using the common key. In the case of a have in common key, a scalable key management plan that modifies the update of the shared common key following state changes (join/leave of devices) is required [4].

4. Security: Within the same spectrum resource application area, there may be individuals or organization with different access rights. Hence, an afforded organization or individuals should not be able to see information which he is not appropriated to.

5. Energy Management: Energy management reaches up-to energy harvesting, conservation, to consumption is an overwhelming issue in the M2M communication context in 3GPP LTE/LTE-A networks. Decreasing energy dissipation and consumption is one of the main problems in M2M communications. The development of novel solutions that maximize energy efficiency is essential. Network protocols will have to deal with inherent characteristics of M2M communications such as long sleep cycles, energy and processing power constraints, time-varying radio propagation environments, and topologies varying with node mobility [8].

3   Cognitive Radio (CR) Technology

3.1   Spectrum Scarcity

Radio spectrum may be one of the most tightly regulated resources of all time. From simple cell phones to garage door opener, nearly almost all wireless machines depends on access to the radio resource spectrum. But access to spectrum has been chronically limited ever since RF transmissions were first regulated in the early 20th century [11]. This all will be exchanged/replaced by new technologies that use spectrum more efficiently and more cooperatively, unleashed by regulatory reforms, may soon overcome the spectrum shortage [12].

3.2   Spectrum Sensing and Sharing

Spectrum sensing is one of the very significant portion CR techniques that enables the secondary users that makes able to measure, sense, learn, and be aware of the portions related to the radio environment, availability of spectrum and power, user requirements and applications, available networks infrastructures, local policies and other operating restrictions [13]. This functionality enables the primary users to adapt to the dynamic environment by detecting and opportunistically using spectrum holes without causing interference to the primary network [14].

3.3   Spectrum Mobility

When the channel state at a particular time becomes very bad or if channel is occupied by licensed users, using the same spectrum band is detected, spectrum mobility issues arise. If the channel bands in use is required by a licensed user, the unlicensed user must vacate those spectrum band and continue its communication in another vacant portion of the spectrum. Several methods have been proposed to design spectrum mobility in order to reduce delay and loss during spectrum hand-off. Spectrum hand-off is handled in IEEE 802.22 by using the method of IDRP, which supports the network to recover its normal activity maintaining an acceptable level of QoS [15].

4   Cognitive Radio in M2M Communications

4.1   Architecture of Cognitive Radio for M2M

As depicted in Fig. 2 below expresses the proposed Cognitive radio M2M networked system architecture. The network parts are categorized into two principal components: the licensed system and unlicensed M2M system [16].

Generally, a cognitive M2M network is only allowed to access the spectrum holes in an opportunistic way, without causing disturbance to the primary network. Cognitive machines communicate with others by opportunistically accessing the spectrum and finding free spectrum bands. At the same time, a cognitive machine carry out a function like data generation/processing/actuation and controlling of the physical appearance. A cognitive AP is an data collect-ing/transfer point in a LA cognitive M2M network. And also, some performance as an packet/data entrance to the surrounding networks, for instance, the Inter-net. A Secondary BS governs the machines that are exchanging information within its network area/scope in a centralized Cognitive M2M system. The alter-native spectrum geo-location database is communicating with all the secondary BSs, and responsible for coordinating the spectrum allocation among multiple cognitive M2M networks [1].

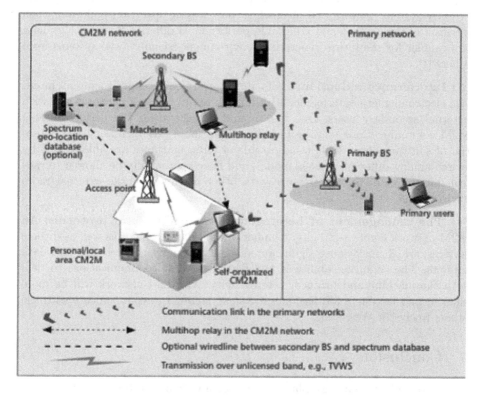

Fig. 2. Cognitive M2M network architecture [1]

4.2 Proposed Solutions of M2M Communication Issues Using Cognitive Radio Technology

The M2M communications main objective is to support a huge numerous smart devices so they can function properly. The usage of this technology to M2M is a capable way to make M2M more efficient in terms of spectrum utilization. Some of the basic challenges are:

(1) Device massiveness: The fundamental practical applications of cognitive radio spectrum is to reach shortcoming of spectrum resource scarcity in present data/package communications. Mitigation/lowering of spectrum congestion is one of the main target for using CR in M2M communications. The main challenge in M2M communications is the ever increasing number of devices/machines want to inter the system. This poses a significant challenge for any existing communication network. CR technology handles large-scale information exchange by utilizing larger portions of the resources.

(2) The need to be green: Cognitive machines in a secondary network has to have the potential of adaptively tuning their receiving/transmission power levels depending on the operating environments, free from assurance of interposing primary system network and meanwhile, not causing spectrum pollution. Such intrinsic context-aware and adaptable performance differs CR technology as a key enabler for the future generations environment-friendly radio systems from others [1].

(3) Interference reduction: Users almost everywhere experiencing an intensive electromagnetic interference within the internal primary networks and with external/secondary users. Due to this and other reasons the performance of M2M communications may be becomes highly poor. By increasing the potential of software dependable re-adjustable of CRs, machines are able to rapidly switch among different wireless modes, and hence potentially be allowed to radical mitigation of the interference with other machines or the external radio environment.

(4) The management of heterogeneous machines and protocols: An M2M network comprises a large number of different machines as well as diverse services, which may cause significant diversity in network protocols and data formats. The cognition ability is beneficial for M2M communications to deal with the machine and protocol heterogeneity. An M2M network will be more efficient and flexible if all machines are smart enough to communicate with the others freely [2]. Weightless.

5   Conclusion

Cognitive radio technology play very important role in the growth of current wireless M2M transceivers technologies. Densification of existing wireless communication networks with the massive addition of devices/machines and a provision for peer communication is one of big challenge. This dramatic development of wireless M2M communication applications have remarkably increases the demand of free spectrum bands. Hence, cognitive radio technology is showing possibility of best achievement for employing the unusable/available frequency spectrum resources with an efficient manner in the way of opportunistic spectrum utilization.

Generally, this work presents a review of how to exploit the existing radio spectrum resources in a dynamic and opportunistic way, by using CR techniques in M2M communication. And also, this distinctive M2M applications that can play a critical role in our future life were illustrated. Finally, the Challenges of

CR technology in M2M Communication and proposed solutions were pointed out in order to initiate further researches.

References

1. Zhang, Y., Yu, R., Nekovee, M., Liu, Y., Xie, S., Gjessing, S.: Cognitive machine-to-machine communications: visions and potentials for the smart grid. IEEE Netw. (2012)
2. Boisguene, R., Chou, S.H., Huang, C.W.: A survey on cognitive machine-to-machine communications. IEEE (2014)
3. Pereira, C., Aguiar, A.: Towards efficient mobile M2M communications: survey and open challenges. Open Access, October 2014
4. Barki, A., Bouabdallah, A., Gharout, S., Traoré, J.: M2M security: challenges and solutions. J. IEEE Commun. Surv. Tutor. **18**, 1241–1254 (2015)
5. Chen, M., Wan, J., González-Valenzuela, S., Liao, X., Leung, V.C.: A survey of recent developments in home M2M networks. IEEE Commun. Surv. Tutor. **16**(1), 98–114 (2014)
6. Zoran, B., Bojkovic, B., Bakmaz, M.: Machine-to-machine communication architecture as an enabling paradigm of embedded internet evolution. In: Recent Advances in Computer Science (2015)
7. Yang, T., Cao, J., Han, Z.: A survey of emerging M2M systems: context, task, and objective. IEEE Internet Things J. **3**, 1246–1258 (2016)
8. Ghavimi, F., Chen, H.-H.: M2M communications in 3GPP LTE/LTE-A networks: architectures, service requirements, challenges, and applications. IEEE Commun. Surv. Tutor. **17**, 525–549 (2014)
9. Ho, C., Huang, C.: Energy-saving massive access control and resource allocation schemes for M2M communications in OFDMA cellular networks. IEEE Commun. Lett. **1**, 209–211 (2012)
10. Corici, A., Steinke, R., Magedanz, T., Coetzee, L., Oosthuizen, D., Mkhize, B., Catalan, M., Fontelles, J.C., Paradells, J., Shrestha, R., Nehls, D.: Towards programmable and scalable IoT infrastructures for smart cities. IEEE, April 2016
11. Kliks, A.: Application of the cognitive radio concept for M2M communications: practical considerations. Wirel. Pers. Commun. **83**, 117–133 (2015). (Open Access at Springer)
12. Staple, G., Werbach, K.: The end of spectrum scarcity. IEEE Spectrum (2004)
13. Xie, S., Liu, Y., Zhang, Y., Yu, R.: A parallel cooperative spectrum sensing in cognitive radio networks. IEEE Trans. Veh. Technol. **59**, 4079–4092 (2010)
14. Liu, X., Zhang, Y., Li, Y., Zhang, Z., Long, K.: A survey of cognitive radio technologies and their optimization approaches. IEEE (2013)
15. Cordeiro, C., Challapali, K., Ghosh, M.: Cognitive PHY and MAC layers for dynamic spectrum access and sharing of TV bands. In: Proceedings of First International Workshop on Technology and Policy for Accessing Spectrum, Boston, MA, USA, August 2006
16. Nekovee, M.: A survey of cognitive radio access to TV white spaces. Open Access: Int. J. Digit. Multimed. Broadcast. (2010)

Author Index

Printed in the United States
By Bookmasters